Arnold Dró,
in Caldy,
January 1959.

Listed Buildings

AUSTRALIA AND NEW ZEALAND
The Law Book Company Ltd.
Sydney : Melbourne : Perth

CANADA AND U.S.A.
The Carswell Company Ltd.
Agincourt, Ontario

INDIA
N. M. Tripathi Private Ltd.
Bombay
and
Eastern Law House Private Ltd.
Calcutta and Delhi
M.P.P. House
Bangalore

ISRAEL
Steimatzky's Agency Ltd.
Jerusalem : Tel Aviv : Haifa

Listed Buildings:
The Law and Practice
of
Historic Buildings, Ancient Monuments, and Conservation Areas

by

Roger W. Suddards
Solicitor, L.M.R.T.P.I.,
C.B.E., F.S.V.A. (Hon.)

with contributions by

David Hicken   and   **Philip Hardman**
B.A. (Hons.) B.T.P., D.M.S.,   *F.C.A., F.T.I.I.*
M.B.I.M., M.R.T.P.I.   *(Grant Thornton)*

and a Foreword by

Sir Desmond Heap
LL.M., Hon. LL.D.

LONDON
SWEET & MAXWELL
1988

Published in 1988 by
Sweet & Maxwell Limited
of 11, New Fetter Lane, London
Computerset by Promenade Graphics Limited, Cheltenham
Printed in Great Britain by
Butler & Tanner Limited,
Frome, Somerset

British Library Cataloguing in Publication Data

Suddards, Roger W. (Roger Whitley), *1930–*
    Listed buildings: the law and practice of historic buildings,
    ancient monuments, and conservation areas.
    —2nd ed.
    1. England. Listed Buildings. Law
    I. Title
    344.204'94

    ISBN 0–421–38130–2

Foreword

By

Sir Desmond Heap, LL.M., Hon. LL.D.

I have always been well pleased when the "fretful star unprofitable and the fever of the world" have been getting me down (as sometimes they have) to dip, yet again, into those wonderfully contemplative writings of Charles Lamb, the *Essays of Elia*, in which he discourses so perceptively, yet so gently, upon such differing matters as *Dream Children, Christ's Hospital Five-and-Thirty years ago, Roast Pig* (early chinese style), and *The Old Benchers of the Inner Temple* where he was born, at 2, Crown Office row, On February 10, 1775.

Of the several *Essays of Elia* one of my favourites has always been *Oxford in the Vacation* and it is with a quotation from "this little sketch" (as Lamb called it) that I want to begin this little Foreword. . . . . . .

> *Antiquity! thou wondrous charm, what art thou? that being nothing, art everything!. . . . What mystery lurks in this retroversion? or what half Januses are we, that cannot look forward with the same idolatry with which we for ever revert! The mighty future is as nothing, being every thing! the past is everything, being nothing.*

Maybe its because so much damage was done in the second world war to the towns and cities of our country that there is now such a strong lobby for the conservation of all things past. It was not always so. But the devastations of bombs and aerial missiles brought home to many the price which our Heritage (as it is now called) was in danger of having to pay in the redevelopment of war-damaged sites and buildings. Whether this attitude is wise (or otherwise) is a debatable matter. The law has provided, in the wake of nineteenth century statutory protection for ancient monuments, for twentieth century protection for listed buildings (in 1962), for conservation areas (in 1967), and for areas of outstanding natural beauty (in 1949), for the solid fact is that it has now became fashionable to indulge in all aspects of this business of protection, preservation and conservation in a big and bigger way than ever before.

Thus, whichever side you embrace, whether you are for or against all this sort of thing, it is essential that you know both your rights and your duties—your *rights* to develop land which contains a protected building; your *duties* to uphold any such protected building which you may happen to own. Which ever camp you are in, *Listed Buildings: The Law and Practice of Historic Buildings, Ancient Monuments, and Conservation Areas* is the book for you.

The title illustrates the broadened sweep of this new and updated edition of Mr. Roger Suddards' earlier book. Since April 1, 1984 the National Heritage Act of 1983 has brought upon the land ownership and the land development scenes a new and doughty fighter for protection and preservation, namely, the Historic Buildings and Monuments Commission for England.[1]

This is a new force. It is one to be reckoned with and it is a further justification (if any were called for) of the burning need for Mr. Suddard's new book.

---

[1] Scotland and Wales continue to have their own respective Historic Buildings Councils under the Historic Buildings and Ancient Monuments Act 1953.

It is clear that the cut and thrust of nothing less than an ongoing battle is now developing between the protectionist lobby on the one side and the Department of the Environment on the other. If any one has doubts about this he need do no more than read *carefully* the current statements of the Secretary of State for the Environment, the Rt. Hon. Nicholas Ridley M.P., on the Government's land development policy in general and on the vexed question of planning control over development in the Green Belt in particular—and especially in the South-East of England. On this the opposing parties have taken their respective stands and are now drawing up their lines of battle. In the last analysis it is Government policy which will settle this issue, but, as planning control of land (and this includes buildings) is an artistic process and not a finite science, there is always room for more than one point of view. Thus, skilful judgment and refined argument are needed for each protagonist and it may be that sophisticated and intelligent use of both judgment and argument may yet win concessions (and thereby some success) which it will be very agreeable to have.

Accordingly, I declare that Mr. Suddards' well-turned book makes a timely arrival on stage. I am sure it will be the success is deserves to be, by which (and for the removal of doubt, as the jargon goes) I mean it will be a monumental, listed and ever-preserved success!

AT THE LAW SOCIETY'S HALL
IN THE CITY OF LONDON
MAY 1988

Preface

To be writing the Preface is like arriving at the weekend. The years of collecting and collating notes, of agonising over what is a fair interpretation of a difficult problem, of writing and re-writing, seems soon to be over. But like every lawyer's weekend, there is a little more to do . . . !

The intention, when preparing this new edition of *Listed Buildings*, has not changed: to present in one book a comprehensive statement of the law and the practice relating to historic buildings, be they listed, in a conservation area, or ancient monuments. The law is stated as at today—September 1, 1987 with occasional later references.

The spirit is the same—and I will quote again the magic words of Harold Nicolson used as part of the preface of one of the best books of the late Alec Clifton-Taylor:

> "Even if Hell exists (which I doubt) and even if Heaven is a reality (which I sincerely hope is not true) . . . I believe that the gift I most appreciate is the gift of seeing beauty. Why should I experience such a spurt of pleasure at seeing the tower of Staplehurst Church catch the sun through fog?"

Now to my thanks . . . My first thanks are to my secretary, Beryl Hull, who has (as with the first edition and other subsequent publications) made clear that which was a garbled manuscript. Without her efficiency and enthusiasm this book would not be published.

Man is not an island—and indeed this book proves it. David Hicken, Chartered Town Planner of Maidstone, Kent, has brought his professional skill to this edition in so many ways. It is valuable to have in a legal textbook the views of a practical town planner with experience both in local government and now in private practice.

June Hargreaves, with her vast fund of knowledge, particularly in archaeology, has kindly read the book and made most helpful suggestions.

Ray Bloomfield of the Diss Village Society has read the book and made very valuable comments resulting in a number of changes which I hope will make the book more interesting to the layman as well as to the lawyer.

Philip Hardman of Grant Thornton, Chartered Accountants, London, has written the chapter on taxation, for which I am most grateful. Tax is an essential part of decision making in respect of listed buildings and Philip's great experience and clear exposition should be valuable in making those decisions.

There are a large number of interested people who I cannot catalogue by name—but my colleague, David Hicken, and I wrote to local authorities and others concerned with listed buildings as we prepared this second edition. The response was marvellous—we received a large number of letters with some fascinating cases and experiences. All have been considered and a great number of points added to the book: we both are most grateful.

One of the benefits we enjoy in dealing with listed buildings is the dedicated work of Miss P. E. Payne, who this year retired from the Civil Service just days after she had completed the text of Circular 8/87 and had superintended the HMSO publication of the "combined" statutes. It is easy to forget the quiet hand of the specialist, and "Pep" Payne did such a lot for the cause of the listed buildings, as do her friends, Michael Ross JP. and Blair Sessions. From all of them I have learnt and continue to learn so much.

My thanks go to Nick Pennington, a solicitor who, though determined to leave the law for other things, has been my constant companion in preparing this edition, carefully editing the work and attending to the boring details of footnotes and case references with efficiency and style. Also thanks to Jonathan Wilson, soon to be a solicitor, who has contributed greatly to the editing process.

To all of them, my friends, and to that dear friend and mentor, Desmond Heap, to whom I am most grateful for again writing a Foreword, I offer my sincere thanks. In saying this, I acknowledge that the mistakes are mine and the responsibility for it lies on my shoulders.

And finally to my wife and family who have put up once again with it all! Without their patience and understanding I should not have been able to finish it all.

September 1, 1987   Roger W. Suddards
                                                         128, Sunbridge Road
                                                         In the City of Bradford

Contents

5. Listed Buildings—The Mechanics of Control

6. Problem Operations and Features—the Nuts and Bolts of Listed Building Control

9. Taxation and Historic Buildings

10. Grant and Loan Facilities

11. Rights of Entry of Officers and Officials

12. Buildings, Conservation Areas and Ancient Monuments—Public Rights

13. Interested Bodies

Appendix

Table of Cases

Table of Statutes

[References in **bold** type indicate where the text of the statute is printed]

xix

Table of Statutory Instruments

Table of Circulars

[References in **bold** type indicate where the text of the circular is printed]

Table of Abbreviations

A.M.A.A.A. 1979	Ancient Monuments and Archaeological Areas Act 1979
B.A. 1984	Building Act 1984
CAC	Conservation Area Consent
C.G.T.A. 1979	Capital Gains Tax Act 1979
CGT	Capital Gains Tax
D.O.E.	Department of the Environment
E.G.	Estates Gazette
F.A.	Finance Act
G.D.O.	General Development Order
H.A.	Housing Act
H.B.A.M.A. 1953	Historic Buildings and Ancient Monuments Act 1953
H.M.S.O.	Her Majesty's Stationery Office
H.P.A. 1986	Housing and Planning Act 1986
I.C.T.A. 1970	Income and Corporation Taxes Act 1970
I.H.T.A. 1984	Inheritance Tax Act 1984
J.P.L.	Journal of Planning and Environment Law
LA	Local Authority
LBC	Listed Building Consent
L.G.A.	Local Government Act
L.G.P. (A). A 1981	Local Government and Planning (Amendment) Act 1981
L.G.P.L.A. 1980	Local Government, Planning and Land Act 1980
LPA	Local Planning Authority
N.H.A. 1983	National Heritage Act 1983
P.H.A.	Public Health Act
RIBA	Royal Institute of British Architects
RICS	Royal Institution of Chartered Surveyors
RTPI	Royal Town Planning Institute
SAVE	Save Britain's Heritage
T.C.A.A. 1974	Town and Country Amenities Act 1974
T.C.P.A.	Town and Country Planning Act
T.C.P. (A). A 1972	Town and Country Planning (Amendment) Act 1972
VAT	Value Added Tax
V.A.T.A. 1983	Value Added Tax Act 1983

1. Introduction

1.01 This book is concerned with two closely interrelated subjects: the statutory basis for the protection and preservation of what is generally termed our "built heritage"; and the practical consequences and effects of the application of those statutory provisions. But first, however, we must set the scene. What, in terms of statute, is our "built heritage"?

On the basis of the King's grave exhortation to the White Rabbit to "begin at the beginning . . . and go on till you come to the end, then stop,"[1] we may best attempt to answer this question by examining briefly the chronological development of statutory provision for "heritage conservation" in the United Kingdom. We start with ancient monuments.

It was not until the latter part of the last century that the desirability of protecting and preserving ancient buildings and structures or their remains, was generally recognised. William Morris took the first really positive steps in this direction by founding the Society for the Protection of Ancient Buildings in 1877, but it was not until 1882 that the first measure of statutory protection was afforded. The Ancient Monument Protection Act of that year marked the start of such protective measures, even though the immediate effects of that Act were only to give the protection of law to 29 such monuments in England and Wales, and 21 in Scotland.[2] Others were added later, as the Schedule which the Act provided for was gradually compiled.

Ninety-seven years, five Acts of Parliament on ancient monuments,[3] and some 13,000 scheduled ancient monuments later, section 61 of the Ancient Monuments and Archaeological Areas Act 1979 provides us with the current definition of what constitutes a monument, and may therefore qualify as an ancient monument:

> "(a) any building, structure or work whether above or below the surface of the land, and any cave or excavation;
>
> (b) any site comprising the remains of any such building, structure of work or any cave or excavation; and,
>
> (c) any site comprising or comprising the remains of any vehicle, vessel, aircraft or other moveable structure or part thereof which neither constitutes nor forms part of any work which is a monument within paragraph (a) above;
>
> and any machinery attached to a monument shall be regarded as part of a monument if it could not be detached without being dismantled."[4]

---

[1] *Alice's Adventures in Wonderland*: The Trial—"Alice's Evidence."
[2] Schedule to the 1882 Act.
[3] See paras. 8.01–8.07.
[4] A.M.A.A. 1979, s.61(7).

1.02   A monument may include the site of a monument, or a group of monuments or any part of a monument or group of monuments.[5]

Thus virtually any edifice may be a monument, although the protection of the law is only actually afforded to those monuments which professional—and, theoretically, public—opinion regards as in some way important to the understanding of our historical, architectural, cultural, and, more recently, technological heritage.

The concept of protecting buildings in more or less daily use for essentially historic or aesthetic reasons is of more recent origin. The 1882 Act, and its successors in 1913 and 1931—and indeed in 1953 and 1979[6]—were mainly concerned with "unoccupied" buildings and structures: henges, castles, bridges, ruins and like structures of essentially antique and historical importance. It was not until 1932 that the desirability of statutory protection for buildings which were, generally, in use, and of architectural or historic interest found currency in law, and even then, as demonstrated in Chapter 2, powers were discretionary rather than mandatory. As we will see, it has taken some 16 subsequent Acts to bring the art of historic building conservation to its present all-embracing level, in which we have in excess of 400,000 assorted buildings subject to various measures of statutory protection under the listed buildings legislation.

The definition of what constitutes a building suitable for listing is as broad as that for a monument: a building may be anything from a street lamp to a railway viaduct, a horse trough to a textile mill; what may be a listed building depends on criteria (considered in detail in Chapter 2) which cover almost any "building" at least thirty years old and which is of:

> "(a) special value within certain types, either for architectural or planning reasons or as illustrating social and economic history (for instance industrial buildings, railway stations, schools, hospitals, theatres, town halls, markets, exchanges, almshouses, prisons, lock-ups, mills);
>
> (b) technological innovation or virtuosity (for instance cast iron, prefabrication, or the early use of concrete);
>
> (c) association with well known characters or events;
>
> (d) group value, especially as examples of town planning (for instance squares, terraces or model villages)"[7]

1.03   It will be apparent from the foregoing that the statutory provisions for the protection of "buildings of special architectural and historic interest" find their ancestry in the statutory provisions for "ancient monuments," and it is not therefore surprising that it is possible for a building or structure to be both a "scheduled monument" and a "listed building," a potentially confusing situation bearing in mind the complexities of both statutory codes. The Secretary of State for the Environment, however, does not regard it as a significant problem, and has indeed seen fit to give guidance on the subject, in Circular 8/87.

---

[5] *Ibid.* s.61(10). There are also exceptions: s.61(8) (referred to also at para. 8.03) and additional provisions regarding land required for the support and preservation of a monument—s.61(9).

[6] See Chap. 8.

[7] Appendix 1 of Department of the Environment Circular 8/87, *Historic Buildings and Conservation Areas—Policy and Procedure*—referred to throughout this book as "Circular 8/87."

"Overlap between listing of historic buildings and scheduling of ancient monuments

49. Section 1 of the Ancient Monuments and Archaeological Areas Act 1979, as amended by the National Heritage Act 1983, gives to the Secretary of State the duty of compiling a Schedule of ancient monuments of national importance by virtue of their historic, architectural, traditional, or archaeological interest. The Secretary of State must consult with the Commission before adding or removing any monument to or from the Schedule. The great majority of scheduled ancient monuments are archaeological sites or monuments whose importance resides in their buried archaeological deposits as well as any standing remains and they are located frequently in agricultural land in the countryside. A further large category within the Schedule are ruins or buildings for which there is often no present-day, readily-apparent economic use.

50. Some buildings are both scheduled and listed. However, section 56(1)(b) of the 1971 Act[7a] provides that the legislative controls relating to listed buildings do not apply to buildings which are "for the time being included in the Schedule of monuments compiled under section 1 of the Ancient Monuments and Archaeological Areas Act 1979." Buildings in ecclesiastical use and occupied dwelling-houses cannot be scheduled but some agricultural buildings, such as medieval barns or dovecotes, are both scheduled and listed, as are some bridges, urban buildings (e.g., market halls or guildhalls) and, to an increasing extent, industrial monuments, where close control of work is necessary. The selection of monuments for scheduling is based upon a concept of national importance and in 1983 the Secretary of State published non-statutory criteria to guide selection. Within the framework of this guide the Commission is now committed to a continuous review and expansion of the Schedule but even an enlarged Schedule is likely to include but a small proportion of the currently known archaeological sites and monuments."

The most recent concept in heritage conservation takes the process **1.04** started in 1882 to what may reasonably be assumed to be a logical conclusion: the recognition of the aesthetic and historic value of whole areas of buildings and the spaces which they enclose or which provide their setting. From 1963 it has been accepted within listed building law that buildings could be listed because of their "group value," rather than on the basis of solely individual architectural or historic merit. As we will see in Chapter 3 this practice remained unchallenged in the courts until 1964 when the Earl of Iveagh questioned the legal validity of group listing, and the Court of Appeal ultimately held that such listing was valid, even though expressing doubt as to whether the Town and Country Planning Act 1947 provisions were adequate for their purpose.[8]

A direct consequence was Duncan Sandys'—later Lord Duncan-Sandys'— Civic Amenities Act 1967 which brought into the statute the concept of

[7a] References throughout this book to "the 1971 Act" are to the Town and Country Planning Act 1971 (as amended).

[8] *Iveagh (Earl of)* v. *Minister of Housing and Local Government* [1964] 1 Q.B. 395; [1963] 3 All E.R. 817.

conservation areas, in which whole groups of buildings and their immediate environment could be "designated" and afforded protection similar to that covering listed buildings. In the same way that subsequent amendments to the provisions of the 1947 Act have refined the measures of protection afforded to individual listed buildings, the Civic Amenities Act 1967 was quite speedily updated—and indeed replaced—by subsequent Planning Acts which tied conservation area practice even more closely to listing and listed buildings practice.

The criteria by which any area may be judged worthy of designation as a conservation area are in a sense more simple than those by which ancient monuments are scheduled or buildings listed. They are, however, equally broad in their scope, a further indication of the inter-relationship and common ancestry of the three codes. Conservation areas may be any

"areas of special architectural or historic interest the character or appearance of which it is desirable to preserve or enhance."[9]

Such areas may or may not contain listed buildings or scheduled monuments; if they do, then the codes concerning such buildings and monuments continue to operate in respect of the structures concerned. Here at least there is no potential for conflict, and the various powers effectively complement one another.

1.05 There is, however, one significant difference. Whereas the scheduling of monuments and the listing of buildings is a function which may only be exercised by the Secretary of State, the designation of conservation areas is essentially a local authority function, with the Secretary of State having solely reserve powers, and only requiring to be notified of designations.

The Local Government, Planning and Land Act 1980, amongst a number of amendments relating to listed buildings law contained in the 1971 Act, makes an important amendment to section 56 thereof. Subsection 3 of section 56 now reads:

"In considering whether to grant planning permission for development which affects a listed building or its setting and in considering whether to grant listed building consent for any works, the local planning authority or the Secretary of State . . . shall have special regard to the desirability of preserving the building *or its setting* or any feature of special architectural or historic interest which it possesses."[10]

The italicised words are the important amendment. We now have a situation in which the concept of area rather than purely building conservation may be applied to individual listed buildings even if they are not within a conservation area.

Perhaps the major event of the early 1980s in the management of our architectural heritage has been the formation of the Historic Buildings and Monuments Commission for England.[11] Known popularly as English Heritage, this body was set up by the National Heritage Act 1983 and its general duties are to secure and promote the preservation and enhancement of ancient monuments, historic buildings and conservation areas in England; also to promote the public's enjoyment and awareness of such. [Throughout

---

[9] T.C.P.A. 1971, s.277(1).

[10] Derived from L.G.P.L.A. 1980, Sched. 15, para. 8.

[11] See also para 13.02, which also indicates the position in Scotland and Wales.

this book the Historic Buildings and Monuments Commission is referred to as "the Commission," save where the distinction needs to be clearly drawn between it and other bodies, *e.g.* the Royal Commission on Historical Monuments (England).[12]]

Most of the Commission's specific functions were taken over from the Secretary of State and include the management and preservation of many buildings and monuments, making grants for their upkeep and repair, acquiring or assuming guardianship of certain sites, advising the Secretary of State on listing and on applications made or referred to the Secretary of State to carry out certain works, carrying out and recording the results of research and archaeological investigation, and providing educational facilities.

It is essential to remember that the Secretary of State retains overall **1.06** financial control, responsibility for broad policy matters, and his quasi-judicial function. Many of the functions of the Secretary of State can now only be carried out after advice from or on the recommendation of the Commission. We note throughout the book where such advice must be sought.

Since the Commission's start in 1984, various new projects have come into being under its auspices, *e.g.* the power to compile a register of historic gardens. The Commission's decisions are made and its activities carried on in consultation with the Ancient Monuments Advisory Committee and the Historic Buildings Advisory Committee.

The Commission superseded the Historic Buildings Council for England and the Ancient Monuments Board for England, although the corresponding bodies for Wales and for Scotland remain in being.

In March 1987 there were in England a total number of 403,623 listed buildings (of which 5,887 were Grade I), 12,875 scheduled ancient monuments and 5,902 designated conservation areas.

Most recently we have the Housing and Planning Act 1986. Schedule 9 of that Act introduces a higher degree of definition into areas of listed building legislation which had previously been vague or open to conflicting interpretations. "Objects within the curtilage" of a listed building are more closely defined, and the defence to a charge of unauthorised works to a listed building, namely that the works were "urgently necessary," is narrowed. A new two-stage process for the granting of listed building consent is introduced, and local planning authorities are given wider powers to take in hand the preservation of a building urgently in need of repair. Further, the problematical "ecclesiastical exemption" and the control of demolition in conservation areas are both tackled in the 1986 Act.

A brief comment should perhaps be made as to the differences in historic building control procedure followed in England, Wales and Scotland. It has already been mentioned[13] that the jurisdiction of the Commission does not extend to Scotland or Wales, but that these two countries have their own corresponding bodies (as indeed they always had) carrying out similar and co-ordinating functions. The law and practice relating to historic buildings is the same in England and Wales for all practical purposes; and in Scotland too, although, as regards the legislation, variations in detail will be found set out in the statutes, to which reference should be made as necessary.

---

[12] See, *e.g.* para. 8.33.
[13] See para. 1.05 and also, para. 13.02.

DOE Circular 14 of 1985 (paragraph 3.3) talks of the need for

" . . . a planning system that works efficiently and effectively, and strikes the right balance between the needs of development and the interests of conservation. It is not to be regarded simply as a means of preventing change."

It is probable that many people do regard historic building controls in this very light, described by Lady Birk as a "pickling policy."[14] Paragraph 3.4 continues:

"If the planning authority considers it necessary to refuse permission, the onus is on them to demonstrate clearly why the development cannot be permitted and the reasons must be precise, specific and relevant to the application."

which as a principle applies as much to consents for historic buildings as to general planning permissions.

Are we going too far? A cautionary note was sounded by Secretary of State for the Environment, Nicholas Ridley, in January 1988 when he said in a speech to the National Association of Conservative Graduates[15]:

"I have a recurring nightmare, that sometime in the next century the entire country will be designated under some conservation order or other. The people actually living there will be smothered with bureaucratic instructions limiting their freedom. We will have created a sanitised, bureaucratised and ossified countryside out of something which has always been, and should always be, a product of the interaction of man and his environment as time goes by."

We are a far cry from the 50 scheduled monuments of 1882. The process of arriving, however, has been and is, complex, as we will see.

---

[14] Baroness Birk, Parliamentary Under-Secretary of State at the Department of the Environment, opening address at the Oxford Conference 1976, in *Journal of Planning and Environment Law*, Occasional Papers (1977), p. 5.
[15] Reported in *Planning Bulletin*, January 8, 1988.

2. Listing

1. GENERAL SUMMARY

Central to planning is a plan; central to listing is the list. The crux is sec- **2.01**
tion 54(1) of the 1971 Act which provides:

> "For the purposes of this Act and with a view to the guidance of local
> planning authorities in the performance of their functions under this
> Act in relation to buildings of special architectural or historic interest,
> the Secretary of State shall compile lists of such buildings, or approve,
> with or without modifications, such lists compiled by [the Historic
> Buildings and Monuments Commission for England . . . or by] other
> persons or bodies of persons, and may amend any list so compiled or
> approved."[1]

There are no lists compiled by other bodies which have been approved by
the Secretary of State: thus the list with which we are presently concerned
is the list compiled by the Secretary of State. It is central government (*i.e.*
the Department of the Environment), and not local government, which has
the responsibility of listing, although in practice, of course, many local
authorities often encourage central government to place on the list buildings with which they are particularly concerned. Some local authorities and
private consultant firms are revising existing lists at the request of and
under the supervision of the Department of the Environment.

The list is not one long document, but a series of lists divided normally in

---

[1] The words in brackets were inserted by the National Heritage Act 1983, which
established the Historic Buildings and Monuments Commission for England
referred to throughout this book as "the Commission."

street alphabetical order, although sometimes (but not often) in grade order. Each list refers to a particular local authority area; when first compiled these related to the former local authority areas, but where a re-survey has taken place the list will now relate to the new local authority area. Buildings included in the list are divided according to their status. Grade I relates to buildings of outstanding national interest (although this Grade is sometimes referred to as having buildings of exceptional interest or outstanding interest or outstanding quality); Grade II contains buildings of "special architectural or historic interest which warrant every effort being made to save them." Particularly important buildings in this section are classified as Grade II*. The grading of a building may affect the grants available to it, but the criteria for making grants has no direct reference to the grading for listing purposes.

The procedure for listing a building is described in detail later, but listing is an order made by the Secretary of State when the civil service head of the branch concerned (being duly authorised to sign on behalf of the Secretary of State) signs and dates the list, that in effect constitutes the listing.

2.02   Buildings appear on the list by one of three methods—first as a result of normal procedures following the methodical re-survey of the country by the DOE investigators. The second is an expedited procedure: spot listing. Spot listing is in particular used for buildings which appear to be in immediate danger of being demolished. The DOE claims that it can spot list a building in less than 24 hours if it is satisfied that it falls into the category of being of "special architectural or historic interest." This was demonstrated in June 1980, when the Secretary of State finally spot listed Billingsgate Market.[2] The Secretary of State has outlined his policy on conservation to be one of retaining buildings of architectural or historic interest wherever possible.[3]

Political considerations have been believed to interfere with spot listing, for example when it was disclosed in 1980 that spot listing had been initially refused in respect of a former potato warehouse in Covent Garden (now listed). It was suspected that the initial refusal was made because the GLC had ambitions to redevelop the building.[4]

But spot listing is not always fast enough. This was demonstrated by the demolition, before the DOE had chance to protect it through spot listing, of the art deco Firestone factory in Brentford. The demolition occurred over August Bank Holiday weekend 1980, and the mechanics of spot listing could not be brought into action because of the holiday.[5] A spokesman for the DOE criticised Hounslow Borough Council for not issuing a building preservation notice in respect of the site.[6] Sometimes spot listing can be too fast and there is evidence of a building being spot listed which it was subsequently felt did not pass the basic test and was then deleted from the list.[6a]

As a result of the Brentford case, the Secretary of State announced that he is determined to review the listing procedure to see where improvements might be made: "I have no intention of standing by while buildings of the

---

[2] *Sunday Times*, June 22, 1980.
[3] (1980) 253 E.G. 1211.
[4] *Period Home* (August 1985) p. 16.
[5] (1980) 255 E.G. 851.
[6] *The Sunday Telegraph*, August 31, 1980.
[6a] Cottages at White Row, Akeham, York.

inter-war period are destroyed without very careful consideration being given to the possibility of preserving them." As a result specific provisions relating to twentieth century buildings are included in Circular 8/87 which at Appendix I sets out criteria for the selection for listing of buildings of the 1919–1939 period. Already the Secretary of State has listed a number of important twentieth century buildings, including Battersea Power Station and the Hoover factory in West London[7] and the Craven Cottage stand at Fulham Football Club.[8]

The third method is as a result of the service of a building preservation notice, as to which see at para. 2.04 below.

It is said that there is evidence of what is called "blanket" listing, *i.e.* list- **2.03** ing a large number of buildings which may eventually be considered of architectural or historic interest, and leaving the merits of their being listed to be determined on a subsequent occasion, when an application is being made for "Listed Building Consent." This allegation would be denied by the Department, for the statute provides that only buildings which pass the test at the time of listing, as being of "special architectural or historic interest," should be included.[9] If blanket listing were the practice, or were to become the practice, then the list would take on a quite different quality and the qualifying words in section 54(1) would be unnecessary, or would need to be amended so as to reflect the fact that the special interest might spring up or have to be proved at a later date. The Minister has indicated that to list a building simply on the basis that it is threatened with demolition would be in excess of his powers.[10]

The inter-relationship of the various codes has been dealt with in the previous chapter. It is essential to see in some detail the derivation of the list in order to be able to assess its correct status. The 1932 Planning Act gave local authorities power to make preservation orders for buildings of special architectural or historic interest, but each order had to be approved by the Minister, who had to consider representations of those involved. There were provisions for compensation for those affected by a preservation order. The 1944 Planning Act empowered the new Minister of Town and Country Planning to prepare lists of buildings of special architectural or historic interest, which lists were for the guidance of local authorities. These powers were strengthened in the 1947 Planning Act, when the Minister was placed under a duty to make lists, and the owners of property had merely to be notified of the inclusion of their buildings in such a list. There was no appeal against the lists, and no compensation if a building was listed. Demolition or major works on a listed building could not be carried out without two months' notice to the local planning authority, and during that period the authority could serve a building preservation order. Such an order had to be confirmed by the Minister, and normally provided for the consent of the local planning authority to be obtained for the execution of any work specified in the order. The order also gave power to the authority to require the restoration of the building to its former state and created a criminal penalty for contravention of the order. Ecclesiastical buildings and ancient monuments were given special treatment.

[7] *The Times*, October 15, 1980.
[8] *The Times*, March 25, 1987.
[9] T.C.P.A. 1971, s.54(1).
[10] (1978) 245 E.G. 860.

2.04   As a result of the Town and Country Planning Act 1968 the procedure was changed. The statutory list became in itself a building preservation order in respect of the buildings on it.[11] There was no need thereafter to have a building preservation order made by the local authority. There was introduced a provision whereby listed building consent (LBC) had to be applied for from a local planning authority in respect of works of demolition, alteration, or extension to a building on the list.[12] In respect of buildings which were not listed, there was a speedy procedure whereby a local planning authority could serve a building preservation notice which would have the effect of putting the building on the list and giving the authorities all the powers of the list in relation to that building until the issue was resolved.[13]

Those provisions were substantially re-enacted in the 1971 Act and they express in general terms the powers and consequences which we shall deal with later. There are the obvious corollaries of criminal offences[14] and powers of the local authority to require restoration work by a document called a listed building enforcement notice.[15] These powers are effectively carried out by the local planning authority (except where it, as a local authority, owns a building so affected) even though the list is in the control of the DOE.

2.05   In trying to ascertain what is the status of the list, one must remember that there is no appeal against listing. There is power to amend the list,[16] and DOE Circular 8/87[17] states that the Department will consider requests to remove buildings from the statutory list where new evidence can be produced to show that they do not possess the special architectural or historic interest ascribed to them. Whilst grounds for listing are given which will show broadly whether the reason for listing is architectural or historical, not all factors which lead the Department to list a building are specified.[18] It thus might be difficult to show that a building should be taken off the list. In February 1978 the Secretary of State, whilst conceding that to list a building "merely on the grounds that [it] was threatened" would be an excessive use of his powers, rejected an allegation that a bus garage in Norbiton had not been properly listed.[19] However, there are cases where the list has been amended by striking off entries where either there was a mistake of description (*e.g.* the wrong number of houses, etc.) or where there has been a genuine misjudgment at listing stage. Where the Department accept either of these cases an order will be made in similar form to an order listing a building, but deleting the entry by amendment. Recent incidents have revealed that mistakes can be made by the DOE. The Odeon cinema, Shepherd's Bush, was listed because of a clerical error, instead of the Liberty

---

[11] T.C.P.A. 1968, s.48.

[12] T.C.P.A. 1968, s.40(4)(*a*).

[13] T.C.P.A. 1968, s.48(1).

[14] T.C.P.A. 1968, s.40; T.C.P.A. 1971, s.55.

[15] T.C.P.A. 1968, s.44; T.C.P.A. 1971, s.96 (as substituted by L.G.P.(A).A. 1981, s.1 and Sched., para. 9).

[16] T.C.P.A. 1971, s.54(1).

[17] At para. 40. Requests to de-list should be sent to the Department's Listing Branch (HSD2), Lambeth Bridge House, London SE1 7SB, and should be accompanied by photographs and a location plan.

[18] [1980] J.P.L. 715–719.

[19] (1978) 245 E.G. 860.

Cinema, Southall, the only art deco Chinese cinema in England, which remains unlisted.[20] In March 1980 Greater London Council wrote to the DOE about a building in Park Street, part of which had been listed, part of which had not. The DOE did not review the listing, but informed the Historic Buildings Council that the original listing had been an administrative mistake and wrote to the council saying "the Department concludes that the building is not of special architectural or historic interest and should not have been included in the statutory list."[21] In 1988 the DOE listed as Grade II a "16th century house" at Sea Palling in Norfolk. The DOE admitted later that this was a mistake as the house had been built between 1983 and 1988, the roof having come from a barn, lintels and doors from demolition sites and the bressumers over two inglenook fireplaces retrieved from a scrapyard. Settlement had been built in. The inspector asserted that the building deserved its Grade II listing "on the grounds of rarity and eccentricity, if not antiquity." The building is being considered at the time of going to press for removal from the list.[21aa]

The "workable non-statutory right" of appeal against listing was referred to in the House of Lords debate on the Bill which became the Housing and Planning Act 1986.[21a] In 1985 notification was made individually in respect of 23,000 new listings: the Department received only some three dozen appeals of which five were successful.

> "The grounds of appeal are very limited. It is not a question of judgment or interpretation of a structure or local plan. It is a question of fact that has to be decided and can be decided without recourse to a full-blown appeals mechanism. I accept that there must always be an element of subjective judgment in the selection of buildings: but in practice, we find that appeals against listing are mostly based on matters of fact rather than interpretation." (Lord Skelmersdale on behalf of the Government.)

A guidance note has been issued[21b] which gives a useful check list of why buildings are listed. In reviewing a listing the Department will ask an expert different from the one who saw the property before listing to visit the property "in the light of what the owner says about it. The inspector will, if you wish, make an appointment to see you when reviewing the case."

2.06 In some people's eyes there has developed, in effect, a presumption that because a building is on the list it has a certain permanent quality of being of "special architectural or historic interest." In recent years "listing" has been emphasised by estate agents as a desirable quality in certain houses, as opposed to its true function, which is a control mechanism.

It is this approach to listing which guides members of the public into thinking that the list has a greater significance than it has. Looking at the threads of legislation from 1932 until the present date, it is clear that Parliament considers the list as a control mechanism and not as a definitive assessment of a quality judgment. Many conservationists believe that it

---

[20] *The Guardian*, September 3, 1980.
[21] *Private Eye*, May 23, 1980.
[21aa] *The Times*, April 11, 1988.
[21a] Lord Skelmersdale *Hansard*, Lords October 13, 1986, col. 599 and 406 and Lord Swinfen, *ibid*. col. 596.
[21b] "How to appeal against listing" DOE September 1987.

should have this latter status, and indeed a SAVE report of December 1975 suggested that listed buildings should be presumed innocent, and condemned only if an overwhelming case against them has been proved: "otherwise they should be discharged unconditionally." The burden of proof should rest with the applicant, who should be required to give reasons for demolition—the test should be "Why demolish?" not "Why save?" Perhaps this introduces a burden of proof which is not implicit in the Act: Lady Birk (sometime Under Secretary of State for the DOE with particular concern for listed buildings) described the procedure as "not a pickling policy," which leaves it in a more neutral position.[22]

The essential, although not the only, difference between the listing of a building and the granting of LBC is the fact that financial considerations are not (nor in practice could they be) taken into account in listing; but these considerations may properly be taken into account in deciding whether or not to grant LBC.

2.07 The question of how far the list takes us—as to whether there is a presumption against demolition, or a protection only, or no presumption, has not been challenged in the High Court: until it is, it is suggested that the effect of placing a building on the list is merely to protect it and not to give it any permanent seal of approval as to quality.

Certain buildings are "deemed" to be listed. They fall into two categories, which can broadly be described as those buildings which were subject to an extant building preservation order under the earlier Planning Acts, unless and until the Secretary of State revokes that order,[23] and secondly those which are the subject of a building preservation notice served under the 1971 Act.[24]

Otherwise, any building can be listed. The point was made forcibly in the Court of Appeal in the *John Walker & Sons Limited*[25] case when Buckley L.J. said:

> "It seems to me that the risk of property being listed as property of architectural or historical interest is a risk which inheres in all ownership of buildings. In many cases it may be an extremely remote risk. In many cases it may be a marginal risk. In some cases it may be a substantial risk. But it is a risk, I think which attaches to all buildings and it is a risk that every owner and every purchaser of property must recognise that he is subject to."

This risk is now alleviated by the provisions of section 54A making provision for a certificate of immunity against listing—see para. 2.49 below.

There are now no buildings which cannot be listed, but different consequences flow in respect of the listing of churches in ecclesiastical use, ancient monuments, and Crown property. Church buildings in use as such have their own code in respect of alteration and extension (but not total demolition)[26]; the ancient monument code overlaps to some extent in prac-

---

[22] Baroness Birk, Parliamentary Under-Secretary of State at the Department of the Environment, Opening Address at the Oxford Conference 1976, in *Journal of Planning and Environment Law*, Occasional Papers (1977), p. 5.

[23] T.C.P.A. 1971, s.54(10).

[24] T.C.P.A. 1971, s.58(4).

[25] *Amalgamated Investment and Property Co.* v. *Walker (John) and Sons* [1976] 3 All E.R. 509; 120 S.J. 252; (1976) E.G. 277, C.A.

[26] See paras. 5.28–5.32 below.

tice with the listed buildings code,[27] and there are special consequences for Crown property.[27a] Buildings cease to be listed when LBC to demolish has been granted, and fully implemented. There is no authority for determining the exact moment at which the listing ceases to be of effect, but it is presumably the time when the last of conditions to be implemented has been fulfilled.

2. WHAT MAY BE LISTED

(a) The building

The answer to this question is set out in the 1971 Act, namely "a building **2.08** which is of special architectural or historic interest," but we must first decide what is a building.

A building is not defined positively in the Act, but negatively, by showing what is "included" in the definition of building, and not what is, in fact, "a building." It includes "any structure or erection and any part of a building structure or erection but does not include any plant or machinery comprised in a building."[28] The General Development Order 1977, Art. 2(1) again gives no positive guidance and merely follows the Act. Section 121(1) of the Building Act 1984 defines "building" for the purposes of building regulations as any permanent or temporary building, which includes any other structure or erection of whatever kind or nature; "structure or erection" including a vehicle, vessel, hovercraft, aircraft or other movable object in certain prescribed circumstances, and "building" includes part of a building. The *Oxford English Dictionary* defines "building" as "that which is built; a structure, edifice."

What is or is not within the definition of a "building" has been a matter concerning the judges for well over a century. Byles J. in 1859 asked:

> "What is 'a building'? Now the verb 'to build' is often used in a wider sense than the substantive 'building.' . . . The imperfection of human language renders it not only difficult, but absolutely impossible, to define the word 'building' with any approach to accuracy . . . I may venture to suggest, that, by a 'building' is usually understood a structure of considerable size, and intended to be permanent, or at least to endure for a considerable time."[29]

The judges have determined from time to time what is or is not a building in interpreting various statutes, and they have given *obiter* opinions on the subject. A summary of some of these decisions gives some further illustration to the suggestion of Byles J., but these lists are not intended to be comprehensive. It should also be remembered that if the edifice is not a building as such, it might fall within the definition of a structure or erection.

Those edifices (to use a neutral word) thought to be a building have **2.09** included a church, a cowhouse, a structure nine feet long, seven feet high,

---

[27] See Chap. 8: Ancient Monuments.
[27a] See paras. 5.34–5.38 below.
[28] T.C.P.A. 1971, s.290.
[29] *Stevens* v. *Gourley* (1859) 7 C.B.(N.S.) 99 at 112 *per* Byles J.

three feet wide, erected some 30 feet in front of the line of street roofed in and fastened securely to the ground, a wooden screen of open trellis work, a hoarding of a permanent nature 156 feet long and 15 feet high for bill posting, statues and monuments, farm walls not appurtenant to farm buildings or used in connection with them, a bandstand where variety entertainments were provided, a model village, a viaduct, and a temporary building.

Those edifices thought not to be a building have included a bird cage, a dog-kennel, a hen-coop, a fence or barrier to prevent the acquisition of prescriptive rights to light, a canal, a bank composed of consolidated earth and covered with grass which has kept out the sea for 2,000 years, four walls erected one foot high, and an incomplete structure.

Whilst the Act does not give a positive definition, a combination of the definitions found in the Act, the above interpretations by the Courts, and the commentary in Circular 8/87 gives a clearer idea certainly of what the Department regards as a "building" which may be helpful until the matter is authoritatively decided by the Courts.

In summary:

2.10   (a) In the definitions section—section 290 (as amended by Schedule 9 to the Housing and Planning Act 1986) " 'building' includes any structure or erection, and any part of a building, as so defined, but does not include plant or machinery comprised in a buiding."

(b) In section 54(9) (as amended by the 1986 Act) a "listed building" means "a building which is for the time being included in a list compiled or approved by the Secretary of State under this section; and, for the purposes of the provisions of this Act relating to listed buildings and building preservation notices, the following shall be treated as part of the building—

(a) any object or structure fixed to the building;

(b) any object or structure within the curtilage of the building which, although not fixed to the building, forms part of the land and has done so since before July 1, 1948."

(c) There is an interesting argument that a "listed building" is a generic term, unrelated to the definition of "a building" as such. Whilst there may be some merit in this argument, we do not consider that it is persuasive. A listed building must first be "a building."

(d) Section 54(2) provides that

"in considering whether to include a building in a list compiled or approved under this section, the Secretary of State may take into account not only the building itself but also—

(a) any respect in which its exterior contributes to the architectural or historic interest of any group of buildings of which it forms part; and

(b) the desirability of preserving, on the ground of its architectural or historic interest, any feature of the building consisting of a man-made object or structure fixed to the building or forming part of the land and comprised within the curtilage of the building."

2.11   (e) Section 28 of the 1971 Act requires local planning authorities to give publicity to any proposal which would affect the "setting" of a listed building. Section 56(3), as amended by the 1980 Act, now

14

requires authorities to have special regard to the desirability of preserving the listed building or its setting when considering planning applications and listed building consent applications which affect a listed building or its setting. Circular 8/87, paras. 25 and 26, observes that the setting of a listed building is often an essential feature of its character. It is important to consider the effect that proposed development may have on its character. It also refers to the importance of the building in its group.

(f) In Circular 8/87 advice is given in Appendix IV on alterations to listed buildings. Some indication may be gleaned from this advice as to what is capable of being listed in its own right, *e.g.* paragraph IV(8):

"Towers, turrets, spires, bell cotes, cupolas, are not only part of the overall design, or indeed its main feature, but frequently make an important contribution to the townscape or landscape."

In paragraph VI(1):

"Staircases, panelling, doors and door cases, mouldings, decorated ceilings, stucco work, wallpaintings of all periods, are part of the listed character of a building and indeed may be the most valuable feature."

In paragraph VII(2):

"Gazebos, temples, follies, grottoes, obelisks, park bridges, statues, urns, vases, ice houses, terraces, ha-has, crinkle-crankle walls and boundary walls and gates and gate piers all contribute to the planned landscape and setting."

(g) It will be seen that the definition of a building excludes plant and **2.12** machinery comprised in a building. This might seem an obvious exclusion, but as Lord Mackay observed in the *Debenhams* case[30]:

"Cases under the Income and Corporation Taxes Act 1970 demonstrate that the word 'plant' is a word of very extensive import and it is obvious that plant or machinery could be fixed to a building and might include structures so fixed."

(h) In *Corthorn Land & Timber Co.* v. *Minister of Housing & Local Government*[31] the divisional court held that any chattel "definitely" affixed to the building was part of the building.

(i) The question of chattels and their fixing is difficult. Two ornamental urns on pedestals in the garden of a listed building were said to have been correctly listed by the DOE, but the Parliamentary Commissioner invited the owner to seek a court ruling to the contrary.[32] Sculptures at Hever Castle, part of the Italian Sculpture Garden which was listed, were removed but, although no issue seems to have been determined in the courts, they were probably not affixed (either "definitely" or not) to the ground but rested by

---

[30] *Debenhams plc* v. *Westminster City Council* [1987] 1 All E.R. 51 at 58 g.

[31] *Corthorn Land and Timber Co.* v. *Minister of Housing and Local Government* (1965) 63 L.G.R. 490; (1966) 17 P. & C.R. 210; [1965] C.L.Y. 3778.

[32] [1980] J.P.L. 715. *Listed Buildings—Planning Law and Planning Reality*, by P. H. Morgan and S. M. Nott, at p. 720. Case reference: Fourth Report of the Parliamentary Commissioner for Administration, Session 1974–75, pp. 68–70. Case No. C/ 278/v/430/J.

their own weight. A statue of the Duke of Wellington for more than 80 years in the garden of an historic Borders mansion was removed but there has been no decision on whether the statue was listed— but the issue there was presumably the same, *i.e.* whether it was "affixed" or, if it was affixed, whether it was in a garden which was not itself part of the curtilage.[33] Tombstones and village pumps are generally accepted not as chattels but structures or erections falling within the definition. Roadways and pavements present greater difficulty: although the interest in floorscape is growing where a pavement is flush with the ground, it is not thought it can be a "structure" and therefore not listable. The nearest we can get to reconciling these issues is to adopt the test as to whether an object is a fixture suggested by Scarman L.J. (as he then was) in *Berkley* v. *Poulett*[34]:

" . . . an object, resting on the ground by its own weight alone, can be a fixture, if it be so heavy that there is no need to tie it into a foundation and if it were put in place to improve the realty. Prima facie, however, an object resting on the ground by its own weight alone is not a fixture."

2.13   (j) When does a building cease to be a building? If neglect or bad occupation has reduced the architectural interest of a building until it is no more than a mere relic of what it was, it probably has ceased to be a building. But a timber framed building can be listable when the frame is complete but the cladding or even the roof covering is largely destroyed. For practical purposes, however, if the roof and most of the walls have disappeared (say, if less than 50 per cent. of the original cubic content is left) it would be difficult to justify listing; however, if that shell had been listed [or non-listed but in a conservation area] and had been deliberately put into this condition, there is little doubt that a listed building enforcement notice would lie and a prosecution be justified: it would be no answer to say: "it is no longer a listed building."

(k) Thus a wide variety of "buildings, structures or erections" can be listed provided that
    (i) they are of suitable quality, and
    (ii) they are not chattels as such but pass the test of "definite" affixion or the object and purpose test in *Berkley* v. *Poulett*, and
    (iii) they have not deteriorated to such an extent that they could not be said to be a building.

Some examples of what have been listed apart from the obvious houses, palaces, public buildings and industrial buildings are:

2.14

Archways	Whipping posts
Gazebos	Gibbets
Temples	Maypoles
Grottoes	Sign posts
Follies	Lamp-posts
Eyecatchers	Bollards

---

[33] Article, *Sunday Telegraph*: "Scots angry over missing statues," January 11, 1987.
[34] (1976) E.C. Digest 754 at 763.

Summer Houses	Pillar boxes
Pounds	Gates and gate-piers
Dovecotes	Railings and fences
Horse gin houses	Raised pavements
Donkey wheel houses	Steps
Bee-boles	Walls, including retaining walls and
Dog Kennels	fortifications (but not earthworks)
Ice Houses	Lych-gates
Windmills	Stiles
Watermills	Boundary stones
Bridges	Hundred stones
Docks	Memorial stones
Locks	Tombs
Tunnel entrances	War Memorials
Lock-ups	Cock pits
Grave watchers huts	Pumps
Fountains	Police boxes or Watchmen's huts
Chairmen's boxes	Surrounds to garden pools and canals
Stocks	Wells houses and retaining walls

(b) The exterior and the features

2.15 We deal in detail with the listable qualities under the section on selection and grading[35] and merely observe here the statutory requirements:

(1) A building must be of special architectural or historic interest.

(2) The Secretary of State may take into account not only the building itself, but

"(a) any respect which the exterior contributes to the architectural or historic interest of the group, and

(b) the desirability of preserving . . . any feature of the building consisting of a man-made object or structure . . . "[36]

These are perhaps self evident, but the qualification as to the object or structure being "man-made" is interesting and perhaps worth remembering. One could get involved into esoteric debates about what is man made or made by God. So far no one seems to have challenged a listing because the Secretary of State, in his discretion, took into account a feature which was other than man made.

(c) The structure

2.16 We have so far considered structures when they are either "parts" of the building but freestanding, or freestanding structures which would not ordinarily be thought of as a building—stocks, whipping-posts, stiles and pumps.

But how far does the listing embrace other buildings or structures which may be physically attached to the building named on the list but which themselves are not separately listed and sometimes may not be of listable

---

[35] See paras. 2.23–2.36 below.
[36] T.C.P.A. 1971, s.54(2).

quality? The answer may be in two directions—whether the other structure is fixed to the building or whether it is within the curtilage of the named listed building.

A definitive answer to the "fixed" point derives from an examination of the majority decision of the House of Lords in *Debenhams plc* v. *Westminster City Council*.[37] This was a rating case where rates would not be chargeable if the rating hereditament was included in the list compiled under section 54 of the Act. Debenhams were the owners of a rating hereditament which comprised two separate buildings, one in Regent Street and one in Kingly Street. They were opposite each other with the back of the Regent Street premises facing the front of Kingly Street, with Kingly Street between them. They were joined by a footbridge over and a tunnel under the street. The Regent Street building was listed but the Kingly Street building was not. Debenhams used the two buildings as a single commercial unit ("Hamleys" the toy shop). In October 1981 Debenhams vacated the hereditament (*i.e.* both units) and it remained unoccupied for the relevant rating year. Debenhams claimed the exemption for both units but the City Council refused to accede to this argument as only the Regent Street building was listed. The issue was could the Kingly Street building be a "structure fixed to a [listed] building"?

The House of Lords held that this expression (from section 54(9)) only encompassed a structure which was either fixed to the main building or within its curtilage, *e.g.* the stable block of a listed mansion house or the steading of a listed farmhouse. The fact that one building was subordinated to another for the commercial purposes of the occupier or that a completely distinct building was connected to a listed building to which it was not subordinate did not make the building a structure fixed to a listed building. Since the Regent Street and the Kingly Street buildings were historically completely independent, the Kingly Street building was not a listed building under section 54(9) of the 1971 Act.

Their Lordships concluded that a different result could lead to difficulties in compiling and construing the list. Would structures adjacent to the "structure" (*e.g.* other buildings in Kingly Street and adjoining streets) be deemed to be listed? Lord Mackay said[38]:

> "Since it is obviously necessary that the list should identify the buildings contained in it, the question whether a particular physical entity is listed or not listed depends on whether on reading the list and taking account of the statutory provisions that entity is to be regarded as a building or part of a building included in the list."

(d) The curtilage

2.17   The question of what is the curtilage is a difficult—and still unsettled—issue. But preceding that debate it is necessary to reflect that if the object or structure is to be treated as part of the listed building, it must form part of "the land." Land is defined in section 290 as "any corporeal hereditament including a building . . . " Broadly, this is a freehold or leasehold, but the

---

[37] See n. 30 above.
[38] *Debenhams plc* v. *Westminster City Council* [1987] 1 All E.R. 51 at 57j.

definition does not specify the extent of the land which compares with the definition contained in section 190(3) which is for compulsory purchase reasons. But the House of Lords envisaged that a listed building "will normally constitute a single holding."[39]

How far across the curtilage or land or garden can the listing extend? We have seen that the setting of a building can be significant: paragraph 8(a) of Schedule 15 to the 1980 Act, provides that the words "or its setting" should be inserted into section 56(3) of the 1971 Act, so that in considering whether or not to grant planning permission for development affecting "a listed building or its setting" or LBC for any works

> "the local planning authority or the Secretary of State, as the case may be, shall have special regard to the desirability of preserving the building or its setting or any features of special architectural or historic interest which it possesses."

The matter is further complicated by the concept of the "curtilage." It will be remembered that section 54(2)(b) provides that the Secretary of State may take into account not only the building itself but also

> "the desirability of preserving, on the grounds of its architectural or historic interest, any feature of the building consisting of a man-made object or structure fixed to the building or forming part of the land and comprised within the curtilage of the building."

The definitions section—section 54(9) (as amended by the 1986 Act) states: **2.18**

> " . . . the following shall be treated as part of the building— . . . any object or structure within the curtilage of the building which, although not fixed to the building, forms part of the land and has done so since before July 1, 1948."

What, therefore, is the curtilage? This phrase hallowed by conveyancers from time immemorial so far as it can be seen has never been definitively interpreted in the English courts, but a case came before the Court of Session in 1950 where the phrase was in issue. The Court of Session held that:

> "the ground which is used for the comfortable enjoyment of a house or other building may be regarded in law as being within the curtilage of that house or building and thereby as an integral part of the same although it has not been marked off or enclosed in any way. It is enough that it serves the purpose of the house or building in some necessary or reasonably useful way."[40]

The problem about the concept of the curtilage is that this definition depends on congruity of occupation, if not of ownership. A test can be taken at the time of listing as set out above: *e.g.* does the ice-house or the gardener's lodge serve the purpose of the house or building? Yes, it does at the time of listing, but suppose that the lodge is sold off to someone with no connection with the house: it might be assumed no longer to be part of the curtilage.

Difficult though the curtilage concept is, the Department decided not to

---

[39] *Ibid.* at p. 60.
[40] *Sinclair-Lockharts Trustees* v. *Central Land Board* (1950) 1 P. & C.R. 195; aff. (1951) 1 P. & C.R. 320.

seek to define the word in the 1986 Act. There have, however, been two helpful cases—the *Debenhams* case above and the *Calderdale* case[41]. In the latter case, three local residents wished to preserve a terrace of 15 four-storey cottages, known as 3 to 31 Nutclough, Hebden Bridge, from demolition by the local council which owned them. The terraced cottages were constructed as mill workers' dwellings. The mill was erected in 1820 and was listed. The terrace was erected in about 1870. Part of the terrace was also used for industrial purposes. There was a stone bridge linking the mill to No 1 Nutclough and giving direct access to Nos. 3 and 5. Until 1973 the land on which the mill and terrace stood were in common ownership. In 1973 the council became the owner of the terrace. Neither the mill nor the bridge nor the terrace were in use. The terrace was not listed. The question for the Court of Appeal was whether or not the terrace was "a structure . . . forming part of the land and comprised within the curtilage of the building" (*i.e.* the mill which was listed).

2.19   Lord Justice Stephenson concluded that the court should take into account the following factors in determining whether a "structure" was within the curtilage whatever might be the conveyancing interpretation. They were:

(1) the physical "layout" of the listed building and the structure;
(2) their ownership, past and present;
(3) their use or function past and present.

Where they were in common ownership and one was used in connection with the other, there was little difficulty in classifying a structure near a building or even some distance from it, as within its curtilage.

In the *Calderdale* case the court held that the terrace was within the curtilage. Lord Justice Stephenson defined the curtilage of a listed building as

"an area of land which includes any related objects or structures which naturally form, or formed, with the listed building an integral whole."

The *Calderdale* case referred to the related objects which "forms or formed" an integral whole. There is yet to be decided a case where disposals of part suggest new separate units of occupation and thus new curtilages. As Stephenson L.J. said in the argument on costs: "The facts of this case were very special: this was a very unusual sort of single unit."

The view of Stephenson L.J. and his tests have to be looked at with some caution because of the comments of the House of Lords in the *Debenhams* case. The *Debenhams* case, it is true, was concerned primarily with structure rather than curtilage, but it is significant that Lord Mackay opined that *Calderdale* was "a very special case on its facts"[42] and doubted the reasons of the court in *Calderdale*. Further, Lord Keith in *Debenhams* observed that "the matter of listing or not listing cannot turn on the business purposes or manner of use of adjoining properties of a particular user."[43]

2.20   Perhaps, however, we are nearer an answer to the difficult question of what happens when the ownership—or indeed perhaps merely the occupation—of an "integral whole" is fragmented. If there is no longer any connection between the fragmented part which contains a structure which might

---

[41] *Attorney-General, ex rel. Sutcliffe* v. *Calderdale Borough Council* (1983) J.P.L. 310.
[42] *Debenhams plc* v. *Westminster City Council* [1987] 1 All E.R. 51 at 60j.
[43] *Ibid.* at p. 55j.

have been considered part of the curtilage and the named listed building, it may be a candidate for de-listing. An application could be made to remove it from the list as it now does not possess the special listable quality which had been ascribed to it when part of the curtilage of the named building.[44]

When Lord Montagu (Chairman of the Commission) rejected in the House of Lords the idea of a definition of curtilage, he referred to significant improvements in listing practices which have been made in the light of the *Calderdale* case. He said[45]:

> "The practice of the department now and my officers is to consider individually all the structures and buildings on a site which can be construed as separate buildings and to list those, and only those, which qualify. The new lists therefore will leave little room for doubt as to whether a building is listed or not . . . "

The Act has been amended so that section 54(9) reads as indicated at para. 2.18 above, thus protecting "any object or structure which although not fixed to the building, forms part of the land and has done so since before July 1, 1948."

This did not, of course, remove the result—regarded by many as a strange anomaly—that listed building consent is not required to erect a building or structure within the curtilage of a listed building[46]; although since the 1986 Act any building or structure so erected will not itself be listable unless it has formed part of the land since before July 1, 1948.[46a] Planning permission is, however, required, and the local planning authority must take into account "the setting." It may well be that when a revision of the General Development Order (which grants certain permissions whether or not they affect the setting of a listed building) is promulgated some of the permissions now available under the GDO will be curtailed. Although section 56(3) requires the local planning authority to take into account the "setting" of a listed building in considering whether to grant LBC, that requirement cannot make a building into a listed building nor force an unlisted building not within the curtilage into the curtilage.

(e) Conclusions

(1) The building must be a building within the legal definition (*e.g.* not **2.21** a hen-coop) or a structure or erection (*e.g.* a lamp-post or pillar box). Of course, something which may not fall within a lawyer's definition of a "building" (*e.g.* a dog kennel) could be listed because it is a "structure or erection."

(2) It must be of the appropriate quality (*i.e.* of special architectural or historic interest).

(3) A chattel cannot be listed unless it

---

[44] Above at para. 2.05 and see Circular 8/87, para. 40.
[45] *Hansard*: House of Lords, Oct 13, 1986, Col. 626.
[46] *Cotswold District Council* v. *Secretary of State for the Environment and Pearson* (1985) J.P.L. 407 (David Widdicombe Q.C. sitting as a deputy high court judge).
[46a] T.C.P.A. 1971, s.54(9)(*a*).

(a) is "definitely" affixed to a building, or

(b) is an object resting on the ground by its own weight alone put in place "to improve the realty."

(4) The listing of a building will not embrace within its listing a separate structure which is not listed unless that separate structure is within the curtilage of the listed building.

(5) A separate structure will be within the curtilage if it is in common ownership and used in connection with the other even if the separate structure is some distance from the listed building. The separate structure must be on "the land."

(6) A separate structure which is not in common ownership with the listed building may be within its curtilage if the three tests in *Calderdale* are satisfied, although some doubt must be cast on the use or function test in view of Lord Keith's comments in the *Debenhams* case. If there is an absence of common ownership (particularly if separated at the time of listing) and the structure is not near the listed building, there seems to be a strongly arguable case that the separate structure is not listed as being within the curtilage and an application could be made for its removal from the list.

(7) It is certainly arguable that a concept of a "moving" curtilage is with us, as opposed to the traditional conveyancers' idea. It could well be argued that as estates are divided up the curtilage becomes smaller—indeed, the definition in the Oxford English Dictionary as "a small court, yard, or piece of ground attached to a dwellinghouse and forming one enclosure with it" could apply. The practical difficulty of this is to know the facts on which it is relied to determine the extent of the curtilage, and to determine the material date on which the curtilage is to be defined.

2.22

(8) The new listings (probably from 1986 onwards) will clearly indicate which buildings within the curtilage are specifically listed.

(9) A building cannot be a listable building if it is almost derelict or a shell unless the main structure is complete even without roof covering or cladding (*e.g.* a timber frame).

(10) There is deemed to be within the listing an object or structure which although not fixed to the building forms part of the land and has done so since before July 1, 1948 (I.C.P.A. 1971, s.54(9)).

(11) Otherwise the erection of a separate structure or erection does not require listed building consent. If it forms part of the land it will only be listed if it falls within the curtilage definition.

Finally, there is some doubt as to who interprets the extent of the listing. The Department takes the view that what is covered by the curtilage provisions in any given case is ultimately a matter for the courts, although the relevant local authority may be prepared to express its own view in the matter. Although at first sight this may seem unhelpful, it is a correct interpretation of the procedure. The Department lists but it is up to the local planning authority to interpret and act—*e.g.* by a prosecution or listed building enforcement notice. If the owner does not agree, then he has to resort to an argument in the magistrates court, or an appeal to the Department, which if not satisfactory, will lead to testing in the courts.[47]

---

[47] SE2/5277/270/68 as reported in the *Estates Times*, January 23, 1987.

3. SELECTION AND GRADING

There are two stages in considering a building for the purposes of the list.   **2.23**

(a) Should the building be *selected* for listing? If so:

(b) In what *grade* should it be placed?

(a) Selection

In considering the answer to the question of selection, it is important to remember the provisions of section 54(2) which provide that the Secretary of State may take into account not only the building itself, but also:

(1) any respect in which its exterior contributes to the architectural or historic interest of any group of buildings of which it forms part; and

(2) the desirability of preserving, on the ground of its architectural or historic interest, any feature of the building consisting of a man-made object or structure fixed to the building or forming part of the land and comprised within the curtilage of the building.

Furthermore, the case of *Iveagh* v. *the Minister of Housing and Local Government*[48] decided that it was proper to consider the interest of the whole of a terrace in deciding whether to list a building forming part of the terrace.

Assuming that which is to be listed passes the test of being a "building," we must give consideration to the basic question of whether its special interest is architectural or historic. This consideration gives rise to particular problems for those concerned with the listing process and raises a number of fundamental questions.

In considering what constitutes "architectural" interest, a view must be   **2.24** taken as to whether the term embraces the art and technique of building in its widest sense, or the design and appearance of a building in a more limited context. The assessment of what constitutes good architectural design will be largely subjective and will inevitably stem from a particular inspector's specialist knowledge and aesthetic judgment, whereas an assessment of vernacular buildings in a particular locality could properly be made against an objective points system, in which pre-determined intrinsic features are awarded a certain score.

The development of modern building techniques has created a number of potentially interesting situations. Could a building which is of great interest structurally be neither of historic nor of architectural interest? Would a novel technological development which was part of an ugly and modern building merit the listing of the building which reflected that technology? Some might aver that certain "point blocks" which were built in the 1960–70 period in the United Kingdom were of significance in the history of the development of concrete as a building material. Would the scarcity value of a particular type of concrete or the fact that the point blocks are no longer being built today, justify the preservation of a last surviving

---

[48] [1964] 1 Q.B. 395; [1963] 3 W.L.R. 974; 3 All E.R. 817; 128 J.P. 70; 107 S.J. 490–851.

example? Could such a building properly be listed? It is neither beautiful nor old, and could not be regarded as "historic", but we believe it could be properly listed as the word "architectural" has the widest meaning and will embrace types of materials, methods of building expression and form, space, mass, light, scale, colour and the like, so long as that which is to be listed is in fact a building.

2.25   The DOE Guidance Notes[49] advise that in selecting a building for its association with technological innovation or virtuosity, it is essential that the information is absolutely accurate and dependable, as most of the buildings in this category are selected on the basis of historical fact, *e.g.* the first example of its type or the first use of a material rather than on aesthetic qualities.

If it cannot claim any architectural interest, then it can only qualify if it is of historic interest. The determination of what constitutes historic interest is eminently debatable and raises many issues. The DOE Guidance Notes suggest that an assessment of historic interest should deal with:

(i)   the importance of the person or event, and
(ii) the importance of the building in relation to that person's life and work or that event. (The transient association of lodgers or tenants, however eminent, should be looked at critically.)

Whilst these guidelines are helpful to a degree, they still nevertheless leave considerable scope for individual interpretation. There is no judicial interpretation of what constitutes "architectural" or "historic" interest in this context, and whilst there appears to be no settled view at the DOE on architectural interest, there is even less on the historic criterion. Perhaps this is as well and encourages flexibility, although it does appear that whilst many properties are associated with famous people, it would seem that literary associations exercise a particularly powerful effect.

2.26   A particularly useful illustration of a building being listed almost entirely for its historical association is found in an article by Paul Bristow[50] in his description of Underhill at Gateshead, which is listed Grade II*. Although it is considered to be largely an unprepossessing Victorian house typical of many in the north east, its particular importance lies in an early tenant, Sir Joseph Swan F.R.S., who lived there from 1869–83. During that time he invented the incandescent electric light bulb and the house was the first in England to be wired for domestic electric lighting. Its importance is thus threefold; it was the home for a considerable period of an important inventor and is the place both of the invention and of the first application of the light bulb on which his fame rests. Paul Bristow considers that whereas one of these associations would have made it listable, the three together give it the high grading.

A further example of a listing for historic interest is St Mark's Railway Station, Lincoln. The inspector (in an LBC case), recommending refusal to demolish, noted that the buildings "are of historic interest because they form part of Lincoln's first railway station."[51] Presumably this was thought (as the Secretary of State agreed with his inspector and refused LBC) to be

---

[49] "Guidance Notes to those concerned in the survey for listing" issued by the DOE in 1985 referred to throughout as "the DOE Guidance Notes".

[50] *Period Home* (January 1985), p. 15.

[51] DOE reference EMP/5311/270/G5 (reported in the *Estates Times* July 3, 1981).

enough: *i.e.* of local historic interest. It could be argued that if the interest
was to be local only, any building of a minute local interest would be
adequate to satisfy the test—what about The Little Puddlecombe Police
Cell? But we have no defined criterion as to whether the historic interest is
local, regional, or national. A challenge in the courts would, however, be
helpful. There may well be found a practical distinction between "architectural" and "historic" citations when the possibility of a demolition and
building of a pastiche occurs.

How the buildings are chosen. The principles of selection as to whether **2.27**
a building should be selected for the list are set out in Circular 8/87, Appendix I, and cover four groups. Each group is here followed by the Department
of the Environment's practical advice on selection, as set out in the Department's notes to those involved in the survey for listing (1985).

"(1) All buildings built before 1700 which survive in anything like their
original condition are listed".
*Any building with its timber frame virtually intact will be list-
able, but where the walling is of other materials the building is
normally listable only where its external features, doorcases, windows and so on, or alternatively its interior features survive well
enough to illustrate its early character. The external features need
not be original, but should either be in keeping[52] or have their own
interest. Full regard should be paid to the state of completeness of
a building, though proper allowance must be made for age and
relative scarcity. Where a building showing fragmentary Roman-
esque features would be listable, one showing fragmentary Jaco-
bean framing probably would not.*

"(2) Most buildings of 1700 to 1840 are listed, though selection is
necessary."
*At the beginning of the eighteenth century a high degree of
inclusiveness should apply, while at the beginning of the nineteenth century a much greater selectivity would be the rule. Pre-
1770 town houses will nearly always be listable, unless denuded
of their interior features (panelled walls, turned balusters, etc.)
and drastically altered. Of the plainer post-1770 town houses, it is
permissible to list only those which either* have exteriors with
several surviving features of value *(such as moulded doorcase,
windows, decorative fan, carved or moulded decoration, or decorative ironwork) or* where the facade *(by itself or as part of a terrace) is architecturally articulated. Such merits as there are will be
enhanced by group value or prominence of siting as well as any
historical associations.*

"(3) Between 1840 and 1914 only buildings of definite quality and **2.28**
character are listed, and the selection is designed to include the
principal works of the principal architects."

---

[52] It may be argued that no guidance is given by the vagueness of the phrase "in keeping." If, *e.g.* no objection is made where eighteenth century sash windows with
pleasant glazing bars have replaced seventeenth century casements, who is to say
that twentieth century steel-frame plate glass windows are or are not equally "in
keeping"? It is suggested that a closer statutory definition of what is meant would
be of greater help; *e.g.* "In harmony with the original style."

25

It should only be necessary for a building to have definite quality and character in one particular aspect, e.g. the architect, the design, decoration, quality of workmanship, planning, social or technological interest, etc. These standards must be distinctly above those applied to buildings of an earlier period. The lists should include the work of the principal architects of the period (e.g. Sir Charles Barry, Sir Edwin Lutyens, A. W. Pugin); however, not all the work of such architects should necessarily be listed and works of the lesser-known architects should not be disregarded.

"(4) Between 1914 and 1939 selected buildings of high quality are listed."

Buildings selected in this category must be submitted for the approval of the assistant chief inspector. There is available for comparison and assessment a photographic record and index of a selection of listed buildings of this period to serve as a body of exemplars and as a guide to further listing. Well-known examples are Battersea Power Station and the Stratford Memorial Theatre.

After 1939, a few outstanding buildings are listed.

2.29 Thus, the principal listing criterion remains the age of the building, not least because the more recent a building is the more selectively it is treated. This is combined with its state of preservation when surveyed and its rarity within a building type, both in its locality and across the country. Appendix I continues:

"In choosing buildings, particular attention is paid to:

(a) Special value within certain types, either for architectural or planning reasons or as illustrating social and economic history (for instance, industrial buildings, railway stations, schools, hospitals, theatres, town halls, markets, exchanges, almhouses, prisons, lock-ups, mills).

(b) Technological innovation or virtuosity (for instance cast iron, prefabrication, or the early use of concrete).

(c) Association with well-known characters or events.

(d) Group value, especially as examples of town planning (for instance, squares, terraces or model villages)."

It should be noted that all the above principles of selection are quoted from Circular 8/87 and have no statutory basis. The only requirement of the statute is that the buildings must be of "special architectural or historic merit."

Paragraph 34 of Circular 8/87 refers to "national criteria" on which the Secretary of State is advised by the Commission; the provision of such advice being one of the Commission's specific functions under the terms of the National Heritage Act 1983. The DOE keep the listing standards under review and they are revised from time to time. Indeed, Paul Bristow, the former Head of Listing at the DOE, acknowledged that the selection process has evolved over a considerable period of time, usually just a little ahead of public opinion, but in some fields, particularly Victorian, industrial and modern buildings, some distance behind. The process of revision has also been ignited in response to a *"cause célèbre"* such as the demolition of the Euston Arch (1961) which *was* listed, and the Firestone factory (1980) which was not.

As far as the selection of buildings from the inter-war period is concerned, **2.30**
Circular 8/87 amplifies at Appendix 1 the criteria for listing as follows:

"The criteria for selecting buildings of the 1914–1939 period for listing
cover two issues: the range of buildings which may be considered, and
the quality of the individual buildings actually selected.

The criteria are designed to enable full recognition to be given to the
varied architectural output of the period. Three main building styles
(broadly interpreted) are represented: modern, classical and others. The
building types which may be considered cover nine categories, as follows:
(a) Churches, chapels and other places of public worship.
(b) Cinemas, theatres, hotels and other places of public entertainment.
(c) Commercial and industrial premises including shops and offices.
(d) Schools, colleges and educational buildings.
(e) Flats.
(f) Houses and housing estates.
(g) Municipal and other public buildings.
(h) Railway stations, airport terminals and other places associated wth
    public transport.
(i) Miscellaneous.
In addition, the selection includes the work of the principal architects
of the period."

The process of revision has been demonstrated by the amendment to the
selection criteria for the inter-war buildings quoted above and by the ministerial announcement that all buildings of special architectural or historic
merit over 30 years of age are now eligible for inclusion in the list, *i.e.* that
there is to be, as in Scotland, a rolling cut-off date whereby all buildings over
30 years old are so eligible.[53]

Lastly, regarding the "group value" of buildings the DOE Guidance Notes
advise:

"The replacement factor must also be kept in mind when selecting
buildings in the group category. A building must not be chosen merely
because its neighbours are good and one is afraid that if it were demolished it would be replaced by an incongruous monstrosity. The design
of new buildings can and should be controlled under general planning
powers and it is not permissble therefore to place a building on the
statutory list simply to ensure a congruity of neighbourhood which
could as well be achieved in a new building. It must be possible to say
that the existing building has some quality in relation to the context
which no new building could have."

(b) Grading

If a building falls within the above principles of selection, then if it is **2.31**
listed it is graded. There is no reference in the 1971 Act to grading. There
has, however, developed over the years a system of grading of buildings

---

[53] Following the recommendations set out in House of Commons Environment
Committee (First Report) on Historic Buildings and Ancient Monuments (1987),
p. xviii, para. 33—*The Times*, April 1, 1987.

included in the list which, whilst it may have no statutory significance as such, has an administrative importance in relation to grants and LBC. In the absence of any contrary reference in Circular 8/87 (or any other relevant reference) it would appear that the decision into which grade a building is placed rests with either the chief investigator or the person authorised to sign on behalf of the Secretary of State. The Department gives guidance as to how it approaches the problem in Circular 8/87, para. 35. It is there said that "buildings are classified in grades to show their relative importance."

The first division in grading is an historic one between secular and ecclesiastical buildings. Secular buildings are divided into Grades I, II* and II, and these grades also apply to redundant Anglican churches, proprietary buildings like college chapels, and churches of other denominations. Anglican churches in use were originally graded A, B or C, but in recent lists the Department has graded by reference to the secular notation.

Dealing firstly with the secular buildings: Appendix I of Circular 8/87 shows the present departmental approach to grading:

"The buildings are classified in grades to show their relative importance as follows:—

Grade I. These are buildings of exceptional interest (only about two per cent of listed buildings so far are in this grade);

Grade II.*These are particularly important buildings of more than special interest (some four per cent. of listed buildings).

Grade II. These are buildings of special interest, which warrant every effort being made to preserve them.

Grade III. A non-statutory and now obsolete grade. Grade III buildings were those which, whilst not qualifying for the statutory list, were considered nevertheless to be of some importance. Many of these buildings are now considered to be of special interest by current standards—particularly where they possess "group value"—and are being added to the statutory lists as these are revised."

2.32 A further complication arises from the fact that many of the older lists were grouped in a slightly different way, and the schedule of listed buildings will normally be found to have been stated in four parts. Part 1 included all the buildings which were afforded statutory protection (*i.e.* Grades I, II* and II). Part 2 of the list included buildings which were formerly Grade III. Part 3 included ecclesiastical buildings, and Part 4 comprised Crown buildings.

There is not necessarily any correlation between grading for listing purposes and qualification for grant purposes. In fact, the terminology is different. Grade I refers to "buildings of exceptional interest," whereas grants towards the cost of repairs of buildings under section 4 of the Historic Buildings and Ancient Monuments Act 1953 are made in respect of buildings "of outstanding architectural or historic interest." There is in theory no reason why a Grade II building, or even an unlisted building, should not qualify for a section 4 grant, and indeed there are cases where grants have been made in respect of unlisted buildings. Nonetheless, it would be expected that whilst scarce national resources are being used for grant purposes, it is more likely that Grade I buildings will be thought of as "outstanding" than Grade II or unlisted buildings. Appendix I of Circular 8/87 refers to 2 per cent. of listed buildings being in Grade I; but as the listing progresses the percentage of

Grade I buildings in relation to the total will no doubt fall—as it is unlikely that many buildings new to the list will be of Grade I standard.

The Department elsewhere[54] defines the "Upper Category," *i.e.* Grades I and II*, as of "paramount or[55] exceptional interest in a national context." For the meaning of "paramount" we might follow the *Oxford English Dictionary's* definition as "above all others in rank, order or jurisdiction"; "exceptional" means, generally, rare or unusual. It is worth noting that 50 per cent. of churches are placed in this "Upper Category."

2.33 The fact that grading is a non-statutory process is further confused by a variety of criteria expressed to differentiate buildings in the most important grade. As we have seen, Circular 8/87 defines Grade I buildings as "of exceptional interest," as does the *English Heritage Monitor (1987)* published by English Tourist Board; John Ayers describes a Grade I building as of "outstanding national interest",[56] as does the *Essex County Council Guide to Historic Buildings*.[57] The phrase "exceptional" is a relative term, but the definition of "outstanding national interest" is perhaps a better guide, as the use of a qualification such as "exceptional" must postulate the question: "exceptional" to whom? The very phrase "outstanding national interest" on the contrary can be quite legitimately read to mean "that which the public will regard as of outstanding interest nationally." With this variety of phraseology we are probably left with the test of "exceptional interest" with all the problems of such a definition, as this is the DOE's own phrase and it is they who invented the process anyway!

The next problem which arises is trying to determine what buildings should or should not be included in the Grade II* category. How does a building qualify for being "a particularly important building"? Presumably it is less than a building of exceptional interest or of outstanding national interest, but it is more important than being merely of "special architectural or historic interest." One interpretation which appears to be adopted by the Department for administrative purposes is to suggest that not only is the exterior "special," but the interior as well. An alternative interpretation is illustrated in the Underhill, Gateshead case referred to at para. 2.26 above, where a multiple historical association justified a higher grading. The majority of buildings are listed solely on their external virtue, and this is right. One of the main purposes of listing is to protect buildings from too hasty demolition. But the demolition is of a building whose external appearance is seen by the members of the public. Most listed buildings are occupied (compared with ancient monuments where occupation precludes scheduling): thus, the average member of the public does not see the interior of a listed building and would not normally be concerned with it.[58]

2.34 There emerges from these considerations a hierarchy of buildings which we categorise as follows:

[54] "Guidance Notes" (see n. 49, above).

[55] In another part of the Notes we read "paramount *and* exceptional interest." If the definitions here given of these two words are accepted, "or" must surely be correct as the two adjectives supply mutually exclusive and therefore alternative tests for entry into the upper category.

[56] John Ayers, "The Historical and Architectural Criteria": address to the Oxford Conference, 1976, in *Journal of Planning and Environment Law*, Occasional Papers (1977), p. 53.

[57] Conservation in Essex No. 4: "*Historic Buildings,*" Essex C.C. (undated).

[58] See also below at para. 4.45.

Grade I—   Buildings of exceptional interest: although most of these may have interiors of considerable significance, this is not necessary in order to qualify for this grading.

Grade II*— Buildings which do not fall into the category of being of exceptional interest but are more worthy than the average building of "special architectural or historic interest." The presence of a fine interior would seem to justify a building being placed in this category as would a strong historical association.

Grade II—   Buildings of "special architectural or historic interest" which warrant every effort being made to preserve them.

In this latter connection it is important to emphasise that the qualification of warranting every effort being made to preserve the building is not a statutory qualification, nor indeed is the whole of the grading process. All that is required under the Act is that a building falls within the category of "special architectural or historic interest."

This leaves, therefore, buildings which may be significant but which do not fall within any of the above gradings. A building which is of ordinary architectural or historic interest should not be listed. A building of architectural or historic merit should not be listed. The three tests must be passed, namely that the building must be of interest, the interest must be architectural or historic, and the building must be of "special" architectural or historic interest. An interesting example of the difference in this terminology is to be found in a ministerial planning decision on an appeal by National Westminster Bank Ltd. against the refusal of LBC to demolish 10 and 12 St. Peter's Street, St. Albans, which had been referred to the Secretary of State.[59] The Secretary of State refused LBC and dismissed the appeal, as he had agreed with his inspector's report. The inspector's report was carefully worded and opened with his description of the building as follows:

> "I am of the opinion in respect of the application for LBC that while the building is not of historical interest or of great architectural merit, its facade makes an important contribution to the attractiveness and interest of the street scene on this side of St. Peter's Street, and to the particular character of the group of buildings of which it forms part, and that it merits retention on that account. . . . "

2.35   In so far as ecclesiastical buildings are concerned, there was for some time a different system of grading for such buildings. The three grades for Anglican churches (including cathedrals) were as follows:

Grade A   (i) Medieval—Exceptional and retaining pristine character.
           (ii) Reformation to 1840—Exceptional.
           (iii) Victorian to 1914—Exceptional.

Grade B   (i) Medieval—More modest buildings than A(i) or those overlaid by subsequent reconstruction.
           (ii) Reformation to 1840—Of particular importance but not exceptional.
           (iii) Victorian to 1914—Of particular importance but not exceptional.

[59] [1974] J.P.L. 552. Ref. SE6/1582/270/17; APP/1582/N/63586, December 10, 1973.

Grade C   (i) Reformation to 1840—Minor or plain buildings, just of statutory quality.

             (ii) 1830 Gothic and standard Victorian—just of statutory quality.

The Historic Buildings Council (as it then was) advised in August 1977 that the use of A, B and C grades for Anglican churches in use be discontinued, that the Grade I, II* and II be introduced and that the grading of Anglican churches be fully equivalent to that of secular buildings. For listing purposes, the following eight categories are recognised[60]:

(i) Churches which are recognisably of pre-Reformation date.

(ii) Churches of post-Reformation date which were built before the 1818 Act though selection is necessary.

(iii) Between 1818 and 1914 churches of definite quality and character apart from those that form part of a group. The selection should include the important works of major architects.

(iv) A selection of churches of 1914 to 1939.

In selecting churches for listing, particular attention should be paid to:

(v) Churches which are important examples of regional church types.

(vi) Churches which contain major paintings, glass, sculpture, monuments or fittings. The DOE Guidance Notes comment that there will be few churches which are listable solely for such features and it will be rare that churches in this category do not already qualify for listing under (i), (ii) or (iii) above.

(vii) Churches which are materially associated with historic events or persons of national importance. Again the DOE Guidance Notes observe that there will be few churches which do not already qualify under (i), (ii) or (iii) above, and only rarely will a person or event be of such importance as to transcend all other considerations. This category may well be an important one for non-conformist churches.

(viii) Churches having group value especially as an integral part of a planned scheme.

2.36 The significance of the grading principles relates more to grants[61] than to any statutory requirements under the Act. Grade I buildings will, in practice, receive more sympathetic consideration for grant than will other buildings. In practice, the grading of buildings, both secular and religious, will affect an LBC decision. In theory this should not be so. There should be no difference in theory in the approach towards a LBC between different grades of buildings, in that the quality of each building should be taken into account as part of the balancing mechanism of deciding whether or not to grant LBC. The grading principle effectively is a shorthand, and so long as the shorthand is recognised as such, then no great harm should arise. The difficulty would arise if those concerned with the granting of LBC's dealt in too blinkered a fashion with the grading, ignoring in the balancing process the fact that a grading might be incorrect. All such aspects have their difficulties, for all judgments in relation to listed buildings are to a degree subjective. In relation to grants the significance of a building being listed as

---

[60] "Guidance Notes" (see n. 49 above).
[61] See Chap. 10 at para. 10.01 below.

Grade I instead of Grade II has been observed. Investigator X may categorise a church building into Grade I, whereas investigator Y may put the same building in Grade II*. What is important is that when the decision is made as to whether or not to grant LBC, the assessment of the building is looked at afresh and is not thought of as a finally prejudged issue. In the relisting process which was carried out between 1984 and 1987, particular care was taken in the administrative process to achieve consistency in grading.

4. DEEMED LISTING

2.37   Deemed listing is a process by which a building is not treated either as part of the overall survey by the Department, nor spot listed, but is deemed to be included in the list and in respect of which all the listed building provisions will apply.

There are two categories of buildings which are deemed to have been listed, namely those which were specifically covered by building preservation orders[62] and those which are the subject of building preservation notices.[63]

(a) Building preservation order

2.38   The building preservation order (see para. 2.04 above) was an order which was made by a local authority (subject to ministerial approval) under the pre-1968 legislation. The purpose of the 1968 legislation was to give the same protection for a listed building to each building included in the list as compared to those buildings which had been the subject of a specific building preservation order.

The powers in relation to building preservation orders are preserved by section 54(10) of the Act[64] which provides that:

> "Every building which immediately before January 1, 1969 was subject to a building preservation order under Part III of the Act of 1962 but was not then included in a list compiled or approved under section 32 of that Act shall be deemed to be a listed building; but the Secretary of State may at any time direct, in the case of any building, that this subsection shall no longer apply to it and the council of the London borough or county district in whose area the building is situated, on being notified of the Secretary of State's direction, shall give notice of it to the owner and occupier of the building."

The Secretary of State has an obligation under section 54(11) to consult with the local, the county, or the district planning authority, and in any case the owner and the occupier of the building before giving a direction under subsection (10). It is estimated that there are very few buildings subject to building preservation orders.

---

[62] T.C.P.A. 1971, s.54(10).
[63] T.C.P.A. 1971, s.58(4).
[64] As amended by the L.G.A. 1972, s.30.

(b) Building preservation notice

The building preservation notice is the "emergency" procedure which is   **2.39**
applicable now. Section 58(1) of the 1971 Act provides that[65]:

> "If it appears to the local planning authority, other than a county plan-
> ning authority, in the case of a building in their area which is not a
> listed building, that it is of special architectural or historic interest and
> is in danger of demolition or of alteration in such a way as to affect its
> character as such, they may (subject to subsection (2) of this section)
> serve on the owner and occupier of the building a notice (in this section
> referred to as a "building preservation notice")—
>
> (a) stating that the building appears to them to be of special architec-
>   tural or historic interest and that they have requested the Secretary
>   of State to consider including it in a list compiled or approved
>   under section 54 of this Act; and
> (b) explaining the effect of subsections (3) and (4) of section 58."

Under section 58(2) of the Act, a building preservation notice cannot be
served in respect of an ecclesiastical building which is for the time being
used for ecclesiastical purposes or a building which is a scheduled monument. A building used, or available for use by a minister of religion wholly
or mainly as his residence, is treated as not being an ecclesiastical building.[66] The building preservation notice comes into force as soon as it has
been served on both the owner and the occupier of the building to which it
relates and remains in force for six months from the date when it is served,
or as the case may be, last served; but it ceases to be in force if, before the
expiration of that period, the Secretary of State either lists the building or
notifies the local planning authority in writing that he does not intend to do
so.[67] During the period that a building preservation notice is in force, the
provisions of the Act (other than section 57) shall have effect as if the building were a listed building.[68] If, following the service of a building preservation notice, the Secretary of State notifies the local planning authority that
he does not propose to include the building in the list, then the authority
must give notice of the Secretary of State's decision to the owner and occupier of the building and may not within 12 months beginning from the date
of the notification serve another notice in respect of the building.[69] If it
appears to the local planning authority to be urgent that a building preservation notice should come into force, it may instead of serving the notice on
the owner and occupier of the building to which it relates, affix the notice
conspicuously to some object on the building and will should be treated for
all the purposes of section 58 and Schedule 11 as service.[70]

There are provisions in section 173 of the 1971 Act in respect of compensation where a building preservation notice is served. Section 173(3) provides that:

---

[65] As amended by the L.G.A. 1985, s.6 and Sched. 2, para. 1(5)(a).
[66] T.C.P.A. 1971, s.58(2)(a) and (b).
[67] T.C.P.A. 1971, s.58(3).
[68] T.C.P.A. 1971, s.58(4).
[69] T.C.P.A. 1971, s.58(5).
[70] See T.C.P.A. 1971, s.283 as to service of notice.

"If the building preservation notice ceases to have effect without the building having been included in a list so compiled or approved, then, subject to a claim in that behalf being made to the local planning authority within the time and in the manner prescribed by regulations under this Act, any person who at the time when the notice was served had an interest in the building shall be entitled to be paid compensation by the authority in respect of any loss or damage directly attributable to the effect of the notice."

The compensation shall include a sum payable in respect of breach of contract caused by the necessity of discontinuing or countermanding any works to the building on account of the building preservation notice being enforced in respect thereto.[71]

5. THE MECHANICS OF LISTING

2.40   The mechanics of listing were described in the decision of Lawton L.J. (as he then was) in the case of *John Walker & Sons Ltd.*[72]

We now describe the processes in detail:

(a) The DOE investigator visits the area to see which buildings might deserve listing. This is the normal process on a survey listing: this step may be dispensed with on a "spot listing" where:

"It would speed consideration of requests to list buildings if they were accompanied by a location plan (such as an Ordnance Survey map extract) and up-to-date photographs of the main elevations of the building (not photocopies or slides), as well as any information the individual or local authority have about the building—for example its date in particular; historical [*sic*] associations, if any; the architect, if known; its group value in the street scene; and details of any interior features of interest" (Circular 8/87, para. 39).

Presumably these items feature in the matters which the investigator is looking for: if an urgent spot listing is to take place there will not be time to verify all these details. The question arises what factors are viewed as constituting a threat so as to induce the DOE to spot list a building. Spot listing will take place if there is a real risk to the future of the property, *e.g.* if it is up for sale by auction or private treaty; but not where the threat is only a vague one, particularly if there are strong signs that the building will in due course be listed anyway. Spot listings are now personally approved by a minister in the DOE. The Department may spot list to enable an owner to obtain the benefit of the VAT exemption if the usual criteria are satisfied. Statistics show that the number of buildings spot listed rose from 744 in 1984 to 1,254 in 1985.

2.41   (b) The report of the investigator is considered by the Chief Investigating Officer.

---

[71] T.C.P.A. 1971, s.173(4).
[72] [1976] 3 All E.R. 509; 120 S.J. 252; E.G. 277, C.A.

(c) The Chief Investigating Officer reports to the DOE administrative officer.

(d) The DOE officer prepares the list of buildings to be listed pursuant to section 54.

(e) The member of the DOE staff gives an internal "provisional acceptance": provisional because it is subject to a check against any other information that might be in the Department relating to the building and affecting its interest. During the provisional period other information—from local authorities, and preservation societies and members of the public—is apparently recorded, but would not affect a provisional listing unless the information related to damage to the building, *e.g.* if it had caught fire or been partially altered. It is strange to see the DOE suggesting that it would take information "from members of the public," few of whom will know about the potential listing of the building.

(f) The selection then becomes unconditional and the decision is made by a Higher Executive Officer, whereas the provisional decision may well have been made by an Executive Officer.

(g) The list is then typed.

(h) The list is presented via the Head of the Branch (a Principal) to be signed on behalf of the Secretary of State by an Assistant Secretary. Only when he signs the list and dates it contemporaneously with his signature is the list "operative."

(i) Letters are prepared for sending to the local authorities concerned indicating that the building has "been selected" for listing (*i.e.* the notification pursuant to section 54(4)).

(j) The local authority then notifies each owner and occupier in accordance with section 54(7) that the building has been included in the list.

(k) The list is registered in the register of local land charges pursuant to section 54(6).

6. THE LISTED BUILDING AND THE GENERAL DEVELOPMENT ORDER

The Town and Country Planning General Development Order 1977[73] is a general order, applicable to all land in England and Wales, providing for the grant of permission for the development of land pursuant to the provisions of section 24 of the 1971 Act. Schedule 1 of the Order sets out in detail the classes of development ("permitted development") for which planning permission is granted. Most are relatively small permissions (*e.g.* house extensions, walls and fences) but some have considerable effect. No application is required so long as the conditions in the Schedule are adhered to. Demolition is not mentioned (as basically it is not development[74]). **2.42**

In the General Development Order there appears in article 4 a provision whereby permitted development can be restricted by a direction (usually known as an "article 4 direction") made by the Secretary of State or the

---

[73] S.I. 1977 No. 289.
[74] See para. 5.01 and 5.20 below.

local planning authority. Generally an article 4 direction made by a local planning authority has to be confirmed by the Secretary of State. In respect of listed buildings (but not unlisted buildings in conservation areas[75]), however, a provision took effect from March 1, 1986[76] whereby the Secretary of State's approval is not required in certain cases:

    (a) a listed building (or a building which for these purposes the Secretary of State deems to be a listed building); or

    (b) development within the curtilage[77] of a listed building.

A local planning authority article 4 direction in respect of such buildings is limited strictly to these categories and cannot be extended and cannot limit certain types of development, *e.g.* some emergency development, maintenance of bridges and drainage works.

There is a further direction which may be made by the local planning authority for a temporary period of up to six months (after which time the approval of the Secretary of State must be given), in respect of "any particular area" where development of Classes I to IV (of Schedule 1) would, in the opinion of the local planning authority, be prejudicial to the proper planning of the area or a threat to the amenities of the area. Classes I to IV include development within the curtilage of a dwellinghouse, sundry minor operations, some changes of use and the erection of some temporary buildings and their uses.

There are provisions for notification to owners and occupiers. Compensation in some circumstances is payable.[78]

Local planning authorities have welcomed this new provison but they are reminded in Circular 14/85 that "permitted development rights should not be restricted without a good reason for doing so."[79] The result of these provisions which remove permitted development rights is to ensure that planning permission is applied for in respect of new development; as for the more general direction, this will give temporary "cover" whilst the local planning authority seek to obtain an article 4 confirmation from the Secretary of State.

7. THE CONSEQUENCES OF LISTING

2.43   The following are the consequences of a building being included in the statutory list:

    (a) The copy of the list relating to a London borough or a county district is deposited with the borough or district council, and outside Greater London, with the county planning authority whose area includes the district or any part of it, and where the district council is not the district planning authority (*e.g.* in a New Town area) with the proper officer of that area;

---

[75] See also below at paras. 3.17–3.19.
[76] As provided by S.I. 1985 No. 1981.
[77] For a discussion as to what is curtilage, see paras. 2.17–2.20 above.
[78] See paras. 5.16–5.17 below.
[79] Paragraph 31.

(b) A copy is registered in the register of local land charges by the local planning authority;

(c) A notice is served by the local planning authority in the prescribed form on every owner and occupier of the building by the London borough or county district stating that the building has been included in the list. The prescribed form is in Town and Country Planning (Listed Buildings etc.) Regulations 1987, Sched. 4;

(d) A copy of the list is made available by the Secretary of State for public inspection free of charge at reasonable times and in a convenient place;

(e) The listing takes effect on the date of the signing of the list, and not **2.44** on the service of the notice.

(f) If permitted development is being carried out and notice of listing is received, the owner must stop. However, he must then consider whether the work he is carrying out would affect the character as a building of special architectural or historic interest. It may be a fine judgment to make.

(g) If any person executes or causes to be executed works for demolition, alteration or extension in any manner which would affect its character as a building of special architectural or historic interest (thus it is not all work which offends—only work affecting the character of the building) without the works having been authorised under the Act, he is guilty of an offence.[80] Under section 55(2A) he may obtain permission *ex post facto*. However, he is still liable in respect of his original offence and the penalties are on summary conviction imprisonment of up to three months or a fine of not exceeding "the prescribed sum" (at present £2,000),[80a] or both; on indictment: imprisonment of up to 12 months or a fine, or both.

(h) Where a local planning authority is of the opinion that works are being undertaken in contravention of section 55, it has the power to serve a listed building enforcement notice under section 96;

(i) The *ex post facto* authorisation of works under (g) above may only be effected on the authority of a LBC in the case of a proposal to demolish, and with effect from November 13, 1980 (the date of the coming into effect of the Local Government, Planning and Land Act 1980) a proposal to alter or extend a listed building.[81]

(j) Permitted development under article 3 of the General Development Order 1977 may be curtailed[82];

(k) The local authority has power to carry out works to unoccupied listed buildings and to recharge the owner;

(l) The local authority has power to acquire compulsorily listed buildings and in the case of a deliberately neglected building with provision for a direction for "minimum compensation";

---

[80] T.C.P.A. 1971, s.55(1).

[80a] The words "the prescribed sum" were substituted by the Magistrates' Courts Act 1980, s.32(2)(9).

[81] L.G.P.L.A., Sched. 15, paras. 6, 7 amend T.C.P.A. 1971, s.55. Works for the alteration or extension of a listed building can no longer be authorised by a planning permission also operating as LBC.

[82] See para. 2.42 above.

(m) If a building has been incorrectly listed, the Secretary of State may amend the list.[83]

8. THE EFFECT OF LISTING ON PLANNING DECISIONS

2.45   This section deals with issues which arise from the relation between the grant of planning permission for development on listed buildings and the effect of listing on planning decisions generally.

Section 56(3) of the 1971 Act, as amended by the Local Government, Planning and Land Act 1980 makes specific reference to the relation as follows:

> "In considering whether to grant planning permission for development which affects a listed building or its setting and in considering whether to grant listed building consent for any works, the Local Planning Authority or the Secretary of State, as the case may be, shall have special regard to the desirability of preserving the building or its setting or any features of special architectural or historic interest which it possesses."

The effect of this subsection has been to encourage a degree of flexibility in planning decisions in respect of development affecting a listed building. This is clearly illustrated in the case of an application for the use of a listed residence for office purposes at The Grange, Codicote Road, Welwyn[84] where an inspector allowed an appeal against a refusal of planning permission. He concluded that although the amount of floorspace to be used for office purposes exceeded the council's policies, he took the view that policies were not inflexible particularly in the case of listed buildings.

The principle of flexibility has even been extended to assist development proposals for a group of unlisted buildings at Jeningsbury Farm near Hertford. A proposal to convert the buildings in question to residential purposes was allowed on appeal[85] because the inspector regarded them as good examples of vernacular architecture and worth retaining, which outweighed the presumption against development in the Green Belt. Such an approach is not unusual and indeed is embodied in many formal policies of local planning authorities where they are seeking to retain good examples of vernacular architecture, such as the oasthouses found in the Weald of Kent.

2.46   The setting of a listed building raises a further consideration in the determination of development proposals. However, this presupposes that the setting of a listed building is easily defined and that it most certainly is not. Certainly it cannot be held to be contiguous with its curtilage and the general extent of the setting is usually a matter of judgment for the local planning authority, a Department of the Environment inspector or the Secretary of State. In a case at 44 West Street, Gravesend[86] the inspector was clearly of the view that "its setting is rather more extensive than its relatively small curtilage." This case also demonstrates the weight attached to listed building and setting considerations in determining a development proposal which "might otherwise be held to be in broad conformity with

[83] See para. 2.05 above.
[84] APP/C1950/A/84/010803/P7.
[85] T/APP/J1915/A/84/016386/P2.
[86] APP/K2230/E/85/801205.

the provisions of the emergent local plan." The inspector generally concluded that

> "the presumption in favour of granting planning permission, contained in Circulars 22/80 and 14/85, ought to be weighed against the equally relevant policy content of Circulars 23/77 and 12/81 as regards the need to preserve both listed buildings and the setting of listed buildings. . . . the merits of the otherwise broadly acceptable retail warehouse proposals . . . would appear to be of comparatively far less importance than the retention of the listed building on the site and its immediate setting."

The appeal was dismissed.

The setting of a listed building in Selby was held to be the principal issue in an appeal[87] against a refusal of permission for the conversion of the house to four dwellings and the erection of three mews houses in the garden land to the rear. The LPA was satisfied with the proposed conversion but the inspector was concerned at the effect of the sub-division on "the expansive quality befitting a grand domestic house" and that the development to the rear would impinge on the setting of the building.

Notwithstanding the considerable importance attached to the setting of a **2.47** listed building, this should not be regarded as an opportunity for a local planning authority to act unreasonably. This principle was clearly demonstrated in a case concerning an appeal[88] to discharge a condition attached by Bristol City Council to a permission for the enlargement and refurbishment of No. 51 Queen Square, Bristol (a listed building) which condition required *inter alia* the prohibition of forecourt parking at Nos. 49 and 50, which though in the same ownership, were in separate occupation. The council argued that Queen Square was an outstanding conservation area, in which 53 of the 74 properties were listed, and that the environmental improvement they were seeking were thus fully justified. However, the appellants drew attention to the ruling of Lord Denning in *Pyx Granite Co. Ltd.* v. *Ministry of Housing and Local Government*[88a] where he stated that

> "conditions to be valid must fairly and reasonably relate to the permitted development. The planning authority are not at liberty to use their powers for an ulterior object, however desirable that object may seem to them to be in the public interest."

The appeal was allowed because the car parking was irrelevant to the planning issues relating to the refurbishment of No. 51.

On a more light-hearted note, it was interesting to note that an inspector considered that the erection of a Herbie Tree in the beer garden of the Squirrel Public House at Alveley in Shropshire constituted development requiring planning permission but that it had "none of the attributes of a natural tree, and by its size, colour and general configuration, is visually discordant when seen in the context and as part of the setting of the listed building."[89]

Many planning authorities regard the lack of a formal mechanism to control the setting of listed buildings, other than the statutory advertisement of proposals requiring planning permission, as a particular deficiency. More-

---

[87] APP/B2735/E/800378 as reported in *Planning Appeals Monthly* (February 1985).
[88] APP/U0110/A/84/012839/P2.
[88a] (1958) 1 Q.B. 554.
[89] APP/J3205/A/85/33569/P2.

over, it seems somewhat anomalous that such powers are extended to local planning authorities in respect of advertisement controls through the provisions of the Town and Country Planning (Control of Advertisements) Regulations 1984 (S.I. 1984 No. 421) by defining areas of special control. Regulation 26(8) requires a local planning authority to

> "exercise their functions under this regulation only in the interests of amenity and for this purpose shall have regard to the general characteristics of their area, including the presence therein of any feature of historic, architectural or cultural interest."

This regulation effectively enables local planning authorities to remove the rights for express consent to display advertisements where they might affect the setting of listed buildings. It is regrettable that the same provisions do not apply to enable local planning authorities to restrict permitted development rights where they might affect the setting of a listed building.

9. THE PROGRESS OF LISTING

2.48   Although the statutory provisions may have changed, and the procedure varied over the years, it may be of interest to consider the progress as opposed to the process of listing buildings. It is as follows:

1946–early 1950s: the first Provisional Lists were produced.

1950s–1969: statutory lists were compiled from the Provisional Lists for all the former district and county borough authorities.

1969–1982: revision of existing lists and issue in the revised formats (*i.e.* instead of the former practice of mere details of address and grade of the building, the new lists including descriptive notes, grade and address, are included in one cumulative statutory list).

In May 1982 the Secretary of State announced details of proposals to accelerate the revision of the lists of historic buildings, and the survey was substantially completed during 1987.[90] By March 1987 the total number of buildings listed was 403,623.

10. IMMUNITY FROM LISTING

2.49   Schedule 15(5) to the Local Government, Planning and Land Act 1980 sought to alleviate the risk of listing by enabling a person to apply to the Department for a certificate stating that it does not intend to list the building within the ensuing five years provided an application has been made for planning permission or permission given. Paragraph 5 of Schedule 15 added a new section 54A to the 1971 Act; section 54A(1) and (2) provide that if such a certificate is applied for and obtained, the Secretary of State is precluded from exercising his powers under section 54 of the 1971 Act to list the building in question, and under section 58 a local planning authority

---

[90] *English Heritage Monitor* (1987), p. 7.

is precluded from serving a building preservation notice, for five years from the date of issue of the certificate. Under subsection (3), notice of any application for a certificate must be given to the relevant district planning authority at the same time as to the Secretary of State.[91]

Recent figures show that approximately 50 per cent. of applications have resulted in immunity certificates being granted, though the numbers of such applications remains fairly low: six certificates issued in 1984, seven in 1985 and in 1986, 16 up to October of that year.

The following points should be noted:

(1) The immunity certificate procedure should, if used, avoid the circumstances which arose in the *John Walker* case, where listing took place (unknown to vendor or purchaser) at the same time as exchange of contracts for the sale of the listed property.[92] If the proposed vendor or purchaser could have then been able to apply for an immunity certificate, the position could have been cleared in advance.

(2) Anyone applying for a certificate runs the risk that his application will bring to the notice of the Department or the local planning authority the existence of a building which might merit listing.

(3) A danger for an owner is that anyone may apply for an immunity certificate so long as the conditions are satisfied—thus a preservation group can apply. But large numbers of buildings have been listed because of the direct intervention of preservation groups. This section therefore does not materially change the former situation: it does provide for the owner a protection (which he had not hitherto) from further pressure if the listing is declined and the immunity certificate issued.   **2.50**

(4) An immunity certificate application should be accompanied by a plan showing the position of the buildings, black and white photographs of each elevation of the building and of any notable interior features, together with details of the date of construction, the architect and information about the architectural or historic interest.

(5) There is no obligation on the Department or the local authorities to notify the owner of the application (if not made by the owner), but it is suggested in Circular 8/87 (para. 44) that this information should be disclosed on a search relating to the land.

(6) There is no time limit to respond imposed on the Secretary of State. Indications from the experience on the first applications are that the turn round of applications for certificates is quite speedy.

(7) An immunity certificate does not prevent the building within the five years from being included in a conservation area with the control on demolition imposed by that code.

(8) Subsection (4) (substituted by the LGA 1985) provides that for the purposes of this section, the words "local planning authority," in relation to a building in Greater London, shall include the Commission.

---

[91] A little credit for this provision is due to The Law Society whose Planning and Development Committee pressed enthusiastically for this provision as an antidote to the results of the *John Walker* case.

[92] See n. 25 above.

11. PROBLEM LISTINGS

2.51 If all the listing processes proceeded as set out above there might be no problems. But from time to time there have been difficulties and it is worth recording the details of the following two cases as cautionary tales.

(a) Carlton Cinema, Swansea

The proposed redevelopment of the Carlton Cinema in Swansea[93] resulted in a complex decision-making process, with the public inquiry being held in three different stages under three different inspectors. The first inspector's report recommended that the cinema was not of sufficient merit to justify its retention. However, the building was listed some three months after the date of the public inquiry and the inquiry was reopened under a different inspector. This inspector considered that "the rarity of listed buildings and other buildings of distinction in the centre of Swansea serves to reinforce the presumption in favour of the preservation of at least the facade," which he had described as "a flamboyant Edwardian Baroque essay" built of Doulton carraware in 1914. The Secretary of State adjourned the inquiry to allow the appellants time to prepare detailed proposals allowing for the retention of the facade. The inquiry was reopened for a third time under a third inspector, who heard conflicting evidence from the appellants on the one hand and the city council on the other hand. His conclusions were accepted by the Secretary of State, who was not satisfied that it would be impracticable to retain the facade and he therefore refused listed building consent for its demolition.

(b) Upper House Barns, Bronylls Village, Near Brecon, Powys

2.52 The practical problems raised by the timescales involved in the processing of listed building consent applications is clearly illustrated in a case concerning a range of eighteenth century Grade II listed buildings at Bronylls near Brecon in Powys.[94] Following the grant of outline planning permission for residential use of a parcel of land in September 1984 on which the "Upper House Barns" were located the owner applied for consent to demolish them in May 1985 to allow the development to proceed unhindered. In view of the apparent advanced state of decay of the building a structural survey was commissioned by the council to assist their deliberation. The report was completed in August 1985, although by July it was apparent that certain elements of the building were extremely unstable and would be very costly to remedy. In September 1985 the LPA recommended that LBC be granted and notified the Welsh Historic Monuments body (CADW) with a copy of the structural report. In January 1986 the council was advised that

---

[93] P84/583 Swansea City Council, Welsh Office, August 28, 1985.
[94] Case report courtesy of the Borough of Brecknock.

the application would be determined by an inspector appointed by the Secretary of State for Wales. The inquiry was held in June 1986 and the inspector's report was received on September 1, 1986 and concluded that "the condition of the west range of buildings is very dangerous . . . and should be demolished with the minimum of delay." The particular concern raised by this case is that the application remained undetermined for 12 months, albeit not an unusually long time for applications following this procedure, whilst it had already been acknowledged at the outset that parts of the building were in an extremely dangerous condition and throughout that period constituted a possible danger to the public.

12. HISTORIC GARDENS

Section 8 of the Historic Buildings and Ancient Monuments Act 1953 (as **2.53** amended by the National Heritage Act 1983[95]) enables the Commission to "compile a register of gardens and other land situated in England which appears to it to be of special historic interest." The register, for which there is no statutory obligation to require it to be kept, lists and grades gardens created before 1939 which still retain their special historic interest. Its purpose is to record their existence so that highway and planning authorities and developers know that they should try to safeguard them when considering new road schemes and new redevelopment generally.

By January 1987 the *English Heritage Monitor* (1987) records that the Commission had published 16 county volumes of the Register of Historic Parks and Gardens. These volumes list 350 parks and gardens which range from major manmade landscapes like Blenheim to quite small gardens such as the one hectare garden at Marsh Court in Hampshire. In format, register entries closely resemble statutory historic building lists and the grading is similar. When the total register, covering the whole of England, is completed, it is expected to include more than 1,200 gardens.

Notwithstanding the attention being focused on historic gardens as a result of the compilation of the register, they remain a particular problem, principally because they have no statutory protection in their own right. Whilst normal planning controls will be sufficient to prevent the development of an historic garden for new dwellings, such as that proposed at the Lutyens house called "The Salutation" in Sandwich, Kent,[96] there is no statutory control over the despoilation of layout, design or form, because they can be neither listed nor be subject to a tree preservation order.

With the rapid growth of public appreciation of gardens there is now a **2.54** sizeable body of public opinion in favour of some form of statutory control over historic gardens in particular and special landscapes in general. Indeed, one might rightfully suggest that a Capability Brown landscaped park or a Gertrude Jekyell garden deserves just as much protection as a listed house from the same period, not only because such landscapes or gardens offer to provide a unique setting for a listed building but because they are intrinsically worth preserving in their own right.

The response of the Commission to proposals by the Department of

---

[95] This section was brought into force on April 1, 1984 by S.I. 1984 No. 208. The detail will be found in Sched. 4 to the 1983 Act, para. 10.

[96] *Period Home* (October 1985), p. 9.

Transport to route a new section of the A34 trunk road through Highclere Park, Hampshire, illustrates three important points. First, it demonstrated the inadequacy of existing control to protect these important environmental assets. Secondly, it highlighted the lack of funds available to tackle not only the threat of major development proposals, but also the long term maintenance problems of gardens. Thirdly, in focusing attention on such an important historic garden or landscape, it served to illustrate the magnitude of the problem which exists in respect of less well known gardens which nevertheless remain an important part of our heritage.

Clearly, the mobilisation of resources required to save Highclere Park is unlikely to be repeated in respect of all historic gardens and it begs the question as to when action will be taken to provide not only a statutory form of control, but also the necessary resources to ensure that historic gardens can be maintained for the benefit of the community and future generations. George Allen suggests that "If the history of listed building controls repeats itself, it will only be after a series of scandalous and tragic losses that any action will be taken."[97]

[97] *Ibid.* p. 9.

3. Conservation Areas

1. GENERAL SUMMARY

Until the middle of this century, measures for the protection of the built **3.01** environment had largely concentrated on the protection of individual buildings against the possibility of demolition. Subsequent to the 1947 Act, these limited measures were extended to afford (still limited) control over the alteration or extension of "buildings of architectural or historic interest," but "the building" remained the basic unit of conservation interest. It was not until 1967 that the concept of "area" conservation found statutory acceptance.

It was perhaps the case of *Iveagh (Earl of)* v. *Ministry of Housing and Local Government*[1] which reached the Court of Appeal in 1964, which marked a further turn of the tide. The Earl of Iveagh owned two adjoining houses in St. James' Square, London, providing an unbroken facade in one corner of the Square. In 1959 the local planning authority made a preservation order under the 1947 Act on the ground that alteration or demolition would be detrimental to the preservation of the character of the Square. The applicants objected and a public inquiry was held. The applicants contended that to fall within the protection given by the 1947 Act a building must have of itself special architectural or historic interest and not derive such interest as part of a group of buildings. The Minister's inspector found that the buildings were not of sufficient quality for the order. The Minister differed from his inspector and confirmed the order. The applicants moved to quash the order. Megaw J. (as he then was) dismissed the application. The

---

[1] [1964] 1 Q.B. 395; [1963] 3 W.L.R. 974; 128 J.P. 70; 107 S.J. 90, 851; [1963] 3 All E.R. 817.

applicants appealed to the Court of Appeal which held that a building might be of special architectural or historic interest by reason of its setting as one of a group.

The Court of Appeal hearing made it clear that there was a divided view as to whether the preservation order protection given in the 1947 Act (and subsequently re-enacted) was adequate where "the group value" was under consideration, and it was apparent that a more general power was required. As a result there was introduced (at the instance primarily of Mr. Duncan Sandys—later Lord Duncan-Sandys—and the Civic Trust) a Bill which became the Civic Amenities Act 1967. The preamble to that Act made it clear that it was an Act "to make further provision for the protection and improvement of buildings of architectural or historic interest and of the character of areas of such interest." The Act required that:

"every local planning authority shall from time to time determine which parts of their area . . . are areas of special architectural or historic interest the character or appearance of which it is desirable to preserve or enhance and shall designate such areas."

They were referred to as "conservation areas." The Act strengthened the law with regard to listed buildings and dealt in some detail with what were then building preservation orders.

3.02   The Civic Amenities Act 1967 was repealed and re-enacted in relation to conservation areas as section 277 of the 1971 Act,[2] with certain provisions of the Town and Country Planning Act 1968 in relation to consultations and the display of site notices also being incorporated.

The legislation was further altered by the Town and Country Planning (Amendment) Act 1972, which gave powers to control the demolition of unlisted buildings in conservation areas[3] and for the making of grants or loans for work in conservation areas of "outstanding interest."[4]

The Town and Country Amenities Act 1974 consolidated the legislation and re-enacted with certain amendments section 277 of the 1971 Act, added sections 277A, which enlarged the demolition control provisions, and 277B which required preservation and enhancement proposals to be prepared by local planning authorities. Additionally the protection of trees was provided for through a new section 61A inserted into the 1971 Act.[5]

Subsequently the view has been taken (e.g. in *Hoveringham Gravels Ltd.* v. *Secretary of State for the Environment*[6]) that the existence of a special form of protection did not cut down the general power under the planning legislation. In this case a burial mound had been scheduled as an ancient monument, but the Court of Appeal held that even if this had not been the case, it would have been open to the planning authority to have refused planning permission because of the existence of the burial mound. The court, by analogy, thought that this principle would apply to a building of special architectural or historic interest.

---

[2] Civic Amenities Act 1967, s.1.

[3] T.C.P.(A).A. 1972, s.8 (repealed by the T.C.A.A. 1974, which inserted similar provisions as an amendment to T.C.P.A. 1971, s.277).

[4] T.C.P.(A).A. 1972, s.10. The term "outstanding" has little practical reference after L.G.P.L.A. 1980 (Sched. 15, para. 27): this swept away the difference which was originally only introduced for grant purposes.

[5] The section was further added to by the L.G.A. 1985 and the H.P.A. 1986.

[6] [1975] Q.B. 754; [1975] 2 W.L.R. 897; 119 S.J. 335; 2 All E.R. 931.

2. WHAT IS A CONSERVATION AREA?

Section 277(1) describes a conservation area as an "area of special archi- **3.03** tectural or historic interest the character or appearance of which it is desirable to preserve or enhance."

The size and nature of conservation areas vary considerably from small groups of buildings to whole town centres. Many nationally well known areas have been designated conservation areas, such as Royal Hospital, Chelsea, Cheyne Walk, The Boltons, Holland Park, Brompton Square, Bayswater, Millbank, St James's, St. John's Wood, and Westminster Cathedral, all in London as well as provincial conservation areas such as Saltaire in Yorkshire.

From the definition given above, it is clear that the most important constituent parts of a conservation area will be those parts which contribute most towards the "character and appearance" of the area. Buildings which can contribute towards the character or appearance of the area are themselves not necessarily buildings of special architectural or historic interest. Consequently it is not necessary for the conservation area to be centred on listed buildings, although it may well be, and very often is. Circular 8/87[7] suggests at paragraph 54: "Pleasant groups of other buildings (*i.e.* other than listed), open spaces, trees, an historic street pattern, a village green, or features of historic or archaeological interest may also contribute to the special character of an area."

This demonstrates the potential range of sizes of the conservation area and their varied potential nature. The criterion for deciding whether a building contributes to the conservation area is different from the criterion for deciding whether to list it; indeed, the character of the conservation area may derive from features other than buildings and which themselves are incapable of being listed, *e.g.* trees, open spaces, and the street pattern. However, it remains necessary for the area to be of special architectural or historic interest and the character or appearance of that area to be one which it is desirable to preserve or enhance.

There is a statutory definition of the word "building" for the purposes of listing, namely "any structure or erection, and any part of a building, as so defined, but [not including] plant or machinery comprised in a building."[8] There is no definition of what is sufficient to constitute a conservation area[9] nor is there anything in the statutes to define what features may make that area special.

The definition is a double definition, *i.e.* to be capable of being a conser- **3.04** vation area an area must pass two tests—it must be (a) an area of special architectural or historic interest, and (b) an area, the character or appearance of which it is desirable to preserve or enhance.

Although (b) would normally apply to an area which qualified under (a), presumably it is theoretically possible for an area to be of special interest under (a) but not to qualify under (b) because, for instance, the buildings might be substantially unused or derelict or subject to confirmed proposals

---

[7] Circular 8/87, para. 54.
[8] T.C.P.A. 1971, s.290, and see the discussion at paras. 2.08–2.14.
[9] T.C.P.A. 1971, ss.290 and 277.

for demolition, so that any realistic possibility of the preservation or enhancement of the area is unlikely.

What then, if anything, is the difference between the meaning of the words "special architectural or historic interest" in the context of specific buildings (*i.e.* for listing) and the same words when applied to an "area"? There are no published guidelines as to what makes an area of special interest, to compare with the detailed guidelines which exist for the listing of buildings. The only help is Circular 8/87, para. 54 (see above at para. 3.03), as to what may be included in a conservation area. Paragraph 54 emphasises that it is the character of areas, rather than individual buildings, which section 277 seeks to preserve or enhance. Ultimately the point may have to be tested in the courts to determine whether there is or is not any distinction.

There is no guidance given as to what types of appearance or character it is desirable to preserve. Is it desirable to preserve or enhance every kind of character or appearance? One would not think of listing a building built five years ago. On the other hand, assuming that there was a remarkably fine group of buildings—perhaps which have been award winning—would one feel justified in making that group a conservation area even though some, or indeed all, of the buildings might have been completed only in the last decade?

In practical terms by April 1987 there had been designated 5,902 conservation areas.[10] There are no statistics available as to the ages of the buildings which are involved in these conservation areas, and indeed it is probably impossible to obtain such statistics. The general impression, however, in the Department is that the majority of conservation areas which have been designated are centred on buildings which were substantially completed before the turn of the last century.

3. THE MECHANICS OF MAKING A CONSERVATION AREA

(a) The duty to determine

3.05   Each local authority has a duty to determine which parts of its area are areas of special architectural or historic interest, the character or appearance of which it is desirable to preserve or enhance and to designate such areas as conservation areas.[11]

The Secretary of State also has power (after consultation with the local planning authority) to designate areas as conservation areas[12]—Circular 8/87 says that this power is intended to be used only exceptionally[13] and has at the date of writing not yet been exercised.

Local planning authorities have a duty to formulate and publish proposals for the preservation and enhancement of conservation areas from time to

---

[10] *English Heritage Monitor* (1987), p. 10.
[11] s.277(1) of T.C.P.A. 1971, and s.277(2) as re-enacted by T.C.A.A. 1974, s.1, and amended by L.G.P.L.A. 1980, Sched. 15, para. 26.
[12] T.C.P.A. 1971, s.277(4) as re-enacted by T.C.A.A. 1974, s.1.
[13] Circular 8/87, para. 57.

time.[14] Such proposals should be discussed at local public meetings, and comments made at such meetings taken into account by the local planning authority.[15]

Paragraph 70 of Circular 8/87 stresses the importance of securing public support and harnessing public enthusiasm for questions of conservation. Local authorities are also advised to set up advisory committees for conservation areas consisting not only of local authority members but also local members of the R.I.B.A.,[16] R.T.P.I.[17] and, for example, where there is thriving commerce in a conservation area, the local Chamber of Trade.[18] The function of such a committee is to advise the local authority on the applications that would affect the character or appearance of a conservation area.[19] The committee has, however, no statutory function.

Local planning authorites are required from time to time to make a review of their conservation areas, to determine whether any additional areas should be designated, and to designate such areas.[20]

(b) Designation by map

It is recommended that the conservation area designation should be by   **3.06**
reference to a map,[21] and nearly all conservation areas so far designated have been by reference to a map, which is often published as part of the publicity procedure.

(c) Notices

Notice of a designation (and indeed of a variation or cancellation) with   **3.07**
particulars of its effect must be published in the *London Gazette* and at least one newspaper circulating in the area.[22] Owners and occupiers of individual buildings in the conservation area do not have to be notified and have no right to object. It behoves those owners and occupiers therefore, who have property in areas which might well be designated as conservation areas, to be mindful of the proposals going before the local planning authority if they seek to object. An objection can only be a political objection in the sense of seeking to dissuade an authority from designating a conservation area, but once designated it will be very much more difficult to persuade an authority to revoke, cancel or limit that area.

A designation as a conservation area is registrable as a local land charge

---

[14] T.C.P.A. 1971, s.277B(1) as amended by T.C.A.A. 1974, s.1, and by L.G.P.L.A. 1980, Sched. 15.

[15] T.C.P.A. 1971, s.277B(2).

[16] Royal Institute of British Architects.

[17] Royal Town Planning Institute.

[18] Circular 8/87, para. 68.

[19] *Ibid.*

[20] T.C.P.A. 1971, s.277(7) as amended by T.C.A.A. 1974 s.1 and L.G.P.L.A. 1980, Sched. 15, para. 26(1).

[21] Circular 8/87, para. 58.

[22] T.C.P.A. 1971, s.277(7) as amended by T.C.A.A. 1974, s.1.

and must be registered as such by the local planning authority.[23] Indeed, to many owners on a sale of their property, this will be the first knowledge of the existence of the conservation area.

Many authorities, however, have sought to involve the public and the owners and occupiers of properties in the making of the conservation area, particularly where it is intended to improve and enhance the areas. Good practice might also include publicity prior to designation by the local planning authority.

There is no specific form of notice for publication—the original Circular 53/67[24] merely provided that "the published notices should describe the areas as clearly as possible, with maps where necessary" and Circular 147/74[24] provided that "the notice . . . must now give particulars of the effect of the designation . . . (and) . . . include information about the control of demolition . . . " No further guidance is to be found in Circular 8/87.

3.08 Many authorities seek to go beyond a statutory type of notice and make it clear what is intended, *e.g.*

> "The effect of designation is that special attention should be paid to the desirability of preserving or enhancing the character or appearance of the area designated. In particular, controls are applied regarding the demolition of buildings (owners are required to apply to the council for listed building consent before carrying out works of demolition to any building or part of a building within the areas); control is also imposed in respect of the display of advertisements and the felling, topping and lopping, etc., of trees within the areas. Penalties apply in the event of violations against this control."[25]

Notification must be given to the Secretary of State and the Commission of the designation of a conservation area, but his consent is not necessary.

Prior to the 1980 Act local authorities were under a duty to review their past exercise of functions relating to the designation of conservation areas "within such period as the Secretary of State might from time to time direct": this has now been changed by Schedule 15, para. 26 requiring a review "from time to time."

4. THE CONSEQUENCES OF A CONSERVATION AREA DESIGNATION

(a) General policy

3.09 The general policy is set out in section 277(8) of the 1971 Act, as amended by the 1974 Act, as follows:

> "Where any area is for the time being designated as a conservation area special attention shall be paid to the desirability of preserving or

---

[23] T.C.P.A. 1971, s.277(9), consequent upon the Local Land Charges Act 1975.

[24] The parts of Circulars 53/67 and 147/74 dealing with conservation areas and listed buildings were cancelled by Circular 23/77, which broadly reiterates the advice and comments given in the circulars referred to.

[25] Taken from an advertisement of Leeds City Council, April 3, 1975.

enhancing its character or appearance in the exercise, with respect to any buildings or other land in that area, of any powers under this Act, Part I of the Historic Buildings and Ancient Monuments Act 1953 or the Local Authorities (Historic Buildings) Act 1962."

This policy is considered important by the courts.[26] But perhaps the weakness of the general statement is the fact that there can be no real definition of what "special attention" means. Many local planning authorities might say that a conservation area policy is not required because it would in any event pay special attention (*i.e.* attention over and beyond that which it would normally pay to any other area) to the sort of area which would be designated as a conservation area.

As can be seen from the *Hoveringham* case[27] the control afforded by special legislation does not preclude or limit the authority from exercising the general control imposed by legislation in relation to the particular circumstances of a particular site or building. Neither does it appear that this general rule was restricted by the existence of a section 52[28] agreement, whereby a local planning authority may enter into an agreement with any person interested in land in their area for the purpose of restricting or regulating the development or use of the land. In a case in relation to non-listed buildings in a conservation area in Windsor[29] the Court of Appeal held that section 52 could not be construed as empowering a local planning authority to bind themselves not to exercise their powers under section 277, which they have a public duty to exercise. It followed that the defendants were not entitled to demolish their buildings (as initially agreed with the authority under a section 52 agreement) without the authority's specific consent under the listed buildings legislation. However, the provisions of the direction contained in paragraph 97(f) of Circular 8/87 would now avoid this situation.[29a]

(b) Development control in conservation areas

Section 28 of the 1971 Act provides that where a planning application is **3.10** made for development which would in the opinion of the local planning authority affect the character or appearance of a conservation area, a notice must be published in a local paper (by the authority, not by the applicant) indicating the nature of the application and stating the place where a copy of the application is open for inspection for a period of 21 days. Such a notice must be displayed on or near the site for seven days (again, by the authority and not the applicant) and the application cannot be determined until 21 days have elapsed after both the date of publication of the press notice, and the date the site notice was first displayed. There is no statutory form of

---

[26] *Richmond Borough Council* v. *Secretary of State* [1978] 37 P. & C.R. 151.
[27] See n. 6 above.
[28] T.C.P.A. 1971.
[29] *Royal Borough of Windsor and Maidenhead* v. *Brandrose Investments Ltd.* [1983] 1 W.L.R. 509; [1983] 1 All E.R. 818; (1983) P. & C.R. 349; [1983] J.P.L. 374; (1983) 266 E.G. 1195.
[29a] See para. 3.14 below.

notice for display to be found in the Listed Buildings etc. Regulations 1987[30] but these regulations prescribe the form of certificate and notice to be given by an applicant in relation to ownership. These notices can be adapted as site notices. Section 28 requires the local planning authority to state in the notice what is the proposal, and where and when the plans can be inspected. The form of notice prescribed additionally provides for an invitation to make representations. Local planning authorities follow, almost invariably, this form. It is suggested that if the invitation was omitted, it would be arguable that the notice would not be bad in view of the provisions of section 28.

The local planning authority must take into account any representations as a result of these notices in determining the application.[31]

Emphasis is laid in Circular 8/87, and indeed in previous departmental circulars, on the point that the policy in relation to conservation areas and planning applications in respect of such areas should be based on control and not on the prevention of development, so as to avoid killing the life of a thriving area which may be in a conservation area.[32]

Paragraph 61 of Circular 8/87 suggests that new buildings should be considered not as separate entities, but as part of the area whose character is to be preserved—to help this aspect plans and drawings may be required showing the proposed development in its setting instead of merely the application in an outline form.

3.11 The Department appears to support in practice this view by the attitude taken on appeals. An application was made in Camden for an infill in a late eighteenth/early nineteenth century street.[33] This application was refused on design grounds. The street was partly in a conservation area. The part under consideration was not, but the council proposed to extend designation. They argued that the proposal was, by reason of its height and alignment with the neighbouring houses, out of sympathy with the street scene. The inspector said that by reason of the diversity which existed in the street: "I see little virtue in requiring the building to conform to the outlines of its neighbours (two original estate buildings). The design would, in fact, due to its complete variance with its immediate neighbours, add interest to the street scene." He allowed the appeal. A speculative scheme in High Wycombe, Buckinghamshire was refused planning permission by the local planning authority and an inquiry was held. The inspector thought the site was suitable in terms of land use and design, would accord with the provisions of the town map, and would enhance the townscape qualities of the conservation area within which it was situated. The proposal could provide accommodation well suited to local needs in a conveniently located position, and the townscape benefit which would be provided, coupled with the appellant's willingness to accept an occupancy condition, would, the inspector felt, override the authority's policy objection. He recommended that the appeal be allowed, and the Secretary of State accepted that recommendation.[34]

---

[30] Town and Country Planning (Listed Buildings and Buildings in Conservation Areas) Regulations 1987 (S.I. 1987 No. 349).
[31] T.C.P.A. 1971, s.29(4).
[32] Circular 8/87, para. 61.
[33] *Planning Appeals* Vol. 1, p. 28. T/APP/5008/A/75/2800/G9.
[34] *Planning Appeals* Vol. 1, p. 67. APP/5136/A/74/8506.

In Barking, the inspector decided that a proposed petrol station and car wash in a conservation area would not be unduly intrusive, particularly as the tranquility of the area was already disturbed by the sustained traffic[35]; and in Gloucester it was thought that the removal of a former postal sorting office, which in itself did not have any particular visual significance, would open up views of a nearby church, and demolition was therefore allowed.[36]

In a case in Bishop's Stortford, Peter Dominic appealed against a decision   **3.12** of the local planning authority to refuse planning permission for the demolition of existing buildings and the erection of three shops with two offices over. The Inspector concluded that the Peter Dominic building dominated the south east corner of Market Square, "and is essential to the character of the conservation area," and furthermore that the application to demolish the building arose from the "failure of the appellants to appreciate its inherent qualities and its outstanding contribution to the street scene" which was enhanced by the reticence of the adjacent building. The inspector concluded that the appellants proposed building would by reason of its "unsympathetic form, ungainly proportions and plain fenestration adversely affect the character of the conservation area by replacing a fine Victorian building by an ugly modern one." The appeal was dismissed on the basis of the architectural merits of the existing buildings and the unsympathetic nature of the design of the proposed replacement building.[37]

This indeed would seem to demonstrate the desire of paying "special attention" to the desirability of preserving and enhancing the character or appearance of the conservation area.

In the Peter Dominic case it is clear that the replacement building was a matter taken into account by the inspector. In practice this frequently happens, and indeed it is difficult to see how "special attention" could be paid if this were not so. Authority for doing this is to be found in *Richmond upon Thames London Borough* v. *Secretary of State for the Environment*[38] where the judge also took into consideration the case of *Kent Messenger Ltd.* v. *Secretary of State* (see para. 4.18 below.)

The question of the economics of a building or development in a conservation area are clearly as acute—if not more acute—than the issue in a listed building consent case. The law on this subject is far from certain, but the subject is dealt with generally in Chapter 4.

(c) Conservation area consent required

Demolition is not as yet considered "development" within the meaning   **3.13** of the Act[39] unless the demolition is, broadly, to precede and be part of new development. The ancient monument and the listed building are specifically dealt with under their respective legislative provisions so that demolition cannot proceed without specific authority. The critical factor so far as conservation areas are concerned and which gave "teeth" to the conser-

---

[35] APP/Z5060/A/85/27343.

[36] APP/U1620/A/85/35495.

[37] *Planning Appeals* Vol. 1, p. 49. APP/5253/A/6394.

[38] Queen's Bench Division, Sir Douglas Frank, sitting as deputy judge of the High Court [1979] J.P.L. 175; (1978) 37 P. & C.R. 151; (1978) 249 E.G. 244.

[39] T.C.P.A. 1971, ss.290 and 22.

vation area principle is the requirement that a building in a conservation area is subject to similar limitations as to demolition as a listed building and that conservation area consent must be obtained for its demolition.[40]

The criterion which the local planning authority must apply is the desirability of preserving or enhancing the character or appearance of the conservation area in which the building is situated.[41]

These general principles are subject to two major comments. First, the control is a control against demolition—the Act does not seek in any special way to prevent extension or alteration of a building in a conservation area, except in so far as planning permission is required or in so far as an article 4 direction has been made withdrawing the planning permission granted by the General Development Order. Secondly there are a number of permissions to demolish granted by the Secretary of State in paragraph 97 of Circular 8/87 which came into operation on April 1, 1987.

3.14   The general rule, however, is incorporated in section 277A (as amended) and applies the control of demolition to a building in a conservation area as if it were a listed building with the exception of:

(a) buildings which are themselves listed;
(b) excepted buildings within the provisions of section 58(2), which provides for
   (i) an ecclesiastical building which is for the time being used for ecclesiastical purposes; or
   (ii) a building for the time being included in the schedule of Ancient Monuments;
(c) a building in relation to which a direction has been applied by the Secretary of State under section 277A(4) which enables the Secretary of State to exempt an individual building or types of building. Such a direction may be given to a local planning authority or to local planning authorities generally.

The direction which has been made by the Secretary of State taking certain classes of buildings outside the ambit of section 277A (namely that these buildings are not subject to the control) is set out in paragraph 97 of Circular 8/87. The direction is a revision of the direction contained in Circular 23/77. It is clearer and no longer directly linked to the General Development Order. The scope has been widened (but more clearly stated) so that consent is required for the demolition of buildings which are likely to have an effect on the character and appearance of the conservation area.

The broad categories of consent thereby given are:

(a) any building (but not a part of a building) with a total cubic content not exceeding 115 cubic metres;
(b) a gate, wall etc. under certain heights;
(c) a building erected since 1914 and used for agriculture or forestry;
(d) an industrial building subject to cubic content restrictions;
(e) a building subject to a discontinuance order or an enforcement notice;
(f) a building agreed to be demolished under a section 52 agreement;
(g) a building which is required to be demolished as a condition of a planning permission;

---

[40] T.C.P.A. 1971, s.277A (as amended by T.C.A.A. 1974).
[41] T.C.P.A. 1971, s.277B.

(h) buildings to be demolished as a result of orders under the Housing Act 1985 or the Pastoral Measure 1983.

Buildings which are themselves listed do not require exempting by this direction as they are already exempt by virtue of section 277A.

5. DEMOLITION OF UNLISTED BUILDINGS IN A CONSERVATION AREA

Unless consent is not required by virtue of section 277A or by the pro-   **3.15**
visions of the direction contained in paragraph 97 of Circular 8/87, an application must be made for conservation area consent (so called specifically in
the Listed Buildings etc. Regulations 1987).[42] A local authority making such
an application must make it to the Secretary of State.[43] There is no general
form of application prescribed in the regulations, but all planning authorities have their own standard application forms. Sufficient identification
(including a plan) and such other plans and drawings as are necessary to describe the works will be required with copies. The local planning authority
will advertise the application unless the application falls within the exceptions relating to the interior of a Grade II (unstarred) building.[44]

Until the coming into force of the Local Government, Planning and Land
Act 1980, a planning permission could in certain circumstances be deemed
to grant LBC to demolish. By virtue of the 1980 Act, Sched. 15, para. 26, this
ceased to be the case, and so, with effect from November 13, 1980 two separate decisions are necessary, although certain authorities will continue to
accept both applications on one form.

It is recommended in Circular 8/87, para. 95, that demolition consent for   **3.16**
an unlisted building in a conservation area, where it is clear that redevelopment of the site will follow, should only be given where there are acceptable
and detailed plans for the redevelopment. Further, to avoid the possibility of
the building being demolished but the development plans not being carried
through, the Circular suggests that the proposed redevelopment should be
subject to an enforceable agreement under section 52 of the 1971 Act.[44a]
This advice will continue to be good, although it is perhaps strengthened by
section 56(5) of the 1971 Act[45] whereby LBC for the demolition of a listed
building may be granted subject to a condition that the building shall not be
demolished before a contract for redevelopment of the site has been made. A
standard wording for such a condition is to be found in Appendix VII to Circular 8/87. This provision applies by virtue of section 277A(8) to a building

---

[42] *Ibid.*
[43] Circular 8/87, para. 101.
[44] S.I. 1987 No. 349, para. 5.
[44a] The provisions of which were extended by s.126 of the Housing Act 1974 which in turn was replaced by s.33 of the Local Government (Miscellaneous Provisions) Act 1982.
[45] *i.e.* the new s.56(5) which was substituted by Sched. 15, para. 10 of the L.G.P.L.A. 1980.

in a conservation area. However, the difficulties of this section and its enforcement will no doubt cause planning authorities to look much more to a section 52 agreement than relying on the fact that a contract for the redevelopment of the site has been made.

There is of course a conflict between the archaeological interests and the commercial need for speed. As an example of the use of section 52 agreements and the approach which some authorities have in relation to historic areas, the Department of Greater London Archaeology are believed to take the view in general that redevelopment within defined areas of archaeological importance should not take place without the conclusion of a definite agreement with the site owner, making adequate time and funding available for the required excavation and recording of archaeological remains, prior to their destruction during the building work. This is in line with the principles of the Code of Conduct for developers issued by the British Property Federation and others. General advice on this subject is given in paragraph 94 of Circular 8/87, which points out that unless otherwise stated the advice on procedural matters in the Circular applies to conservation area consents as well as to listed building consents.

It has been pointed out that, because the operation of section 57 (acts causing or likely to result in damage to listed buildings) does not extend to unlisted buildings in conservation areas, it seems quite possible that small but significant acts of demolition (e.g. the removal of a cornice) will be beyond the control of the local planning authority.[46] It is often difficult to draw the line between demolition (which does require conservation area consent) and alteration (which does not require conservation area consent for an unlisted building in a conservation area): this matter is discussed in full at paras. 5.20–5.21 below.

The principles applicable to the consent to demolish a listed building do not apply to a non-listed building in a conservation area. The test as to whether or not consent should be granted in respect of a listed building is that regard should be had to the character of the building itself as one of special architectural or historic interest. The test in relation to a non-listed building in a conservation area is the effect on "the character or appearance of the conservation area in which the building is situated." This was given recognition in The Town and Country Planning (Listed Buildings and Buildings in conservation areas) Regulations 1977, Schedule 3 (repeated in Schedule 3 to the Listed Buildings etc. Regulations 1987) in the reference to section 96 of the Act which draws this distinction in respect of the demolition of unlisted buildings in conservation areas, which are dealt with in regulation 10. Thus, in enforcement notice proceedings,[47] the test is not the building itself but the effect of the loss of the building on the character and appearance of the conservation area. Paragraph 61 of Circular 8/87 points out that when considering consent for a new building in a conservation area, its design not as a separate entity but as part of a larger whole will be important, and that to this extent detailed rather than outline plans may be called for; conservation areas, however, will sometimes be drawn widely and it will probably not be necessary to insist on detailed applications throughout the area.

---

[46] Charles Mynors, "Urban Conservation and Historic Buildings," London Borough of Kensington and Chelsea (1984), p. 10.
[47] See paras. 5.40–5.43.

6. THE GENERAL DEVELOPMENT ORDER AND ARTICLE 4 DIRECTIONS IN CONSERVATION AREAS

Article 4. Article 4 of the General Development Order 1977[48] provides that: **3.17**

> "If either the Secretary of State or the appropriate local planning authority is satisfied that it is expedient that development of any of the classes specified in Schedule 1 to this Order . . . should not be carried out in any particular area, or that any particular development of any of those classes should not be carried out, unless permission is granted on an application in that behalf, the Secretary of State or the appropriate local planning authority may direct that the permission granted by Article 3 of this Order shall not apply to:
> (i) all or any development of all or any of those classes in any particular area specified in the direction, or
> (ii) any particular development, specified in the direction, falling within any of those classes."

Consent. Although a local planning authority may, without the consent of the Secretary of State, make an article 4 direction in respect of a listed building or a building within the curtilage of a listed building,[49] this freedom does not apply to conservation areas where such consent must be obtained.

Temporary order. A provision is contained in article 4(3)(b) of the General Development Order whereby in "a particular area" a local planning authority may make a temporary order withdrawing Classes I to IV inclusive from permitted development.[50]

Departmental advice. Advice to local planning authorities on the use of article 4 directions is given in Circular 8/87—see paragraph 64 and Appendix II. Basically the advice is that a local planning authority should gauge the attitude of the local population in a conservation area and should normally only make an article 4 direction if the attitude is largely uncooperative. Although article 4 says that a direction made under it can apply to "any particular area," it is stressed in Circular 8/87 that the mere existence of a conservation area is not sufficient justification for making a blanket article 4 direction in relation to it. Broadly, a local planning authority should make a direction only in two circumstances: **3.18**

(i) known existing or potential threats to the character of the area from permitted development,[51] or
(ii) where a direction would assist a positive policy of the local planning authority for the improvement of the area.[52]

Even where a case for a direction exists, the ambit of the direction should be

---

[48] Town and Country Planning General Development Order 1977 (S.I. 1977 No. 289).
[49] See para. 2.42 above.
[50] *Ibid.*
[51] Circular 8/87, para. 2, App.II.
[52] *Ibid.*

narrow rather than broad, *i.e.* it should only apply to those classes of permitted development that are genuinely relevant and the geographical boundary of the order should be drawn as tightly as possible and not automatically made to include the whole conservation area.[53]

3.19 *Departmental approval.* There appears to be a greater readiness in the Department to approve article 4 directions and to extend the range of them, particularly if there is an active conservation scheme in progress and grant aid is provided. East Lindsey D.C. had an article 4 direction approved in Horncastle which even extended to include external painting schemes; though that council's attempt to have an article 4 direction approved to prevent stone cladding, roof and window alterations in a Louth conservation area was unsuccessful in respect of the windows.[54]

At Tixall Gatehouse, Stafford, where there was felt to be an urgent need to provide control over the setting of this Grade I listed building, an article 4 direction was made, approved and served in the record time of one week.[55] This was at a time when consent from the Secretary of State was required for an article 4 direction in respect of a listed building.

Compensation. The local planning authority, of course, will be concerned as to the financial consequences of making an article 4 direction. An article 4 direction withdraws the permission granted by the General Development Order and makes it necessary to apply to the local planning authority for a specific permission. If this is refused, or granted subject to conditions, the owner is entitled to compensation on the footing that permission already granted has been revoked or modified. Article 4 directions do not enable the Secretary of State or the local planning authority to withdraw permission which had been given and acted upon.

7. TREES IN A CONSERVATION AREA

3.20 Trees which are not subject to a tree preservation order but which are in a conservation area, are given protection by section 61A of the Town and Country Planning Act 1971 introduced by section 8 of the 1974 Act. The Act contains no definition of "tree" but Lord Denning M.R. in *Kent C.C.* v. *Batchelor*[55a] suggested that a distinction might be drawn between mature trees and saplings, with only trees having a diameter greater than seven inches or eight inches being protected.

Broadly, the protection given is the same as for a tree outside a conservation area which is subject to a tree preservation order. The purpose of the requirement is to give the authority a final opportunity to make a tree preservation order, if appropriate. The difference is one of mechanics, namely that by section 61A anyone intending to do any act which would be prohibited under section 60(1)(*a*) (*i.e.* if the tree was protected by a tree preservation order) must give six weeks notice of such intention to the local planning authority. If after six weeks of such notice being given the local

[53] Circular 8/87, para. 3, App.II.
[54] Both cases courtesy of East Lindsey D.C.
[55] Courtesy of Stafford B.C.
[55a] *The Times*, October 7, 1976 (C.A.); [1976] J.P.L. 754, C.A.

planning authority has not responded, or if it grants consent, work may proceed. It seems that in giving consent, conditions cannot be imposed. If the local planning authority is not willing it may make a tree preservation order.

Penalties for contravening the requirements given in the notice are similar to penalties for breach of a tree preservation order (including a duty to replant).[56]

The local planning authority (which, in the case of urban development areas, will be the relevant urban development corporation) must keep a register of applications available for public inspection.[57] The Secretary of State may by regulations exempt certain classes of tree from the operation of section 61A by reference to their location, size, species or other designation.[58]

Section 174 of the 1971 Act is an enabling provision as to compensation payable in respect of loss or damage caused or incurred in consequence of the refusal of any consent required under a section 60 tree preservation order. The provision is nowhere expressed to apply to trees protected under section 61A, but it is worthwhile to note that the measure of such compensation, following the decision of the Court of Appeal in *Bell* v. *Canterbury City Council*,[58a] is the diminution in the value of the land resulting from the refusal, and not merely the commercial value of the timber which the owner can not realise.

Town and Country Planning (Tree Preservation Order) (Amendment) and (Trees in Conservation Areas) (Exempted Cases) Regulations 1975 were made on the February 11, 1975 and provide in regulation 3 that section 61A of the Town and Country Planning Act 1971 shall not apply where the act is— **3.21**

(i) the cutting down, uprooting, topping or lopping of a tree in the circumstances mentioned in section 60(6) of the 1971 Act (*i.e.* the cutting down, topping or lopping of trees which are dying or dead or have become dangerous, or the cutting down, topping or lopping of any trees in compliance with any obligations imposed by or under an Act of Parliament or so far as may be necessary for the prevention or abatement of a nuisance);

(ii) the cutting down of a tree in the circumstances mentioned in paragraph (1) or (2), or the cutting down, uprooting, topping or lopping of a tree in the circumstances mentioned in paragraph (3), of the Second Schedule to the form of Tree Preservation Order contained in the Schedule to the Town and Country Planning (Tree Preservation Order) Regulations 1969 (S.I. 1969 No. 17) (as amended by the 1975 Regulations) (which broadly relate to woodlands schemes approved by the Forestry Commission);

(iii) the cutting down of a tree in accordance with a felling licence granted by the Forestry Commissioners;

(iv) the cutting down, uprooting, topping or lopping of a tree on land in the occupation of a local planning authority and the act is done by or with the consent of that authority;

---

[56] T.C.P.A. 1971, s.61A as introduced by T.C.A.A. 1974, s.8 and T.C.P.A. 1971, s.62.
[57] T.C.P.A. 1971, s.61A(7), (as introduced by T.C.A.A. 1974, s.8).
[58] T.C.P.A. 1971, s.61A(4) and (5).
[58a] *The Times*, March 11, 1988 (C.A.).

(v) the cutting down, uprooting, topping or lopping of a tree having a diameter not exceeding 75 millimetres or the cutting down or uprooting of a tree having a diameter not exceeding 100 millimetres where the act is carried out to improve the growth of other trees.

8. PAINTING AND STONE-CLEANING IN CONSERVATION AREAS

3.22   The painting[59] of the exterior of a building in a conservation area presents some difficulties and is dealt with in some detail in paragraph 4 of Appendix II of Circular 8/87. The issue of painting is also dealt with in relation to "development" in the General Development Order 1977. The problem is best tackled in stages.

(1) Painting the exterior of a building will only be development within section 22(2)(a) of the 1971 Act if it would "materially affect the external appearance of a building."

(2) If, therefore, painting in a particular case does not "materially affect the external appearance" of the building, it will not be development and not be therefore subject to control. Whether or not it does so affect the appearance must depend not just on the nature and extent of the painting but on the result and appearance on the building. Generally speaking, however, there is no question but that external painting is not subject to development control unless it falls within the specific reference in section 22(4), whereby the "use for the display of advertisements of any external part of a building which is not normally used for that purpose" is brought within control as involving a material change in the use of that part of the building.

(3) If painting as such is to be development, then it may be permitted development under the General Development Order, Sched. 1, Class II, para. 3: "The painting of the exterior of any building or work otherwise than for the purpose of advertisement, announcement, or direction." In such a case it will not normally be controlled, but it can be brought under control by an article 4 direction.

(4) Circular 12/73 (para. 2 and Appendix D, the latter quoted as Appendix II to Circular 8/87) comments on this, suggesting that a strong case will be needed for including painting in an article 4 direction. Such a case might be established in an area with a formal townscape "where continuity, form and colour is an essential part of the local character."

3.23   (5) If painting is to be included in an article 4 direction it is suggested that the local planning authority should publish a colour code of acceptable colours, and this has been done freqently and to good effect.

(6) In the case of *Royal Crescent at Bath*[59a], the problem was tested in connection with the painting of the front door of a building situated

---

[59] See also para. 6.06.
[59a] [1972] J.P.L. 650.

60

in a conservation area. The owner wished to paint it a canary yellow and did so and was then subject to an enforcement notice requiring the painting to be altered, the premises being in a conservation area. The enforcement notice was not upheld (on other grounds) but the ability of the local planning authority to make an enforcement order in these circumstances was not challenged.

(7) There is a prohibition on painting a listed building whether in a conservation area or not if this would affect its character as a building of special architectural or historic interest. Thus, for instance, a white painted barn could be repainted white without consent. However two stone properties in Sleaford (in fact which were in a conservation area) had been painted. The result was described by the inspector as follows: "I am satisfied that the painting of the stonework of the facade, by obscuring the colour, texture and scale of the stonework, has inevitably had a very detrimental effect on the appearance and character of this listed building, of the group of listed buildings of which it forms part, of the generally attractive street scene, and of the surrounding conservation area." The Secretary of State dismissed the enforcement notice appeal and refused to grant LBC for the works enforced against.[60]

(8) Stone-cleaning[61] is a subject which involves basic town planning questions such as whether it requires planning permission at all—and whether or not it requires listed building consent. It certainly would not require conservation area consent for an unlisted building within a conservation area. Strangely there appear to be no cases in the courts and no reported ministerial decisions in England. However the matter has been considered carefully in Scotland—where the legislation is expressed in similar terms to that in England—and the following conclusions seem to emerge[62]:

  (a) The first question is whether stone-cleaning is development. The reporter (the equivalent of an English inspector) held in a case relating to a building in Downside Road, Glasgow[63] that whilst a colour change on stone cleaning had affected the building's external appearance, he did not consider the change to be "material"—so escaping the provisions of the Act defining "development" by virtue of (the English) section 22(2)(a) of the 1971 Act. Equally in a further appeal[64] relating to a building in Clarence Drive, Glasgow, the reporter took the view that the effect of stone-cleaning had been to restore the building to a condition closely resembling that which it must have possessed when originally built. He regarded the cleaning as "maintenance"—and as such not involving development.

  (b) But even if the stone-cleaning does not require planning permission, it still may require listed building consent as section

3.24

---

[60] J.P.L. 782: (APP/5312/F/77/26); see also [1981] J.P.L. 607 considered at para. 4.46 below.

[61] See also para. 6.05.

[62] We are indebted to Eric Young and his article in *Estates Gazette* (August 1, 1987), Vol. 283, p. 540.

[63] P/ENA/SL/199, October 3, 1985.

[64] P/ENA/SL/201, November 25, 1985.

55 does not refer to "development" in relation to a listed building, but "works"—of which term there is no definition. The George Hotel in George Street, Edinburgh was proposed to be stone cleaned.[65] The local planning authority's policy on the cleaning of listed buildings was to weigh the visual desirability of clean buildings against the adverse effects which some methods of stone-cleaning can have. The Secretary of State accepted that the determining issue was whether the risk of damage could be regarded as justifiable. He stated that in general, he accepted the planning authority's policy of seeking to protect sandstone buildings from the severe damage whch could be caused by abrasives or acid used in stone-cleaning. "Had the listed building had a begrimed or shabby appearance, cleaning might have been justified, but here the building had a well-maintained appearance and a pleasant patina which blended well with the stonework of most of the buildings in the vicinity." He therefore dismissed the appeal.

9. CONTROL OF ADVERTISEMENTS

3.25   Circular 8/87 (para. 67) advises local planning authorities to be flexible in the way they apply the control of advertisements regulations to conservation areas. This again is to take account of the fact that the conservation area may well include an area of thriving commerce. Section 63 of the 1971 Act, however, requires the Minister to make regulations to control the display of advertisements in the interest of amenity or safety and enable such regulations to provide for regulating the dimensions, appearance or position, and requiring planning consent for the display, of advertisements; also for the constitution of advisory committees. Currently operative regulations under the 1971 Act are, in fact, general advertisement control regulations made in 1984 and include specific advice as to conservation areas. Circular 11/84 incorporates advice[66] given on this topic since 1962, and observes that the Secretary of State has now given up the power to call in any particular application for advertisement consent or to give directions requiring consultation by LPA's in exercise of their functions.[67]

10. URGENT REPAIRS TO A BUILDING IN A CONSERVATION AREA

3.26–   Section 101 of the Act is a new section, substituted by the 1986 Act,
3.27   which amended and strengthened the powers existing before April 1, 1987. The section covers both listed buildings and certain unlisted buildings in a conservation area. The subject is fully covered in relation to listed buildings[68] but there are some differences which should be noted:

[65] HGJ/2/LA/50, December 19, 1984.
[66] The "explanatory memorandum" referred to in para. 3.
[67] Para. 12.
[68] See Chap. 7.

(a) The section only relates to those unlisted buildings in a conservation area for which the Secretary of State has made a direction if it appears to him that the preservation of the building is important for maintaining the character or appearance of the conservation area.[69] The Secretary of State must consult the Commission before giving such a direction.

(b) Either the Secretary of State or the local planning authority may, if of opinion that works are urgently necessary for the preservation of the building, execute the works. The Commission, if authorised by the Secretary of State, may carry out the works but he has indicated that he will only do so where the conservation area is of national rather than of local significance and the building in question is so important that failure to carry out emergency repairs to it may affect the character of the area.[70]

In other respects the rules in respect of a notice under this section in relation to a building in a conservation area follow those in relation to listed buildings, details of which will be found at paras. 7.10–7.13 below. The provisions of sections 114 and 115 relating to non-urgent repairs to a listed building are not applicable to non-listed buildings in a conservation area.

11. FINANCIAL ASSISTANCE

There are a number of provisions by which the Secretary of State or the local planning authority (frequently as agent of the Secretary of State) may provide conservation moneys to the owners of properties in conservation areas by way of grant or loan, and they are dealt with more particularly in Chapter 10. **3.28**

---

[69] T.C.P.A. 1971, s.101(2).
[70] Circular 8/87, paragraph 126.

4. Listed Building Consent—The Criteria for Consent to Demolish, Alter and Extend

1. GENERAL SUMMARY

4.01 Listing is too often considered to be a permanent freezing of a building. This was never the intention nor in practice should it be the way in which listing should operate. Sir Hugh Casson, in giving evidence for Barclays Bank in connection with a building at 39/40 Lombard Street, London, summarised—in our view quite correctly—the relationship between listing and the granting of LBC. He said:

> "While the facade is not distinguished, in my view the Inspectorate was correct in listing the building as Grade II. Listing, however, means no

more than it says. It permits time for study and for second thoughts. Such study should properly balance the practicabilities of preservation with the visual loss to the street of demolition."[1]

Similarly Lady Birk denied that listing was "a pickling policy" (1977).[2]

The DOE Circular 8/87 is a reminder that in considering any application for LBC, local planning authorities are required by section 56(3) of the 1971 Act to have special regard to the desirability of preserving the building or any features of special architectural or historic interest which it possesses.[3] This circular gives perhaps the most up to date departmental thinking on the question of the criteria to be taken into account by local planning authorities or the Secretary of State when considering LBC applications, and certain aspects are also firmly stated in Circular 22/80.[4] Circular 8/87 is used as an index of the points which are to be taken into account and endeavours to relate those items to reports of decisions by the Secretary of State. The criteria for decisions are not necessarily closed—as time goes on, and the subject obtains a greater and more comprehensive coverage of recorded decisions—a greater sophistication of criteria may emerge. No case has yet been taken to the High Court which tests these criteria.

There are two problems in ascertaining the practical consequences of policies expressed in Circular 8/87. First, obtaining details of ministerial decisions on LBC appeals and "call-ins," which might be expected to reveal the Secretary of State's interpretation of stated policies. Secondly, the limited number of LBC appeals and call-ins.[5] Access to data on relevant cases is complicated by the fact that the DOE does not maintain any central, publicly accessible "register" of such cases. Appeal and call-in case records are kept at individual DOE regional offices,[6] and copies of inspectors' reports and Secretary of State's decision letters are available on payment of copying charges.[7] The publication of details of decisions thus depends largely on the goodwill of those parties, the vigilance of the press and publishers, and in some respects, the notoriety and/or publicity value of the cases themselves.

The statutory requirement for consideration of whether to grant LBC is for a local planning authority to have "special regard to the desirability of

---

[1] [1976] J.P.L. 445; Ref. B/5002/270/14 April 9, 1976.

[2] Opening address to Oxford Conference in 1976, reported in *Journal of Planning and Environment Law Occasional Papers*, (1977) p. 5.

[3] L.G.P.L.A. 1980 extends s.56(3) to include the setting of a listed building; see para. 4.03 below: "Provisions in the Act."

[4] Circular 22/80: *Development Control—Policy and Practice*. Para. 17 thereof refers.

[5] Midgley, J.B, *Restoration and Renewal*, Leeds Polytechnic, August 1980.

[6] Although listing is done centrally by the Department of the Environment, LBC appeals and call-ins are processed, and decisions and recommendations made at the Department's regional offices unless the case is of particular national significance or of such importance that either the Secretary of State of his own volition, or at the request of a Member wishes to look at it, or the regional controller refers it to the Minister. In every LBC appeal or call-in case, however, the actual decision is that of the Secretary of State.

[7] The first ten pages of such copies are normally free, the charge thereafter being 8 pence per sheet.

preserving the building or its setting or any features of special architectural or historic interest which it possesses" (section 56(3), T.C.P.A. 1971).[8]

4.02   Circular 8/87 observes that it should be remembered that the number of buildings of special architectural and historic interest is limited. Accordingly, it contends, the presumption should be in favour of preservation, except where a strong case can be made out for granting consent after the application of the criteria mentioned below.[9]

This attitude is reflected in, for instance, a decision on the application of the Post Office for LBC to demolish Red Barracks, Barrack Road, Weymouth. The Secretary of State refused the application, saying, "the Department has always made it clear in its Historic Buildings and Conservation Circulars that there should be a presumption in favour of preserving listed buildings, except where a strong case is established for their demolition."[10]

The Department may have always made its attitude clear, but the question is: is its attitude correct? There is almost a suggestion (although, it must be emphasised, nowhere expressed as such by the DOE) that a burden of proof is placed on the applicant to dislodge a presumption of preservation. However desirable this may be thought to be by the DOE, it does not seem to flow from having "special regard to the desirability of preserving the building . . . " The words "burden of proof" or "onus of proof" do not frequently enter the planning context. But for the purpose of this argument we take the definition as being a burden which lies on the party who substantially asserts the affirmative of the issue. Perhaps a reasonable analogy can be drawn with the rule relating to a planning application, when an applicant has a right to have a decision in his favour unless there is a positive planning argument to the contrary.[11] The words of Circular 14/85, although they relate primarily to planning applications, are certainly worth remembering here:

> "There is therefore always a presumption in favour of allowing applications for development, having regard to all material considerations, unless that development would cause demonstrable harm to interests of acknowledged importance.
> . . . If the planning authority consider it necessary to refuse permission, the onus is on them to demonstrate clearly why the development cannot be permitted and the reasons must be precise, specific and relevant to the application."[12]

It may be difficult to draw the distinction between shifting the burden of proof and "having special regard." but "having special regard" is but one matter to take into account. We do not believe that the statute imposed or intended to impose a burden of proof on the applicant. If the issue is finely balanced, then it is suggested that the general rule should prevail that the applicant is entitled to his decision so long as the local planning authority

---

[8] T.C.P.A. 1971, s.56(3), as amended by L.G.P.L.A. 1980, Sched. 15, para. 8. See para. 4.03 below.

[9] Circular 8/87, para. 91.

[10] [1979] J.P.L. 496. Ref. SW/P/5192/270/129. December 19, 1978.

[11] See Circular 22/80, para. 3 (replacing Circular 9/76): local planning authorities are asked "always to grant planning permission, having regard to all material considerations, unless there are sound and clear-cut reasons for refusal."

[12] Paragraph 3.4—see also Introduction at 1.06 above.

has had special regard, and not merely a passing consideration, to the desirability of preserving the building.

2. PROVISIONS IN THE ACT

There is very little statutory guidance as to what criteria are to be used when considering applications for LBC.   **4.03**

Section 56(3) of the 1971 Act, as amended by para. 8 of Schedule 15 to the Local Government, Planning and Land Act 1980 provides that:

> "in considering whether to grant planning permission for development which affects a listed building or its setting and in considering whether to grant LBC for any works, the local planning authority or the Secretary of State, as the case may be, shall have special regard to the desirability of preserving the building or its setting or any features of special architectural or historic interest which it possesses."

The inclusion of the "setting" of a listed building, by the 1980 Act, as one of the factors to be taken into account, is not a new practice, although it has not previously been a statutory requirement.

Section 56(4) and (4A) refers to the conditions which may be attached to a grant of LBC including "the preservation of particular features of the building," repairing any damage caused to the building during execution of the works, and reconstruction of the building with the use of original materials, where possible, after the works have been carried out.[13-14] Section 56(4B) provides that a condition may be attached to a LBC reserving specified details of the works for subsequent approval by the L.P.A.

Section 56(5) provides that

> "LBC for demolition may be granted subject to a condition that the building shall not be demolished before a contract for the carrying out of works of redevelopment of the site has been made, and planning permission has been granted for the redevelopment of the site for which the contract provides."[15]

3. THE DEPARTMENTAL CRITERIA FOR CONSENT

The guidance provided by the Secretary of State on criteria which should be employed by local authorities when considering applications to demolish (or alter) listed buildings, is set out in Circular 8/87.[16] This guidance is accepted as a basis for consideration, but it should be remembered that even though it is clearly given with every good intention, it is not statutory. Other factors may thus also be relevant. It is divided into four sub-paragraphs, which shall be considered individually. The four sub-paragraphs are: **4.04**

[13-14] L.G.P.L.A. 1980, Sched. 15, paras. 9, 10 amends T.C.P.A. 1971, ss.56(4) and 56(5). S.56(4B) is added by H.P.A. 1986, Sched. 9, para. 3.

[15] *Ibid.*

[16] Circular 8/87, para. 90.

"(a) the importance of the building, both intrinsically and relatively bearing in mind the number of other buildings of special architectural or historic interest in the neighbourhood. In some cases a building may be important because there are only a few of its type in the neighbourhood or because it has a fine interior, while in other cases its importance may be enhanced because it forms part of a group or series. Attention should also be paid to the contribution to the local scene made by a building, particularly if it is in a conservation area; but the absence of such a contribution is not a reason for demolition or alteration;

(b) in assessing the importance of the building, attention should be paid to both its architectural merit and to its historical interest. This includes not only historical associations but also the way the design, plan, materials or location of the building illustrates the character of a past age; or the development of a particular skill, style or technology;

(c) the condition of the building, the cost of repairing and maintaining it in relation to its importance, and whether it has already received or been promised grants from public funds. In estimating cost, however, due regard should be paid to the economic value of the building when repaired and to any saving through not having to provide alternative accommodation in a new building. Old buildings generally suffer from some defects, but the effects of these can easily be exaggerated;

(d) the importance of any alternative use for the site and, in particular, whether the use of the site for some public purpose, would make it possible to enhance the environment and especially other listed buildings in the area; or whether, in a rundown area, a limited redevelopment might bring new life and make the other listed buildings more economically viable."

Paragraph 89 of Circular 8/87 adds that, before LBC to demolish will be granted, evidence will be required that every possible effort has been made to continue the present use or find a suitable alternative use for the building. Further, it must normally be shown that the freehold has been offered for sale on the open market. There must be exceptional reasons to justify the offer of a lease or the imposition of restrictive covenants which would limit the chances of finding a new use. Local authorities are directed to set an example themselves in respect of buildings within their ownership.

4. THE IMPORTANCE OF THE BUILDING: PARAGRAPH 90(*a*)

4.05   The first criterion stated in Circular 8/87 is:

"the importance of the building, both intrinsically and relatively bearing in mind the number of other buildings of special architectural or historic interest in the neighbourhood. In some cases a building may be important because there are only a few of its type in the neighbourhood or because it has a fine interior, while in other cases its importance may be enhanced because it forms part of a group or series. Attention should also be paid to the contribution to the local scene made by a building, particularly if it is in a conservation area; but the absence of such a contribution is not a reason for demolition or alteration."

The problem is one of differing subjective judgments, even among experts on aesthetics. As was said by Forbes J. (as he then was): "experts do tend to differ and for every expert that one could find who said, looking at pure aesthetics, that something was exceptionally fine one might quite easily find another expert who took exactly the opposite view."[17]

Should the building have been listed in the first place? It is always open to the applicant to claim that the building should not have been listed.[18] This is simply an assertion that the building should not have been regarded as of special architectural or historic interest. An example of this is 6/8 East Parade, Leeds,[19] where an application for LBC was made in 1977 for the demolition of three Georgian buildings—former dwellinghouses later used as shops and offices. The building was listed and in a conservation area. The applicant's proposal to erect a new office building on the site was supported by Leeds City Council. The inspector reported that the properties were structurally sound with several original internal features surviving. It appeared that owing to differences in floor levels it would not be possible to carry out new development behind retained facades. If the property was to be restored, it could only be on the basis of three separate units. The front elevations had been altered by the addition of unsympathetic shop windows, while other parts had been changed by extensions and uncharacteristic new additions, so that the premises now possessed no historic or architectural merit. In the inspector's view the value of the buildings did not match the strategic importance of the site. This was an area covered by a local authority planning brief, which called for retention of the better buildings and improved pedestrian access. The opportunity to enhance the overall streetscape of East Parade outweighed the loss of these listed buildings. Other examples of the period could be seen in nearby Park Square. The proposed new development would provide a more satisfactory link with adjoining listed buildings than did the existing premises. The Secretary of State granted LBC.

Given that it is agreed that a building *is* properly listed, sometimes the **4.06** importance in a larger group—the street scene—plays a part in the decision making. An application by the National Westminster Bank Ltd. for LBC to demolish 10/12 St. Peter's Street, St. Albans, was refused by the local planning authority. An appeal ensued[20] and in his report the inspector said: "I am of the opinion in respect of the application for LBC that while the building is not of historic interest or of great architectural merit, its facade makes an important contribution to the attractiveness and interest of the street scene on this side of St. Peter's Street, and to the particular character of the group of buildings of which it forms part and that it merits retention on that account." For that and other reasons the inspector recommended that LBC should not be granted, which view was shared by the Secretary of State. It is perhaps a pity that this case was not taken to the High Court, bearing in

---

[17] *Winchester City Council* v. *Secretary of State for the Environment* (1978) 3 P. & C.R. 455 at 473.

[18] See para. 2.05 above.

[19] [1977] 244 E.G. 985.

[20] [1974] J.P.L. 552. Ref. SE/6/1582/270/17; APP/1582/A/63583, December 10, 1973.

mind that the test adopted by the inspector and the Secretary of State appears not to be the test as set out in the statute, but more a conservation area test. Nonetheless, it demonstrates the attitude in relation to the street scene.

4.07   The street scene was also important in another banking case in connection with Barclays Bank Ltd., whose application to demolish the facade of 39/40 Lombard Street, London, was refused.[21] The inspector in that case observed: "No. 39/40 Lombard Street is a massive four-storey stone building situated on the south side of the street at its eastern end and forming the corner of Gracechurch Street. It is constructed in the full Victorian classical 'palazzo' style, with profuse ornamentation and a crowning heavy cornice and balustrade . . . No. 39/40, situated as it is at the curved end of Lombard Street, plays an important role in the street scene." For this and other reasons the Secretary of State granted LBC for the demolition of the building with the exception of the facades facing Lombard Street and Gracechurch Street, together with sufficient depth of the existing building to ensure their stability.

In an application by Nottinghamshire County Council for consent to demolish three listed buildings in Castle Hill, Worksop (in a conservation area), the Secretary of State agreed with the inspector's report that although it was desirable to keep the buildings which contributed to the appearance and character of the street containing many similar old buildings[22], in this particular case the cost of repair and rehabilitation was not economically viable because the buildings were in such poor condition. LBC was granted.

Consent to demolish may be given in circumstances where the "street scene" around a listed building has deteriorated. The demolition of two listed school cottages in Colchester was allowed because their surroundings had been demolished and redeveloped.[23] The cottages themselves were capable of restoration, yet the inspector advocated demolition, quoting Development Control Policy Note 7: "An old building can be destroyed, as surely by changes in its surroundings as by direct assault . . . " Similarly, when considering whether to grant consent for the demolition of an unlisted building in a conservation area, the test to apply relates not to the building itself but to the effect that its loss would have on the conservation area.

5. THE ARCHITECTURAL MERIT AND HISTORIC INTEREST OF THE BUILDING: PARAGRAPH 90(b)

4.08   The second criterion mentioned in Circular 8/87 is the architectural merit and historic interest of the building:

"in assessing the importance of the building, attention should be paid to both its architectural merit and to its historical interest. This includes not only historical associations, but also the way the design,

---

[21] [1976] J.P.L. 445. Ref. 8–3/5002/270/14. April 9, 1976.
[22] [1979] 250 E.G. 48. Ref. EMP/1935/270/5. February 1, 1979. See also APP/5034/80/ 08935 (*Estates Times*, December 4, 1981).
[23] [1979] 250 E.G. 993. Refs. APP/5214/E/78/116; and APP/5214/A/78/08348. May 9, 1979.

plan, materials or location of the building illustrates the character of a past age; or the development of a particular skill, style or technology."

There are few cases which appear to rely specifically on this criterion. An interesting case, however, is reported in connection with the proposed demolition of the City of London Club, 19 Old Broad Street, London.[24] This was designed by Philip Hardwick, R.A. In giving his decision in 1976 on an appeal for non-determination, the Secretary of State said: "The front elevation appears to be stuccoed, but is, in fact, faced in stone and decorated with cream oil paint. The ground floor is channelled with a centre doorway with flat hood supported on festooned consoles and symmetrically flanked with three fine tall rectangular windows on each side, the original sashes having been replaced with more recent metal casements." The inspector noted that the building was considered by the Victorian Society to be the finest remaining example in London of Philip Hardwick's work. Except for the addition of the attic storey (apparently designed by his son, P. C. Hardwick) and the substituted casements to the front elevation, the building seems to have been virtually unchanged since its completion. The Secretary of State said: "It is thought to be one of the few surviving pieces of Philip Hardwick's work and is regarded by the Secretary of State as a fine example of an early Victorian gentlemen's club, as well as being an elegant building in itself and the only one of its kind in the City." The Secretary of State dismissed the appeal and refused LBC for the demolition of this building, as he considered it to be both a building of particular architectural and historic interest and an irreplaceable part of the City scene; and the arguments put forward that its demolition should be allowed, to enable redevelopment of the site to take place, were not in his opinion sufficiently cogent to override the importance of retaining this building.

It is perhaps significant that in this decision the Secretary of State also said that he "would not be justified in dealing with this appeal otherwise than in accordance with his present policies for the preservation of buildings of special architectural or historic interest." He concluded by asserting that by "the standards now applicable he considers [the building] to be both a building of particular architectural and historic interest and an irreplaceable part of the City scene." This perhaps is a reference to one of the then Secretary of State's predecessors, who permitted the demolition of the Euston Arch designed also by Philip Hardwick.

6. THE CONDITION OF THE BUILDING: PARAGRAPH 90(c)

The third criterion mentioned in Circular 8/87 is the condition of the building: **4.09**

"the condition of the building, the cost of repairing and maintaining it in relation to its importance, and whether it has already received or been promised grants from public funds. In estimating cost, however, due regard should be paid to the economic value of the building when repaired and to any saving through not having to provide alternative

[24] [1976] J.P.L. 450. Ref. JLC/L/VC1 70–01/0207. December 16, 1975.

accommodation in a new building. Old buildings generally suffer from some defects but the effects of these can easily be exaggerated."

The condition of the listed building perhaps raises the most difficult issues, both for the applicant for LBC and for the local planning authority or Secretary of State. It is obvious that a route to demolition lies by way of neglect. The owner of a listed building may well allow the building to deteriorate to such an extent that it might fall down of its own accord; or hope that if it gets into a condition whereby an economic restoration is impossible, he will be able to persuade the local planning authority or the Secretary of State that he should be granted consent to demolish it. Obviously we have moved on from the stage when that simple proposition was accepted. Local planning authorities up and down the country are generally watchful, and mindful of people who deliberately let buildings decline so that this argument can be put forward.

But should an owner be penalised by his being required to spend money to maintain a building he does not want, for the good of future generations? Put another way, should the owner be able to obtain the advantage of a release from his obligations as "a trustee for the future" and so be enabled to achieve a cleared site? The problem tends to mix facts with morality. Whether this should or should not be is a matter for individual judgment, but three cases demonstrate the problems which the Secretary of State and the local planning authorities have in this connection. This range of cases includes a building which is in good condition, a building which is in poor condition without blame to anybody, and a building which is in poor condition where there is a belief that it has been deliberately allowed to deteriorate. The result of such a review may not square with morality, but then results often do not.

4.10   The first case refers to an appeal by the British Gas Corporation for consent to demolish a listed building within the Sheffield Metropolitan District Council area, being the former Gas Offices, Commercial Street, Sheffield.[25] The inspector concluded that:

"the original Gas Office building has architectural merit, both from an external design and workmanship point of view, and also having regard to some internal features relating to the Board Room and Cash Hall. The classical style design of the Victorian era could contribute to the evolving character of this part of the town centre of Sheffield, assuming that adjacent redevelopment is suitably designed. For these reasons I am of the view that the former Gas Offices are properly listed as Grade II building of special architectural or historic interest and that these premises should, if possible, be preserved. I note the various schemes, and related valuations submitted by the appellants, indicating that the refurbishing of this listed building and redevelopment of the remainder of the site, would result in a financial loss. In addition, there is now a surfeit of office space in Sheffield and no prospective occupant for the building has been found. However, there are other considerations that in my view outweigh the above factors. The structural condition of this listed building is good generally, and these premises could be so maintained pending an improved climate, economically and from the urban

[25] Appeal by British Gas Corporation. *Planning Appeals*, Vol. 3, p. 119—Ref. APP/ 5098/A/75/3580 and E 75/65.

redevelopment point of view, which could favour rehabilitation. The nature of the building is such that, if rehabilitated, the premises will have a very considerable future life."

The inspector recommended that the appeal against LBC refusal be dismissed and the Secretary of State agreed.

Where the structural condition of the building is virtually beyond recall, **4.11** this is clearly a matter which is taken into account. This was significant in connection with the application of LBC to demolish Nos. 3 and 5 and the buildings known as Queen's Hotel, Micklegate, York.[26] The Secretary of State, having called in the application because of the Grade II* grading of the buildings and a great deal of public concern over the proposals, was also "concerned at the danger to the public and the owner's contractors, the risk to the buildings themselves, and also to the internal features, many of which are no less important than the exterior." The Secretary of State continued:

> "The reports of surveys commissioned by the owners and by the various societies have been considered. A common element in all the reports was fear about the structural condition of the buildings. It is clear that differential settlement has taken place and is continuing; that the timbers have been attacked by beetle; and that the outer skin of the front wall of the hotel is inadequately bonded to the supporting piers; and that the brickwork has been the subject of serious and progressive decay. He is also advised that deep piling would be required to support the buildings or any that replaced them . . .
>
> Although it is accepted that there are techniques which might be used to arrest the deterioration of the buildings and prepare them for the difficult task of restoration, the Secretary of State is not persuaded that any of the schemes put forward offer a reasonable hope of preservation. There are strong grounds for believing that the structural condition of the group is worse than was at first realised, and that the works necessary to effect restoration are so extensive that they could result in premature collapse. Also the evidence suggests that the end result of restoration, even if it were technically successful, would be unacceptable on aesthetic grounds . . .
>
> The Secretary of State is of the opinion that these buildings are outstandingly important not only individually but also as a group and for the contribution they make to the townscape of Micklegate, and agrees with objectors that demolition should only be permitted on condition that they are replaced in replica. He also takes the view that any new buildings should incorporate both the internal fittings which are being removed with consent and as many of the external features and materials as can be salvaged from the originals. He also considers that he himself should approve the details of the replacement buildings before they are erected."

Accordingly, consent to demolish was given subject to a number of con- **4.12** ditions, comments in relation to which are made below at paras. 5.08–5.11.

Another case where neglect had not been deliberate and LBC was granted, was that of an application to demolish a row of nineteenth century weavers cottages where it was concluded that any attempt at restoration would "pre-

[26] [1974] J.P.L. 493. Ref. YH/1869/270/58P. May 8, 1974.

serve a shell, but not the outward appearance, ambience or atmosphere of the original dwellings."[27] Again, in a case concerning Burgh Hall, Melton Constable, the evidence showed that the North wing was in a poor state of repair, that rehabilitation would be expensive, that no grants were available, and the local authority were not prepared to press for repairs. In these circumstances the Secretary of State granted consent to demolish the wing.[28]

A case where the cost of restoration was not allowed to outweigh the advantage of conservation of a building not in a serious condition was that of Lutterworth Hall, Leicestershire.[29] The hall was a good example of an early nineteenth century villa possessing a facade with characteristics of the Greek Revival style. The inspector felt that the condition of the building was not serious and that demolition ought not to be allowed, especially since an industrial company was prepared to buy the hall for offices. The Secretary of State agreed and refused LBC, criticising the applicants, Harborough District Council, for allowing the building to fall into disrepair through neglect, contrary to the advice of what is now paragraph 91 of Circular 8/87: where the local authority themselves owned a listed building, they should be careful to set a good example to others.[30]

The interesting question is whether or not the kind of case in Micklegate, York quoted above can be distinguished from the sort of case where neglect has obviously been permitted. Morally one can take a view about this kind of case, but at the end of the day when the Secretary of State is presented with the problem of whether or not to grant LBC, does it matter? Should the owner be castigated because he has apparently permitted the building to decay? The moral argument is an interesting one, but what should be the relevant question for the Secretary of State? This is not an easy question to answer, and there is little evidence to show what is the view of the Secretary of State.

4.13 However, perhaps an interesting example of "deliberate neglect" is a case in Yeovil, where the Yeovil District Council had applied for consent to demolish Hendford Manor, Yeovil. The Secretary of State ordered an inquiry, and in his report,[31] the inspector commented "Despite the advice contained in Circular 61/68, repeated in Circular 23/77, paragraph 65, [now, Circular 8/87, para. 91], the council, as a matter of policy, have not properly maintained Hendford Manor even though it was listed as along ago as 1970 [the decision was in 1978] and its present sad condition is a direct result of this action." It is understood that only approximate estimates of the cost of rehabilitation had been put forward and the market for sale had not been properly tested. The inspector's opinion was that it had not been established that the expenditure of public funds need be so great as to warrant the loss of an exceptionally rare, valuable and important building in a town notably lacking in properties of similar calibre. The inspector concluded: "The council should accept the consequences of their previous policy (however

---

[27] [1977] 242 E.G. 304, quoted at [1980] J.P.L. 722.

[28] E1/5320/411/2, May 14, 1986.

[29] [1979] 252 E.G. 76. DOE Ref. EMP/5303/270/45, June 26, 1979; see also DOE Ref. E1/5382/270/96 where the demolition of a sixteenth century farmhouse was refused LBC as it was not beyond repair, though empty for 17 years (see *Planning Appeals Monthly* (May 1981)).

[30] See paras. 4.37–4.38 below.

[31] *Planning Appeals*, Vol. 3, p. 258. (Ambit, 1979) Ref. SW/P/5367/270/15 South West Region.

well-intentioned) and, by repairing the building in the same manner as would be expected by a private owner, set an example to others." The Secretary of State agreed with the inspector's recommendation of refusal of consent to demolish. He also refused consent for the demolition of Baynards Park, Cromleigh, which, it was claimed, was being deliberately allowed to deteriorate by its owner, who wished to obtain LBC to demolish and replace it with a modern bungalow. *Private Eye*[32] observed: "if the four applications to demolish have had little effect, his [the owner's] policy of deliberate neglect certainly has. The once grand mansion is now in a parlous state of repair." Soon afterwards, as a result of most of the building being destroyed by a fire, LBC for demolition was granted.[33]

The fact that the preservation of a building would hinder or restrict a **4.14** redevelopment operation which is otherwise acceptable, for which planning permission has been given, does not prevent the refusal of LBC to demolish, particularly if the building is of good quality and the retention only causes inconvenience to the redevelopment rather than insuperable obstacles. This was the outcome of the case in relation to the City of London Club referred to above.

However, redevelopment proposals which have been approved may be sufficient to justify LBC to demolish. One large redevelopment had been approved before the listing and the merits of the building were not great enough "to justify abandoning the basic planning objective." This view was taken by the Secretary of State in connection with an application by MEPC to demolish a group of buildings in Boar Lane, New Station Street, Alfred Street and Briggate, Leeds, which was called in.[34] The demolition was needed to create a pedestrian deck linking a pedestrianised area to the north of Boar Lane with a proposed redevelopment to the south.

The inspector felt that the architectural importance of the buildings was not so great as to justify abandoning the basic planning objective of developing the area to the south of Boar Lane as an extension of the pedestrianised area to the north. He felt that without the pedestrian deck, while continuity could be provided with other pedestrian links, it was doubtful whether they would provide a link of adequate width and attraction to ensure the success of the area to the south. The Secretary of State said that he accepted these conclusions "with the greatest reluctance." He said that had the scheme been a new redevelopment scheme he would have had no hesitation in refusing LBC, but that the principle of the pedestrian deck which must involve the demolition of some of the listed buildings was part of the Comprehensive Development Area proposals first put forward in 1966. He felt he would not be justified in requiring the scheme to be completely recast and he had been guided principally by the view that the local authority and the developer "could reasonably have thought that the ministerial decision of 1968 (when the properties were included in a Comprehensive Development Area approved by the Secretary of State) justified them in preparing a scheme on the lines they did."

An application for consent to demolish a Baptist Chapel and Manse in Husbands Bosworth, Leicestershire (where planning permission had already

[32] *Private Eye*, August 17, 1979.
[33] [1980] J.P.L. 485. Ref. SE2/5393/411/1 November 14, 1979.
[34] *Planning Appeals*, Vol. 1, p. 141. Ref. YH/5114/270/2P.

been granted for the redevelopment of the site as old people's homes), was granted conditionally upon a contract for redevelopment being made.[35]

4.15   Similarly, consent to demolish has been granted where demolition was essential for access to a new development for which planning permission had already been given. Such a decision arose in Bridport, where West Dorset District Council sought LBC for the demolition of several buildings in St. Mary's Place and South Street, Bridport.[36] It is understood that the buildings were in a conservation area, but planning permission had already been given for a new development at the rear of the buildings. It was essential that access to the development be provided through South Street. An alternative to demolition of the buildings was to provide the access to the south of the buildings, but this would "add to the cost of the scheme to an unacceptable degree." However, one of the revised plans for the access enabled some of the affected buildings to be saved. It was this plan which was accepted by the Secretary of State, who refused LBC for the buildings which would not be affected by it, eight in total, and granted LBC for the remaining eight, all in South Street.

Thus the present approach to the importance of the state of repair of a listed building in relation to LBC to demolish appears to be:

(1) a state of good repair is a strong factor against granting LBC;

(2) a state of bad repair resulting from natural causes is a strong factor in favour of granting LBC;

(3) a state of bad repair brought about through neglect may well give rise to a presumption against granting LBC; and

(4) local authorities ought to take a lead in keeping listed buildings in good repair.

7. ECONOMIC FACTORS: PARAGRAPH 90(c)—THE VIEW OF THE COURTS AND THE DEPARTMENT

4.16   The question of how far economic factors should be taken into a planning decision seems now to have been settled with the Department following in its decisions the views of the courts. The courts have discussed this matter, but at first instance: there has been no decision of the Court of Appeal which would be welcome in resolving this difficult aspect of planning law. Although most of the decisions referred to below were decided before the views of the courts were expressed generally on economic considerations, there is on the whole a consistency about the departmental decisions and the views of the courts.

(a) The attitude of the courts

In so far as the courts are concerned, a start is made with *J. Murphy & Sons* v. *Secretary of State for the Environment*,[37] where the Secretary of

---

[35] (1981) 253 E.G. 436.

[36] *Planning Appeals*, Vol. 1, p. 141. Ref. SW(P) 5191/270/23.

[37] [1973] 2 All E.R. 26; [1973] 1 W.L.R. 560; 117 S.J. 304; [1973] 71 L.G.R. 273; [1973] J.P.L. 362.

State's decision granting the London Borough of Camden planning permission was challenged *inter alia* on the ground that he had failed to have regard to a material consideration (the high cost of developing the site). The application was dismissed. Ackner J. (as he then was) said:

> "The planning authority exercises no paternalistic or avuncular jurisdiction over would-be developers to safeguard them from their financial follies. If it had such jurisdiction, planning inquiries would last even longer than they do now, and the problems of establishing whether or not a particular development was or was not economically justifiable would be countless."

In *Sovmots Investments Limited* v. *The Secretary of State for the Environment*[38] (the *Centre Point* case) Forbes J. (as he then was), after summarising the *Murphy* case, stated:

> "If Mr. Justice Ackner was intending to say that cost can never be a relevant consideration either in a planning appeal or on a compulsory purchase order (and that I am told is how this decision is interpreted in Whitehall), then I find myself unable to agree with him. Of course planning is concerned with land use, but the Minister charged with the overall duty of considering applications for planning permission and the confirmation of planning proposals for particular areas must, it seems to me, be entitled to bear in mind the likelihood of the proposed development being carried into effect."

The decision of Forbes J. was reversed in the Court of Appeal,[39] but the point mentioned above was not discussed, nor was it in the House of Lords,[40] which reversed the decision of the Court of Appeal.

However, in the case of *Hambledon & Chiddingfold Parish Councils* v. **4.17** *Secretary of State for the Environment*[41] Ackner J. qualified his statement in the *Murphy* case. He said:

> "Notwithstanding my own natural affection for consistency, and while I still think the decision was correct, I might have stated a general proposition too widely. Nevertheless, it was clear from the Secretary of State's decision letter that he had considered the question of costs and so the point was not relevant."

This leaves the view of the courts in the uncertain position that economic factors probably can be a relevant factor in making a planning decision.

In the case of *Brighton Borough Council* v. *Secretary of State for the Environment*[42] the *Murphy* and the *Sovmots* cases were referred to. Sir Douglas Frank Q.C. dealt with one ground of appeal to the court, a claim that the inspector had been wrong in taking into account financial considerations when forming his opinion on a planning rather than a listed building issue. The inspector had allowed an appeal against refusal of planning permission to trustees of a private school intending to develop part of a playing field by building houses and flats: the benefit likely to accrue from the

---

[38] [1976] 2 W.L.R. 73; [1976] 1 All E.R. 178; [1975] 74 L.G.R. 95; 119 S.J. 612.
[39] [1976] 3 All E.R. 720; [1976] 3 W.L.R. 597.
[40] *Sovmots Investments Ltd.* v. *Secretary of State for the Environment* [1977] 2 All E.R. p. 385 H.L.
[41] [1976] J.P.L. 502.
[42] [1979] 249 E.G. 747. Queen's Bench Division, June 29, 1978.

money derived from the development must in this case, he felt, be taken into account. Sir Douglas Frank Q.C. felt that, as a generalisation, it might be true that financial considerations are not relevant to planning but, in his opinion, Forbes and Ackner JJ. had both made it clear that they did not mean to say that financial considerations can never be relevant. Restoration and maintenance of a building are important planning matters, he concluded, and the Inspector was justified, on these grounds, in taking into account financial considerations.

The case of *Niarchos (London) Ltd.* v. *Secretary of State for the Environment*[43] was referred to in the *Brighton Borough Council* case: here Sir Douglas Frank Q.C. held that the Secretary of State was wrong on the facts of the case in not taking into account financial considerations involved in his decision, namely that a building in central London could not be used economically as a dwelling house, and would stand empty if it could not be used as offices. Sir Douglas said that financial circumstances were not generally relevant, but in "these cases" they might be.

In *Godden* v. *Secretary of State for the Environment*,[43a] Stuart Smith J., in the Queen's Bench Division in 1987 reviewed a refusal to permit the demolition of a listed building in Beach Street, Folkestone. The building had little architectural merit but was of historical interest as it was the sole survivor of buildings which had formed part of the original fishing village. One of the first grounds of complaint was that the Secretary of State should only have looked at the surrounding area as it existed and not at some hypothetical future development of the area. But Stuart Smith J. said that the Secretary of State was not wrong to take potential development in the area into consideration. It was a matter for him what weight was attached to it and it seemed no undue weight was attached. As far as the second ground of complaint was concerned, that in considering the question of economic value of the building he should have confined himself to the value of the building alone and not to its site, the judge examined the arguments of cost and value of restoration v. replacement. The judge held that it was "entirely reasonable and a relevant consideration to take account of the alternative proposals for the site involving the retention of the listed building and to weigh the rival proposals as a whole."

Webster J., in considering an application to quash the permission for the extension of Covent Garden Opera House, London, held that the planning authority was entitled to regard the financing of the improvements to the Opera House as a material consideration in permitting new offices in a conservation area.[43b]

(b) The attitude of the Department

4.18   Circular 8/87 clearly suggests that the cost of repairing and maintaining the building in relation to its importance, and whether it has already received or been promised grants for public funds, are relevant criteria.

---

[43] [1977] 76 L.G.R. 480; [1977] 245 E.G.; [1977] J.P.L. 247.
[43a] [1988] J.P.L. 99.
[43b] *The Planner*, February 1988.

Indeed, Circular 8/87 goes on to say that "In estimating cost, however, due regard should be paid to the economic value of the buildings when repaired . . . "[44] This is borne out by the decisions and the attitude of the Department over the years. One case concerned a shop in Fowlmere.[45] The inspector considered that the building had been altered so much that it possessed little intrinsic merit, and its importance lay chiefly in the contribution which it made to the village scene on account of its materials, siting, and mass form. "To repair and convert the building to residential use would in my opinion be unlikely to prove economically viable, and the objections to restoring it to a shopping use are soundly based." He was confident that an appropriate replacement building could be secured by negotiation and the Secretary of State agreed with his recommendation that LBC be granted for demolition. This also was the substance of the decision in the case of *Kent Messenger Ltd.* v. *Secretary of State for the Environment*[46] where the inspector recommended that LBC should be granted, summarising the economic arguments by reporting: "It seems to me therefore, that there is some substance in the applicants' submission that the retention and repair of the building would be uneconomic."

Typical of these cases was an application by Reading Borough Council for LBC to demolish a disused cemetery chapel. The structural condition was poor and possibly dangerous. The cost of reinstatement would be (1981 prices) £93,700; even to retain the roofless shell of the building as a landscape feature was likely to cost £24,000. The inspector reported that the building was properly listed. The surrounding cemetery was still in use. The council was not prepared to spend a large sum of public money on a building which was no longer required for its original purpose, had been unused for many years and for which there seemed no prospect of funding an appropriate alternative and economically viable use. There were, it said, more deserving cases on which the limited funds available for restoration work should be spent. The inspector recommended the grant of LBC and the Secretary of State agreed.[47]

Similarly, consent was granted for the demolition of unlisted buildings in **4.19** a conservation area because the development proposals appeared to blend reasonably and the old buildings could not be modernised and let at a realistic cost. Rugby Borough Council refused LBC for the demolition of six houses in a conservation area.[48] The inspector, after saying that he did not consider the cottages were of such architectural interest or significance in the street scene as to justify their preservation at all costs, said that he thought that having regard to the total price at which the units upon conversion could be offered, the size of the units and characteristics which could not be overcome, there was little likelihood of modernisation schemes being carried out. LBC for demolition was granted. This appeared also to be the reasoning behind the finding of the High Court in *Thanet Dis-*

---

[44] Para. 90(c).
[45] *Planning Appeals*, Vol. 1, p. 143. Ref. SE6/5142/411/1/.
[46] [1976] J.P.L. 372.
[47] D.O.E. reference SE2/5128/270/67 reported in *Estates Gazette*, July 25, 1981. See also N/5102/270(P)/9 *Planning Appeals Monthly* June 1981 (demolition of a hospital).
[48] *Planning Appeals*, Vol. 2, p. 257. Ref. WMR/P/5397/270/6.

trict Council v. *Secretary of State for the Environment.*[49] Certainly this was the view expressed by the Secretary of State (disagreeing with his inspector) who said: "the present state of disrepair of the building and its location in the surroundings . . . make it unlikely that, if restored, it would be disposed of and beneficially occupied for any worthwhile period."

Trustees of a night refuge in Crispin Street, London E1 appealed against decisions of Tower Hamlets to refuse LBC (now conservation area consent) to demolish a 95-year old unlisted building within a conservation area and redevelop the site with six-storey offices. The appeal premises had been empty for two years but were in reasonable structural condition.

The inspector agreed that the estimated £350,000 for repairs and refurbishment could not be justified on the basis of a capital value of the property of £257,000, but "a lot of the work specified—though desirable—was not essential." The appellants were looking for a 12 per cent. return which the inspector (in February 1987) considered high. In the end, however, the appeal failed because of design characteristics.[50]

4.20   Not always, however, is the economic argument the determinant factor. Often the economic argument appears to be referred to as the "beneficial use" of the property. Perhaps the phrase "beneficial use" can be interpreted in this context to mean that there is a sensible economic use. The former West Suffolk County Council refused LBC for the demolition of the silk mill at Glemsford and granted planning permission for residential development of the site.[51] The mill was situated in a conservation area and was recognised by the inspector as being of industrial and sociological historic interest, but that because of widespread structural failures, subsidence, and inadequate foundations, he was satisfied that it was of no beneficial use, requiring an unrealistic expenditure to convert it to a suitable use. He therefore recommended consent for demolition of the mill be granted and that planning permission be given for the residential development. The Secretary of State did not agree, and commented on his inspector's report that: "He appears to have relied too heavily on the lack of the mill's beneficial use and the cost of conversion which it is thought should not be overriding factors in deciding whether to give consent to the demolition of a listed building." The Secretary of State felt that investigation should be made as speedily as possible into the financial and practical aspects of converting it into some other use and dismissed the appeal.

4.21   Where the cost of reinstatement is similar to that of erection of the new building, the (implied but in our view, incorrect) presumption against demolition appears to operate if there are sound commercial prospects for restoring the premises, and LBC will be refused. This was the case where it was proposed to demolish the Old Grammar School, Berwick upon Tweed: the school occupied a prominent position on a major distributor road through Berwick town centre on the edge of a conservation area.[52] In the case of a listed Regency property in Cheltenham, conversion to office use was allowed by the inspector on appeal. It was felt that the proposed office use was a better economic proposition than the building's conversion to

---

[49] [1978] J.P.L 251.

[50] APP/E5900/E/86/801505.

[51] *Planning Appeals*, Vol. 1, p. 142. Ref. APP/2239/A/74/2967, 2761, APP/2239/E/74/32.

[52] (1981) 253 E.G. 436.

flats, and that this was a factor to take into account in maintaining the character of a listed building.[53]

Again, at Bushey, it was shown that alternative uses for certain listed cloisters were difficult to find, and that extensive works were necessary to make them viable. The building was not particularly noteworthy in itself, and its admitted contribution to the conservation area was outweighed by its poor condition, leading the inspector to grant consent to demolish.[54]

By implication the economic argument has been established as a factor in the decision-making by the inclusion in paragraph 17 of Circular 22/80[55] of the following: "The Secretaries of State will not be prepared to grant LBC for the demolition of a listed building unless they are satisfied that every possible effort has been made to continue the present use or to find a suitable alternative use for the building. They would usually expect to see evidence that the freehold of the building has been offered for sale on the open market." The very use of words such as "continue the present use," "suitable alternative use," and "offered for sale on the open market" must indicate a continuation or new economic use, and a prospective sale at an uneconomic price, or no price at all.

(c) Evidential considerations

Consideration should also be given to what in fact constitutes admissible **4.22** evidence of cost and economic value.

In the case at Bridport[56] it was said that the alternative to the demolition of the buildings was to provide the access to the south of the buildings, although this would "add to the cost of the scheme to an unacceptable degree." What is an acceptable and what is an unacceptable degree?

Some guidance is available on how evidence as to cost and the economic value should be presented. Consent was sought for the demolition of the Royal Oak Public House, Biggleswade.[57] The estimated cost of repair and adaptation put forward were not related to specific proposals but were based on an estimated cost per square metre and differed widely. The inspector doubted the use of estimates on that basis for the sort of work required. There were obvious difficulties of comparability where the rate per square metre was based on what had been the rate elsewhere. The Secretary of State commented that although the possibly uneconomic cost of restoring the building to its former condition was not in itself thought to provide a compelling reason for demolition, the building was not of such merit as to warrant retention and consent was granted.

Similarly, in an appeal against the refusal of the Borough of Hove to give **4.23** consent to demolish 1–6 Victoria Terrace, Hove,[58] the inspector, after con-

---

[53] T/APP/B1605/A/84/14004/P7, reported in E.G. (March 1984). Similar considerations influenced the decision in relation to Robinwood Mill, Todmorden (YH/5112/270/141) reported in *Estates Times*, March 20, 1987.

[54] APP/N/1920/E/83/607 reported in *Chartered Surveyor Weekly* (June 12, 1986).

[55] Circular 22/80: *Development Control—Policy and Practice*, para. 17.

[56] Referred to in n. 36.

[57] *Planning Appeals*, Vol. 3, p. 257. Ref. APP/5214/E/76/120.

[58] *Planning Appeals*, Vol. 3, p. 256. Ref. APP/5205/E/76/138, SE/1239/270/49. This point considered also in SW/P/5225/270/29 reported in 2 *Planning Appeal Decisions*, p. 33.

sidering the merits of the buildings, turned his attention to financial matters. Whilst he did not disagree with the manner in which estimated costs for rendering the buildings sound for their previous uses had been deduced, he did not fully accept the financial implications drawn on behalf of the appellants. He identified the estimated costs for normal refurbishment as consisting of maintenance work to keep any such accommodation in a reasonable condition and improvement works which would enhance the property beyond its former standards. He considered that most of the items of expenditure ought to be disregarded in assessing any additional costs necessarily incurred due to the age and type of construction of the buildings. In addition, the costs included items extending beyond what he considered necessary reasonably to preserve the most important historic visual qualities of the buildings. The costs of refurbishment directly attributable to the retention of historic features were thus likely to be considerably less than those proposed on behalf of the appellants, so much so that he was not convinced that alternative accomodation in a new structure of a similar scope and standard would be appreciably different in cost. He concluded that the possibilities of retaining the buildings had not been fully explored and was unconvinced that their demolition ought, out of economic necessity, to be permitted. He therefore recommended refusal of consent and the Secretary of State agreed.

It is submitted that if these are the conclusions which were to be drawn from these two cases, then they depart from reality. An owner of a listed building has the building. He cannot say to his contractor: "ignore the costs necessarily incurred due to the age and type and construction of the buildings; only present me with a bill which will keep the accommodation in reasonable condition." Indeed, Circular 8/87 does not say this. That Circular says that "the condition of the building, the cost of repairing and maintaining it in relation to its importance" and the economic value of the building when repaired, are relevant.[59] It is difficult to see how the Hove decision can be justified in terms of practical realities.

8. ECONOMIC FACTORS: PARAGRAPH 90(c)—CONCLUSIONS

4.24   It is not easy to draw conclusions, but it is suggested that the following is the present state of the law in relation to the application of economic factors to the determination of an LBC application:

(1) Economic factors are relevant in making a planning decision.

(2) Economic factors have always been considered as relevant in determining LBC applications (at all events by the Secretary of State, and by implication by the High Court).

(3) The lack of financial viability on conversion for re-use of a listed building is a criterion which might lead to a consent.

(4) One test of financial viability after conversion for re-use is whether there will be an economically beneficial use—if there will not be this would be a criterion which would lead to consent.

(5) The arguments for demolition are reinforced if the replacement building proposed will be appropriate in the street scene.

[59] Circular 8/87, para. 90(c).

(6) But lack of financial viability is, on its own, not necessarily a reason for consent, nor is it an overriding factor.

(7) The financial benefit likely to accrue from development may be taken into account.

(8) If the cost of reinstatement is similar to that of erection of a new building, it seems that LBC will not be granted if there are sound commercial prospects for the restored premises.

(9) No consent is likely to be forthcoming unless:
   (a) every effort has been made to continue the existing or to find a suitable alternative use, and
   (b) usually evidence is forthcoming that the freehold has been offered for sale on the open market—without success (*i.e.* no sale, or offers, at very low prices—well below the market value had the property not been listed).

(10) On the admissibility of evidence of cost and economic value, the following conclusions emerge from analysing the Biggleswade and Hove decisions:
   (a) The estimated costs of refurbishing the building in issue are relevant but a generalised per square metre cost is not acceptable.
   (b) The additional costs incurred due to the age and type of construction of the buildings must be ignored.
   (c) Only the cost of maintenance work to keep accomodation in a reasonable condition should be considered.
   (d) Improvement works which would enhance the property beyond its standard at the time of the application should be ignored.

9. ALTERNATIVE USES FOR THE SITE: PARAGRAPH 90(*d*)

" . . . the importance of any alternative use for the site and, in particular whether the use of the site for some public purpose would make it possible to enhance the environment and especially other listed buildings in the area; or whether, in a rundown area, a limited redevelopment might bring new life and make the other listed buildings more economically viable." **4.25**

There has been some uncertainty as to whether or not this is a valid criterion, but it was accepted by the Secretary of State in dealing with an application for demolition on a listed building in the Banbury Town Centre Conservation Area. Planning permission had been given by the former Oxfordshire County Council in January 1974 for redevelopment of the site containing a white fronted Victorian building with a new terrace office building. This building was subsequently listed along with many others in the conservation area. The appeal related to the demolition of the building. The inspector felt the proposal should be considered in the light of the criteria set out in Circular 61/68 (now 8/87). In this respect he noted that the building was listed not because of special architectural importance, but because of its group value. Concerning the proposed replacement building, the inspector thought that this would "be in harmony with its setting and

83

would form an unobtrusive unit within the row of old buildings . . . unlike the existing one . . . it would occupy the full width of its curtilage, and by closing the only gap in the row of buildings would turn this into an uninterrupted terrace. Whilst the existing house is obstrusive and disrupts the continuity of the row, the proposal would be of a design and materials in sympathy with those of the adjacent buildings." He recommended that LBC for demolition be granted, and the Secretary of State agreed with him.[60]

4.26 One of the most celebrated recent decisions in this sphere was that of the Secretary of State in the Mansion House case in the City of London. The proposal was for the clearance of nearly four acres of Victorian buildings and the erection of a glass tower block. Refusing LBC the Secretary of State commented:

> "The proposed new office building would dominate the appeal site and the surrounding area to a wholly unacceptable extent because of its height and bulk and because of the stark conflict between it and the scale and character of neighbouring buildings. Such domination of this focal point at the centre of the City would fundamentally and irreversibly alter the character of what is for millions of people the historic centre of the City of London."[60a]

The importance of any alternative use for the building is clearly a significant criterion in decision making. Norfolk County Council wanted to extend their law courts, by a partial demolition of one building and complete demolition of granaries at the rear.[61] The inspector considered these granaries outdated. He said: "I cannot see them serving any future useful purpose. With the small openings, low ceiling heights, great depth of structure, there is little prospect of conversion to domestic or office use." He accepted that the present courts were inadequate and that new ones should be built, and LBC for demolition of the granaries was granted. However, this principle cannot successfully be invoked unless it can be shown that all possibilities of disposal have been fully explored.

Eastleigh Borough Council wanted to demolish a house and outbuildings in Leigh Row, Eastleigh.[62] The inspector concluded that although there were no agreed alternative uses for the buildings, apart from rehabilitation of the farm house for some form of residential accommodation and the continuation of storage use of the barn, it was impossible to believe that alternative uses would not readily emerge in the future. In his opinion, retention of the buildings would not frustrate possible future plans for the extension of the Civic Centre and the buildings could, if restored, provide a valuable adjunct to it. He recommended that consent should not be given, and the Secretary of State agreed.

4.27 It should be remembered that there are a number of commercial publications offering a service for those endeavouring to dispose of historic buildings. These are in place of the quarterly list formerly produced by the Historic Buildings Bureau. Such information exchanges are important and were significant in a case in Scotland where the congregational board of the

---

[60] *Planning Appeals.* Vol. 2, p. 256. Ref. APP/5352/E/76/1.
[60a] (City of London) Marsham Street 22/5/85, reported in *Planning Appeals Monthly*, May 1985.
[61] *Planning Appeals.* Vol. 1, p. 143. Ref. SE6/1278/411/1.
[62] *Planning Appeals.* Vol. 3, p. 254. Ref. SE2/1070/270/2.

84

Allan Park South Church were refused LBC for the demolition of the church in Stirling.[63] They appealed and served a listed buildings purchase notice on the local planning authority, Stirling District Council. The grounds of the appeal were that since the amalgamation of the congregations of South and Allan Park Churches in 1970, the South Church building had become surplus to requirements. Up to that time the appellants held that the church had been maintained, and had been widely advertised for sale. Several enquiries were received which were referred to the then planning authority, Stirling Town Council, who informed them that they would probably require any prospective developer to make provision for vehicle parking, loading and unloading. At no time were enquirers informed by the local planning authority that the building was listed, and the appellants were also oblivious of this fact. However, dry rot was detected in the upper hall of the church, so an application for planning consent to demolish was made—only then did the church board discover the property was listed. The local planning authority submitted that they considered the church to be a good example of Gothic Revival architecture, and their main reason for refusal was that they thought the church to be of considerable architectural merit and high townscape value. While accepting that the church had been advertised for sale, they pointed out that the services of the Historic Buildings Bureau, despite being brought to the attention of the church board, had not been utilised. The building had been listed in 1965 and notification to the owners had been carried out by the Scottish Development Department. The reporter recognised the architectural qualities of the church, which he considered to be a good, but not outstanding, example of its category, which together with its townscape value made him feel that further efforts should be made to secure its preservation—he did not consider that the owners had been deprived of reasonably beneficial use of the land without a further round of advertisements being undertaken and the services of the Historic Buildings Bureau being enlisted. He therefore recommended that the appeal be dismissed and that the listed building purchase notice be not confirmed, with which view the Secretary of State concurred.

Although the importance of alternative use is a criterion, it is not (in the **4.28** same way that the economic aspect is not the overriding criterion: para. 4.24 above) the only criterion, nor an overwhelming consideration. Finding an alternative use does not automatically mean that preservation must follow. With regard to barns, for example, Essex County Council in 1985 went so far as to rule that that it would no longer be permissible to convert historic barns for housing in that county.[64] We should be wary of "adapting unsuitable buildings for unnecessary uses." These were the words of the Inspector in a case where the Secretary of State was considering applications by the City of Kingston upon Hull for consent to demolish a listed building and 18 unlisted buildings within the Old Town Conservation Area, Hull.[65] The inspector held that whilst it would be physically possible to build a court complex (which was the purpose of the applicants) and retain the application buildings, he was of the opinion that decayed and derelict buildings of uncertain life could hardly be retained in close proxi-

---

[63] *Planning Appeals.* Vol. 2, pp. 260/261. Ref. HB/PN/CC/1, Scottish Development Department.

[64] *English Heritage Monitor* (1986), p. 8.

[65] *Planning Appeals*, Vol. 3 p. 256. Ref. YH/5267/270/17P.

mity to a major prestige project and would prejudice the courts in carrying out their function with dignity in their proper setting. Chapel Lane, he said, presented itself as a narrow back lane, lined with decaying, inferior, industrial premises of unattractive appearance and lacking any form of appeal. Had it not been in a conservation area he considered that it was most unlikely that anyone would have taken notice of it. After considering the views of objectors the inspector concluded that adapting unsuitable buildings for unnecessary uses instead of providing modern purpose-built accommodation was not likely to encourage organic growth and would not serve the true aims of conservation. The Secretary of State agreed with the inspector's recommendation that consent be granted for the demolition of the majority of the unlisted buildings.

In a case in Camden in 1983 the inspector, whilst finding certain Georgian houses to be worthy of retention for their value and good condition, also found the proposed development to be satisfactory in the context of the conservation area and gave consent to demolish.[66]

A persuasive test was put forward by the inspector in 1984 considering the future of certain derelict buildings in the Maida Vale Conservation Area. In his opinion, the proposed development "should be measured against the buildings as they probably appeared after the conservation area was designated but before they fell into their present state."[67]

10. CHURCHES

4.29   Churches represent a particularly interesting and perhaps difficult problem. Because a church is such a purpose-built structure, it may well be that the finest features, those most worthy of preservation, are those which would conflict directly with the secular use, and this may justify consent to demolish. An application was made to demolish St. Cuthbert's Church and Presbytery and adjacent house in Bedford Street, North Shields.[68] The inspector considered that the arched sanctuary, lancet windows and a cornice, would conflict with any secular use, and yet if they were covered up or removed the objective of preservation would be defeated. With its strong ecclesiastical character the building would be unacceptable and incongruous as premises for a social club. The inspector found it difficult to justify the estimated expenditure to reinstate the church which he did not think of sufficient architectural or historic character to warrant retention at any cost. In addition, there appeared to have been no interest shown in the church from any religious organisation since religious services ceased, and there were other disused churches in the area. He recommended grant of LBC to demolish and the Secretary of State agreed.

There also seems to be a feeling for the dignity of a church building, and the suggestion that demolition may be preferable to the indignity of the proposed alternative. North East Derbyshire District Council had applied to the Secretary of State for consent to demolish the former Methodist Church on land at High Street, Eckington.[69] The former chapel in its present con-

---

[66] APP/X5210/A/83/005536.
[67] APP/X5990/A/84/23536.
[68] *Planning Appeals*, Vol. 3 pp. 254/255. Ref. N/5101/270(P)/6.
[69] *Planning Appeals*, Vol. 3 p. 255. Ref. EMP/5173/270/4.

dition was considered by the Inspector to be of limited interest with the proposed inner relief road alignment detracting from its setting. Putting aside the question of the road proposals, he was not convinced that, on balance, the expenditure of substantial funds was justified to restore the building externally and to convert it internally for any foreseeable use. The uses suggested were, in most cases, incompatible with the residential nature of the area and would cause problems with regard to vehicular access and parking. In addition, many uses he considered to be incompatible with the dignity that a preserved chapel and family monument should warrant. In his opinion, a major change in the road alignment to preserve some setting for the building was unwarranted and he therefore recommended grant of consent, with which view the Secretary of State agreed.

11. REPLACEMENT, REPLICA AND PASTICHE

LBC may, as we have seen, be granted subject to conditions, one of which **4.30** may be in respect of the reconstruction of the building or any part of it following the execution of any works, with the use of original materials, so far as practicable, and with such alterations of the interior of the building as may be specified in conditions.[70] The growth in interest in buildings of architectural or historic interest has led to intense debates on questions of replacements and replicas and whether they should be encouraged or discouraged following the grant of listed building consent for demolition.

Indeed, such interest has even resulted in a philosophical debate being aired in an appeal decision in respect of students' accommodation at an Oxford College. This particular case raised the issue of whether a replica facade to replace a demolished building in the sensitive St Aldate's in Oxford[71] was desirable. On balance, it was decided that the best solution was for a well designed modern building to act as a replacement.

However, there are a number of points arising from consideration of these issues which merit further investigation and discussion.

(a) Rehabilitation versus replacement

The first and basic issue arises with the consideration of whether a listed **4.31** building should be retained and rehabilitated or replaced. Naturally such decisions are not reached without considerable detailed argument about the architectural or historic interest of the building in question and whether its replacement is justified for a multiplicity of planning, land use, amenity or design reasons.

However, such decisions are becoming increasingly difficult to reach because the choice is not often so simple, given the weight attached to the arguments of facadism, replica and pastiche which are increasingly introduced into the debate.

---

[70] L.G.P.L.A. 1980, Sched. 15, para. 9, amending T.C.P.A. 1971, s.56(4).
[71] APP/5353/E/82/260 SE.

(b) Facades

4.32   At first blush the retention of a facade of a listed building, which is often the most visible and therefore perhaps the most important element of the building, represents an attractive solution. Its retention would often result in minimal disruption to the streetscene and the townscape would therefore remain largely unaltered. However, notwithstanding the technical difficulties which often arise with solutions designed to retain facades, it raises a number of fundamental issues. Should the facade remain listed or does the loss of the original building devalue it to such an extent that it should no longer be worthy of listing? Does the new building attached to the facade automatically become listed because of its attachment? Does a single wall facade constitute a sufficiently significant element of the original building or should a greater proportion of the building be retained (*e.g.* facade and one room depth)?[71a]

If facades are considered an acceptable solution or compromise, it begs the question as to whether the facade is preserved throughout the construction period of the new building behind or whether it should be dismantled and re-erected at the end of the construction taking place, so as to ensure that it is not damaged beyond repair.

(c) Replicas

4.33   If it is not possible or desirable to retain the original facade or building, it may be possible to propose a replica of the original, which for the purposes of the continuity of the streetscene or the retention of an important landmark, may merit some consideration. However, for many reasons the introduction of a replica does not always find support. In the eyes of some, there are no sound or logical reasons why a new building should be a replica of an original. The proposed new building has often been designed to perform a different function from the building which it is to replace and is very likely to benefit from modern design and construction techniques which bear no relation to those used on the original building. For all these reasons a replica is often regarded as merely a pastiche and undesirable.

These issues were carefully considered in an appeal decision involving the erection of replacement flats at Haverstock Hill in the London Borough of Camden. The inspector concluded that the rehabilitation of the buildings to be demolished which dated from 1820 and which were in a conservation area, would be too expensive due to the condition and layout of the buildings. He was of the opinion that the replacement buildings were satisfactory and he rejected contentions that the existing structure was a "local landmark building" and that the proposals were a pastiche. He considered that the design proposed, which was clearly twentieth century, satisfactorily respected the scale and proportions of the surroundings.[72]

However, in a case where the owners of the Hackney Empire had demolished the hall's ornate twin domes without consent, but had offered to

---

[71a] See para. 4.07.
[72] APP/X5210/A/84/021565.

replace them with glass fibre substitutes, they were ordered to restore them as closely as possible to the originals at a likely cost (at 1984 prices) in excess of £200,000. Clearly the importance of the materials used and the method of construction was a major consideration in this decision even though it is feasible that the glass fibre substitutes could have been designed to have an almost identical appearance to the original. Thus it appears that the integrity of the original building in this case was of overriding importance.[73]

In all these instances the introduction of a replica would have been likely to maintain the architectural interest, but it is most doubtful whether the "historic interest" would have been maintained to the same degree in a replica building for the simple reason that such interest largely disappears if the original building is removed. The only common factor which remains is the geographical location and this is much less interesting than the actual house where the great man lived or worked or where the treaty was signed.

(d) Dismantling buildings

On the other hand, it would be possible to dismantle an "historic" listed **4.34** building and re-erect it elsewhere, but the loss of its true geographic location would also devalue it in no small measure. The same objections could be raised about re-erecting a building which is listed for its "architectural" interest, although this is not likely to diminish to the same degree if such a building was relocated.

Undoubtedly the biggest and most important loss involved with dismantling and re-erecting listed buildings is the original "setting" of the building in question,[74] which is often almost impossible to recreate.

Nevertheless, the dismantling of listed buildings for re-erection elsewhere does constitute a more acceptable solution than the loss of the building altogether, but it is not our role to adjudicate between the relative merits of replacement, replica or relocation.[75]

(e) Reinstatement of parts

An example of this was put forward in respect of Queen's Hotel, Mickle- **4.35** gate, York,[76] where an application for LBC to demolish Nos. 3 to 5 Micklegate, York was granted subject to conditions which in effect provided for the replacement of the original materials. This matter is further considered at para. 4.11 above.

In one case a condition was imposed that certain specific features should

---

[73] Reported in the *Evening Standard* (July 31, 1984).

[74] TCPA 1971, s.56(3) as amended by the L.G.P.L.A. 1980.

[75] It is worth noting that Lord Clark in his autobiography *The Other Half* (John Murray (1977), p. 171) notes of Japanese buildings in Nara: "many of these buildings are extremely ancient—eighth or ninth century—but as the Japanese very sensibly remake their old buildings every fifty years or so, imitating exactly the originals, they look quite new."

[76] APP/5353/E/82/260(SE).

be salvaged. Medway Ports Authority applied for consent to demolish the early nineteenth century Quadrangle Storehouse, Sheerness Dockyard, to allow construction of a container terminal.[77] The inspector was convinced that the continued prosperity of the Port and the Isle of Sheppey would be best served by allowing the redevelopment. The Secretary of State agreed, subject to the building's clock tower being carefully dismantled and re-erected on a site to be agreed with the Swale District Council. He requested that consideration be given to the careful salvage and safekeeping of any materials such as doors, window frames, Yorkshire floor slabs, cast iron beams etc. which might be capable of use in the area for display in a maritime museum or other suitable location.

Inevitably linked to the aesthetic arguments expressed above are the legal consequences in relation to the list. The general provisions about the list are to be found at paras. 2.08–2.22 above; the conclusions on whether LBC should be granted are set out at para. 4.24 above. How then do these provisions and conclusions tie up with the aesthetic arguments about replicas?

(f) Conclusions

4.36   It is suggested that the following may reflect recent trends in the law and practice in relation to replacements, replicas and pastiches.

   (1) As a first assumption, let us concede that the building was at the time of listing and remains properly listable.
   (2) What is the result of the proposed work—does it amount to an application for demolition, alteration or extension?
   (3) Probably in all cases mentioned above it will amount to a demolition of part in view of the present state of the cases on demolition.
   (4) Thus LBC will be required.
   (5) It is proper for the LPA to impose conditions on the LBC: the broad provisions in section 56(4A) will be applicable as to preservation of particular features, the making good of any damage caused to the building by the works, and the reconstruction of the building or any part of it with the use of original materials and with such alterations to the interior of the building as may be specified.
   (6) Such conditions may be imposed on an LBC for demolition or alteration or extension.
   (7) Thus all the works specified in paras. 4.30–4.35 above could be, and often are, incorporated as conditions to an LBC.
   (8) It must follow that the building remains a listed building. That proposition might seem doubtful in relation to a demolition consent but still the listing remains.
   (9) The question then will arise as to whether, after the works have been carried out, the building remains of listable quality. There could be serious arguments as to whether it does.
   (10) To do the work in the absence of a LBC could well be a criminal offence, as well as potentially giving rise to an enforcement notice: so the moral must be to obtain the LBC first.
   (11) Thereafter there is no reason why the application to de-list should

---

[77] *Planning Appeals*, Vol. 3, p. 259. Ref. SE2/1527/270/5 and SE2/1527/422/1.

not be made, on the ground that there is new evidence that the building is not (now) of listable quality.

(12) A prudent landowner who sees no advantage in his reconstructed building being listed might well be advised to apply quickly after reconstruction.

12. LOCAL AUTHORITIES

The principle that local authorities have special responsibility to take a **4.37** lead in historic building conservation is carried through into practice. In the case of the Town Hall of Buckingham which the owner, Aylesbury Vale District Council, wished to demolish, consent was refused by the Secretary of State.[78] Here local authority ownership was a significant factor in the refusal. Having commented on the architectural townscape qualities of the building, its role in the social life of the area, the fact that there were no proposals to replace the building, and expressed the view that the county council's and objectors repair estimates were more realistic than those of the applicants, the inspector commented:

"Whilst the obligations of owners of listed buildings are clear and planning authorities are given sanctions to enforce them, local authorities who are themselves owners of listed buildings have been given advice on their special responsibilities in the example which they set to other owners. It was pointed out that there had been some flagrant cases of demolition of buildings in local authority ownership." ·

Consent to demolish was refused.

A similar case which has already been discussed at para. 4.12 above is that of Lutterworth Hall, Leicestershire, where the local authority, as owners of the building, were criticised for setting a bad example by allowing the building to deteriorate. This view was also followed in the earlier case of Yeovil District Council (also mentioned at para. 4.13 above) when the inspector (supported by the Secretary of State) commented: "The council should accept the consequences of their previous policy (however well-intentioned) and, by repairing the building in the same manner as would be expected by a private owner, set an example to others."

An apparently blatant case (where the "special responsibility" did not seem to be applied) occurred in 1984, where the local government ombudsman reported to the Department that the council, who wished to redevelop land in the medieval city centre (a part of which land did not belong to them) induced their own chartered surveyor agents to apply to them for planning permission.[79]

Local authorities have problems in relation to the constraints within **4.38** which they work. Boothferry District Council wanted to demolish Nos. 2 to 8 Pinfold Street, Howden, Humberside, which were unlisted buildings in a conservation area.[80] The inspector considered that the demolition and use of the site as an open space would have detrimental effects on that part of the conservation area. In his opinion, if restoration and conversion could

---

[78] *Planning Appeals*, Vol. 2, pp. 258/259. Ref. E1/5132/270/41/Pt. II.
[79] Reported in *Period Home* (May, 1984), p. 39.
[80] *Planning Appeals*, Vol. 3, p. 258. Ref. YH/5262/443/ZP.

not be achieved and, therefore, if demolition was accepted, residential development would be preferable to use as an open space. He noted that from the schemes considered by the council, a satisfactory redevelopment by them was unlikely to be possible because of the constraints within which they worked. The greater freedom available to a private developer could result in a more sympathetic form of development. The Secretary of State agreed with the inspector's recommendation that consent be withheld.

Paragraph 17 of Circular 22/80, already referred to, noted the concern of the Secretary of State about "the number of applications to demolish being submitted by local authorities in respect of their own buildings." The circular reminded local authorities of the advice given in paragraph 24 of Circular 23/77 (now re-stated in Circular 8/87, paras. 19–24), concerning "New Uses for Old Buildings": planning authorities were encouraged to consider relaxation of land use, density and daylighting standards, and other controls where such action would secure a new and viable use for a redundant building; as a starting point to preserve wherever possible the original use, but otherwise to promote new uses for redundant buildings, both within their own ownership and those of others; and to make use of, and advise other owners to make use of, the services of the Department's Historic Buildings Bureau (now, the Buildings at Risk Unit of the Commission) in disposing of such buildings.

The duty of care on the part of a local planning authority in considering a LBC application was interestingly demonstrated in a case considered by the Ombudsman.[80a] The Feering and Kelvedon Preservation Society successfully brought an Ombudsman case against the Braintree District Council for allowing the demolition of a massive six-octagon shafted seventeenth century chimney stack at the White Hart Public House in Kelvedon, Essex, which was listed Grade II. The Ombudsman found maladministration in that the planning officer accepted the brewery surveyor's opinion of unsafeness without consulting the county council's specialist advice team. The Ombudsman suggested that the council should have obtained its own specialist advice from whatever source it normally obtained it and not merely rely on the view of the building owner or his professional adviser, however competent.

13. BALANCING THE FACTORS AND THE PUBLIC INTEREST

4.39   In balancing the factors as to whether or not LBC should be granted, the public interest is relevant. Consent has been granted on the basis that the public interest would be better served by the grant than by the refusal of consent.

An application was made for the erection of a vicarage house in a conservation area on land adjoining a listed building. The inspector said that the main issues raised at the inquiry related to the effect of the proposed devel-

---

[80a] Commission for Local Administration in England—report by local ombudsman (investigation into Complaint No. INV/262/A/86, Braintree DC). Courtesy of Essex C.C. Planning Dept.

opment on Manor House, a Grade II listed building in the Ringwood Conservation Area, the effect on other neighbouring properties and the adequacy of the site. The inspector had reservations about the neighbourliness of a large house on the appeal site, but against these reservations considered the arguments relating to the need for a new vicarage. He said: "I am therefore driven, despite my reservations and with some reluctance but with little doubt to the conclusion, that on balance the public interest would be best served by permitting the erection of the parsonage house as proposed on this site.[81]

Similarly, this factor was taken into account when Carlsberg Brewery Ltd. applied for LBC to demolish a warehouse in Northampton.[82] This application was called in and the inspector felt that the building was "of some historic interest, but its architectural merits are at the best dubious." He found that it was a prominent edifice which from most viewpoints was in a deplorable state and would remain so unless extensive and costly works of reinstatement were carried out. The appellants were not able readily to find a use for the building, as it had low floor heights and poor daylighting, but the inspector considered this to be partly because they had designed the new brewery complex on the assumption that the warehouse would be demolished. Notwithstanding this, he felt that the public interest would now best be served by its demolition providing it was replaced by a new building. However, until such a building had received planning permission, and the appellants were ready to start it, he recommended that LBC should be refused for the time being, with which view the Secretary of State agreed and LBC was refused.

At Shillingham Manor Farm, Saltash, Cornwall, an application to demol- **4.40** ish a listed barn was approved. The balancing of the different criteria is well summarised in the Secretary of State's decision:

> "The expensive repair work necessary to ensure the preservation of the building would need to be so extensive that much of the original workmanship and character of the rubble walling would be lost and the historical and architectural value of the building would be considerably diminished. There appears to be no use for the building even if repaired or converted."[83]

With the coming into effect of the Local Government, Planning and Land Act 1980, a LBC may now be granted subject to

> "a condition that the building shall not be demolished before a contract for the carrying out of works of redevelopment of the site has been made, and planning permission has been granted for the redevelopment for which the contract provides."[84]

This provision perhaps effectively puts an end to the argument as to whether the Secretary of State was wrong in considering the character of the replacement building as in *Kent Messenger* v. *Secretary of State for the*

---

[81] [1981] J.P.L. 614.
[82] *Planning Appeals*, Vol. 2, p. 260. Ref.EMP/1458/270/39.
[83] SW/P/5155/270/9.
[84] L.G.P.L.A. 1980, Sched. 15, para. 10, inserting a new s.56(5) to T.C.P.A. 1971.

Environment[85] and *Richmond upon Thames LBC* v. *Secretary of State for the Environment.*[86]

14. THE CURRENT POSITION

4.41   Subsequent to Circular 22/80, Circular 8/87 sets out a clear and detailed policy statement on the Department's approach to LBC. It is worth quoting this policy in full, as it is clearly of significance.

> "19. New uses for old buildings may often be the key to their preservation. Controls over land use allocation, density, plot ratio, daylighting and other controls should be relaxed where this would enable historic buildings to be given a new lease of life. A sensitive and sensible application of the Building Act 1984 and the fire safety legislation is also extremely important. This advice is particularly important at the present time when the future of so many old buildings is threatened by neglect and decay if not by wanton destruction or redevelopment proposals. Local authorities are asked to help owners find ways of keeping their buildings in economic use and thus in repair.
>
> 20. The best use for an historic building is obviously the use for which it was designed and wherever possible, this original use, particularly if it is a residential use, should continue. If the use of the building has been changed from its original purpose, it should be considered whether it can revert to it. But in many cases it must be accepted that the continuation of the original use is not now a practical proposition and it will often be essential to find appropriate alternative uses. In considering whether a use is appropriate, authorities should pay particular attention to the architectural and historic features of the building and endeavour to find a use which will preserve them. If, for example, a large house with fine staircases and plaster ceilings can only be converted into flats with excessive subdivision that will destroy the internal features of interest, then a use needing large rooms such as offices, which will enable the staircases and ceilings to be left intact, might be preferable. Even if internal alterations are not proposed, it is important to find a use which will not damage the fabric of the building or result in damage from increased floor loadings. Unsympathetic development in close proximity to a listed building can mar its appearance or make its future use unattractive or untenable or, on some occasions, physically damage its structure, for example if it brings heavy traffic close to the building.

4.42

> 21. The greatest problems arise when large buildings, built for needs which have long ceased to exist, become vacant, eg mills, maltings, breweries or former military establishments. Because of their bulk and position in the townscape or landscape, their demolition would cause a radical change in the appearance and ambience of the locality. This is particularly important when the buildings are along a waterfront of historic interest. Several successful conversion schemes have been carried out. Old warehouses and granaries, etc., are now being used for housing,

---

[85] [1976] J.P.L. 372.
[86] [1979] 37 P. & C.R. 151.

workshops, squash courts, restaurants, hotels, community and art centres. Alternative uses are also sometimes needed for historic buildings found in gardens or parks. Redundant churches pose a sensitive problem as there are many people who sincerely believe that a once-consecrated building should not be used for purposes which they regard as incompatible with years of worship. Nevertheless, unless funds are available to retain a redundant church in good repair, the acceptance of a suitable alternative use may be the only means to preserve both the building itself and its contribution to the character and appearance of the area, and a reminder of its earlier purpose.

22. Changing patterns of farming and rural life also mean that new uses must be found for buildings such as stables, coach houses, barns and oast houses that play such an important part in the history and appearance of the countryside. All possible solutions should be explored. If these buildings are used as workshops, craft studios or as holiday accommodation they can often make a contribution to the rural economy by providing employment.

23. Local authorities should therefore be flexible in dealing with planning applications for changes of use of buildings of architectural or historic interest. It is suggested that they should, wherever possible, make a survey of such buildings in their area and make a provisional assessment of the types of new uses which they would be prepared to accept. This is particularly important when the buildings are empty, either in their entirety or on the upper floors. With this information available, authorities should be able to respond more quickly when applications for a change of use are submitted.

24. Authorities are reminded that when owners are having difficulties in disposing of historic buildings, help is available from the Buildings at Risk Unit of the Commission (25 Savile Row, London W1X 2BT; Tel: 01–734 6010 Ext 853). (The Society for the Protection of Ancient Buildings offers an analogous service to their members also extending to buildings not on the statutory list.) Authorities are asked to keep in mind the possibility of using listed buildings themselves and to draw attention to the availability of premises in their areas if they receive enquiries from potential employers."

There are many decisions emerging which emphasise the importance of **4.43** testing the market and finding alternative uses. Indeed, it is apparent that many appeals are lost simply because they have failed to demonstrate that they have undertaken a thorough marketing exercise. One example is a called-in case for Edgbaston,[87] which concerned an application for LBC to demolish a substantial Victorian property in large grounds. The physical feasibility of the building and successful rehabilitation of the house was unquestioned. But the Secretary of State agreed with his inspector that a case for demolition had not been established, particularly in view of the complete absence of serious attempts to find alternative uses for the building by the simple expedient of offering it for sale in the open market. He

[87] (1981) 253 E.G. 744 and see DOE Reference APP/5226/E/80/52 where an appeal against the refusal of LBC for demolition of a listed warehouse at *Gloucester Docks* was refused as the Secretary of State was "not convinced that every effort had been made to find an alternative use, where necessary taking steps to dispose of the building in order to achieve this"—reported in *Estates Gazette*, June 27, 1981.

said: "Until the market value of the house or its site (or both) are tested, I would regard consent for its demolition as premature." Similarly, the Secretary of State agreed with his inspector in respect of St Marks Railway Station, Lincoln, where the inspector said that British Rail had not made a sufficiently strong case to justify demolition. He said he was not satisfied that all the possibilities for use of the buildings, after they became surplus to railway requirements, had been fully explored.[88]

In a case at Godmanchester[89] an appeal was dismissed because the Secretary of State concurred with his inspector's conclusions that "although its repair and rehabilitation would not be economically viable for the appellant, there is now a strong possibility of the property being purchased and repaired in an acceptable manner by the Civic Society." The same emphasis is reflected in a case at Crawley[90] where consent to demolish two listed buildings was refused because "they were capable of being repaired at reasonable cost and could be sold at a price that reflected the land's potential value," even though it was acknowledged that "neither had any real architectural or historic merit." The demolition of the Old Grammar School in Berwick[91] was refused consent because the Secretary of State said that it "was difficult to accept that an alternative use could not be found for the building." A proposal to demolish a cottage in Kimbolton, near Huntingdon[92] failed because the inspector accepted evidence that a financially viable scheme of renovation could be achieved, whilst a further proposal to demolish a row of cottages in Chertsey[93] was rejected because of the lack of a detailed survey and economic assessment of the potential of the structure and any effort to sell the premises for renovation.

However, in a case at Dean Clough Mills in Calderdale[94] LBC to demolish a nineteenth century mill extending to 74,000 square feet was granted because the alternative uses were considered to be either "unrealistic expectations" (office use in the face of unknown surplus of better located space), or "beyond the bounds of serious consideration" (squash courts). Considerable weight was attached in this case to the generation of small business and other job opportunities which could arise from its demolition by improving access to the other buildings in the group.

15. OTHER BUILDING REQUIREMENTS

4.44   It should not be forgotten that compliance with building regulations and fire regulations is as necessary in dealing with the preservation of a listed building as with any other building.[95] The Alliance Building Society applied

---

[88] (1981) 253 E.G. 852. (See also *Estates Times*, June 12, 1981 reference YH/5111/270/31P) and *Estates Times*, July 3, 1981; and paras. 4.25–4.28 above.

[89] APP/5140/E/83/052.

[90] SE2/5403/270/14 reported in E.G. Planning Appeals (May 26, 1984).

[91] APP/E2910/E/84/800362 reported in *Planning Appeals Monthly* (May 1985).

[92] E1/5140/411/10 reported in *Planning Appeals Monthly* (December 1984).

[93] SE2/5389/411/1 reported in *Planning Appeals Monthly* (December 1984).

[94] YH/5112/270/91P.

[95] An excellent paper on *Fire safety in historic buildings* by Alan Parnell and David H. Ashford, has been published by the Society for the Protection of Ancient Buildings and the Fire Protection Association (obtainable from S.P.A.B.—see para. 13.05 below).

for consent to demolish 30 Westgate Street, Gloucester.[96] This was refused, and on appeal the inspector considered the premises to form part of a fine group of buildings within an attractive conservation area, the character of which should be preserved or enhanced. He considered the appellant's costs of rehabilitation to be too high, possibly reflecting an unduly pessimistic assessment of the work necessary. He not only considered the cost of rehabilitation to be broadly comparable with the cost of redevelopment, but criticised the appearance of the proposed new building.

With regard to the rehabilitation scheme put forward at the inquiry, he was of the opinion that the listed building status of the existing premises warranted a relaxation of some aspects of the normal building bye-laws and fire regulations and that relaxation would probably be forthcoming. The Secretary of State agreed with the inspector's recommendation that the appeal be dismissed and permission refused. (It is understood that a modified refurbishment scheme was subsequently put forward which found acceptance, and the building was rehabilitated, being subsequently occupied by the applicants.)

16. ALTERATIONS AND EXTENSIONS

4.45 LBC is required for any works for the alteration or extension of a listed building "in any manner which would affect its character as a building of special architectural or historic interest." The meaning of these words is discussed more fully at paras. 2.23–2.30 above.

Potentially, any alteration to a listed building may require consent, internal alterations included. This applies regardless of the grade of the building. It is sometimes said that the difference between Grade II and Grade II* buildings is that the latter contain particularly fine interiors. This supposition has no statutory basis to it; buildings in Grade II* are merely particularly important examples of Grade II buildings. It is therefore wrong to assume that unstarred Grade II buildings do not require consent for internal alterations; grading is only a quasi-statutory designation for administrative purposes.[97] There is, however, a difference drawn between the requirement to notify the Secretary of State of an application for demolition extension or alteration in respect of Grade II* and Grade II (unstarred) buildings. This appears in the Circular 8/87, para. 86. What matters for the purposes of LBC is the effect of the works on the character of the building. This matter is discussed more fully at paras. 5.20–5.21 below.

As a broad principle, it is stated in Circular 8/87 that alterations which affect the character of a building as one of special architectural or historic interest should be kept to a minimum, and that repair is preferable to replacement where this is possible.[98] This is perhaps the equivalent of the principle on applications for demolition consent that in cases of doubt the balance should be in favour of preservation.

4.46 Whilst most of the cases of painting buildings[99] seem to have related to buildings in conservation areas, an appeal was heard in 1980 relating to an

---

[96] Taken from correspondence. Ref. SW/APP/5226/E/76/140.
[97] See also para. 2.31 above.
[98] Circular 8/87, Appendix IV.
[99] See also paras. 3.22–3.23 above and para. 6.06 below.

enforcement notice served by Dover District Council alleging that the painting of the brickwork front elevation, the erection of shutters to the windows and the erection of a vertical fillet to the party wall line of the front elevation of 15 New Street, Sandwich, had been executed in contravention of section 55. This property was in a conservation area but the district council's view that the appeal works had harmed the appearance and character of the listed building, the streetscape and the outstanding conservation area was accepted by the inspector and the Secretary of State.[1]

Nalgo House, The Crescent, Taunton, is a listed building. The National Association of Local Government Officers which occupies Nalgo House removed the weathered clay tiles and replaced them with modern machine-made concrete tiles without permission. This resulted in an enforcement notice. On an appeal by NALGO the Secretary of State concluded that he was "satisfied that the works carried out to the building constitute a contravention of section 55 in that they affect its character as a building of special architectural or historic interest, but LBC was not obtained; that the works have seriously harmed the character of the listed building and therefore LBC should not be granted."[2] A number of cases on alterations have come to the Department on enforcement appeals.[3]

The meaning of alteration has been taken to include the removal of a painting from the Hall of Woodperry House, a Grade II* listed building in Oxfordshire; the details of this case are set out at para. 5.24 below in the section dealing with interiors. On the other hand, it was held in a case concerning the laying of two strips of York stone paving in the garden of a listed residential property at The Boltons, London SW10 that "the placing of additional objects or structures on land within the curtilage of a listed building is not the carrying out of works for the demolition, alteration or extension of any of the existing structures and accordingly is not within section 55(1)."[4]

Painting the exterior of a listed building in such a manner that its character as a building of special architectural or historic interest was affected might well require listed building consent since repainting was capable of being an alteration.[5]

4.47   There is no reason why the criteria applicable on applications for consent to demolish should not also be applied to alterations, except that the difference of scale may make them inappropriate. For example, if it could be shown that certain alterations were necessary if a use were to be found for a

[1] [1981] J.P.L. 607. See also a case relating to conversion of a window in a Grade II building to a door (APP/5091/A/80/05323 reported *Estates Times*, October 16, 1981. Further similar cases are discussed at paras. 3.22–3.24 above.

[2] D.O.E. reference SW/APP/5365/F/80/55, 68 and 69, reported in *Estates Times*, July 10, 1981.

[3] See paras. 5.40–5.46.

[4] APP/5021/F/74/7. For a full discussion of the curtilage problem, see paras. 2.17–2.20.

[5] *Windsor and Maidenhead Borough Council* v. *Secretary of State for the Environment: The Times* January 6, 1988. Where Mann J. (as he then was) held that having regard to the possible meaning in ordinary language of the word "alteration" and having regard to purpose of s.55(1), he was justified in concluding that repainting was capable of being an alteration; and that in any case the critical question would be whether the repainting affected the character of the building as a building of special architectural or historic interest. See also para. 6.06 below.

listed building, that would be a relevant consideration just as it would on an application to demolish. The criteria for consent to demolish relate broadly to the building as a whole, and are therefore unlikely to be appropriate except for very major alterations; the detailed guidelines on alteration in Circular 8/87 are more likely to be relevant.

It should, however, be remembered that the provisions of para. 8(2) of Schedule 11 to the 1971 Act, whereby an appeal against refusal of consent or grant subject to conditions may include a claim that the building is not of special architectural or historic interest and should be removed from any list, apply to applications for alteration just as for demolition.

The effect of alterations to a listed building are sometimes difficult to quantify, particularly where such buildings have been subject to numerous accretions over a long period of time. This particular issue was highlighted by the problems encountered by the Borough of Watford in dealing with an application for LBC for the improvement and refurbishment of a range of buildings and the removal of rear sections at 129–151 High Street and 1A Carey Place, Watford.[6] The group of timber framed listed buildings had been altered over a considerable period of time and the local planning authority took the view that until "opening up" works had been undertaken it was not possible to provide the detailed plans and elevations showing the building in its finished form with its timber frame exposed. In effect, the local planning authority resorted to dealing with the application almost in "outline" form, but by requiring the applicants to enter into a section 52 agreement[7] to provide a controlled and staged "opening up" process, with the subsequent submission of detailed drawings at each stage of the process, the local planning authority adopted an unusually novel but pragmatic method of dealing with a problem which must face many local planning authority. Whilst this approach may not be that which was strictly intended by section 55 of the Act, it nevertheless demonstrates a practical approach to and an understanding of the problems of dealing with alterations to listed buildings.

---

[6] Application Ref. 9/385/86LB, by courtesy of the Director of Technical Services, Borough of Watford.
[7] See para. 3.16 above.

5. Listed Buildings—the Mechanics of Control

1. GENERAL SUMMARY

5.01 This chapter deals with the mechanics of the application for LBC to demolish, to alter, and extend. Whilst most of the chapter is devoted to demolition (which in practice causes many of the contentious problems) a note is added at the end of the chapter as to the differences in relation to applications for alterations and extensions. Such applications can create very difficult problems, but the *procedure* is now almost identical to that in relation to demolition.

It is not intended to undertake a full discussion of what can or cannot be

100

done without planning permission under the ordinary planning law. However, a brief summary of the position helps to show precisely the extent of additional control in the case of listed buildings.

Under section 22 of the 1971 Act planning permission is required for development, other than permitted development. Development is defined as

> "the carrying out of building, engineering, mining or other operations in, on, over, or under land, or the making of any material change in the use of any buildings or other land."[1]

Whether or not demolition *is* development is a vexed question.[2] The answer depends on the circumstances, and on what one means by "is." Certainly demolition can amount to development, because it may involve engineering operations; see *Coleshill & District Investment Co. Ltd.* v. *Minister of Housing and Local Government*.[3] But it should be noted that the test of development is not the end product, but the operations involved in reaching it; the fact that a building may cease to exist as a result of demolition does not itself mean that development has taken place—what matters is what operations are involved. This is, of course, only a partial answer, and there is no clear statement of principle in the cases as to whether demolition *per se* constitutes development.

The fact that it is a "building" which is being demolished is not conclusive. This is more important in the context of listed buildings than it is in the course of the ordinary planning law, because many listed buildings are not buildings in the normal sense of the word; there are, *e.g.* lamp posts and bird baths which are listed buildings, and it is easier to imagine the demolition of these without involving engineering operations than it is the demolition of a house. Only in exceptional circumstances does demolition of itself amount to development: the *Coleshill* decision is based on its own unusual facts. No case has tested the particular circumstances of the demolition of a listed structure, but we would adopt a cautious view that the demolition at all events of lamp posts and bird baths might be "other operations." **5.02**

An interesting point arose with the view expressed by the Secretary of State in a listed building enforcement notice in respect of 6 Mark Square, Stafford.[4] In that case, the Secretary of State said that he considered it beyond the powers provided in the Act under the enforcement procedures to require the reinstatement of property damaged or destroyed by accident. The essence of an enforcement notice is that it is triggered by a breach of planning control which may itself, particularly in relation to a listed building, constitute a criminal offence.

---

[1] The traditional definition is extended by s.1 of the Town and Country (Planning) Minerals Act 1981 which extends the meaning of mining operations to include "the extraction of minerals from a mineral-working deposit."

[2] See also para. 2.42 above and paras. 5.20–5.21 below.

[3] [1969] 2 All E.R. 525, H.L. For a full discussion on this point, see the paper by Sir Iain Glidewell who considered the relationship between *Coleshill* and *Iddenden* [1972] 3 All E.R. 882—"Development—some current legal problems" contained in *"Development Control—Thirty Years On"* J.P.L. Occasional Papers, (1979).

[4] [1981] J.P.L. 443, APP/5373/F/79/33.

Demolition works are only authorised if:

(a) the local planning authority or the Secretary of State has granted written consent (LBC) for the execution of the works and the works are executed in accordance with the terms of the consent, and
(b) notice of the proposal has been given to the Royal Commission on Historical Monuments,[5] and either
   (i) for at least one month following the grant of consent and before commencement of the works reasonable access has been made available to the Commission for the purpose of recording the building, or
   (ii) the Commission have by their Secretary or other authorised officer stated in writing that they have completed their recording of the building or that they do not wish to record it.[6]

5.03   Where the demolition or the alteration or extension requires a specific grant of LBC to authorise it, the procedure for obtaining this is dealt with in paragraph 76 of Circular 8/87. Although it may be in certain areas *applications* for both planning permission and LBC will still continue to be made on the same form, it is necessary for the authority to treat these separately and to give separate decisions. It should be noted that the setting of a listed building is a matter over which control is to be exercised in the consideration of both applications for listed building consent, and applications for planning permission. Provision is made to this effect in section 56(3) of the 1971 Act, amended by the 1980 Act.[7]

LBC normally is granted for the continuing benefit of the building, and although the local planning authority has power to impose a condition to limit the benefit of the consent to a specified person or persons this rarely happens.[8]

Personal planning permissions are granted very rarely, if at all, and it is believed that personal LBC's are granted even more infrequently. Indeed, the theory must be that the legislation is more concerned with the building than with the individual owner. Perhaps the spirit of William Morris' dictum is to be borne in mind: " . . . these old buildings do not belong to us only . . . they belong to our forefathers and they will belong to our descendants unless we play them false . . . we are only trustees for those that come after us."

There are certain special cases which will be treated separately: they are:

(a) Ancient monuments—dealt with at para. 5.27 below and in Chapter 8;
(b) Ecclesiastical buildings—dealt with at paras. 5.28–5.32 below.
(c) Listed buildings and non-listed buildings in conservation areas within a compulsory purchase area—dealt with at para. 5.33 below;
(d) Buildings which have become dangerous structures—dealt with at para. 5.39 below and in Chapter 7.

---

[5] See para. 13.03 below.
[6] T.C.P.A. 1971, s.55(2).
[7] See above at para. 2.11.
[8] T.C.P.A. 1971, s.56(6) and Sched. 11, para. 1(2).

2. PROCEDURE

The procedure for obtaining LBC is to be found in Schedule 11 to the 1971 **5.04** Act as amended by Schedule 15 to the 1980 Act and in the Town and Country Planning (Listed Buildings and Buildings in Conservation Areas) Regulations 1987, which also provide for the form of an application for LBC, how it should be made, the advertisement of it by the LPA, and the time for dealing with it.

Applications for LBC should be made to the district planning authority, or in Greater London to the London Borough Council, the City of London Common Council or the London Docklands Development Corporation, for which special provisions are applicable and are dealt with at para. 5.07 below.

The application should be accompanied by plans and drawings illustrating the proposal.[9] Perhaps it should be emphasised how important it is to ensure a good quality of drawings and plans. We believe that many LBC cases are lost because of inadequate presentation; and this is not necessarily always the fault of the applicant. Although section 56(4B)[10] provides an "outline" LBC procedure (but not so named), an applicant often proceeds directly to the detailed stage and there seems to be little guidance as to how much detail will be required to satisfy a LPA. It will be safest to err on the side of too much detail, although this may prove to be an expensive waste of resources for an applicant, if the application is ultimately unsuccessful.

A certificate must also be provided stating that the applicant is the owner, or has notified the owner of the application[11]; *i.e.* equivalent to a certificate under section 27 of the 1971 Act for an ordinary planning application. The prescribed form of notices and certificates as to ownership, etc., are contained in Schedule 2 of the 1987 regulations. Owner includes the owner of the freehold, or of a lease with at least seven years unexpired at the relevant time.[12] Under regulation 5 of the 1987 Regulations, local authorities are required to advertise in a local newspaper applications for LBC's made to them, to display a notice on or near the site the subject of the application, and to take into account any representations they receive. The requirements for such publicity do not apply to applications for LBC for works affecting only the interior of a Grade II unstarred building (see below and paras. 5.20–5.26).

Retrospective consent is possible, as provided for by section 55(2A) which **5.05** enables a LPA or the Secretary of State to give written consent for the retention of works for the demolition, extension or alteration of a listed building, where those works have already been executed without such consent.

Schedule 11, para. 7(2) gives the Secretary of State power to direct that local planning authorities should notify bodies of persons specified by him of any applications they receive for LBC and of their decision. Such a direction is given in paragraph 81 of Circular 8/87 which requires that notice of

---

[9] Town and Country Planning (Listed Buildings and Buildings in Conservation Areas) Regulations 1987, reg. 3(1).

[10] Added by Sched. 9 of the H.P.A. 1986—below at para. 5.08.

[11] Town and Country Planning (Listed Buildings and Buildings in Conservation Areas) Regulations 1987, reg. 6(1).

[12] *Ibid.*, reg. 6(5) and C.L.A. 1975, s.6(1) and (2).

all applications for consent to demolish a listed building, and the decisions taken thereon, should be given to the following bodies:

> The Ancient Monuments Society,
> The Council for British Archaeology,
> The Georgian Group,
> The Society for the Protection of Ancient Buildings,
> The Victorian Society, and
> The appropriate Royal Commission on Historical Monuments.

Except in the case of The Royal Commission on Historical Monuments (who are notified because of the possible need to record the building, should consent to demolish be granted), the notifications of the applications should be accompanied by the relevant extract from the list describing the building. Any representations received in response to these notifications must be taken into account when the application is being considered. (Paragraph 81 suggests that the representations "should" be taken into account—surely they "must" be taken into account?)

It is noteworthy that there is no provision whereby the local planning authority is required to wait for a specific period after notifications to the six bodies. Presumably it is expected that the six bodies will respond in adequate time for the decision to be given in eight weeks. The application may not be determined by the local planning authority until 21 days have elapsed after both the date of the press advertisement and after seven days from the date on which the site notice was first displayed.

Paragraph 82 of Circular 8/87 contains the further direction that local planning authorities shall notify the Commission (i.e the HBMC) of all applications for listed building consent to alter, extend or demolish, first, any Grade I or II* building outside Greater London and, secondly, any grade of listed building in Greater London. There are supplementary directions relating to the London Docklands.

5.06   The decision must be given within eight weeks, although the period can be extended with the consent of the applicant. The Secretary of State may direct that applications be referred to him,[13] and he must in any case be notified of the application in accordance with Schedule 11, para. 5,[14] before LBC is granted, so that he can decide whether to call in the application for his own decision. A local planning authority cannot grant LBC unless it has notified the Secretary of State of the application and given details of the works for which consent is required[15]; such notification is made to the DOE regional office, and in so doing local authorities are asked to send copies of any representations received, particularly from the societies named above, and to send recent photographs.[16] The Secretary of State has directed that, with the exception of various specified types of demolition work, the need to notify him shall not apply to applications for consent to demolish, alter or extend certain minor Grade II (unstarred) buildings, other than a building in respect of which a grant has been made under section 4 of the Historic Buildings and Ancient Monuments Act 1953, or a building in

---

[13] T.C.P.A. 1971, Sched. 11, para. 4(1).
[14] As amended by L.G.A. 1985, Sched. 2 and H.P.A. 1981, Sched. 9, para. 6.
[15] T.C.P.A. 1971, Sched. 11, para. 5(1).
[16] Circular 8/87, para. 87.

respect of which such a grant has been applied for but the application has not been decided.[17]

If the Secretary of State calls in an application he must, before determining the application, afford either the applicant or the authority an opportunity of appearing before and being heard by a person appointed by him. The local planning authority may not determine the application until 28 days after notifying the Secretary of State, unless before the expiration of 28 days from notification the Secretary of State has advised the authority that he does not intend to call in the application. If the Secretary of State considers that he needs more than 28 days to make up his mind, he may so notify the authority, who must not determine the application before the Secretary of State advises the authority of his decision whether or not to call in the application. There is no time limit on the Secretary of State for this further consideration.[18]

The decision of the Secretary of State on a called-in application is final, save of course on an appeal to the High Court by a person aggrieved under the provisions of sections 244–246 of the 1971 Act.[19]

Notice of the decision (whether of a local planning authority or one called in by the Secretary of State) must be given in writing, and if the decision is a refusal of LBC or a grant of consent subject to conditions, the reasons for the refusal or the conditions must be stated.[20] The local planning authority must when it gives such a decision point out to the applicant:

(i) that he has a right of appeal to the Secretary of State;
(ii) the possibility of serving a purchase notice if the building is incapable of reasonably beneficial use;
(iii) that in certain circumstances there is a right to claim compensation (but not on refusal of demolition consent).[21]

3. LONDON PROVISIONS

Prior to the abolition of the Greater London Council, all the London borough councils had to notify the Greater London Council of all the London borough council applications, other than those they intended to refuse, and could not grant consent until authorised to do so by the Greater London Council as to how the application should be determined.   **5.07**

The functions of the Greater London Council, with some modifications,

---

[17] Circular 8/87, para. 86.

[18] In 1986 Lord Elton reported in the House of Lords that out of 2,057 applications for LBC which came in for consideration, only 34 proved substantial enough to call in (H.L. *Hansard* (July 30, 1986) Col. 856).

[19] For an authoritative discussion on the role of the Courts in development control see the paper by Mr. Peter Boydell, Q.C. in *"Development Control—Thirty years on"* published as J.P.L. Occasional Papers 1979.

[20] Town and Country Planning (Listed Buildings and Buildings in Conservation Areas) Regulations 1987, reg. 3(5). Reasons have acquired a particular significance since Simon Brown J. found that a decision of the Secretary of State in connection with property used by the Inner London Education Authority was invalid because of the absence of reasons—see *The Times*, March 30, 1988.

[21] Town and Country Planning (Listed Building and Buildings in Conservation Areas) Regulations 1987, reg. 3(5) and Sched. 1, Pt. II.

were transferred from April 1, 1986, under section 6 of, and Schedule 2 to, the Local Government Act 1985, from the Greater London Council to the Commission.

In Greater London, paragraph 6 of Schedule 11 to the Town and Country Planning Act 1971, as amended by paragraph 17 of Schedule 2 to the Local Government Act 1985, requires London borough councils to notify the Commission of any application for listed building consent which they do not determine to refuse, and provides that they shall not grant consent until the Commission either authorises them to do so or directs them how to determine it.

The other principal difference for notification procedures in Greater London is that which requires all local planning authorities in London to notify the Commission of all applications for listed building consent to alter, extend or demolish *any* grade of listed building. Outside Greater London, local planning authorities are only required to notify the Commission of applications in respect of Grade I or Grade II* buildings. (These arrangements do not apply to the London Docklands Development Corporation who follow the procedure for authorities outside Greater London).[22]

Where the Commission has given a London borough council a direction to refuse consent which the authority are unwilling to accept, the council may within 28 days from the date of the direction being made, notify the Secretary of State of the application for him either to call in or to give notice that he does not intend to do so.

It is, however, expected that the Commission and the local planning authority will have made every attempt to reconcile differences of opinion in order to reach a solution before any application is referred to the Secretary of State. Where the Secretary of State decides not to require reference of the application to him, the Commission's direction will stand.

4. CONDITIONS IN A LISTED BUILDING CONSENT

5.08 LBC may be granted unconditionally, or subject to conditions.[23] Under section 56(4A) conditions may in particular include:

"(a) the preservation of particular features of the building, either as part of it or after severance therefrom;

(b) the making good, after the works are completed, of any damage caused to the building by the works;

(c) the reconstruction of the building or any part of it following the execution of any works, with the use of original materials so far as practicable and with such alterations of the interior of the building as may be specified in the conditions."

Schedule 9 of the Housing and Planning Act 1986 adds subsection (4B), as follows:

"(4B) Listed Building Consent may be granted subject to a condition reserving specified details of the works (whether or not set out in the application) for subsequent approval by the local planning auth-

---

[22] T.C.P.A. 1971, Sched. 11, para. 6(1) (as amended by L.G.A. 1985, Sched. 2).
[23] T.C.P.A. 1971, s.56(4).

ority or, in the case of consent granted by the Secretary of State, specifying whether the reserved details are to be approved by the local planning authority or by him."

In the St. Aldates, Oxford case[24] the Secretary of State allowed LBC to demolish on condition that various historic interior fittings be carefully dismantled and stored so that they could be refitted in the replacement building.

An application for the demolition of a barn in Aylesbury Vale, subject to a **5.09** condition ensuring its re-erection, met with a suggestion by the inspector that the consent should be delayed until expert advice could confirm the possibility of removal of the timber framed structure. The Secretary of State disagreed and allowed the appeal, as he was convinced that its removal was practicable.[25] In a case involving buildings containing cruck frames at Tring, Hertfordshire, the Secretary of State, whilst not imposing a condition requiring retention of the frames for possible future use, expressed the hope that the buildings concerned would be carefully demolished with a view to the crucks being preserved for eventual re-erection elsewhere. In deciding, following an inquiry, to grant LBC for the demolition, the Secretary of State accepted that the cost of repairs was substantial, that the remains of the crucks were in poor condition, that demolition would not preclude investigation of the history of the timber frame construction of the buildings, and that the dilapidated appearance of the property detracted from the conservation area in which it was located. The local authority (Dacorum District Council) supported the proposal to demolish.[26]

Under section 56(5) (added by the 1980 Act) there is a new provision whereby "listed building consent for the demolition of a listed building may be granted subject to a condition that the building shall not be demolished before a contract for the carrying out of works of redevelopment of the site has been made, and planning permission has been granted for the redevelopment for which the contract provides." An example of this being imposed will be found in the decision of the Secretary of State in relation to the demolition of a Baptist Chapel and Manse at Husbands Bosworth, Leicestershire.[27]

Although it may be considered reasonable as a question of principle that **5.10** the architectural and other merits of the proposed new development should be taken into account in considering whether to grant LBC to demolish, the problem was always that demolition might not be followed by the proposed development. Circular 8/87 at paragraph 95 suggests that LBC should not normally be granted for demolition as a prelude to redevelopment unless there are available acceptable and detailed plans for that development. It is suggested that the question of enforceability of the redevelopment might be resolved by an accompanying agreement under section 33 of the Local Government (Miscellaneous Provisions) Act 1982, or section 52 of the 1978 Act[27a] (i.e. one specifically enforceable). This, it contends, is particularly appropriate in the case of demolition within a conservation area, where the

[24] See para. 4.30 above.

[25] APP/5132/E/79/128 reported in *Planning Appeals Monthly*, 1981.

[26] DOE reference E1/5252/270/17, Eastern Charles House. Additional information supplied by Dacorum District Council.

[27] 1981 257 E.G. 436.

[27a] See para. 3.16 above.

subsequent development, and the risks of unsightly gaps, may be more important than in the case of an isolated listed building. It will be interesting to see how the new section 56(5) helps with this problem. The intention is obviously excellent, but the bald words of section 56(5) leave a lot of questions unanswered. The whole of the site? How is the contract to be approved? What if the contract is rescinded? So far, however, the subsection has not met with any pitfalls in its application; again, the St. Aldates, Oxford decision[28] is a case in point.

5.11   Local planning authorities, and the Secretary of State, try from time to time to impose conditions which will have the effect of preserving parts of the building. An interesting example is one arising from an application by the Medway Ports Authority to demolish the early nineteenth century Quadrangle Storehouse at Sheerness Dockyard to allow construction of a container terminal.[29] The Inspector was convinced that the continued prosperity of the port would best be served by allowing the redevelopment. The Secretary of State agreed, subject to the building's clock tower being carefully dismantled and re-erected on a site to be agreed with the Swale District Council. He requested that consideration be given to the careful salvage and safe keeping of any materials such as doors, window frames, Yorkshire floor slabs, cast iron beams, etc., which might be capable of use in the area for display in a maritime museum or other suitable location. Obviously the intentions behind such conditions are worthy, but are conditions framed in this way really enforceable? Was the alternative site "under the control" of the applicants? No doubt the owners were happy to get their consent and comply with the conditions, but it is submitted that conditions on these lines are suspect. Did they in fact comply with the criteria set out in Circular 5/68 (Now replaced by Circular 1/85) "The Use of Conditions in Planning Permissions": namely that conditions should be necessary, relevant to planning, relevant to the development to be permitted, enforceable, precise and reasonable?

Perhaps when suspect conditions such as these are in contemplation, the use of a section 52 agreement might be considered, but there are presently practical difficulties in the Secretary of State imposing a section 52 agreement on an appellant.[30]

Mention should also be made of the time limits for listed building consents introduced by the Local Government, Planning and Land Act 1980. The normal time limit was set at five years, but the period can be longer or shorter. If consent is allowed to lapse an application for further consent may be made; although the danger for the applicant will be that the LPA's policy may have changed since the original consent was issued.

The Housing and Planning Act 1986 has added section 56B which provides that any interested person may apply to the LPA for the variation or discharge of conditions attached to a LBC. On such an application the local planning authority (or the Secretary of State) may vary or discharge the conditions attached to the consent and may add new conditions upon the variation or discharge. The important aspect is that the consent itself is still valid.

---

[28] See para. 4.30 above.
[29] *Planning Appeals*, Vol. 3, p. 259. Ref: SE2/1527/270/5 SE2/1527/422/1.
[30] See para. 3.16 above.

5. PRESUMPTION AS TO REFUSAL

Unless the local planning authority give notice of their decision, or the **5.12** applicant agrees to an extension of the decision period, or the application has been referred to the Secretary of State within the eight week period or any agreed extension thereof, LBC is treated as having been refused,[31] which would enable the applicant to appeal to the Secretary of State. This provision has now been extended by the Housing and Planning Act 1986 to include applications for approval of details of works required under a condition of a LBC already granted.

6. RIGHTS OF APPEAL[32]

The applicant has a right of appeal to the Secretary of State where the **5.13** local planning authority refuse LBC or grant it subject to conditions, or if no decision is given within the prescribed eight weeks or any such extended period as the applicant may have agreed to.[33] The applicant may appeal within six months of the receipt of the decision.[34]

The notice of appeal may include a claim that the building is not of special architectural or historic interest and ought to be removed from any list.[35]

Unless the appeal relates to an application to demolish any listed building, to alter or extend a Grade I or Grade II* listed building, or to an enforcement notice in connection with either case, the Secretary of State may appoint someone to determine the appeal instead of doing so himself.[36] In practice, most listed building appeals have so far been determined by the Secretary of State himself. Before determining the appeal, the Secretary of State must, if either party so desires, afford both the appellant and the local planning authority the opportunity of appearing before and being heard by a person appointed by him.[37] There is no reason why the written representation procedure should not be used for an LBC case on the usual conditions.

The appeal procedure corresponds with the planning appeal procedure under section 36 of the 1971 Act, except that the appellant may include in

---

[31] T.C.P.A. 1971, Sched. 11, para. 9 (as amended by H.P.A. 1986, Sched. 11, para. 9).

[32] Procedure on listed building appeals is governed by the Town and Country Planning (Inquiries Procedure) Rules 1974 where the final decision is to be taken by the Secretary of State, and by the Town and Country Planning Appeals (Determination by Appointed Persons) (Inquiries Procedure) Rules 1974 where jurisdiction is transferred to an inspector (both as amended by S.I. 1986 No. 420). See also the Town and Country Planning (Enforcement Notices and Appeals) Regulations 1981.

[33] T.C.P.A. 1971, Sched. 11, para. 8(1). Under Sched. 11, para. 9 an application is deemed to be refused if after eight weeks no decision has been given, and no notice has been given that the application has been referred to the Secretary of State.

[34] Town and Country Planning (Listed Buildings and Buildings in Conservation Areas) Regulations 1987, reg. 8(1).

[35] T.C.P.A. 1971, Sched. 11, para. 8(2).

[36] T.C.P.A. 1971, Sched. 9, para. 1(1), and Sched. 11, para. 8(6); T. & C.P. (Determination of Appeals by Appointed Persons) Regulations 1986 (S.I. 1986 No. 623).

[37] T.C.P.A. 1971, Sched. 11, para. 8(4).

his appeal the ground that the building is not of special architectural or historic interest, and should not be listed. The Secretary of State may, in determining the appeal, remove the building from the list.[38] His decision is final, save of course on an appeal to the High Court by a person aggrieved under the provisions of sections 244–246 of the 1971 Act.

Circular 2/87 (Awards of Costs Incurred in Planning and CPO Proceedings) governs the costs aspect of appeals relating to listed buildings as well as general planning appeals. The Circular reiterates the principle that there is always a presumption in favour of allowing planning applications, and that a LPA may lay itself open to an award of costs against itself where by its refusal it is shown to have acted unreasonably in any way causing the applicant to incur unnecessary expense. Equally, where it is shown that for any reason it was unreasonable for an appeal to have been brought, the appellant may become liable for costs. Experience following the publication of Circular 2/87 suggests that costs are being taken much more seriously in decision making on listed building appeals, both by the appellants and the local planning authorities. In a recent planning appeal the costs of the third parties were awarded against the local planning authority.[38a] Costs applications should be made at the inquiry before the proceedings are over, and as from March 2, 1987 all applications are determined by the inspector unless the appeal itself is to be decided by the Secretary of State.

7. NOTIFICATION TO OTHERS OF DECISION

5.14   Where LBC to demolish is granted, local planning authorities are asked in Circular 8/87, para. 117:

(i) to include a statement in their decision notice to indicate that the applicant must permit the Royal Commission on Historical Monuments to record the building before demolition. The recommended wording is:

"Attention is drawn to section 55(2) of the Act, the effect of which is that demolition may not be undertaken (despite the terms of the consent granted by the local planning authority) until notice of the proposal has been given to the Royal Commission on Historical Monuments,[39] and the Commission subsequently have either been given reasonable access to the building for at least one month following the grant of consent, or have stated that they have completed their record of the building or that they do not wish to record it";

(ii) to send the applicant a form on which he can notify the Royal Commission of the proposal to demolish the building;

(iii) to give the Royal Commission advance warning by immediately sending them a copy of the decision notice.

However, the above three requirements do not apply to demolition of unlisted buildings in conservation areas.

---

[38] T.C.P.A. 1971, Sched. 11, para. 8(3).

[38a] APP/G4240/A/87/65338 reported in *Chartered Surveyor Weekly*, January 28, 1988.

[39] T.C.P.A. 1971, Sched. 11, para. 9.

8. REVOCATION OF LISTED BUILDING CONSENT

The local planning authority can, if it appears expedient to them having **5.15** regard to the development plan and other material considerations, make an order revoking or modifying LBC.[40] Such an order revoking or modifying the consent does not take effect unless it is confirmed by the Secretary of State, except under the procedure specified below.

Where the owner and the occupier and all persons who in the opinion of the local planning authority will be affected have notified the authority that they do not object, the authority must advertise the fact that the order has been made and specify a period during which persons affected by the order should give notice to the Secretary of State that they want an opportunity to be heard, and also specifying a period at the expiration of which the order will take effect without confirmation if no notice has been given.[41] A copy of the advertisement must be sent to the Secretary of State within three days of publication.[42] If no person claiming to be affected by the order gives notice to the Secretary of State, and if the Secretary of State has not directed that the order be submitted to him for confirmation, the order takes effect accordingly and no compensation will be payable.[43-44] This procedure does not apply to an order which revokes or modifies consent granted by the Secretary of State.

Where an order is submitted to the Secretary of State for confirmation, notice must be served on the owner, the occupier, and any other person who in the authority's opinion will be affected by the order, and, at the request of any such person, an opportunity to be heard by a person appointed by the Secretary of State must be given both to that person and the local authority.[45] The Secretary of State may himself make an order revoking or modifying consent. Except where an order takes effect without compensation,[46] compensation must be paid to a person who has incurred expenditure or abortive works or has otherwise sustained loss or damage.[47]

9. COMPENSATION FOR REFUSAL OF LISTED BUILDING CONSENT

A local planning authority is liable to pay compensation under section **5.16** 171 of the 1971 Act in certain limited circumstances on the refusal of an application for LBC. The principal points are:

(a) The application must be for consent to the alteration or extension of a listed building. It is not clear whether demolition of a part of a building is to be regarded as demolition or alteration. Circular 23/77 suggests (though this was not re-stated in Circular 8/87) that

[40] T.C.P.A. 1971, Sched. 11, para. 10(1).
[41] T.C.P.A. 1971, Sched. 11, para. 12(1) and (2).
[42] T.C.P.A. 1971, Sched. 11, para. 12(4).
[43-44] T.C.P.A. 1971, Sched. 11, para. 12(5).
[45] T.C.P.A. 1971, Sched. 11, para. 10(3).
[46] See n. 43–44 above.
[47] T.C.P.A. 1971, s.172.

because "building" is defined by section 290(1) as including any part of a building, the demolition of part of a building should be regarded as the demolition of a building for the purposes of section 55 (the need for LBC) and section 277A (CAC for demolition in a conservation area).[48] It is thought that this is probably correct, because in both sections 55 and 277A there are references to "demolition" alone; however, in section 171 the word "demolition" is not mentioned, the section being limited to cases of "alteration or extension of a listed building." Although it is often assumed that demolition and alteration are mutually exclusive categories, the Act does not say so; partial demolition probably falls within "demolition" for the purposes of section 55 and 277A, but that need not prevent it from being "alteration" for the purposes of section 171.

(b) Either the works in question must not constitute development within the meaning of section 22 or they must be permitted development under a development order.[49]

Section 22(2)(a) provides that works for the maintenance, improvement or other alteration of any building which affect only the interior of the building or which do not materially affect its external appearance, do not amount to development. This of course does not mean that LBC will not be needed for such works, but it does mean that compensation may be payable if it is refused.

5.17

(c) The Secretary of State, either on an appeal or an application referred to him for his decision, must have refused the consent or granted it subject to conditions.[50]

Although it is the local planning authority who are liable to pay the compensation (including the London Docklands Development Corporation in the case of a development area falling within its jurisdiction), the decision to refuse consent or grant it subject to conditions must be that of the Secretary of State. This requirement effectively rules out from the compensation provisions refusals which do not justify the expense of an appeal in view of the likely measure of compensation.

(d) It must be shown that the value of a person's interest in the land "is less than it would have been if LBC had been granted, or had been granted unconditionally, as the case may be."[51]

In assessing the value, it must be assumed that any subsequent application for consent would be determined in the same way, but if on a refusal of consent the Secretary of State undertook to grant consent for some other works to the building in the event of an application being made, regard must be had to that undertaking.[52]

The measure of compensation will be the difference between the value of a person's interest in the land, assessed as above, and the value of his interest had consent been granted, or granted unconditionally as the case may

---

[48] Circular 23/77, para. 66.
[49] T.C.P.A. 1971, s.171(1)(a).
[50] T.C.P.A. 1971, s.171(1)(b).
[51] T.C.P.A. 1971, s.171(2).
[52] T.C.P.A. 1971, s.171(3).

be.[53] Valuation assumptions are written into the section.[54] No compensation will be payable if a purchase notice is served and takes effect under section 180, section 188 or section 190.[55]

Compensation is only payable under section 171 in respect of a building which is the subject of a building preservation notice if and when the Secretary of State includes the building in a statutory list. Nonetheless, a *claim* for compensation may be made before the listing of the building[56]; and such claim may include a sum payable in respect of a breach of contract caused by the necessity of discontinuing or countermanding any building works because of the notice.[57]

10. LISTED BUILDING PURCHASE NOTICES

Where LBC is refused or granted subject to conditions, or where consent is revoked or modified after being granted, any owner of the land may in certain circumstances serve a notice on the council of the London borough or county district in which the land is situated, requiring the council to purchase his interest in the land ("listed building purchase notice").[58]   **5.18**

To justify the service of a listed building purchase notice, the owner of the land must claim and be able to show the "section 190" conditions:

(a) that the land has become incapable of reasonably beneficial use in its existing state; and

(b) (in a case where consent was granted subject to conditions with respect to the execution of works, or where it has been modified by the imposition of such conditions) that the land cannot be rendered capable of reasonably beneficial use by the carrying out of the works in accordance with those conditions; and

(c) in all cases, that the land cannot be rendered capable of reasonably beneficial use by the carrying out of any other works for which consent has been granted, or for which the local planning authority or the Secretary of State has undertaken to grant such consent.[59]

"The land" means the building in respect of which consent has been refused, or granted subject to conditions, or modified by the imposition of conditions, and in respect of which a notice under section 190 has been served, together with any land comprising the building, or contiguous or adjacent to it, and owned with it, being land as to which the owner claims that its use is substantially inseparable from that of the building, and that it ought to be treated, together with the building, as a single holding.[60]

Where a question arises as to what is or would in any particular circumstances be a reasonably beneficial use of land, no account is to be taken of any prospective use of that land which would involve the carrying out of

---

[53] T.C.P.A. 1971, s.171(2).
[54] T.C.P.A. 1971, s.171(3).
[55] T.C.P.A. 1971, s.171(4).
[56] T.C.P.A. 1971, s.173(1).
[57] T.C.P.A. 1971, s.173(4).
[58] T.C.P.A. 1971, s.190.
[59] T.C.P.A. 1971, s.190(1).
[60] T.C.P.A. 1971, s.190(3).

any new development or of any works requiring LBC which might be executed to the building, other than works for which the local planning authority or the Secretary of State have undertaken to grant such consent.[61] In confirming a listed building purchase notice the Secretary of State need not have regard to any history of decay of the building (*Leominster Borough Council* v. *Minister of Housing and Local Government*).[62]

5.19   Within three months of the service of a listed building purchase notice on the appropriate council, the council must serve notice on the owner, stating either:

> (1) that they are willing to comply; or
>
> (2) that another local authority or statutory undertaker specified in the notice has agreed to comply in their place; or
>
> (3) that for reasons specified in the notice they are not willing to comply and have not found any other local authority or statutory undertaker who will agree to comply in their place, and that they have transmitted to the Secretary of State a copy of the purchase notice and of the council's notice in reply.[63]

In the first two cases above, *i.e.* the council is willing to comply, or others are willing to comply in their place, the council or other authority are deemed to be authorised compulsorily to acquire the owner's interest and are deemed to have served a notice to treat at the date of service of the council's notice.[64] In the third case above, *i.e.* where neither the council nor others are willing to comply, the council must transmit to the Secretary of State a copy of the purchase notice, together with a copy of their notice in reply. The procedure thereafter is the same as for a purchase notice on refusal of planning permission (for which see sections 180–183 of the 1971 Act).[65] If the Secretary of State is satisfied that the conditions in section 190 (set out as conditions (a) to (c), above) are fulfilled, he must confirm the notice; and he has the power to confirm the notice in respect of part only of the land, if he is only satisfied that the conditions are fulfilled in respect of part of the land.[66] But before confirming a notice he must be satisfied that the land is contiguous or adjacent to the building and is required for preserving the building or its amenities, or for affording access to it, or for its proper control or management.[67]

Where the notice was served because LBC was refused or granted subject to conditions, the Secretary of State may if it appears to him expedient, grant LBC for the works, or revoke or amend the conditions imposed on the consent, instead of confirming the listed building purchase notice.[68] Similarly, where the purchase notice was served because LBC had been revoked or modified, the Secretary of State may cancel the order that revoked the consent, or may revoke or amend conditions imposed by an order that modified LBC, instead of confirming the purchase notice.[69]

---

[61] T.C.P.A. 1971, s.190(2).
[62] (1971) 218 E.G. 1419.
[63] T.C.P.A. 1971, s.190 and Sched. 19, para. 1(1).
[64] T.C.P.A. 1971, s.190 and Sched. 19, para. 1(2).
[65] T.C.P.A. 1971, s.190 and Sched. 19, para. 1(3).
[66] T.C.P.A. 1971, s.190 and Sched. 19, para. 2(1).
[67] T.C.P.A. 1971, s.190 and Sched. 19, para. 2(2).
[68] T.C.P.A. 1971, s.190 and Sched. 19, para. 2(3).
[69] T.C.P.A. 1971, s.190 and Sched. 19, para. 2(4).

If the land could be rendered capable of reasonably beneficial use within a reasonable time by carrying out other works for which LBC ought to be granted or by the carrying out of development for which planning permission ought to be granted, the Secretary of State may direct that such consent or planning permission shall be granted if an application is made, instead of confirming the purchase notice.[70]

Where a notice is confirmed, the council or other authority are deemed to be authorised to acquire compulsorily, and are deemed to have served a notice to treat on such date as the Secretary of State may direct.[71]

If, before the end of a certain period of time which is either nine months from the service of the purchase notice, or six months from the transmission of the notice to the Secretary of State, whichever is the sooner, the Secretary of State has neither confirmed the notice, nor taken any other action as indicated above, and has not notified the owner that he does not propose to confirm the notice, it is deemed to be confirmed at the end of the period.[72]

11. DEMOLITION, ALTERATIONS AND EXTENSIONS: THE GENERAL PRINCIPLES

5.20 We have referred earlier to the problem of whether demolition is redevelopment,[73] and the difficulty of drawing the line between what is demolition (which, *e.g.* requires conservation area consent in the case of unlisted buildings in conservation areas) and alteration (which does not).[74]

We now seek to set out the principles on which these problems are to be determined:

(a) Demolition may amount to development requiring planning permission,[75] but generally it does not require planning permission.

(b) Demolition of a listed building requires listed building consent,[76] and demolition of a scheduled ancient monument requires scheduled monument consent.[77]

(c) Demolition of an unlisted building in a conservation area generally[78] requires conservation area consent, whereas an alteration or extension to an unlisted building in a conservation area does not require consent.

(d) Demolition is not a term which is defined in the Act, nor is there a definition or guidance in the regulations nor in Circular 8/87.

(e) The problem arises in determining the line between demolition and partial demolition (a phrase not used in the Act) and the line

---

[70] T.C.P.A. 1971, s.190 and Sched. 19, paras. 2(5) and 2(6).
[71] T.C.P.A. 1971, s.190 and Sched. 19, para. 3(1).
[72] T.C.P.A. 1971, s.190 and Sched. 19, para. 3(2).
[73] See also para. 2.42 and paras. 5.01–5.02 above.
[74] See also paras. 3.15–3.16 above.
[75] See para. 5.01 above and the *Coleshill* decision.
[76] T.C.P.A. 1971, s.54.
[77] See paras. 8.16–8.17 below.
[78] For exceptions to the general rule, see paras. 3.13–3.14 above.

between demolition and the removal of materials which is required for the purpose of an alteration or addition to a listed building.

(f) If demolition only is concerned, *i.e.* there is no extension or alteration involved, then listed building consent or conservation area consent will be required, however small the extent of the demolition. "Building" includes in its definition "part of a building." Partial demolition cannot be justified as avoiding the need for LBC or CAC on the grounds that only a few stones are removed: they might be the vital ones. But this will not apply to free standing structures built after 1948 within the curtilage nor to the other exemptions in the Direction in Circular 8/87 (as to which see paras. 3.13–3.14 above).

5.21

(g) Mr. Justice Comyn in considering this question of demolition or alteration/extension in relation to addition to an old farm house, involving "keying–in" or marrying the extension to the existing building, concluded that not every piece of work by way of alteration or extension necessarily amounted to demolition.[79] He thought any court would be prepared to overlook and be prepared to treat as an extension rather than demolition "something small by way of interference with a listed building." In the event he found that what had been proposed did amount to demolition and quashed, on the application by a neighbour for judicial review, decisions of the local planning authority granting planning permission and listed building consent. The decisions of the authority would have been in order if the words stood simply as stated in section 55: "demolition of a building or alteration or extension" but the decisions were bad because the interpretation section of the Act defined "building" as including "a part of a building."

(h) To adopt the criterion of Comyn J. we must then determine what is "something small." There is no authority on this subject, but we suggest two tests: a qualitative and a quantitative test.

(i) Applying a qualitative test we would expect the DOE to view as alterations and not as demolition: the replacement of one type of roofing material with another (*e.g.* asbestos tiles for slate), the removal of part of the fabric of a building purely to facilitate the carrying out of alterations or extensions (particularly the removal of part of the roof or wall to enable an extension to be constructed), new windows in enlarged openings or new doors.

(j) To apply a quantitative test it might be helpful to consider a 10 per cent. of the cubic content basis—10 per cent. or under would not be demolition. The genesis of this (perhaps not unreasonable) basis is that 10 per cent. is that element of the cubic content of a Grade II (unstarred) listed building which does not require listed building consent.[80] A further example of the use of 10 per cent. as a "de minimis" criterion is the direction which exempts the necessity for a conservation area consent in relation to the demolition of 10 per cent. of a building used for an industrial process.[81]

---

[79] *R. v. North Hertfordshire D.C., ex p. Lorana Olcott Sullivan* [1981] J.P.L. 752.
[80] Direction contained in para. 86 of Circular 8/87.
[81] Direction contained in para. 97 to Circular 8/87.

12. ALTERATIONS AND EXTENSIONS: THE MECHANICS OF CONSENT

Alterations and extensions are little different from demolition in relation **5.22** to the mechanics of obtaining consent. Publicity need not be given to an application for the alteration of the interior of a Grade II unstarred listed building. Conservation area consent is not required for an alteration or an extension to an unlisted building in a conservation area. Otherwise the procedure for obtaining consent to alter or extend a listed building is the same as for a demolition.[82]

13. INTERIORS: THE PRINCIPLES

Not all alterations or extensions require LBC; section 55(1) states that **5.23** consent must be obtained for any works for the alteration or extension of a listed building "in any manner which would affect its character as a building of special architectural or historic interest." It follows that works for the alteration or extension of a listed building in a manner which would not affect its character as a building of special architectural or historic interest will not require LBC (indeed if such works are not development or are permitted development they would require no specific permission or consent whatsoever).

Clearly it is important to know what is meant by the phrase "in any manner which would affect its character as a building of special architectural or historic interest." Neither the Act nor Circular 8/87 offers any guidance on the point, presumably because it is really a question of subjective judgment whether particular works affect the architectural or historic interest of the building. The Act does not make the local planning authority nor the Secretary of State the arbiter on this point. As regards listed buildings, there is no provision equivalent to section 53 whereby an interested person may apply to have the question determined whether proposed operations would or would not constitute or involve development and thereby require planning permission.

The important point is that it is not the works themselves that must be considered, but the manner in which they affect the building. Hence an inspector in determining an appeal against a refusal of listed building consent for the conversion of a stable block to a dwelling at Milwich Hall near Stafford concluded that

> "the conversion to residential accommodation in the manner proposed would secure preservation of and improvement to the structure of the stable block without harm to its appearance or to the character of Milwich Hall. For these reasons, it is considered that there are no grounds on which listed building consent for the proposed works should be withheld",[83-85]

---

[82] The question what is or is not an alteration as regards listed buildings has been discussed in various cases concerning VAT liability. See Chap. 9.

[83-85] APP/5373/A/79/11330 and 5373/E/80/37 dated January 21, 1981 (courtesy of Stafford Borough Council).

although the appellant in this case failed to convince the inspector that there were any circumstances to justify the grant of planning permission for the proposed use in that particular area, and he dismissed the planning appeal.

5.24   The manner in which works affect the building is an issue which has been particularly important in respect of the interiors of buildings. This is evidenced by the growth in interest in the details of interiors of buildings, and this in turn is reflected in decisions emanating from the Department of Environment. Two particular cases illustrate the point in question. In the first case, it concerned an application to remove a mural sculpture which was originally in the centre lounge of the Midland Hotel, Morecambe, a Grade II* listed building, which had been created by Eric Gill. Permission had been given in 1977 for the sculpture to be removed to another room. At the time of the appeal it was stored in pieces. The Secretary of State ruled that in spite of alterations to the hotel, the remaining interior features were an integral part of the design (by Oliver Hill) and should remain *in situ*.[86]

In the second case, an application for consent to remove a painting of Westminster Abbey from the hall at Woodperry House, a Grade II* listed building at Woodperry, Stanton St. John, Oxfordshire, was refused by South Oxfordshire District Council with support being lent by the Georgian Group. The Secretary of State supported his inspector's appraisal and concluded that

> "the Westminster painting is important architecturally and historically and that it is a good and unspoilt example of an eighteenth century decorative scheme with a local connection. It forms an extremely attractive centrepiece to the overmantel and serves as a splended focal point to the hall and is entirely appropriate to its setting . . . its removal would be seriously detrimental to the character of Woodperry House as a building of special architectural or historic interest."[87]

Although this example is concerned with a particular painting, it raises many issues of wider concern, not least of which is that it draws a useful distinction between a painting which is merely hanging on a wall and a painting which occupies an integral part of the original design of the room in which it is located. It appears that such a distinction proved in this case to be the determining issue as to whether it constituted a fixture as specified in section 54(9) of the Act.

5.25   The key lesson to be drawn from these examples is that the evidence adduced from exacting historical research proved to be critical in determining the association of the fixtures in question with the listed building. Thus where it is known what features of a building were regarded as important on the listing of the building, it is logical to assume that alterations or extensions affecting those features would affect the character of the building as one of special architectural or historic interest and would therefore require LBC. This principle can only be treated as a guideline for a number of reasons:

[86] DOE reference APP/5292/E/80/187 reported in *Planning Appeals Monthly*, May 1981. See also a case on the removal of a picture forming part of a chimney piece APP/5355/E/80/155 reported in *Planning Appeals Monthly* June 1981.

[87] APP/Q3115/E/84/800390 dated May 23, 1985 (courtesy of South Oxfordshire District Council).

(1) the building may not yet have been listed; it may be the subject of a building preservation notice which will rarely contain any descriptive material;

(2) the factors which were considered important in deciding to list may not be known—in the case of those buildings which were listed prior to the DOE's 1982–87 survey the inspector's notes on "list description" may not necessarily have been incorporated into the list;

(3) there may have been subsequent changes to the building, or its site, or its setting (whether or not such changes required LBC themselves) which may mean that the factors decisive on listing have been reduced in importance or that new factors should now be taken into account;

(4) the listing inspector may have failed to appreciate certain features of the building, or may have been mistaken as to certain features;

(5) the list description is not intended to be a justification or explanation for listing; its purpose is partly to serve as a record of features existing at that date, and partly as an aid to identifying the building in question, but the DOE certainly do not regard it as exhaustive.

(6) Most local authorities do not have a detailed record of interiors and until proposals are submitted their officers may not be aware of any special features.

The Technical Digest on Alterations to Listed Buildings set out in Appen- **5.26** dix IV of Circular 8/87 gives specific advice on interiors in the following form:

"VI. Interiors

1. Interior features of interest should be respected and left *in situ* wherever possible. Staircases, panelling, doors and doorcases, mouldings, decorated ceilings, stucco work, wall paintings of all periods, are part of the listed character of a building and indeed may be the most valuable feature. Whatever the grading, interiors should be inspected even if they are not referred to in the list description.

2. Repairs to important interiors can be considered grantworthy by the Historic Buildings and Monuments Commission for England.

3. The form of the Building Regulations 1985 enables local authorities to adopt a flexible approach to the requirements (including fire safety provisions) when staircases of note and panelling or timber framing are liable to be affected.

4. New internal walls should not cut through mouldings or enriched plaster decoration but be shaped around them to allow for reinstatement at a later date.

5. Timber-framed buildings can be much damaged by interior alteration. Later C17 and C18 brick or stone buildings often have entirely timbered and panelled interiors and these deserve careful treatment.

6. Survivals of early roof structures are often important and as few as possible of their members should be renewed.

7. Good chimney-pieces are part of the decorative history of a build-

ing and often central to the design of a room. There is no excuse for their removal if this is simply because a chimney is redundant. If there is absolutely no alternative, then the chimney-piece should be saved for use in another position.

8. Every care should be taken that no interior feature of interest is unnecessarily removed or inadvertently damaged when a building is standing vacant or is in the process of conversion. If a rebuild is required then interior features of note should be carefully dismantled and re-set wherever possible."

Regardless of what features were considered important by the Department on listing, it is thought that the question of whether an alteration or extension would affect the character of a building as one of special architectural or historic interest falls to be determined according to the criteria generally applicable on listing, and that the criteria to be applied should be those applicable as at the date of the proposed alteration or extension.

Circular 8/87 sets out detailed guidelines on the technical aspects of alterations.[88] The Circular states that these are "to assist local authorities in deciding on the suitability of alterations to listed buildings" and they should not be regarded as doing more than that. In particular the guidelines on suitability are not an attempt to define what alterations require LBC; only after it has been decided that LBC is needed for certain alterations should the guidelines on suitability be considered. Logical though this may be, the distinction may not always be obvious. On the subject of doors, for example, the circular says: "Original doorways or any surviving doors up to the mid-Victorian period are of value and should be retained." This does not mean that the alteration of original doorways or pre-Victorian doors will always require LBC. Consent will obviously be required where doors or doorways are of such significance in the first place that their alteration must affect the character of the building as one of special architectural or historic interest. One can conceive of cases, however, where the door is so insignificant its alteration or substitution would not possibly affect the character of the building as being of special architectural or historic interest.

14. ANCIENT MONUMENTS

5.27   The provisions of section 55 do not apply to "a building for the time being included in the schedule of monuments compiled and maintained under section 1 of the Ancient Monuments and Archaeological Areas Act 1979."[89]

The provisions for the authorisation of works affecting ancient monuments (it is an offence to effect certain specified works without such authorisation) are contained in section 2 of the Ancient Monuments and Archaeological Areas Act 1979. These are considered in Chapter 8.

---

[88] Circular 8/87, Appendix IV.
[89] T.C.P.A. 1971, s.56(1)(b).

15. ECCLESIASTICAL BUILDINGS

Ecclesiastical buildings have always presented particular problems in **5.28**
planning terms. There are three main aspects to this issue. The first is that
no one is sure what the term "ecclesiastical" covers—whilst one would
expect that all Christian denominations of all kinds might fall within this
definition, what about buildings of non-Christian religions? The second is
that churches in the Anglican community have, since 1913, been treated in
a special way. The third aspect is that churches are so essential a part of our
rich architectural heritage. There are probably 20,000 or so churches belong-
ing to Anglicans, non conformists and Roman Catholics alone. Of these,
over 12,000 are listed and 2,500 or so are listed Grade I (or A—a category of
listing once used, most such former gradings having now been replaced by
the Grade I category). The general practice as to listing and grading is set out
above at paras. 2.23–2.36.

To understand the present situation it is as well to look at two major
influences: the special treatment of the Church of England and the *Howard*
case.[90] The basis lies in the exception afforded in section 56 of the Act to

> "an ecclesiastical building which is for the time being used for ecclesi-
> astical purposes or would be so used but for the works [of demolition,
> alteration or extension]."[91]

This exemption originates from an agreement in 1913 between the then
Archbishop of Canterbury, Archbishop Davidson, and the government,
largely it seems in response to the assurances given by the Archbishop as to
the Church's future good conduct.[92] Church buildings of denominations
other than the Church of England were also exempted at the same time. It
does not appear that churches other than the Church of England gave such
assurances.

The debate has continued to rage as to whether the Church of England **5.29**
has been of good conduct; the conservation lobby castigates the Church of
England for its destructions whilst the General Synod (a decision on the
morning after the York Minster blaze) affirms that it is in favour of maintaining the exemption. At all events the Church of England established and
maintained a Faculty Jurisdiction. This is an internal procedure unique to
the Church of England deriving from its own ecclesiastical courts. A faculty
is required to be issued by the chancellor of the diocese in which the Church
is situated to introduce ornaments into a church and for repairs and alterations to its fabric. There is a provision for advertisements. Anyone with an
interest recognised by law may apply for a faculty—usually a resident of the
parish or the Parochial Church Council. If an application is contested, there
will be a hearing by the consistory court at which the chancellor (invariably
a lawyer) presides. For minor work it is not necessary to go to the chancellor: an archdeacon's certificate is all that is required. The procedure is governed by the Faculty Jurisdiction Measure 1964[93] which incidentally does
not affect Cathedrals or Royal Peculiars (*e.g.* Westminster Abbey, the

---

[90] *Attorney-General (on the relation of Bedfordshire County Council)* v. *Trustees of
the Howard United Reformed Church, Bedford* [1976] A.C. 363, H.L.
[91] T.C.P.A., 2.56(1)(*a*).
[92] See Charles Mynors' article, [1985] J.P.L. p. 599.
[93] A "measure" has the authority of an Act of Parliament.

chapels of the Oxford and Cambridge colleges and the Temple Church). The Church of England also has its own system relating to redundant churches which may, after appropriate periods, procedures and publicity, authorise the total demolition of churches.[94]

In the *Howard* case[95] the House of Lords held that a congregational church was an ecclesiastical building within the meaning of section 56(1)(a) since it was owned by a church, been built as a church, and had been used by a church for 200 years. It was held that the phrase "or would be so used but for the works" [of demolition] meant that the exemption in section 56 did not apply to total demolition (for which listed building consent—or indeed conservation area consent—would be needed) but did exempt partial demolition if some part of the building would continue to be used for ecclesiastical purposes.

5.30   This led to a procedure where it was possible to demolish a listed church or a non-listed church in a conservation area by means of obtaining planning permission for the erection of a new building or the use of a church hall for services thus ensuring the continuity of ecclesiastical use. If the new building was to be attached to an existing church building, then listed building consent would also be required as it would have amounted to an extension. Of course if the ecclesiastical use could be continued in a part of the existing listed building which could be separated from that which was going to be demolished, so much the easier. There were outcries about St. Francis Xavier's Church in Liverpool (where this procedure was intended, relying on the retention of one small chapel) and Jesmond Methodist Church which was intended to be demolished except for the attached Sunday School building.[96]

These and other problems led the government to take soundings as to whether the ecclesiastical exemption should be preserved. This led to new agreements between the government, the Church of England and the Churches Main Committee in 1986. The Churches Main Committee represents all Christian and Jewish Churches in the United Kingdom. These agreements were mentioned in the debate on the Housing and Planning Bill which became the 1986 Act. Although some matters remain to be further clarified, the changes in the Act and the indications of the government now form the new basis of the control over churches. Broadly the ecclesiastical exemption remains but the opportunity has been taken to improve the whole of this branch of the law.

5.31   Thus the present situation[97] is that:

> (a) Listed building consent (or if appropriate conservation area consent) is necessary for the total demolition of a listed (or non-listed in a conservation area) church except for demolition of a Church of England church pursuant to a pastoral or redundancy scheme.[98]
>
> (b) When total or partial demolition of a Church of England listed church (or non-listed in a conservation area) is proposed pursuant

---

[94] Pastoral Measure 1983.

[95] See n. 90 above.

[96] See n. 92 above.

[97] This is an analysis of Lord Skelmersdale's speech in the House of Lords on October 13, 1986 and its subsequent repetition in Circular 8/87, para. 103.

[98] Pastoral Measure 1983 and the Direction contained in Circular 8/87, para. 97. See also para. 103.

to a scheme under the Pastoral Measure 1983 the Church of England will ask the Secretary of State for the Environment if he wishes to hold a non-statutory local public inquiry into any proposal to demolish, wholly or partially, in circumstances where the Commission, the Advisory Board for Redundant Churches, the local planning authority or a national amenity society, give reasoned objections to the proposal.[99]

(c) If there is such an inquiry (as mentioned in (b) above) the Church Commissioners have undertaken to accept a recommendation from the Secretary of State that—

(i) if the church is of sufficient importance to be vested in the Redundant Churches Fund it will be so vested, or

(ii) if it is not of such importance, then the Church Commissioners will make further efforts to find an alternative use and will consult further with the Secretary of State before demolition.[1]

(d) In considering the recommendation which he will make the Secretary of State will take into account:

(i) the financial implications of retaining a church building, and

(ii) the architectural and historic interest of the church, and

(iii) other planning and social factors.[2]

(e) In case of works for partial demolition of a church or for its alteration or extension, the ecclesiastical exemption will still continue to apply and listed building consent or conservation area consent will not be required if the ecclesiastical use is to continue during the works or will only be interrupted temporarily whilst the works are to be carried out.[3] This will remain the position until an order is made under section 58AA (see below) which will only be done after further consultations with the churches.[4]

(f) LBC is required for a proposal which would materially affect the architectural or historic interest of a church, such as a spire, tower or cupola, except in relation to a Church of England church.[5]

(g) The ecclesiastical exemption will apply to proposals which will have a "lesser effect" than in (f): *i.e.* LBC will not be required whether the church be that of the Church of England or not.[6]

(h) All churches have undertaken to consult the local planning authority and in England, the Commission, before undertaking any significant external works which remain exempt from listed building control.[7]

(i) Planning permission is required already (and will continue to be required) for material external alterations and extensions to all churches; local planning authorities are required to take into account the effect of the proposed development on a listed building

---

[99] *Ibid.* para. 103(ii).

[1] *Ibid.* para. 103(i).

[2] *Ibid.* para. 103(ii).

[3] See the *Howard* case (above n. 90) and the notes above.

[4] Circular 8/87 para. 105.

[5] *Ibid.* para. 103(i).

[6] *Ibid.* para. 103(i).

[7] *Ibid.* para. 103(vi).

or its setting when considering whether planning permission should be granted. No further controls—*e.g.* listed building controls—over external alterations and extensions are presently contemplated.[8]

(j) A building which is used or available for use by a minister of religion wholly or mainly as a residence from which to perform the duties of his office shall be treated as not being an ecclesiastical building and thus not entitled to the exemption.[9]

5.32   There is still left unanswered the extent of the ecclesiastical exemption—what churches are exempt. The Churches Main Committee represents all Christian and Jewish Churches in the United Kingdom. As the Churches Main Committee are signatories to the above agreements it presumably can safely be assumed that all these denominations are churches within the exemption. But it is still a partially open question as posed by Lord Cross in the *Howard* case,[10]

"is the expression ('ecclesiastical buildings') confined to Christian buildings or does it extend to synagogues and mosques? Does it make a difference whether the building was built as a church or not?"

Perhaps the reference in section 58AA to "different religious faiths or denominations" points us in a more general direction?

Section 58AA of the Act (inserted by the 1986 Act[11]) provides for the Secretary of State to order that specified cases may be restricted or excluded in relation to ecclesiastical buildings from sections 56(1) and 58(2). The order may make provision (*inter alia*) for buildings generally, different provision for different areas, for buildings of different religious faiths or denominations. The further discussions which will no doubt lead to an order under section 58AA may also cover objects or structures within the curtilage of the church.

16. HOUSING ACT CASES

5.33   The Housing Act 1985 contains special provisions for listed buildings and buildings in conservation areas which are subject to a compulsory purchase order under Part IX of the Act. The provisions of the 1985 Act are summarised in Circular 8/87 at Appendix V.

17. CROWN LAND

5.34   Although section 266(1) of the Town and Country Planning Act 1971 does not preclude a "building which for the time being is Crown land" being listed, there was until 1984 no formal provision by which the Crown in respect of Crown land could seek LBC. This has now been remedied by the

---

[8] *Ibid.* para. 103(v).
[9] T.C.P.A., s.56(1).
[10] See n. 90 above.
[11] H.P.A. 1986, Sched. 9, para. 5.

Town and Country Planning Act 1984, which came into force on August 12, 1984, in its provisions affecting Crown land. In particular, it renders redundant the procedure by which disposing departments sought an informal opinion from local planning authorities about appropriate uses of surplus Crown land. The detailed provisions of the Act are fully explained in Circular 18/84—Crown Land and Crown Development and by the Town and Country Planning (Crown Land Applications) Regulations 1984. Section 1(1) of the Act enables the Crown to dispose of Crown land or an interest in such land with the benefit of (inter alia) planning permission, listed building consent or conservation area consent.

Furthermore, it is known that planning permission and possibly listed building consents and conservation area consents have been granted in the past in respect of Crown land in which there was no other interest and that their validity may be thought to be in doubt. Subsection (8) removes this doubt by providing that such permission and consents shall be deemed to be valid, and always to have had effect as provided for in subsection (3).

(a) Buildings of special architectural or historic interest

Whilst these "enabling" provisions are intended to assist the Crown, there are no provisions introduced to *require* a Crown developer to seek listed building consent to demolish, alter or extend a listed building. However, Circular 18/84, Pt. IV, para. 31 provides that departments must consult the local planning authority in a manner prescribed in Part IV, paragraph 9 of the Circular (see below) about any proposal to demolish a listed building (other than one scheduled as an ancient monument or held in departmental care under the provisions of the Ancient Monuments and Archaeological Areas Act 1979—for which different procedures apply (see below)) or to alter or extend a building in a way which would affect its character as a building of special architectural or historic interest. The local planning authority are asked to advertise such proposals and to notify those bodies listed in Annex B to the Circular and local amenity societies, in the same way as they would if application had been made for listed building consent. **5.35**

If the local planning authority do not themselves wish to make representations, but where, following advertisement and notification, objections are received, the objections should be passed on to the developing department. The department in question then has discretion to decide whether to proceed in the light of the objections or alternatively to consider whether "the substance of the objections is such that it would be appropriate for the Secretary of State to decide whether the proposal should proceed."[12] If they so decide the developing department then forwards the objections to the Department of the Environment for consideration. In that case and in cases where the Department of the Environment have been notified by the developing department of unresolved disagreements between themselves and the local planning authority, the method of dealing with them is set out in Part IV, paragraph 25 of the Circular. The procedures identified involve either written representations exchanged between all bodies expressing views; or a

[12] Circular 18/84, Pt. IV, para. 32.

meeting between representatives of the developing department and the local planning authority, chaired by an officer of the Department of the Environment (this would only be appropriate if there were no other interested bodies); or finally a non-statutory public inquiry may be held and determined by the Secretary of State.

Special consideration needs to be given to listed buildings which are used as hospitals in the green belt. Guidelines for the future use of redundant hospital sites in the green belt are contained in Circular 12/87.[12a]

If the proposal involves the demolition of a listed building, departments are required to give at least one month's notice, before commencing demolition, to the Royal Commission on Historical Monuments or, in Wales, to the Royal Commission on Ancient and Historical Monuments in Wales, to enable the Commission to consider whether to make a record of the building.

(b) Unlisted buildings in conservation areas

5.36   Developing departments are required to consult the local planning authority, in the manner prescribed in paragraph 9 of Circular 18/84, about any proposals to demolish a building in a conservation area, except where the building is included in one of the descriptions of buildings set out in paragraph 97 of Circular 8/87.

Where the local planning authority object to the proposed demolition and the matter cannot be resolved to the satisfaction of both parties, the department is required to advise the Department of the Environment and the procedures for resolving the disagreement are substantially the same as those set out above.

(c) The consultation process

5.37   This is described in Circular 18/84 on Crown Land and Crown Development (Part IV):

"9. When the formal stage of consultation is reached, the developing Department will send to the local planning authority four copies of a statement of their proposal marked Notice of Proposed Development by (Department) sufficient to enable the authority to appreciate its nature and extent.

They will also supply four copies of a location plan showing the relationship of the proposed development to adjoining property and, except where the proposal involves only a material change of use, four copies of plans of the proposed development.

10. The Notice will make it clear whether the proposal is submitted with all relevant details, or in outline only to be followed by the submission of details. If it is in outline, the Notice will specify which, if any, of the reserved matters as defined in the General Development Order, *i.e.* siting, design, external appearance, means

[12a] "Redundant Hospitals in Green Belts: Planning Guidelines," dated April 29, 1987.

of access and landscaping of the site, are included. The local planning authority will not be expected to ask at this stage for further details except where this is essential to enable them to form a view on the proposed development.

11. When the Crown does not hold all the interests in the land, the developing Department will advise the owner, any agricultural tenant and any other tenant with seven or more years of his tenancy to run of the submission and contents of the Notice of Proposed Development.

12. The local planning authority will treat the Notice in the same way as they would a statutory planning application but are recommended to keep a non-statutory addendum to Part II of the register in respect of Notices of Proposed Development."

(d) Crown lands and section 52 agreements

In view of the increasing use of section 52 agreements in the planning process, a cautionary note in relation to Crown lands may be thought worthwhile. The essential feature of a section 52 agreement, which is intended to regulate or restrict, either permanently or temporarily, the use of land is that it is directly enforceable by the local planning authority against the owner for the time being when the LPA wishes to enforce a breach—without the necessity of bringing into an action any intervening owners. But this advantage can only be obtained if the agreement is registered as a local land charge.

5.38

Although the Town and Country Planning Act 1984 widened the provisions relating to Crown land as described in the preceding paragraphs, it is to be noted that the 1984 Act specifically did not make reference to section 52. The basic legal principle is that a statute does not apply to the Crown unless it specifically so states.

The consequence of this must be that whilst a Crown department may enter into an agreement with a local planning authority—it cannot have the same effect as a section 52 agreement—indeed it is strictly not registrable as a local land charge.

There are two solutions to this problem. One is for the Crown land department to enter into a section 52 type agreement with the local planning authority—and this agreement would, for enforceability reasons, have to be under seal—whereby the appropriate Secretary of State would agree to procure that on any subsequent disposal of the land the purchaser would enter into a new agreement under seal with the local planning authority in similar terms. The other possibility might be to deal with it by condition on the listed building consent or the conservation area consent. The latter solution might be rather more risky than the first in view of the remaining doubt about positive conditions. Although the *Grampian* case[13] suggested that a planning condition might be drawn so that the planning permission did not have effect until work carried out by some third party was effected, that principle has not been tested specifically in the listed buildings area. The former solution would in our view be preferable.

[13] *Grampian Regional Council* v. *City of Aberdeen D.C.* [1984] J.P.L. 590.

18. PUBLIC HEALTH ACT CASES

5.39   If a building is subject to an order under sections 77 or 78 of the Building Act 1984 the owner of the building has the choice of demolishing it instead of carrying out works to remedy the danger. It is contended by the Secretary of State that this does not release the owner from the obligation of obtaining LBC if the dangerous structure is listed. Similarly, if a listed building is subject to a notice served by the local authority under section 79 of the 1984 Act because it is a ruinous or dilapidated building which is seriously detrimental to amenity, then LBC is still needed for its demolition. Circular 8/87 suggests that owners should be reminded of the need for LBC under these circumstances, and the local planning authority must consider whether or not they should use their powers under sections 101, 114 and 115.[14]

19. LISTED BUILDINGS ENFORCEMENT NOTICE

5.40   Carrying out works without LBC (in breach of section 55(1)) or in contravention of a condition attached to a consent (in breach of section 55(4)) can lead either to prosecution or the issuing of an enforcement notice or both. However, in relation to an enforcement notice, the Secretary of State considers it beyond the powers provided in the Act to require reinstatement of property damaged or destroyed by accident.

Section 96 of the Act, which provides for listed building enforcement notices (together with section 97 relating to appeals against such notices), has been amended, particularly in relation to the steps which a local planning authority may require to be taken for remedying a contravention, by section 1 of the Local Government and Planning (Amendment) Act 1981.

The original wording of section 96 provided that a listed building enforcement notice was to specify the alleged contravention, and the steps required by the local planning authority to restore the building "to its former state or, as the case may be, it would have been in if the terms and conditions of any LBC for the works had been complied with."[15] The revised section 96(1)(b) expands the range of steps which the local planning authority may require to be taken, where it may not be necessary to require faithful restoration—a provision which was found in practice sometimes to be inappropriate. The requirements are now as follows:

"(i) for restoring the building to its former state; or
(ii) where the authority consider that such restoration would not be reasonably practicable, or would be undesirable, for executing such further works specified in the notice as they consider necessary to alleviate the effect of the works which were carried out without LBC[16]; or
(iii) for bringing the building to the state in which it would have been if the terms and conditions of any listed building consent which has been granted for the works had been complied with."

---

[14] Circular 8/87, para. 107 and section 56C.
[15] T.C.P.A. 1971, s.96(1), as substituted by L.G.P.(A).A. 1981.
[16] As DOE Circular 26/81 points out in para. 15, the power of a local authority under section 96(1)(b)(ii) is new.

Where a requirement is imposed in the terms stated in (ii) above, section 96(7)[16a] provides that LBC shall be deemed to be granted for any works of demolition, alteration or extension of the building executed as a result of compliance with the notice.

Copies of the notice must be served on the owner/occupier of the building **5.41** and on any other person whose interest in the building is, in the opinion of the authority, materially affected by the notice, the service of which is to take place not later than 28 days after the date of issue of the notice, and not later than 28 days before the date specified in the notice as the date on which it is to take effect.[17] The local planning authority may withdraw a listed building enforcement notice (without prejudice to their power to issue another one) at any time before it takes effect, and if they do withdraw such a notice, every person on whom the notice has been served must be notified of the fact.

Section 96 confers no power on a local planning authority to require the *improvement* of a building to restore an historic appearance. In *Bath City Council* v. *Secretary of State*[18] the roof of an hotel was composed of two-thirds Welsh slate and one third asbestos cement slates. The owners decided to re-cover the whole roof entirely with asbestos slates, and an enforcement notice was served requiring *all* the asbestos slates to be replaced by Welsh slates. Woolf J. (as he then was) quashed the enforcement notice.

A further point has been found to arise in practice as to the content and wording of the notice. It would seem that the Department of the Environment encourage a local planning authority as a general rule to be somewhat more specific than to require restoration in a manner or with materials "to be agreed by the local planning authority." Does this mean that the authority is to specify materials by name, or even manufacturer?

An owner or occupier who has incurred expenses in complying with an enforcement notice is able to recover them from the person who carried out the works to which the notice relates.[19]

Of course it is often the case that a number of enforcement notices are served. The demolition and storage of materials pending sale in America of the listed barn at Stagbatch Farm, near Leominster gave rise to enforcement notices being served on the site owners, the contractors and an antique company responsible for the resale. The barn was dated about 1620 and was found to have been properly listed. About 75 per cent. of the structural frame had been safely recovered and it was accepted that the only way to satisfy the requirements of the notice was to re-erect it on the original site. At 1985 prices £3750 had been paid for the salvageable fabric and a contract had been entered into to sell the same at a profit—this justified the dealer being brought into the enforcement proceedings as a person with an "interest." The appellant argued that rebuilding of the barn would have resulted in a replacement of better quality—thus going beyond the requirements of section 96. The Secretary of State determined that there might be some improvement, but concluded that the antique company was in the best pos-

---

[16a] Inserted by s.7 of the L.G. & P. (Amendment) Act 1981. Subss.(2)–(6) of s.96 (as amended) of the 1971 Act contain substantially the same provisions as subss.(2)–(5) of the original s.96.

[17] T.C.P.A. 1971, s.96(3), as substituted by L.G.P.(A).A. 1981.

[18] *The Times*, March 25, 1983; [1983] J.P.L. 737.

[19] T.C.P.A. 1971, s.96(2).

ition to restore the barn as they had made a photographic survey of it during its dismantling, upheld the enforcement notice and allowed six months to rebuild.[20]

Some authorities, faced with a situation which would justify both the service of an enforcement notice and the institution of a prosecution might be tempted to back the situation both ways. The South Lakeland District Council did this in relation to the Crown Inn at Flookburgh in Grange-over-Sands.[20a] The prosecution was dealt with first; the enforcement proceedings thereafter. The Secretary of State in dealing with the listed building enforcement notice stated:

> "The Secretary of State notes the Inspector's conclusion and recommendation. However, in view of the judgment given in the Crown Court at Barrow, on appeal against the conviction in the Magistrates Court, and in that it was found that the alteration was to a very nominal extent and did not justify a conviction, the present appeal must, in the Secretary of State's opinion, succeed on ground (b) of section 97(1) of the Act. Accordingly, the Secretary of State allows your client's appeal and hereby directs that the listed building enforcement notice issued on December 21, 1984 be quashed."

5.42   If the whole of a building is demolished, then there is a question as to whether or not an enforcement notice would lie at all on the grounds that there is no building left to be the subject of an enforcement notice. It is understood that the view of the Department is that if there is a substantial part of the building left, then this can be the subject of a valid enforcement notice. There is no authority on where the dividing line (if there be a dividing line) comes between what can be the subject of an enforcement notice and what cannot.

Much will depend on the intent of the owners. An accident is one thing; a deliberate act is another. In the middle of all this comes a mistake such as the Monkspath Hall, Solihull, case,[21] where the defendant company's bulldozer driver mistakenly demolished an eighteenth century Grade II listed farmhouse instead of farm buildings across the road. Driver and company were successfuly prosecuted and there was an order in the High Court for the company to pay for the costs of rebuilding and preservation of still-intact parts of the hall (estimated in 1985 at £200,000), and also the costs of the hearing and the professional fees involved, but this was a result of a breach of the contractual relationship between the council (which commissioned the demolition of the other building) and the contractors.

In the end there are two factors which are taken into account in practical terms in relation to listed buildings enforcement notices. They are "wilfulness' and "the 50 per cent. rule." Neither has statutory effect and neither can be relied on as constituting a defence to a listed building enforcement notice. But in practice local planning authorities rarely serve enforcement notices unless those responsible for the building have wilfully damaged it. If

[20] APP/C1815/F/86/162—July 13, 1987—reported in *Planning* (July 31, 1987) and *Chartered Surveyor Weekly* (August 6, 1987).

[20a] APP/X0990/F/85/19.

[21] *Solihull B.C.* v. *D. Doyle Contractors (Birmingham) Ltd.*, reported in *The Times*, November 7, 1985, and also *The Times*, May 19, 1981.

there is less than 50 per cent. of the building left—a broad test—but thought to be 50 per cent. of the cubic content—the Department will rarely, it seems, uphold a listed building enforcement notice.

With those two, albeit unofficial, criteria in mind, the result seems to be: **5.43**

(a) If all that is left is a heap of assorted rubble, a listed building enforcement notice will not lie or is unlikely to be upheld;

(b) if all the basic structural parts of the building are there but not in place, it seems now more likely that an enforcement notice might lie (see the Stagbatch farm, Leominster decision above at para. 5.41;)

(c) if the "building" is on site but less than 50 per cent. by cubic content is in place, it seems unlikely that—particularly in the absence of a wilful act—a local planning authority would serve a listed building enforcement notice or that the Department would uphold it;

(d) if the roof was off but otherwise the "building" was substantially in place, an enforcement notice would probably lie and be upheld;

(e) if there were parts of the building missing—perhaps because of accidental damage, then it is unlikely—particularly in the absence of wilfulness and if there was difficulty in reproducing the craftsmanship—that an enforcement notice would lie or be enforced (see the Stafford case below at para. 5.46).

20. APPEAL AGAINST ENFORCEMENT NOTICE

Under section 97(1)[22] a person on whom a listed building enforcement   **5.44**
notice is served, or any other person with an interest in the building, (which includes a person who, at the date of issue of the notice, occupies the land or building by virtue of a licence in writing and continues so to occupy when the appeal is brought),[23] may appeal to the Secretary of State against the notice on any of the following grounds:

(a) that the building is not of special architectural or historic interest;

(b) that the matters alleged to constitute a contravention of section 55 (of the Act) do not involve such a contravention;

(c) that the contravention of that section alleged in the notice has not taken place;

(d) that the works were urgently necessary in the interests of safety or health or for the preservation of the building, that it was not practicable to secure safety or health or, as the case may be, the preservation of the building by works of repair or works for affording temporary support or shelter, and that the works carried out were limited to the minimum measures immediately necessary;

(e) that listed building consent ought to be granted for the works or that any relevant condition of such consent which has been granted ought to be discharged or different conditions substituted;

(f) that copies of the notice were not served as required by section 96(3) (of the Act);

[22] As amended by the L.G.L.P.A.(A.)A. 1981 and the H.P.A. 1986.
[23] T.C.P.A. 1984, s.4(2).

(g) except in relation to such a requirement as is mentioned in section 96(1)(b)(ii) or (iii) (of the Act), the requirements of the notice exceed what is necessary for restoring the building to its condition before the works were carried out;

(h) that the period specified in the notice as the period within which any step required thereby is to be taken falls short of what should reasonably be allowed;

(i) that the steps required by the notice for the purpose of restoring the character of the building to its former state would not serve that purpose;

(j) that the steps required to be taken by virtue of section 96(1)(b)(ii) (of the Act) exceed what is necessary to alleviate the effect of the works executed to the building;

(k) that the steps required to be taken by virtue of section 96(1)(b)(iii) (of the Act) exceed what is necessary to bring the building to the state in which it would have been if the terms and conditions of the listed building consent had been complied with.

5.45   On an appeal against an enforcement notice served by Lincoln City Council in respect of the erection of external shutters to the sash windows of a house, the inspector concluded that although the house would look marginally better without the shutters, the appellant, who had restored the previously dilapidated building, should be given the benefit of the doubt and allowed to retain the shutters; the Secretary of State allowed the appeal.[24]

Change of materials or use of inappropriate materials is often the subject of enforcement action by local planning authorities. Buckingham City Council served an enforcement notice in respect of works which replaced the rendering on the front of a building with a "Mock Tudor" finish which, in the words of the inspector, "produced a facade which is not even an hybrid of good architectural styles and which is unacceptable." The appeal against the enforcement notice was dismissed, although the period for compliance was extended.[25] By contrast, an enforcement notice served by Shepway District Council in relation to roofing alterations at the Barn, Home Farm, Newington, was quashed on the inspector's recommendation. The notice required that Kent peg roofing tiles be replaced by the available original tiles and additional matching tiles; however, three-quarters of the original tiles had been removed from the roof before service of the building preservation notice, which made the building subject to the listed building controls. Consequently it was only the removal of the remaining 25 per cent. against which the local planning authority could enforce, and the inspector considered that such enforcement would serve no useful purpose and would be absurd.[26]

5.46   A similar case arose in Stafford where an enforcement notice was served alleging that the pilaster mouldings, console brackets and flat cornice hood had been removed from the doorway of a Grade II listed building which was of red brick construction with a slated roof. The local planning authority did not dispute that the original cornice hood projected into the inside of a bend in the highway and had been damaged on occasions by vehicles and had deteriorated to a point beyond which it was impossible to repair or replace

---

[24] *Planning Appeals*, Vol. 2, p. 262. Ref: APP/5311/F/76/4.
[25] *Planning Appeals*, Vol. 2, p. 262. Ref: APP/918/F/74/3.
[26] *Planning Appeals*, Vol. 3, p. 259. Ref: APP/5281/F/77/34.

it. The Secretary of State considered that in view of the extent of the damage already caused by vehicular impact, the eventual removal of the cornice, console brackets and pilasters, could not reasonably be regarded as an alteration affecting the character of the listed building and that therefore the action is unlikely to have constituted a contravention of section 55. He also considered it beyond the powers provided in the Act under the enforcement procedures to require the reinstatement of property damaged or destroyed by accident. Accordingly, he allowed the appeal and quashed the enforcement notice. He also awarded costs to the appellant, as he felt that the council ought to have realised in the particular circumstances of the case that the removal of the cornice, console brackets and pilasters could not reasonably be regarded as an alteration affecting the character of the building.[27]

The remaining subsections of section 97 provide for the conduct of appeals, and the Secretary of State's powers in respect thereof, and amend the original section 96 so as to bring its provisions into line with those relating to the conduct of "ordinary" enforcement notice appeals under section 88 of the 1971 Act (as amended by the Local Government and Planning (Amendment) Act 1981).

By virtue of these amendments the Secretary of State's powers on appeal include power to make regulations prescribing time limits for the making of an appeal, and for dismissing an appeal if it is made outside that time limit, or for allowing it if the local planning authority fail to comply with any requirements and regulations made by virtue of section 88 of the Act. The detailed provisions for appeals against listed building enforcement notices are contained in the Town and Country Planning (Enforcement) (Enquiries Procedure) Rules 1981 which apply the same procedure to these appeals as to ordinary enforcement notice appeals. The Secretary of State may also correct immaterial defects in the notice, quash the notice, grant LBC for the works to which the notice relates, discharge or substitute conditions, grant planning permission, or remove the building from the list.[28]

There is a right of appeal from a decision of the Secretary of State to the High Court on a question of law[29] but in relation to the merits of the grant of planning permission or LBC his decision is final.[30]

21. CRIMINAL MATTERS

There are five principal sanctions by way of criminal prosecutions in relation to listed buildings, and unlisted buildings in conservation areas. There are also specific criminal penalties in relation to ancient monuments but these are dealt with separately in Chapter 8.

5.47

(a) Section 55—unauthorised work to a listed building

"(1) . . . if a person executes of causes to be executed any works for the demolition of a listed building or for its alteration or extension in

---

[27] [1981] J.P.L. 443, APP/5373/F/79/33.
[28] T.C.P.A. 1971, s.97(4) and (5), as substituted by L.G.P.(A).A. 1981.
[29] T.C.P.A. 1971, s.246(1), as substituted by L.G.P.(A).A. 1981.
[30] T.C.P.A. 1971, s.97(6), (7), as substituted by L.G.P.(A).A. 1981.

any manner which would affect its character as a building of special architectural or historic interest, and the works are not authorised under [this section] he shall be guilty of an offence.

(6) In proceedings for an offence under this section it shall be a defence to prove the following matters—

(a) that works to the building were urgently necessary in the interests of safety or health or for the preservation of the building,

(b) that it was not practicable to secure safety or health or, as the case may be, the preservation of the building by works of repair. or works for affording temporary support or shelter,

(c) that the works carried out were limited to the minimum measures immediately necessary, and

(d) that notice in writing justifying in detail the carrying out of the works was given to the local planning authority as soon as reasonably practicable.[31]

(5) A person guilty of an offence under this section shall be liable:

(a) on summary conviction to imprisonment for a term not exceeding three months or a fine not exceeding £1,000 or both; or

(b) on conviction on indictment to imprisonment for a term not exceeding 12 months or a fine, or both

and in determining the amount of any fine to be imposed on a person convicted on indictment, the Court shall in particular have regard to any financial benefit which has accrued or appears likely to accrue to him in consequence of the offence."

These provisions also apply to demolition of unlisted buildings in conservation areas (section 277A(8)).

(b) Section 57—acts causing or likely to result in damage to listed buildings

5.48 "(1) where a building [not being an ecclesiastical building or a scheduled monument] is included in a list, . . . then if any person who, but for this section, would be entitled to do so, does or permits the doing of any act which causes or is likely to result in damage to the building [other than excepted works, *i.e.* authorised by planning permission or the subject of LBC] he shall be guilty of an offence and liable on summary conviction to a fine not exceeding level 3[31a] on the standard scale."

There is a further provision whereby a person who is convicted under this section and fails to prevent any damage or further damage resulting from the offence, is liable on summary conviction to a daily fine of £40. Section 57 does not apply to damage to unlisted buildings in a conservation area.

---

[31] Subs. (6) was radically altered by the 1986 Act.
[31a] See para. 5.52 below.

(c) Section 98—non-compliance with a listed building enforcement notice

"(1) . . . where a listed building enforcement notice has been served on **5.49**
the person who, at the time when the notice was served on him,
was the owner of the building to which it relates then, if any steps
required by the notice to be taken have not been taken within the
period allowed for compliance with the notice, that person shall be
guilty of an offence and liable on summary conviction to a fine not
exceeding 'the prescribed sum' [at present £2,000][31b] or on conviction on indictment to a fine."

There is a provision for the substitution of a subsequent owner (if he
became the owner before the period for compliance with the listed building
notice had expired) to be brought before the court. If the original owner
proved he took all reasonable steps to comply and the fault lies with the
subsequent owner, then the original owner is entitled to be acquitted and
the subsequent owner may be convicted.

There is a daily penalty provision similar to that in relation to section 57.
It must be proved that the defendant has not done "as soon as practicable
everything in his power to secure compliance." In this case the defendant
may be brought before the magistrates where the daily penalty is a maximum of £200 a day or he may be indicted when a fine of unlimited amount
may be imposed.

(d) Section 58—non-compliance with a building preservation notice

If a building preservation notice is served[32] and, whilst it is in force, an act **5.50**
is done which would be an offence if it was a listed building, the criminal
provisions of section 55 (see para. 5.47 above) will be applicable. The provisions of section 57 (para. 5.48 above) do not however apply to an "act
causing or likely to cause damage" in relation to an unlisted building which
is the subject of a building preservation notice.

(e) Non-compliance with a dangerous structures notice

The law relating to dangerous structures and listed buildings has been **5.51**
reconciled by provisions in the 1986 Act.[33] A local planning authority must
consider the provisions contained in sections 101 and 114 of the Act before
making a dangerous structure order. If LBC is not obtained before the works
are carried out, then a prosecution may be commenced under section 55 (see
para. 5.47 above). Of course the defences in section 55 will be avail-

---

[31b] The words "the prescribed sum" were substituted by the Magistrates' Courts Act
1980, s.32(2)(9).
[32] See para. 2.39 above.
[33] See section 56C and Chap. 7.

able to the defendant. These provisions apply to listed buildings, unlisted buildings in conservation areas (where demolition is the act complained of) and buildings the subject of a building preservation notice. Section 57 prosecutions could also lie—except in relation to buildings subject only to a building preservation notice.

(f) Criminal sanctions generally

5–52   There are other criminal sanctions in relation to listed buildings but these (*e.g.* failure to permit entry) are only an application of the criminal offences relating to planning law generally.

There are a number of points which relate to this aspect of listed building legislation, many of them arising from the experience of prosecutions.

(a) Where there is a choice of prosecuting before the magistrates or before a Crown Court (which is the meaning of the phrase "on indictment") it is up to the prosecution so to elect. It would be expected that the more serious the case the more likely it would be that it will be dealt with at the Crown Court. In certain circumstances the defendant may, if prosecuted in the magistrates court, opt for trial at the Crown Court. This he must do on the opening of the case. He will usually do it if he feels he will fare better with a jury which will be involved on a trial in the Crown Court.

(b) The prosecution may also opt between a section 55 and a section 57 prosecution. In a section 55 prosecution it must be shown that the act complained of would "affect" the character of the building. There is no such requirement on section 57—only damage need be shown. But section 57 prosecutions may only go to the magistrates and the penalties are lower than on a section 55 prosecution.

(c) A prosecution may be commenced by anyone so long as he can persuade a magistrate to issue a summons. This requires him to show a prima facie cause. Most prosecutions will be by the local authority which is also the local planning authority. But some of the most successful prosecutions have been initiated by the Society for the Protection of Ancient Buildings.

(d) Magistrates are limited to the maximum fine (and in the case of imprisonment to the maximum period). Level 3 (mentioned in section 57) is a now standard scale of maximum fine for summary offences (*i.e.* those triable by the magistrates). This idea was introduced by the Criminal Justice Act 1982 so as to enable the levels to be increased by order of the Secretary of State. Level 3 is presently a maximum of £400.[34] The Crown courts however have no limit and it will be seen that the Crown court in relation to a prosecution under section 55 (only: not the other offences) may fine a defendant to reflect the financial benefit accrued or likely to accrue to him. Although there is no mention in the Act, any court may order the defendant to pay the costs of the prosecution—but this is discretionary.

(e) Section 55 creates an absolute offence, *i.e.* it is not necessary for it

[34] Criminal Penalties, etc. (Increase) Order 1984 (S.I. 1984 No. 447).

to be shown that the defendant knew that the building was a listed building. The divisional court pointed out that intent need not be proved—there was a discretion whether to prosecute or not and to refrain from punishment by either fine or imprisonment in appropriate cases.[35]

(f) It was held in *Maltglade* v. *St. Albans*[36] which concerned the service of a building preservation notice, that *actual* service of the notice must be proved where it was important to establish the date from which the notice took effect; service through the ordinary course of post could not be presumed.

(g) Sometimes the circumstances would justify both enforcement proceedings and a criminal prosecution. But this may not be wise as the criminal prosecution might deter the Secretary of State from confirming a listed building enforcement notice.[36a]

(h) Some examples of prosecutions (all under section 55) which have all led to convictions are:

5.53

Date of Conviction	Nature of Offence	Penalty imposed
1975	Demolition of listed building	Crown court. Fine, £10,000 and £1,000 costs[37]
1980	Removal of pantiles from roof of Clock Tower, Walton	Fine £50 and £40 costs[38]
1981	Demolition of a C18 listed cottage, Portsmouth: defendant claimed he was ignorant of listing	Fine £500[39]
1981	Demolition of listed almshouses at Welby	Fine £1,000 and £2,000 costs[40]
1985	Demolition of listed Monkspath Hall, Solihull—defence of mistake did not succeed	Bulldozer driver. Fine £1,500; Company (of which he was a director) £2,000. (See Note at end of table)[41]
1985	Demolition of a listed house in Royston. Defence of urgent necessity did not succeed	Fine £5,000 on one defendant. £1,000 on another. Both to pay costs[42]

---

[35] R. v. *Wells Streets Stipendiary Magistrate, ex parte Westminister C.C.* [1986] 3 All E.R. 4.

[36] [1972] 3 All E.R. 129.

[36a] See para. 5.41.

[37] R. v. *Endersley Properties Ltd.* (1975) 32 P. & C.R. 399.

[38] Courtesy of Elmbridge Borough Council.

[39] *The Times*, September 25, 1981.

[40] Private prosecution brought by the Society for the Protection of Ancient Buildings in respect of the demolition of Welby Almshouses, Grantham, Lincolnshire.

[41] *The Times*, (May 19, 1981).

[42] Reported in *The Planner* (August 1986), p. 4.

1986	Removal of shop front from an unlisted building in a Conservation Area	Fine £1,500 and £500 costs[43]
1986	Removal of chimney pieces, panelled doors and staircase from listed building	Divisional court held lack of knowledge that it was a listed building no defence (see (e) above). Case sent back to magistrate to complete[44]
1986	Removal of windows in a listed building by a window replacement company	Fine £500 and ordered to pay costs[45]

Note

Monkspath Hall, Solihull: In addition to the penalties recorded, an action was brought in the High Court for the defendant company to pay for the costs of rebuilding and preservation of the still intact parts of the Hall (estimated in 1985 prices at £200,000) with the costs of the hearing arising out of a breach of the contractual relationship between the Council and the contractor.[46]

22. ALTERNATIVE ENFORCEMENT PROCEDURES

5.54   Additional to criminal proceedings and the enforcement provisions under the Listed Buildings and Ancient Monuments legislation, is the possibility of injunction proceedings. At Stagbatch Farm, Leominster, an interim injunction was granted in the High Court to restrain a dismantled 500-year-old cruck-framed barn from being exported to the United States, pending a High Court action to determine the future of the building.[47]

There is no equivalent provision in the listed building legislation to a "stop notice" under section 90 of the 1971 Act, whereby a local planning authority may follow up a planning enforcement notice with a notice compelling the person on whom it is served forthwith to suspend the operations complained of. Clearly, however, it is always open to the local planning authority to apply to the High Court for an injunction having the same effect, as we have just seen.

This aspect of the law is in a state of development. There seems more and more enthusiasm to establish civil rights—with civil remedies which can be much more direct and speedy.

In ecclesiastical cases, where work has been carried out without a faculty, it is possible for a parishioner or any interested party to petition for a faculty authorising the restoration of the building to its previous state; or to oppose a retrospective confirmatory faculty sought by the church authorities. Moreover, orders for costs in this connection are enforceable through the county court.

---

[43] T/APP/A5270/C/85/1185/86.
[44] See n. 35 above.
[45] Courtesy of Hove Borough Council, October 22, 1986.
[46] See n. 21 above.
[47] *The Times*, August 12, 1986.

6. Problem Operations and Features—The Nuts and Bolts of Listed Building and Conservation Area Control

During the course of research and preparation for the second edition of **6.01** this book, it became apparent that many of the day to day practicalities of dealing with listed buildings or particular features of listed buildings are of considerable importance to practitioners in the field. This not only includes the owners of the buildings, but local planning authority officers dealing with listed building applications, members of local amenity groups and local parish councils.

In an attempt to develop this aspect this chapter has been prepared on the basis that some readers will find guidance from a collection of cases dealing with some of the down to earth aspects of listed building control.

1. CANOPIES

6.02 The addition of canopies to listed buildings continues to cause problems for local planning authorities, particularly as they are often erected without consent in the first place. North West Leicestershire District Council has been particularly active in this field and has successfully served listed building enforcement notices to secure the removal of advertisement canopies at a property in Ashby-de-la Zouch.[1] The inspector's analysis of the issues involved is very thorough and raises some interesting points about the method of fixing canopies to the building and his conclusions read as follows:

"The canopies attached to this Grade II listed building obscure the incised lintels over the windows and cover part of the windows. The effect of this is to alter the visual proportion of the windows which are a specific feature of a Georgian window. While the method of fixing, by two clips and two screws to each canopy, does not constitute any structural alteration to the fabric of the building, the creation of the canopies does materially affect the appearance of the building and the terrace in which it is situated.

The structural connections to the building do not in themselves alter the character of the building, for if the canopies were removed the fixing clips or holes would not alter the character of the building; the obscuring effect of the canopies does however materially affect the appearance of the building. By the obscuring of detail and visually altering the proportion of the windows, I consider that the canopies do constitute an alteration to the building and as such contravene section 55(1) of the 1971 Act and as such ground (b) fails.

As I conclude that the erection of canopies would contravene section 55 of the 1971 Act then, as the canopies have already been erected, it follows that a contravention has taken place, as such therefore ground (c) must fail.

Dutch style canopies are not a traditional Georgian feature and their introduction, which obscures detail and the proportions of the building, is detrimental to the character of the building and to the facade of the terrace in which they are situated.

Whilst I appreciate that some of the detailing obscured by the canopies can be seen from the pavement directly below the canopies, it is from the longer range that the architectural value of the appeal premises and the terrace can be appreciated. From such viewpoint the character of the appeal premises and the terrace are adversely affected by the canopies which introduce a non-traditional feature at first floor level as well as obscuring some of the detailing of the facade; for such reasons I consider ground (e) fails.

Restoration of the building to its original appearance could be achieved by the simple expedient of removing the canopies, a matter of removing two screws per canopy and lifting the canopies off their retaining clips. Whilst it is accepted that the fixings do not in themselves affect the structural condition of the building, the removal of the

[1] APP/G2435/F/84/68.

canopies is a necessary operation to restore the building to its former condition; accordingly ground (g) fails.

To say that the removal of the canopies would not serve the purpose of restoring the building to its former state is not valid. While the fixing of the canopies does not affect the structural integrity of the building, the visual appearance of the building has to be taken into account. As such the removal of the canopies must serve to restore the building to its former appearance and for that reason ground (i) must fail.

The use of the first floor windows of the appeal premises for display purposes, besides having limited visual impact, does not in my opinion warrant or justify the installation of the canopies. Whilst accepting that confectionery products would require protection from sunlight, in my opinion this unusual form of display at first floor level, behind barred windows containing some bulls-eyed glass panes, is of doubtful commercial or visual merit.

In view of the ease by which the canopies could be removed, I consider that the period for the compliance with the notice is more than sufficient."

In a further case involving first floor canopies on a listed Georgian building in Newbury,[2] the appellant's arguments that the canopies were required to advertise the business premises were set aside by the Secretary of State, who did not consider the business interests of the appellant to be relevant to the effect the proposal would have on the listed building. He was concerned that the canopies would detract from the appearance of the listed building and have a harmful effect on the Newbury Town Centre Conservation Area, whose character was largely dependent on the unchanged and uncluttered appearance of the period buildings within it.

2. SIGNS[2a]

6.03 The application of signs to listed buildings or unlisted buildings in a conservation area often involves commercial considerations and it is not unusual for public houses to figure at the forefront of this contentious activity.

The reader will not therefore be surprised to learn that Trafford Metropolitan Borough Council refused permission for the retention of five red plastic canopies, 20 brass wall lights and a total of 15 illuminated and non-illuminated board and canopy signs at a public house in Altringham.[3] The pub was large and occupied a very prominent position in a conservation area. The Secretary of State was concerned that the materials used in the door and window canopies contrasted sharply with the colours of the appeal building. Furthermore, the combination of signs and wall lights gave the building a cluttered appearance which was detrimental to the visual amenity and character of the conservation area. The signs at the upper level were considered to be unduly prominent and unrelated to the main fenestration of the building. The appeal was dismissed.

---

[2] APP/G0310/E/85/801164.

[2a] Signs are subject to a double form of control in that they are also governed by Regulations as to control of advertisements—see para. 3.25 above.

[3] PLUP/5088/175/132.

Notwithstanding this resounding defeat for the brewing industry, it was successful in winning an appeal against the London Borough of Harrow which had refused listed building consent for a hanging sign and the erection of illuminated and non-illuminated signs on a listed pub.[4] The council's contention that the modern signs introduced an obtrusive commercial element into a predominantly residential street and that they were not in keeping with the listed building, was not accepted by the Secretary of State.

He took the view that the signs, although not traditional in style or construction, did not have an unduly harmful effect on the appearance of the building. He was of the opinion that the hanging sign was sufficiently distant from the building to have little effect and he allowed the appeal with the exception of two black swan-necked lamps which illuminated the name sign on the front elevation of the public house.

3. CLADDING AND RENDERING

6.04   The application of new materials to the external elevations of properties constructed in traditional materials is undoubtedly one of the activities causing most concern to local planning authorities and conservationists alike. The desire of the householder to lend his property individuality often runs into conflict with the principles of conservation and two particular cases illustrate the wide gulf which exists between conservationists and the householder in some instances.

In a case within the Kirklees area of West Yorkshire[5] the owner of an end-of-terrace stone listed building had not only replaced the windows with small paned windows with top opening lights, but had covered the external elevations with swirl textured white render, which was also interspersed with randomly placed projected stones. The Secretary of State concluded that these works were inappropriate and detracted from the character of the listed building.

In a second case, the owner of a small terraced property in the South Highfields Conservation Area in Leicester[6] had applied imitation stone cladding to the front elevation of this property without planning permission. The conservation area was also subject to an article 4 direction[6a] and the inspector concluded as follows:

> "The work which has been carried out on the appeal property has retained the string course, lintels and cills. The appearance of the house has, however, been fundamentally changed as a result of the obliteration of the characteristic red brickwork. The cladding used has a predominantly light colour which emphasises the difference in appearance between the appeal property and the adjoining premises. I therefore consider that the cladding has had an unacceptable effect on the appearance of Churchill Street and if retained would damage the efforts the authority is making to retain and enhance the character of the South Highfields Conservation Area.

[4] APP/M5450/E/84/800605.
[5] APP/J4715/E/85/800678.
[6] T/APP/U2425/A/84/021265/P3.
[6a] See paras. 3.17–3.18 above.

Although I accept that the appellant did not understand the need to obtain planning permission for this work when it was begun, I consider that in this case the authority has given widespread publicity to its policies and proposals. I also note that the appellant was advised to stop the work before its completion and to apply for a grant towards the costs of reinstatement, brick cleaning and repointing. Since this advice was not followed, I do not consider that the cost and inconvenience involved in the removal of the stone cladding can be sufficient reason to set aside the clear policies which apply in this case."

The inspector dismissed the appeal despite the fact that the appellant was supported by many of the local residents.

4. CLEANING OF LISTED BUILDINS[7]

The cleaning of listed buildings is an issue which continues to cause **6.05** some local planning authorities consternation and particularly as to whether the act of cleaning requires listed building consent. The practice among local planning authorities varies, *e.g.* whilst Bath City Council does not require applications for consent to clean listed buildings, Edinburgh City Council does.

Clearly the critical issue remains whether the cleaning process in question is regarded as an alteration which would affect its character as a building of special architectural or historic interest. Naturally the appropriateness of a particular cleaning process will vary from building to building depending upon the external materials to be cleaned. For example, sandblasting is unlikely to be appropriate for a soft textured brick or stone and could irrevocably damage the surface being cleaned, thereby materially affecting the character of the building of special architectural or historic interest.

Appendix IV to Circular 8/87 (Technical Digest on Alterations to Listed Buildings) gives brief advice on cleaning as follows:

"Cleaning of stone, brick or terracotta facades should only be carried out by specialised firms or under close supervision, as details can all too easily be blurred or obliterated by crude techniques."

In the light of this advice and practice generally it is evident that the question of whether the cleaning of a listed building requires LBC will depend upon two factors:

(i) the materials to be cleaned;
(ii) the cleaning process to be used.

It is therefore essential that there is a dialogue between the owners of listed buildings, cleaning contractors and the local planning authority before cleaning works commence. In particular, owners of listed buildings should be encouraged to discuss proposals for cleaning before they undertake such work so that a considered assessment can be made of the likely effects of the work proposed on the character of the listed building.

It therefore remains, in our view, a matter of judgment based on the facts

---

[7] See also para. 3.24 above.

of each case whether a cleaning process would required listed building consent.

5. PAINTING OF LISTED BUILDINGS[8]

6.06   The painting of a building does not amount to development within the meaning of section 22 of the Town and Country Planning Act 1971, unless it can be said to "materially affect the external appearance of the building." Furthermore, if it is deemed to constitute development it would normally constitute permitted development by virtue of the provisions of Schedule 1, Class II(3) to the Town and Country Planning General Development Order 1977.

It is an arguable point as to whether the application of paint in itself could irrefutably be said to affect the character of a building as one of special architectural or historic interest. Notwithstanding the esoteric arguments which might be advanced in this direction, experience generally supports the view that the painting of a listed building would usually require consent.

In a case at Hexham in County Durham,[9] Tynedale District Council refused listed building consent for the painting of the front stonework of a shop in white and the woodwork in signal red. The property was located in a conservation area and the council argued that the colour scheme was out of keeping with neighbouring properties and had destroyed the architectural quality of the building. The Secretary of State concurred with the council stating that the paintwork gave the appeal building an unbalanced appearance and that it had a harmful effect on the conservation area.

The matter seems now to have been settled by the Divisional Court, which further considered the matter in *Windsor and Maidenhead Borough Council* v. *Secretary of State for the Environment,*[9a] a case in which the Secretary of State had said that because the facade of the building in question was already painted, the action of repainting could not therefore be said to have constituted works of alteration. Mann J. disagreed, holding that having regard to the possible meaning in ordinary language of the word "alteration" in section 55 of the 1971 Act and having regard to the purpose of that section, repainting *was* capable of being an alteration.

The City of York, with its rich heritage of buildings, has been mindful of the problems of painting listed buildings or buildings in conservation areas for many years. It has specifically addressed those problems by introducing a local bye law—under the provisions of section 30 of the York Corporation Act 1969—which controls the painting of the fabric of buildings within the city walls and within the city's conservation areas. This section specifically excludes windows, window frames, doors, door frames, guttering or fallpipes to allow reasonable maintenance of these features. The council sought to exercise this control because of the often irreversible damage which can be caused by the application of cement-based paints to the original fabric of a building. (This danger is highlighted in Appendix IV to Circular 8/87.)

However, experience has shown that the York Corporation byelaw could

---

[8] See also paras. 3.22 and 4.46 above.
[9] APP/B2925/E/85/801501.
[9a] *The Times* January 6, 1988.

only be used to control "the colour or combination of colours or pattern" and could not be used to exercise control over the first time painting of a building. The City of York is seeking to remedy this weakness through the promotion of further legislation.

It is also very interesting to note that at the time of the 1969 Act, all the principal firms of painters and decorators in the City of York were advised of the contents of section 30 and to April 1986 some 342 applications had been received under the terms of the section. It has been estimated that over 30 per cent. of the proposed painting schemes have been modified following discussions with the applicants and it has not been necessary to use the powers of prosecution invested in the Act. Indeed, the scheme has been regarded as extremely successful based upon the co-operation of owners with a local planning authority which has used its powers sympathetically. Clearly this is an example for other local authorities to follow.

6. REINSTATEMENT OF ORIGINAL FEATURES

The architectural and or historical integrity of listed buildings is regarded **6.07** by many conservationists to be of paramount importance and it is therefore interesting to compare some appeal decisions in respect of the reinstatement of original features on listed buildings.

In a case at Bridlington in East Yorkshire[10] the removal of a Victorian shop front to a Georgian building brought an opinion from the Georgian Society to the effect that upon removal of the shop front the elevation should be restored to its original condition. The inspector disagreed with this view and saw the determining issue as to whether the proposals put forward were sympathetic to the character of the listed building, having regard to the fact that it had previously been altered. He concluded that the scheme of refurbishment was beneficial and he allowed the appeal.

The use of plastic gutters and downpipes on a restaurant conversion of a listed building in Allerdale, Cumbria[11] was in breach of a condition requiring that the rainwater goods should be in cast iron of similar design to the existing. The council were concerned about the unsympathetic qualities of plastic goods, but the appellant had used them because the requirements of the condition were unduly onerous and costly. The Secretary of State noted that the plastic gutters and downpipes which had already been placed on the building were not prominent and toned in well with the building's stonework. He allowed the appeal and discharged the condition.

However, the removal of castellations and a parapet wall from a listed hydraulic tower in Liverpool[12] were considered by the City Council adversely to affect the architectural integrity and character of the building. The Secretary of State noted the appellants' arguments that these features had been removed for safety reasons following the deterioration of the soft chalky mortar between the stonework and several stone falls. Indeed, the Secretary of State accepted that the work might have been justified at the time on public safety grounds, but took the view that as a listed building of special interest which was also an important local landmark, the tower

[10] YH/5268/270/36P.
[11] APP/R0905/E/84/800327.
[12] APP/Z4310/F/84/000087.

should be reinstated as required by the City Council. The appeal was dismissed.

7. ROOF MATERIALS

6.08 *Reconstituted roof materials.* The replacement of roof materials on listed buildings is a recurring problem for owners and local planning authorities alike. The most contentious issue arises through the desire to use machine made or reconstituted roof materials which are often cheaper and more readily available than handmade or secondhand materials. Two specific examples serve to illustrate the views of local planning authorities and inspectors from the Department of Environment.

In a case where the Cotswold District Council had refused consent for the use of reconstituted stone slates on a house,[13] the Secretary of State concurred with that view and considered that modern slates would not be satisfactory. In particular he was concerned that the slates would be of "reconstituted, machine made material, mainly regular in size and would be markedly different from the variety of size, thickness, colour and texture of the natural material."

A similar view was taken in a case at Filkins in West Oxfordshire,[14] where a proposal to strip the natural stone slates from the roofs of four cottages owned by the district council was refused consent and a subsequent appeal dismissed. The inspector's observations are particularly valuable and highlight the importance attached to the distinctive qualities of traditional materials.

> "I note that a natural material which was the raison d'être behind the building of these houses would be replaced by an artificial product. No matter how cleverly contrived to match the original effect of Cotswold stone roofing, the social, historic and architectural integrity of the initial concept would be impaired. For this reason I consider the proposed use of concrete tiles undesirable. It would greatly detract from the reasons which led to the buildings being listed in the first place. To this must be added the resulting visual quality. It is clear to me, if only from the many examples of concrete-tiled roofs in the village, using the kind of tiles suggested, that they lack the ruggedness of form, surface colour and texture of the original work. The constructional approach is different, whether in relation to the random sizes of stone slates, requiring considerable care in the laying, or the manner of treating the roof valleys. Even allowing for the effects of weathering over the years the appearance would not match the singular qualities of the traditional roofing."

Even the extra cost of re-roofing in natural materials (£6,300 per house as opposed to £4,000 per house at 1985 prices) was not considered sufficient reason to override the inappropriateness of the proposals.

6.09 *Thatch.* As a traditional roofing material, thatch is often regarded as being particularly attractive from an aesthetic point of view and recent appeal decisions appear to support the retention of thatch for aesthetic reasons. In a

---

[13] SW/APP/F1610/E/84/800142.
[14] SE2/5356/411/2.

146

case at Daventry[15] a proposal to replace thatch with tiles was held to be unacceptable by the Secretary of State, who considered that the beauty of the group of buildings of which the appeal house formed part would be best preserved by the re-thatching of the roof. He did not accept the appellant's argument that thatch was a fire hazard provided that all normal safety precautions were taken.

In a second case, the Secretary of State supported Chichester District Council in its refusal of consent for the replacement of straw thatch with hand made clay tiles at a house in the West Burton Conservation Area.[16] The council contended that the architectural character of the listed building depended to a large extent on its thatched roof and were concerned that the re-roofing proposals also involved the loss of "eyebrow" windows, which were an attractive feature of the appeal building and which were to be replaced by ill-proportioned tiled dormers. The Secretary of State concluded that the loss of these features and the thatched roof would be seriously detrimental to the character of the listed building and dismissed the appeal.

Finally in a case at Stansfield in the Borough of St Edmunsbury[17] the Secretary of State supported the borough council's refusal of listed building consent to replace thatch with reclaimed red/brown clay plain tiles. All the arguments put forward by the appellant in respect of problems securing the services of a thatcher within a reasonable period, the length of time it takes to thatch a building, the maintenance problems associated with thatch, the expense and the insurance costs, were not considered sufficiently strong to override the importance attached to the use of thatch in the locality and it was concluded that its replacement would fundamentally affect the external appearance of the listed building and detract from its essential character.

8. TECHNOLOGICAL INNOVATION

Listed buildings are increasingly subjected to pressures for change or alterations as a result of technological innovation. Two particular examples, i.e. bank service tills and solar panels, serve to illustrate the problems of incorporating modern technology into listed buildings constructed in traditional materials.   **6.10**

9. BANK SERVICE TILLS

Bank service tills are often a source of concern to local planning authorities, not least because they need to be primarily located on the external elevation of a building if they are to serve the purpose for which they are intended. This creates potential conflict with the need to protect the character of listed buildings. An example of this concern is reflected in the decision of the London Borough of Harrow[18] to refuse LBC for a second service till at a bank, the first having been installed prior to the building having   **6.11**

---

[15] APP/12810/E/84/800127.
[16] APP/L3815/E/85/800962.
[17] APP/E3525/E/86/801302.
[18] APP/M5450/A/85/032896.

been statutorily listed. The council was concerned that the combined effect of two closely located and matching designed service tills would adversely affect the appearance and symmetry of the bank building. In dismissing the subsequent appeal, the Secretary of State accepted the argument that the proposal would disrupt the major architectural elements of the building and so diminish its visual impact and significance.

10. SOLAR PANELS

6.12   Although the installation of solar heating panels into the roof of a listed farmhouse was refused by the High Peak Borough Council,[19] the Secretary of State supported the inspector's view that as the existing roof tiles were almost as dark as the panels would be, and although they would be readily visible, they would not adversely affect the character of the listed building.

It is interesting to speculate how such a proposal might be viewed in an area of the country where the prevailing colour of the roofscape is much lighter than that found in the High Peak. Furthermore, it is evident that this particular inspector placed considerable emphasis on the colour of the solar panel, but appears to have attached less weight to the texture and form of the panels and their relationship with the traditional roof tiles.

11. WINDOWS

6.13   Judging by the number of appeal cases which have been published, the installation of new windows into listed buildings or buildings within conservation areas probably creates more conflict between owners and local planning authorities than any other single form of alteration.

Taking a balanced view of the large number of appeals which are determined, it is evident that local planning authorities are experiencing some degree of success in their efforts to control the replacement of traditional sash windows with aluminium framed or UPVC windows in listed buildings. However, such success is often recorded after the service of enforcement notices and in many instances applications are submitted in retrospect after the works have been carried out.

A typical case of the many which have been determined involved the London Borough of Haringey enforcing against the installation of new double-glazed windows in a dwelling in the Tower Gardens Conservation Area,[20] which was covered by an article 4 direction removing permitted development rights to make alterations to the appearance of the buildings.

The inspector took the view that the new aluminium framed windows were quite different from those in the rest of the terrace and because of their size and prominence were a visually disturbing feature in the street scene. In dismissing the appeal the inspector ruled that the windows should be replaced or permanently altered so as to look like the original wooden sashes, but conceded that the materials and the manner in which that could be achieved should be left to the appellant.

[19] APP/T1030/E/84/800618.
[20] T/APP/Y5420/C/85/3159/86.

The requirements of an enforcement notice upheld in respect of a Grade II **6.14** listed Georgian terrace house were far more stringent than those reported above. Bath City Council had taken enforcement action against the installation of three UPVC windows on the front elevation of the building[21]; the windows were double-glazed with mock glazing bars between the two panes. The Secretary of State was concerned that the windows seriously detracted from the character of the appeal building and the terrace of which it formed part. Furthermore, he concluded that acceptable standards of security and sound insulation could be achieved by the use of locks and internal secondary glazing. The notice required the reinstatement of vertical sliding timber sash windows each sub-divided into six panes by thin glazing bars and the appeal was dismissed.

South Hams District Council were also successful in an appeal against an enforcement notice concerning the removal of traditional vertical sliding sashes from the second floor of a listed building in Dartmouth.[22] The appellants argued that severe maintenance problems were experienced with timber windows in exposed coastal locations but these were not accepted as being incapable of solution and the Secretary of State upheld the appeal because he thought that the windows adversely affected the character of the building.

The London Borough of Southwark successfully enforced against the installation of aluminium framed double glazing in a Georgian house in the Holly Grove Conservation Area.[23] Notwithstanding the fact that the new windows were of a similar shape, style and size to the timber framed sliding sashes they replaced, the Secretary of State stated that the alterations detracted from the appearance of the appeal premises despite the effort made to replicate the original windows. He was not satisfied that it was necessary to replace the original windows with double-glazed units in the interests of health, safety or for the preservation of the building. These interests could have been safeguarded by the replacement of decayed window frames by replicas of traditional design and materials.

Notwithstanding the successes recorded by local planning authorities in **6.15** the above cases, there are instances where appeals have been allowed particularly if the area in question has already been infiltrated by modern windows. This point is very well illustrated by two cases involving Hove Borough Council. In the first case enforcement action had been taken against replacement windows (UPVC) in a principal elevation of Brunswick Terrace in Hove, a Grade I listed seafront terrace.[24] The appellants argued that the replacement windows were of greater aesthetic quality than those which they had replaced which in any event were not original. The council refuted this argument because they did not resemble the traditional timber sliding sashes found elsewhere in the building and therefore detracted from the continuity of the terrace as a whole. The Secretary of State observed that as the windows were only visible from a distance, the materials used in their construction were not readily noticeable. In allowing the appeal he acknowledged that the appeal windows were not of a type indigenous to the

---

[21] SW/APP/P0105/F/85/9.
[22] SW/APP/V1125/E/84/71–72.
[23] APP/A/5840/F/85/14.
[24] APP/F1420/F/84/121.

appeal building, but did not regard them as out of keeping when seen against the multiplicity of window types in the terrace.

In the second case, the offending replacement aluminium windows were located on the fourth floor of a listed building in Hove.[25] The council argued that they were highly visible from an adjacent square and significantly different from those prevailing in the area. The inspector's report concluded that the replacement windows had altered the overall appearance of the appeal building and had not enhanced the character of the conservation area in which the building was located; nevertheless the Secretary of State took the view that although the windows were at variance with the main fenestration in the building, they were no more harmful than those they had replaced. The appeal was allowed.

6.16   Finally the details of a case involving velux windows in the roof of a listed building in Chorley New Road, Bolton[26] serve to demonstrate the aesthetic problems of incorporating this type of modern window into such buildings, but also show the importance attached to the economic use of listed buildings by the Secretary of State.

The case involved an appeal against an enforcement notice requiring the removal of two velux windows, a section 36 appeal against the refusal of planning permission for their installation and an appeal against the refusal of listed building consent for their installation. In each case the appeals were allowed based upon the following analysis of the merits of the case:

> "The planning merits of the development the subject of the enforcement notice are relevant also to consideration of the appeals against refusal of planning permission and listed building consent. I agree with the Council's appraisal of the quality of the listed building and the character of its surroundings. The roof lights interrupt the plane of the roof and when seen from the north side of Chorley New Road they disturb the balance of the pair of former dwellings, which is comprised of the appeal premises and the neighbouring property. However, the dominant elements of the facade of the building are the red brick walling and the regularly spaced windows and doors. I consider that in this instance the slated roof is a subordinate element within which the Velux windows, by virtue of the low pitch of the roof, are not particularly conspicuous, even when open. The works of conversion which the appellants have undertaken have served to restore 51 Chorley New Road, to put the listed building to a useful purpose in the furtherance of a commercial business, and seem likely to ensure its future for a number of years to come. I am unable to determine, on the evidence which I heard, the extent to which the viability of the conversion depends upon the retention of the rooflights, but I have no doubt that they enhance the usable office space within the building and thereby contribute to the benefits which have stemmed from the appellants' enterprise. In my opinion, this consideration outweighs the small adverse impact of the rooflights upon the appearance of the listed building and the surrounding area. I find no reason to question the Council's policy to preserve the attractiveness of Chorley New Road, but in the special circumstances of this case I consider that the velux windows ought to be permitted."

[25] APP/F1420/F/85/53.
[26] APP/N4205/F/84/23, APP/N4205/N/84/012283, APP/N4205/F/84/800178.

12. DEMOLITION

Whilst the question of demolition is dealt with in much greater detail **6.17** elsewhere in this book,[27] the following examples are given to demonstrate some of the arguments which are used to secure or resist total demolition or partial demolition of buildings at appeal.

13. TOTAL DEMOLITION

It is very usual for the decision on whether to allow the total demolition **6.18** of listed buildings to hinge on the question of the economic benefits which might not otherwise arise if LBC was refused for the demolition of specific listed buildings. This is very well illustrated by a widely reported case involving proposals to demolish listed buildings in Elliot Street, Clayton Square and Deane Street in Liverpool[28] for the re-development of the site as a shopping centre. The comprehensive redevelopment proposals submitted by Wimpey Property Holdings were the subject of an inquiry to consider both the compulsory purchase order made by the city council and applications for listed building consent. The inspector felt that the merits of the proposed retail development in improving the attraction of Liverpool as a regional shopping centre and in providing a greater variety of shops were not sufficiently strong arguments to outweigh the value of the listed buildings. The Secretary of State did not agree with his inspector and considered that apart from the listed buildings issue, the development of the site in the manner proposed was satisfactory and that the scheme had both interest and merit. The completion of the scheme would bring the City Centre Plan to fruition and would attract investment to the area. He recognised that the development could not proceed without the demolition of the listed buildings and he took the view that the area would continue to decline without the revitalisation offered by the redevelopment scheme. He regretted the loss but considered that the benefits outweighed the loss of the listed buildings; he allowed the appeal and the compulsory purchase order was also confirmed.

The need carefully to balance the conflicting policies aimed at promoting **6.19** development on the one hand and preserving listed buildings on the other, was clearly recognised in an appeal decision involving retail warehouse proposals on a site at West Street, Gravesend, Kent,[29] which also included a listed building with the appeal site. The inspector's conclusions are particularly succinct on this important issue:

"I generally conclude that the presumption in favour of granting planning permission, contained in Circulars 22/80 and 14/85, ought to be weighed against the equally relevant policy content of Circulars 23/77 and 12/81[30] as regards the need to preserve both listed buildings and the settings of such buildings. In this particular instance, the merits of the

[27] See above at paras. 5.20–5.21.
[28] PNW/5091/12/17.
[29] SE2/5277/270/68.
[30] Both circulars now substantially consolidated in Circular 8/87.

otherwise broadly acceptable retail warehousing proposals subject of the first appeal would appear to be of comparatively far less importance than the retention of the listed buildings on the site and its immediate setting. There would appear to be no immediate prospect of reconciling the retention of the small group of buildings with the use of the land for development which might otherwise be held to be in broad conformity with the provisions of the emergent local plan."

The Secretary of State agreed with his inspector and dismissed the appeal.

It is also clear that proposals to secure the total demolition of listed buildings have to be supported by unequivocal evidence that no alternative uses can be found. Two cases illustrate the emphasis given by the Secretary of State on fully exploring alternatives before consent is granted.

In a case involving a proposal to demolish a row of cottages in Chertsey[31] in the area of Runnymede District Council, the appeal failed because the appellants had not produced a detailed structural survey, nor had any economic assessment of the potential of the structure been undertaken and no effort had been made to sell the premises for renovation. Not even the support of the district council and the county council's historic buildings architect were sufficient to support the appellant's contention that the buildings were not capable of repair at reasonable cost.

A similar conclusion was reached by an inspector determining an appeal against the decision of Mid Suffolk District Council to refuse listed building consent for the demolition of a thatched timber framed cottage.[32] The inspector took the view that the building was basically sound and that it was an uncommon example of its period. Although no scheme for renovation had been prepared, the inspector thought that funding would be forthcoming from the local planning authority.

14. PARTIAL DEMOLITION

6.20   The question of whether minor works to a listed building or unlisted building in a conservation area amount to partial demolition often raises many esoteric arguments. This is well illustrated in a case involving the installation of a new shop front in Bridport on an unlisted building in a conservation area.[33] West Dorset District Council claimed that listed building consent was required for its demolition or partial demolition, but not for its alteration or extension.

The Secretary of State took the view that any demolition work undertaken during the installation of the shop front was minimal and incidental to the main purpose of altering the building. He concluded that the works involved did not therefore amount to demolition or partial demolition within the meaning of the 1971 Act. He quashed the enforcement notice and allowed the appeal.

---

[31] SE2/5389/411/1.
[32] APP/W3520/E/84/800425.
[33] APP/F1230/F/85/46.

15. WORKS HIDDEN FROM VIEW

The fact that proposed alterations to a listed building are largely hidden **6.21** from view does not in itself constitute sufficient reason to guarantee the grant of listed building consent. The decisions which have emerged from local planning authorities and the Secretary of State are not consistent and appear to depend on the weight attached to the integrity of the building in question.

In a case at Chester,[34] the Secretary of State overruled the city council which had refused alterations at the rear of a restaurant occupying an eighteenth century listed building in Lower Bridge Street. The Secretary of State took the view that the works were largely hidden from view and that as they would enable the restaurant to function more efficiently, drawing on the advice embodied in Circular 23/77, they were acceptable and he allowed the appeal.

However, the decision of Edinburgh City Council to refuse consent for the erection of a rear staircase to a listed building was fully supported by the reporter.[35] He was not convinced by the fact that the development could not be seen from the public highway and considered that the quality of the appeal building was worth conserving in its own right and should therefore be altered as little as possible. The strength of this argument was reinforced by the fact that the building was in an outstanding conservation area where policies for rear staircases on listed buildings were consistently applied by the council.

[34] APP/X0605/E/84/800546.
[35] P/PPA/LA/365 (Scottish Development Department).

153

7. "Problem Buildings": Redundancy, Neglect and Disrepair

1. GENERAL SUMMARY

7.01   Listing is essentially an action through which society attempts to protect, from what it sees as unsympathetic change, that portion of the built environment which it perceives as being an important aesthetic or historic factor in the quality of life which it enjoys. However, the vast majority of buildings which are listed for this reason are also integral parts of an overall economic system upon which much of this quality of life depends, and all such buildings have, to some extent, to be capable of adaptation or role change in order to meet changing economic demands and circumstances.

In listing buildings, the Secretary of State does not concern himself with this latter factor, and consequently he has no regard to the economic consequences of his actions, notwithstanding that implicit in a listing is a restriction on the physical—and therefore in all probability the economic—adaptability of the buildings concerned.

Similarly, in the consideration of applications for LBC there have been obvious presumptions in favour of the use of aesthetic, architectural and

154

historic criteria as principal determinant factors.[1] Despite various recommendations of the Secretary of State in respect of the consideration of financial and economic implications and consequences[2] and of alternative use potential,[3] economic factors have been clearly secondary to aesthetic ones.

If to the foregoing considerations is added the fact that society expects the owners of the buildings it seeks to preserve to meet the ongoing costs of their "preservation" (public grants, though they run into millions of pounds a year, represent only a minor contribution to the overall cost of implementing conservation policies), it is inevitable that situations will arise on which buildings cease to be physically, or economically, capable of sustaining the use for which they were originally intended. They become redundant, are neglected, and fall into disrepair. They may even be neglected whilst in use. Whatever the circumstances, they become "problem buildings."

Initially it should be stated that nowhere in the listed buildings legislation is there an obligation cast on an owner or occupier to keep the building in repair. There are sanctions if a building falls into disrepair but nowhere is there a positive obligation, nor is it primarily a criminal offence to fail to repair (unless it is a breach of a specific notice or order served in accordance with the 1971 Act or the various Public Health Acts here considered).

There are no simple instantaneous remedies for problem buildings. There are, however, a number of options available to both local authorities and to building owners. The principal purpose of this Chapter is to consider their options. Additionally, consideration is given to certain options for owners of buildings which they suspect might become subject to the various statutory listing and conservation measures.

We set out the statutory provisions in detail but demonstrate in the Tables which appear at the end of this Chapter the options which are open as follows:

(1) to the DOE and to local authorities in respect of a listed building appearing to be in need of repair;

(2) to local authorities in respect of a building which is dangerous, defective, ruinous, dilapidated or unfit;

(3) to the owner of a "redundant" listed building;

(4) to the owner of a non-listed building not in a conservation area, suspecting that it is of a type likely to be listed and wishing to avoid the consequences: building not in beneficial use;

(5) the same: building in beneficial use but use change, demolition or major alteration is possible in the future; and

(6) to the owner of a non-listed building which is unlikely to be listed, but which is located in an area likely to be designated as a conservation area.

---

[1] Circular 8/87, paras. 4, 5 and 90(a) and (b).
[2] Circular 8/87, para. 90(c).
[3] Circular 8/87, paras. 19–24; Circular 22/80, para. 17.

2. COMPULSORY ACQUISITION OF LISTED BUILDINGS IN NEED OF REPAIR

(a) General

7.02   Section 114 of the 1971 Act empowers the Secretary of State, in circumstances where it appears to him that reasonable steps are not being taken properly to preserve a listed building,[4] either himself to acquire the building,[5] or authorise the council of the county, county district, or (in the case of a building situated in Greater London) the Commission or the London Borough Council, so to acquire the building. An order may not be made in respect of an excepted building (*i.e.* ecclesiastical or a scheduled monument), compulsorily to acquire the building.[6]

Additionally, the Secretary of State may either acquire, or authorise any of the above authorities to acquire, any land comprising or contiguous or adjacent to the building which appears to be required for preserving the building or its amenities, or for affording access to it, or for its proper control or management.[7] It is provided that the Secretary of State shall consult with the Commission before making or confirming a compulsory purchase order.[8]

(b) Repairs notice as preliminary to section 114 action

7.03   A repairs notice made and served under the provisions of section 115 of the Act is a pre-requisite for any compulsory acquisition under section 114. The procedures for making and serving such a notice, and for any ensuing compulsory purchase action, are described at para. 7.06 below and in Table 1.

(c) Consequences and applications of repairs notice procedure

7.04   Although the principal purpose of a repairs notice under section 115 is to facilitate the commencement of section 114 compulsory acquisition proceedings, it would however appear that such notices are capable of being used primarily for the purpose of persuading the owners of listed buildings to which they apply to effect requisite repairs—the implied consequences of non-compliance being the probability of compulsory acquisition. Any local authority can serve a repairs notice; only the Secretary of State can undertake, or authorise the undertaking of, compulsory purchase proceedings under section 114.

---

[4] Other than a building "excepted" under T.C.P.A. 1971, s.58(2) *cf.* s.114(3).
[5] T.C.P.A. 1971, s.114(2).
[6] T.C.P.A. 1971, s.114(1) and s.56(1).
[7] T.C.P.A. 1971, s.114(1).
[8] N.H.A. 1983, Sched. 4, para. 19.

It is, however, apparent that (although clearly this was not the intention of the Act) the provisions of sections 114 and 115 may be used by owners to divest themselves of buildings which have become a liability. An owner may well deliberately neglect his listed building in the hope that either the Secretary of State, or more probably the local authority, will serve a repairs notice, and on his not complying with its requirements, the Secretary of State will start, or authorise, compulsory puchase proceedings. The owner himself may be able to force the pace by serving a purchase notice on the authority which has served the repairs notice, although he cannot do this until the expiration of three months from the service of the repairs notice and is precluded if within that period the authority serving the repairs notice begins the compulsory acquisition procedure.[9]

7.05 Even the provisions of section 117 (whereby minimum compensation only may be payable in respect of a listed building deliberately left to fall into disrepair) (see para. 7.09 below) may not prompt a reluctant owner to effect requisite repairs, especially when the cost of so doing may produce a lower value than might be obtained with even minimum compensation on compulsory acquisition.

It is also significant to remember that if a repairs notice is served and compulsory acquisition is effected as a result of non-compliance, the responsibility for the subsequent repair and upkeep of the listed building (at least until, and if, it is disposed of by the acquiring authority) devolves upon the acquiring authority.

For this reason in particular the incidence of the service of repairs notices is relatively low. Moreover, although there is no statutory obligation for the serving authority (be it the Secretary of State or a local authority) to follow non-compliance with a repairs notice by compulsory acquisition, the authority risks a purchase notice being served on it by the owner. There may be a moral or face-saving obligation; in the emotive circumstances which frequently surround neglected listed buildings, the Secretary of State or a local authority would face much criticism if it "threatened" to acquire a building in order to preserve it, and then failed to do so when the owner ignored the notice. Equally difficult is the situation where a local authority compulsorily acquires a building, the subject of a repairs notice, and then re-sells. If the purchaser contracts to do the repairs and fails to do so, the authority has a problem and may need to acquire compulsorily again. A better way might be to lease and require the lessee to carry out the repairs; on doing so satisfactorily the authority will then dispose of the freehold to him.

In practice, it is unlikely that a repairs notice would be served without any prior consultation with an owner, and thus the service of such a notice must generally be regarded as a last resort when all efforts at informal persuasion have failed.

As there is nothing in the 1971 Act to the contrary, it would appear that a repairs notice may be served in respect of an unoccupied listed building, notwithstanding the probability that action under section 101 of the Act[10] may be more appropriate in such circumstances. As we have explained above at para. 3.27 the purpose of a section 101 notice is to effect urgent repairs to prevent further deterioration: tarpaulins and breeze block are the

---

[9] T.C.P.A. 1971, s.180(5).
[10] See paras. 7.10–7.13 below (Urgent repairs of unoccupied listed buildings).

consequences of a section 101 notice, rather than the longer term consequences of a section 115 notice.

(d) Repairs notice procedure

7.06   (i) A repairs notice must be served at least two months prior to the initiation of compulsory purchase proceedings in respect of a building to which section 114 applies, *i.e.* a listed building which is not an excepted building by virtue of section 58(2) of the Act.[11] The notice is to be served on the owner of the building.

(ii) The notice may be served by either the Secretary of State (this would be the procedure in the case of a notice relating to a listed building owned by a local authority; the Act does not preclude such action); by the Commission (who would be more likely to serve than the Secretary of State); by the county or district council in whose area the building is situated; in Greater London, by the Commission; by the appropriate London borough; by a planning board; or by a development corporation.

Whilst a notice under section 115 may be served by any of the above, only the Secretary of State may initiate or authorise any subsequent compulsory purchase under section 114—see para. 7.08 below.

(iii) There is no prescribed form of notice. The notice must however specify[12]:

(a) the works which the Secretary of State, the Commission or the local authority consider "reasonably necessary for the proper preservation of the building" and

(b) the effect of sections 114–117 of the Act (see below).

Two cases, though decided under section 101 (urgent repairs) may give a guide as to the required content of the notice *i.e.* the works should be specified in detail and not merely "such steps as shall be necessary . . . "[13]

The specification of works required will result from a survey or investigation of the building by the serving authority. Such a survey may be taken under powers conferred by sections 280 and 281 of the 1971 Act (rights of entry and supplementary provisions thereto, described in Chapter 11); an owner who wilfully obstructs an authorised entry shall be guilty of an offence.

(iv) The demolition of a building after the service of a repairs notice does not prevent the serving authority from being authorised compulsorily to acquire the site of the building under section 114 powers.[14]

(v) The serving authority may withdraw the notice at any time but must notify any person served with the notice that they have done

[11] T.C.P.A. 1971, s.115(1).
[12] T.C.P.A. 1971, s.115(1)(a) and (b).
[13] *R.* v. *Secretary of State for the Environment, ex p. Hampshire C.C.* [1981] J.P.L. 47; and *R.* v. *Camden L.B.C., ex p. Comyn Ching* (1984) 47 P. & C.R. 417.
[14] T.C.P.A. 1971, s.115(2).

so.[15] This of course might prompt the owner to serve a purchase notice under section 180(4).

(e) The owner's response

(i) On receipt of a repairs notice, it would appear that an owner has **7.07** four options:
- (a) to undertake (or at least commence) the works specified as necessary in the notice, within two months of receipt;
- (b) to undertake works which he considers necessary (but which do not necessarily accord with those specified in the notice);
- (c) to take no action at all and wait for compulsory purchase proceedings to be initiated;
- (d) to consider serving a purchase notice; but which he cannot do until the expiration of three months from the service of the repairs notice.

(ii) In the case of option (i)(a), such action should remove the threat of compulsory acquisition under section 114, as the Secretary of State's authority under that section can only arise "where it appears to him that reasonable steps are not being taken for properly preserving"[16] the building.

(iii) In the case of option (i)(b), which may well arise where the owner considers the works specified in the notice are more than are required for the proper preservation of the building, it would appear that an owner is at liberty to proceed with such works as he considers necessary (subject, of course, to such works not amounting to alterations or extensions requiring LBC).

An owner would be ill-advised so to proceed without first consulting the serving authority—such consultation may well produce a mutually acceptable solution, and the consequent withdrawal of the notice. However, if such a solution were not to be achieved, the owner could still proceed with repairs which he considered necessary and, if compulsory purchase proceedings were still initiated, he could, at the appropriate point therein (see para. 7.08; (iii), below) apply to a magistrates court for an order staying the proceedings, on the grounds that reasonable steps had been taken for properly preserving the building.

(iv) In the case of option (i)(c), such inaction could be expected to result, at the end of two months, in the commencement of compulsory purchase proceedings. This may well be the option chosen by an owner who wished to divest himself of responsibility for the building.

(v) If the compulsory purchase proceedings do not materialise, the owner may serve a purchase notice after waiting three months.

(vi) Again, if the compulsory purchase proceedings are abandoned, then the owner may serve a purchase notice.

---

[15] T.C.P.A. 1971, s.115(3).
[16] T.C.P.A. 1971, s.114(1).

(f) Compulsory purchase under section 114

7.08

(i) In a situation where, two months after the service of a repairs notice under section 115, it appears that reasonable steps are not being taken for properly preserving the building, and the notice has not been withdrawn, if the Secretary of State is satisfied "that it is expedient to make provision for the preservation of the building and to authorise its compulsory acquisition for that purpose."[17] he may compulsorily acquire the building, or authorise the council of the county or county district, the Commission, the London borough in which the building is situated, the planning board or development corporation, compulsorily to acquire the building.[18]

(ii) The procedure for compulsory acquisition under section 114 is that applicable by virtue of the Acquisition of Land Act 1981.

(iii) Any owner, lessee or occupier (other than a tenant for one month or less) has the right to object to the confirmation of an order made under the 1981 Act, in the manner and during the time prescribed in the notice required to be served on such persons under section 12(1) of that Act, whereupon the Secretary of State must either afford to the objector an opportunity of being heard by a person duly appointed for the purpose, or cause a public local inquiry to be held, where any other objectors have the right to be heard.[19]

(iv) Any person having an interest in the building may, under section 114(6) of the 1971 Act, "within 28 days after the service of the notice . . . apply to a magistrates' court acting for the petty sessions area within which the building is situated for an order staying further proceedings on the compulsory purchase order; and, if the court is satisfied that reasonable steps have been taken for properly preserving the building, the court shall make an order accordingly."

(v) If such an order is granted, then by implication the compulsory purchase order cannot be proceeded with, as the powers under section 114 can only be used where reasonable steps are not being taken properly to preserve the building.

(vi) If the magistrates court does not make an order (because it is not satisfied that reasonable steps are being taken) any person aggrieved by the magistrates' decision may appeal to the crown court, and that court may grant an order if it is satisfied that reasonable steps are being taken.[20]

(g) Compensation on compulsory acquisition under section 114

7.09
If the building sought to be acquired is a "normal" building to which section 117 will not apply, then the usual rules of compensation flowing from the Acquisition of Land Act 1981 will apply. However, the provisions

---

[17] T.C.P.A. 1971, s.114(4).

[18] T.C.P.A. 1971, s.114(2) and (1).

[19] *Middlesex County Council* v. *Minister of Local Government and Planning* (1953) 2 P. & C.R. 227, C.A.

[20] T.C.P.A. 1971, s.114(7).

regarding compensation on the compulsory acquisition of a listed building deliberately left derelict are set out in section 117 of the Act.

(i) If an authority[21] proposing to acquire a building under section 114(1) is satisfied that it has been deliberately allowed to fall into disrepair for the purpose of justifying its demolition and the development or re-development of the site or any site adjoining, it may include in the compulsory purchase order which it submits to the Secretary of State for confirmation a direction for minimum compensation.[22]

(ii) The Secretary of State may also include such a direction in a case where he is making a compulsory purchase order under section 114(2), and is satisfied that the building has been deliberately allowed to fall into disrepair for the purposes stated in (i) above.[23]

(iii) Notices[24] stating the effect of a compulsory purchase order including a direction under section 117 must specify that such a direction is included in the order, and explain the meaning of "direction for minimum compensation."[25] There is no prescribed form of notice.

(iv) Such a direction limits the compensation which would be otherwise payable by assessing it on the assumption that LBC would only be granted for works for the restoration of the building to a proper state of repair and for maintaining it in that state.[26]

(v) Where a direction for minimum compensation is included in a compulsory purchase order under section 114, any person having an interest in the building may within 28 days of the service of the notice of the order[27] apply to the magistrates' court for the area in which the building is situated for an order that the direction should not be included. If the court is satisfied that the building has not been deliberately allowed to fall into disrepair for the purposes mentioned in (i) above, the court shall make such an order.[28] If a person applying for such an order from the magistrates' court is aggrieved by the court's decision, there is a right of appeal to the Crown Court.[29]

3. URGENT REPAIR OF UNOCCUPIED LISTED BUILDINGS

Under section 101 of the Act, which was substituted in the 1986 Act and amended and strengthened the powers existing before April 1, 1987, local authorities are empowered to execute any works which in the opinion of the authority are urgently needed for the preservation of a listed building,[30]

7.10

---

[21] As referred to in T.C.P.A. 1971, s.114(1).
[22] T.C.P.A. 1971, s.117(1).
[23] T.C.P.A. 1971, s.117(2).
[24] Acquisition of Land Act 1981, s.12(1).
[25] T.C.P.A. 1971, s.117(3).
[26] T.C.P.A. 1971, s.117(4).
[27] See n. 24 above.
[28] T.C.P.A. 1971, s.117(5).
[29] T.C.P.A. 1971, s.117(6).
[30] T.C.P.A. 1971, s.101(1) as substituted by H.P.A. 1986, Sched. 9.

other than an excepted building.[31] In London the Commission has concurrent powers with the London boroughs.[32]

The procedures leading to, and for the undertaking of, action under section 101 are illustrated in Table 1. It should be noted that the Secretary of State also has the power to take such action,[33] and has power to authorise the Commission so to do, although he has indicated that he will authorise the Commission only where the building is of exceptional interest.[34] It is believed that the Secretary of State first used his power to serve a section 101 notice in respect of Barlaston Hall, Staffordshire[35]; and in December 1987 the Commission was authorised for the first time to serve a notice and carry out repairs, at Revesby Abbey, a neglected Grade I listed Victorian mansion near Boston, Lincolnshire.[35a]

The Secretary of State may also direct that section 101 should apply to an unlisted building in a conservation area if he is satisfied that the preservation of the building is important to the character or appearance of the area.[36] Local planning authorities or members of the public may ask the Secretary of State to make such a direction.[37]

The works may consist of or include works for affording temporary support or shelter for the building. These expenses thus may be of a continuing nature.

If the building is occupied works may be carried out only to those parts which are not in use. This is a new provision in the section and will obviate the problem which previously existed under the old section—what was occupation? The words "in use" have a clearer perception in rating law and interpretation will no doubt be drawn from them.

The owner must be given at least seven days notice in writing of the intention to carry out the works and the notice must contain a description of the works.

The costs of carrying out the works may be recovered from the owner[38] and the owner may appeal against a notice requiring payment of the cost of works, on three grounds:

(a) that some or all of the works were unnecessary for the preservation of the building,

(b) in the case of works for affording temporary support of shelter, that the temporary arrangements have continued for an unreasonable length of time, or

(c) that the amount specified in the notice is unreasonable or that the recovery of it would cause him hardship.[39]

Ground (c) may well be of relevance in a period of economic constraint. Whilst undoubtedly intended to provide for cases where some helpless individual owning a crumbling Georgian mansion simply could not afford to

---

[31] T.C.P.A. 1971, s.101(3), referring to s.58(2).
[32] Circular 8/87, para. 127.
[33] T.C.P.A. 1971, s.101(5).
[34] Circular 8/87, para. 126.
[35] J.P.L. [August 1982].
[35a] Reported in *Planning* January 8, 1988.
[36] T.C.P.A. 1971, s.101(2).
[37] Circular 8/87, para. 125.
[38] T.C.P.A. 1971, s.101A(1)–(3).
[39] T.C.P.A. 1971, s.101A(4).

effect repairs even if willing to do so, it may well be much more relevant to the firm owning two large factories, and having to choose between expensive repairs to one which was listed and redundant, and capital investment in another that was not listed and in full production. The Secretary of State is the final arbiter in such matters.[40]

In respect of works and the costs thereof, Circular 8/87 gives local authorities some indication of the considerations to which the Secretary of State would have regard in the event of an owner making representations: **7.11**

"(i) Any work done on a building under section 101 should be the minimum required for its preservation and be carried out at a reasonable cost: expensive permanent repairs should not be carried out under these powers. It is considered that only emergency repairs, for example to keep a building wind and weatherproof or to prevent damage by vandals, which should not involve an owner in great expense would be appropriate. Inexpensive repairs done in time often arrest the deterioration of a building.

(ii) The financial circumstances of the owner should be taken into account at the outset and any sums authorities wish to recover from him should not be unreasonable in relation to his means.

(iii) Special care is needed when dealing with large buildings, especially those owned by charities. Even limited repairs to a large building are likely to prove expensive and may be beyond the owner's means. Since local authorities have already been asked not to involve owners in great expense under section 101, this is particularly important where a large building like a church is empty and in need of repair.

(iv) Churches need special care, not only because they are usually large and the available resources limited, but because of the problems of redundant churches. In the case of a Church of England church, the Pastoral Measure puts an obligation on the diocesan authorities to keep the building in good repair during the waiting period between a declaration of redundancy and the drafting of a redundancy scheme. If an authority contemplate action under section 101, they are advised to first discuss the condition of the building with the diocesan authorities to see if the problems can be resolved.[41]"

In one of the few decisions on this section there are some interesting comments on how the Secretary of State interprets what is now section 101A. This was a case for determination by the Secretary of State for the Environment following representations under the then section 101(7)(a), (b) and (c) of the 1971 Act against a notice served under section 101(6) of that Act by the Hampshire County Council seeking reimbursement of the sum of £1,356 expended by that council in executing works urgently necessary for the preservation of the listed building at 29/31 Bell Street, Romsey, Hants.[42] The Secretary of State said: **7.12**

"The Secretary of State is anxious that local planning authorities should use the powers given to them by section 101 in cases where prompt and effective action can save the building from further deterio-

---

[40] T.C.P.A. 1971, s.101A(4) and (5).
[41] Circular 8/87, para. 129.
[42] [1978] J.P.L. 637 SE2/5240/480/2 May 10, 1978.

ration. In the opinion of the Secretary of State a notice under section 101 should describe in as much detail as possible the work which the authority consider is urgently necessary so that the owner knows what he has to do to comply with its terms or is forewarned of the work which will be done by the council if he fails to do it himself. Such a notice also gives the owner the opportunity to discuss other possible solutions which will achieve the same effect with the council or to dispute that at the time the works are not urgently necessary. It is also important that the works specified should be capable of being completed so that one account for their total cost can be sent to the owner and he is not involved in a continuing liability.[42a] For the powers of section 101 to be properly exercised, the work must be urgently necessary at the time the notice is served and it is not considered that the fact that one notice has been served specifying certain work to be done, enables an authority to recover cost of works done to the building which are in addition to those covered by the notice unless a further notice under section 101(4) is served describing the additional work subsequently considered necessary.

It has been considered whether or not the amount referred to by the county council should be recoverable from the owner but it has been concluded that recovery would not be justified and would cause the owner hardship because, at the time of the service of the original notice, there was a conflict of view as to the necessity for the preservation of the building between the district council, the local authority primarily responsible for the control of the demolition of listed buildings, and the county council.

While it is legitimate to take section 101 action while the future of a building is under discussion so that the question of demolition is not decided by its collapse in the meantime, it is, in the Secretary of State's opinion, unreasonable to carry out work of the type undertaken by the council when it has already been indicated that the building may be demolished when a satisfactory scheme of redevelopment has been approved. The Secretary of State therefore serves no notice for the recovery of costs in this case."

7.13 Hampshire County Council applied to the High Court for an order of certiorari, but the application was dismissed by the court on June 25, 1980. There were a number of grounds, but two comments from the judgment of Donaldson L.J. (as he then was) are particularly important:

"We considered the decision letter to be slightly inaccurate in referring to the owner wishing to carry out the works herself and to 'comply with its terms.' It is inaccurate in that the notice does not call upon the owner to do any work. The intention of the seven days notice is to enable the owner to discuss the nature of the works and to be aware of what the county council propose doing. It does therefore serve a purpose. The Secretary of State is right in saying that it is important to go into some detail in describing the works contemplated. It must however be borne in mind that this is an emergency procedure and hence not to be compared with section 115 of the Act. It would have been enough if the estimate had been included with the notice. But the

---

[42a] But see now the provisions of s.101 (as amended): para. 7.10 above.

notice did not give a clue and the owner was entitled to some notice of
the works contemplated . . .

.   We decline to define 'hardship.' It clearly covers the personal circumstances of the owner and it is submitted by the county council that it
could include a great disparity between the cost of the works and the
resultant value of the building."[43]

4. LOCAL AUTHORITY OPTIONS IN RESPECT OF "DANGEROUS" LISTED BUILDINGS

(a) General powers relating to all buildings (other than buildings in London)

The Building Act 1984 makes certain provisions in respect of buildings or   **7.14**
structures, or parts of such, which appear to local authorities to be in such a
state of repair or are being used to carry such loads, as to be dangerous. Leaving aside for the present the difficult issue of what constitutes a "dangerous
building" (see para. 7.17 below) the relevant powers are as follows:

(i)   Where the authority considers the danger to be such as to warrant
immediate action for its removal, it may take such steps as are
necessary to remove the danger by virtue of section 78(1) of the
1984 Act. This power is qualified by requirements for the giving of
notice of proposed action under the section to owners and occupiers,[44] power of recovery of the expenses of such action from
owners,[45] and a number of provisions regarding any subsequent
court proceedings for the recovery of such expenses.[46]

(ii) Where an authority considers the danger to be less than such as to
require urgent action, application may be made by the authority to
a magistrates' court under the provisions of section 77 of the 1984
Act,[47] for an order requiring the owner:

(a) where danger arises from the condition of the building, to
execute any works necessary to obviate the danger, or, if the
owner elects, to demolish the building or any dangerous parts
of it, and remove the resultant rubbish, or

(b) where danger arises from overloading, to restrict the use of the
building until works (in respect of the danger thus created)
have been executed to the satisfaction of the court, and the
order has been withdrawn or modified.[48]

Failure to comply with an order under section 77 within the time specified
in the order (the Act does not stipulate any particular period to be stated in
an order) may result in the local authority executing the works. In such cir-

[43] See [1980] J.P.L. 731.
[44] B.A. 1984, s.78(2).
[45] B.A. 1984, s.78(3) and (4).
[46] B.A. 1984, s.78(5), (6) and (7).
[47] This section is now to be read in conjunction with T.C.P.A. 1971, s.56c: see para.
7.19 below.
[48] B.A. 1984, s.77(1), and see para. 7.19 below.

cumstances the authority have power to recover expenses reasonably incurred from the owner, who may also be liable to a fine for non-compliance not exceeding £50.

(b) General powers relating to all buildings in London

7.15   Similar powers to those described in para. 7.14 above, are provided in respect of buildings in London by sections 61 to 67 of the London Building Acts (Amendment) Act 1939.[49] The powers are exercisable as appropriate by the councils of the London boroughs, or the common council of the City.[50]

(c) Powers of entry for investigating dangerous buildings

7.16   (i) Outside London, sections 95 and 96 of the Building Act 1984 provide a range of powers of entry for purposes under that Act (in this respect, section 77, described at para. 7.14; (ii) above). Sections 95 and 96 do not, however, extend to entry pursuant to powers under section 78 of the 1984 Act (para. 7.14; (i) above). Although it is implicit in section 78 that entry may be effected for the purpose of carrying out works considered necessary by the authority, there does not appear to be any provision in the 1984 Act in respect of entry necessary for ascertaining whether or not the building is dangerous in the first place.

(ii) Within London, section 139 of the London Building Acts (Amendment) Act 1939, as extended by section 9, London County Council (General Powers) Act 1955, provides a range of powers of entry of authorised persons in respect, *inter alia*, of the powers referred to in para. 7.15 above.

(d) Definition of a dangerous building

7.17   Neither the Acts referred to, nor, so far as can be ascertained, do any other Acts, provide a statutory definition of what constitutes a dangerous building. Whilst logic might suggest that any building, or part of any building, which is likely to collapse on either its occupants or on passers by, might be considered dangerous, who is to pronounce upon the scale, or the urgency, of the (alleged) danger? It is true that structural engineers have sophisticated techniques for measuring movement in buildings, and these might be used as a test, as might tests and calculations of floor loadings. One might possi-

---

[49] London Building Acts (Amendment) Act 1939, s.61 (information and survey of dangerous structures); s.62 (certification of dangerous structures); s.63 (arbitration in respect of s.62 certification); s.64 (enforcement proceedings); s.65 (Court orders notwithstanding arbitration); s.66 (expenses of authorities); s.67 (power to remove inmates of dangerous structures).

[50] London County Council (General Powers) Act 1958, s.15(1).

bly disagree with Allan's suggestion that the "assessment of the structural safety of a building is a subjective affair."[51] Reported case law on the subject is sparse and not, apparently, wholly conclusive. In *London County Council v. Herring*[52] it was held[53] that a structure need not be dangerous to the public in order to be considered to be in a dangerous state; in *London County Council v. Jones*[54] a reasonable apprehension of danger was sufficient for such a view to be taken.[55]

(e) Dangerous listed buildings

Whilst the law regarding the options of local authorities in respect of **7.18** dangerous buildings in general is reasonably clear (notwithstanding the absence of any precise criteria for the determination of what constitutes "danger") distinct problems are created when consideration has to be given by a local authority to the possibility of using these powers in respect of a dangerous listed building.

The principal problem arises where an authority consider a listed building to be so dangerous as to warrant its immediate removal. The appropriate power, under circumstances in which a listed building was not involved, would be section 78 of the Building Act 1984 (see para. 7.14; (i) above). However, section 83 of the Public Health Act 1961 prohibits the use of any power under the Act where it would be "unlawful under the law relating to ancient monuments or to town and country planning."

Under section 55 of the Town and Country Planning Act 1971 it is unlawful to demolish (or alter), with certain exceptions,[56] any listed building without such demolition (or alteration) being "authorised" by the grant of LBC. The procedures for obtaining such consent are described in Chapter 5, and it may be seen from that description that it may take between four and eleven weeks (or possibly more) to obtain such consent and be in a position to commence demolition works.[57] Thus an argument that action under section 78 of the 1984 Act is "urgently necessary" may be negated by a local authority having first to obtain LBC in order to avoid conflict with section 83 of the 1961 Act.[58]

---

[51] Allan, G.E., *Conservation of Buildings of Merit* [1977] J.P.L. 569.

[52] [1894] 2 Q.B. 522.

[53] Noted at *Halsbury's Statutes* (3rd. ed.), Vol. 20, p. 186, in respect of definition of dangerous structure in London Building Acts (Amendment) Act 1939, s.61.

[54] [1912] 2 K.B. 504.

[55] See n. 53, above.

[56] T.C.P.A. 1971, s.56.

[57] An application for LBC must be advertised for 21 days before a decision as to its determination is taken by the local planning authority. The authority must then convey their recommendation and certain other papers to the Secretary of State, and may not decide the application until either 28 days have expired, or the Secretary of State has indicated that he does not wish to "call in" the application. Once such conditions have been fulfilled, and consent has been granted up to 28 days notice has to be given to the Royal Commission on Historical Monuments before demolition can commence—see paras. 5.01–5.03 above.

[58] For an extreme example of a protracted application for consent to demolish, see the Upper House Barns, Brecon case noted above at para. 2.52.

Section 55(6) of the 1971 Act[59] does provide that

"In proceedings for an offence under this section it shall be a defence to prove the following matters—

(a) that works to the building were urgently necessary in the interests of safety or health or for the preservation of the building,

(b) that it was not practicable to secure safety or health or, as the case may be, the preservation of the building by works of repair or works for affording temporary support or shelter,

(c) that the works carried out were limited to the minimum measures immediately necessary, and

(d) that notice in writing justifying in detail the carrying out of the works was given to the local planning authority as soon as reasonably practicable."

This provision might appear to give a local authority wishing to pursue its powers under the Public Health and Building Acts a defence in any prosecution under the Planning Act, arising from its having demolished a listed building without consent. However, this is only a defence; it does not alter the fact that an offence would have been committed by the authority, and as section 83 of the Public Health Act 1961 prohibits the use of any power which would be unlawful under planning law, it can only be taken that action by a local authority under section 77 of the 1984 Act, without LBC, would in any event be *ultra vires*. There would also be an additional problem for any authority taking such action and being prosecuted under section 55 as a result: with the building removed, and with it, the physical evidence of the danger which gave rise to its removal, the authority could have difficulty in substantiating a defence of urgent necessity.

7.19   Where the dangerous condition of a listed building is considered by a local authority to be less than warranting urgent action by it under the 1984 Act, action under section 77 may be appropriate. Such action may, however, cause problems for owners, as well as for the authority seeking the relevant order from the magistrates' court. To overcome this difficulty, the Housing and Planning Act 1986 has added section 56C to the 1971 Act, whereby a LPA must consider whether they should exercise their powers under sections 101, 114 and 115 before taking any steps with a view to making a dangerous structures order, and a new subsection to sections 77 and 79 of the Building Act 1984, to provide that these sections have effect subject to the relevant provisions of the 1971 Act.[60-61] This makes it plain that works specified in a dangerous structure order require listed building consent.

Paragraph 107 of Circular 8/87 suggests that authorities taking action under these dangerous structure provisions should remind owners of the need to obtain LBC or give notice under section 55(6)(d). Would the owner have any defence if he merely gave notice to the local planning authority of intent to demolish (because of urgent need) and then proceeded to do so? As the action giving rise to the order under section 77 of the 1984 Act would have been based on the local authority's implied contention that the condition of the building was less serious than to warrant urgent action, could the defence of urgent necessity indicated in section 55(6) of the 1971 Act be used in any subsequent proceedings? Logically if the section 77 procedure is

---

[59] As amended by H.P.A. 1986, Sched. 9.
[60-61] H.P.A. 1986, Sched. 9.

used, the case is unlikely to fall within the defence offered in section 55(6). But it may not be quite so clear cut as the words "urgently necessary" seem to imply a subjective judgment which might make the subsection applicable if the owner thought the demolition was urgently necessary.

With such doubt existing, the owner's only option in such circumstances would be to elect to demolish the building after obtaining LBC. Clearly the court would have to have regard to the probable time needed to obtain such consent in stating the period for compliance, but that is an issue which would be readily resolvable. More difficult to resolve would be the issue of the owner's position if he were to be refused LBC for demolition, or more particularly that of the local authority which, if the owner failed to comply with the order (because of refusal of consent), has the sanction under section 77 of the 1984 Act of executing the order themselves and recovering from the owner the costs of so doing.

(f) Dangerous listed buildings in London

The issues raised in paras. 7.18–7.19 above apply substantially to action **7.20** taken by local authorities in London under the powers described in para. 7.15 above save that the provisions of section 83 of the Public Health Act 1961 do not apply to London. The provision in section 83 prohibits the use of any power under the Act where it would be "unlawful under the law relating to . . . town and country planning." Therefore, whilst demolition pursuant to an order under the London Building Acts (Amendment) Act 1939 might constitute an offence if LBC had not first been obtained, it would not be *ultra vires* if the action were taken by a London borough council or the common council of the City.

5. LOCAL AUTHORITY OPTIONS IN RESPECT OF "DEFECTIVE" PREMISES

(a) Defective premises in general

Section 76(1) of the Building Act 1984 provides that where it appears to a **7.21** local authority that any premises are in such a state (in the section referred to as a "defective state") as to be prejudicial to health, or a nuisance[62-63] and unreasonable delay in remedying the situation would be occasioned by taking action under sections 93–95 of the Public Health Act 1936 (in respect of statutory nuisances as defined in section 92 of that Act) the local authority may serve on any person upon whom it would have served an abatement

---

[62-63] Nuisance: see *Halsbury's Laws* (4th ed.), Vol. 34, para. 337. The definitions of public nuisance and private nuisance in respect of buildings revolve very much around the extent to which a building is in a ruinous condition and the extent to which it is considered to represent a danger (to third parties). As noted at para. 7.17 above there is no precise definition of "danger" in respect of buildings..

notice under section 93, a notice stating that the authority itself intends to remedy the "defective state" of the premises, and specifying the defects which it intends to remedy.

Nine days after the service of a notice under section 76(1) the local authority may take the action specified in their notice, unless within seven days of the service the person on whom the notice was served serves a counter-notice stating that he intends to remedy the defects specified in the notice. In such a case the local authority can take no action in respect of their notice unless the person serving the counter-notice fails to execute the works within a reasonable time, or fails to make progress to the satisfaction of the local authority.[64]

Section 76 makes provisions for the recovery of expenses of action under the section by the local authority and provides for matters to be considered by the court in such action for recovery of expenses.[65] Section 76 powers are also applicable in Greater London by virtue of the Greater London (General Powers) Act 1967, s.25.

(b) Defective listed premises

7.22   It would appear that the application of section 76 to listed buildings throws up problems not dissimilar to those produced by the application of section 78 powers, discussed at paras. 7.18–7.19 above. Section 76(6) states that a notice may not be served, or works proceeded with, by an authority if the works would contravene a building preservation order under section 29 of the Town and Country Planning Act 1947. Section 29 of the 1947 Act was replaced by section 30 of the Town and Country Planning Act 1962, and this itself was repealed and not replaced in the Town and Country Planning Act 1968. In consequence building preservation orders no longer exist; section 76(6) of the Public Health Act 1961 however has not subsequently been amended or repealed to recognise the fact.

Allan[66] suggests that "since all buildings subject to such orders are now listed buildings or deemed to be listed, the prohibition" (in what is now section 76(6)) "cannot apply and the subsection must be regarded as repealed by implication."

It would, however, seem that a different interpretation is possible. Section 40(10) of the Town and Country Planning Act 1968 provides that all buildings which were subject to building preservation orders immediately before the commencement of that part of the Act would be deemed to be listed, and this provision is repeated in section 54(10) of the 1971 Act.[67] As building preservation orders have been replaced by deemed listing, a problem arises in connection with section 76(6) which would appear still to apply in respect of notices and works under section 76. This might result in there being contravention of a deemed listing, and the powers and restrictions applied thereto by sections 54 and 55 of the 1971 Act.

If this latter supposition is correct (and there are no cases reported to indicate the contrary), then action by a local authority under section 76 in

---

[64] B.A. 1984, s.76(3).
[65] B.A. 1984, s.76(4) and (5).
[66] Allan, G. E., *Conservation of Buildings of Merit* [1977] J.P.L. 569.
[67] para. 2.38 above.

respect of a listed building may well be an offence under the 1971 Act, if LBC is not obtained first; and *ultra vires* by virtue of section 83 of the Public Health Act 1961 (considered at paras. 7.18–7.19 above).

6. LOCAL AUTHORITY OPTIONS IN RESPECT OF "RUINOUS AND DILAPIDATED" BUILDINGS

(a) Ruinous buildings in general

7.23 Section 79(1) of the Building Act 1984 provides that if a local authority considers a building to be seriously detrimental to the amenities of the neighbourhood because of its ruinous or dilapidated condition, it may serve notice on the owner requiring him either to undertake such works of repair or restoration as they consider necessary in the interests of amenity, or to demolish the building and remove resultant rubbish in order to achieve this aim.

This section does not apply to inner London, which is covered by the provisions of the London Government Act 1963.[68]

(b) Ruinous listed buildings

7.24 So far as a local authority is concerned, because their action under this section is only to require an owner to take action, it would appear that when the action concerns a listed building the authority is not prohibited from acting because of section 83 of the 1961 Act (paras. 7.18–7.19 above). It would, however, seem to be fair that an authority serving a notice under section 79 of the 1984 Act in respect of a listed building should make the person served with the notice aware of the possible need to obtain LBC before carrying out any works required by the authority.

7. LOCAL AUTHORITY POWERS UNDER THE HOUSING ACTS

7.25 In common with all other buildings which are houses or dwellings, listed residential buildings may be subject to powers of local authorities under the Housing Act 1985, where such premises are considered to be either unfit, or require substantial repairs (capable of implementation at reasonable expense).[69] In housing action areas or general improvement areas,[70] authorities may serve improvement notices on the owners of dwellings not having standard amenities and considered capable of improvement at reasonable expense.[71]

---

[68] s.40(1) and Sched. 2, Pt. I, para. 36.
[69] H.A. 1985, ss.189, 190.
[70] H.A. 1985, Pt. VIII.
[71] H.A. 1985, Pt. VII.

Alongside these powers, local authorities have certain powers and duties to make grants under the Acts to facilitate such works as are necessary. These grants are considered in Chapter 10.

8. "PROBLEM BUILDINGS"—OWNER'S OPTIONS

7.26   This concluding section on options and remedies for problem buildings consists of a series of Tables and accompanying notes. Their purpose is to provide owners of listed (or possibly listable) buildings and their professional advisers, with an "instant" basic appraisal of various possible courses of action depending on particular circumstances, and of the implications of the principal stages of options indicated.

Where appropriate, the notes to each Table cross-reference to specific chapters, from which additional information may be obtained on the matter referred to. Some cross-references are also included in the Tables themselves.

Attention is in particular drawn to the provisions of Table 5 in respect of "immunity certificates" under section 54A of the 1971 Act. Owners considering this course of action should have special regard to the implications of the immunity certificate provisions. The matter is dealt with at paras. 2.49–2.50 above.

We conclude with Tables 4 and 5 which deal with the situation of the owner of a non-listed building not in a conservation area, who suspects that it is of a type likely to be listed and wishing to avoid the consequences. Table 6 which follows deals with the situation of a non-listed building in an area likely to be designated as a conservation area.

9. TABLES

7.27   1. Options open to the DOE and to local authorities in respect of a listed building appearing to be in need of repair.

2. Options open to local authorities in respect of a building which is dangerous, defective, ruinous, dilapidated or unfit.

3. Options open to owners of "redundant" listed buildings.

4. Options open to the owner of a non-listed building not in a conservation area, suspecting that it is of a type likely to be listed and wishing to avoid the consequences; building not in beneficial use.

5. Options open to the owner of a non-listed building not in a conservation area, suspecting that it is of a type likely to be listed and wishing to avoid the consequences; building in beneficial use but use change/demolition/major alteration possible in future.

6. Options open to the owner of a non-listed building which is unlikely to be listed but which is located in an area likely to be designated as a conservation area.

172

TABLE 1

Options open to the DOE and to local authorities in respect of a
listed building appearing to be in need of repair (1)

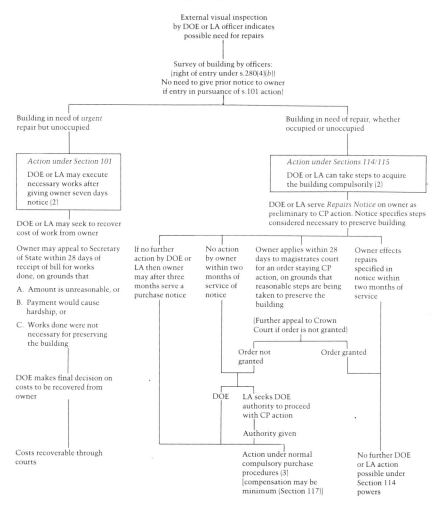

External visual inspection
by DOE or LA officer indicates
possible need for repairs

Survey of building by officers:
(right of entry under s.280(4)(b))
No need to give prior notice to owner
if entry in pursuance of s.101 action)

Building in need of *urgent*
repair but unoccupied

Building in need of repair, whether
occupied or unoccupied

Action under Section 101

DOE or LA may execute
necessary works after
giving owner seven days
notice (2)

Action under Sections 114/115

DOE or LA can take steps to acquire
the building compulsorily (2)

DOE or LA may seek to recover
cost of work from owner

DOE or LA serve *Repairs Notice* on owner as
preliminary to CP action. Notice specifies steps
considered necessary to preserve building

Owner may appeal to Secretary
of State within 28 days of
receipt of bill for works
done, on grounds that

A. Amount is unreasonable, or

B. Payment would cause
hardship, or

C. Works done were not
necessary for preserving
the building

If no further
action by DOE or
LA then owner
may after three
months serve a
purchase notice

No action
by owner
within two
months of
service of
notice

Owner applies within 28
days to magistrates court
for an order staying CP
action, on grounds that
reasonable steps are being
taken to preserve the
building

Owner effects
repairs
specified in
notice within
two months of
service

(Further appeal to Crown
Court if order is not granted)

Order not
granted

Order granted

DOE makes final decision on
costs to be recovered from
owner

DOE   LA seeks DOE
authority to proceed
with CP action

Authority given

Costs recoverable through
courts

Action under normal
compulsory purchase
procedures (3)
[compensation may be
minimum (Section 117)]

No further DOE
or LA action
possible under
Section 114
powers

(1) Other than listed buildings "excepted" under s.58(2), T.C.P.A. 1971.

(2) This and subsequent action under the powers referred to is taken by the authority
initiating the action. Normally such actions are undertaken by the district planning authority.

(3) If acquiring authority is satisfied that building has been deliberately allowed to
fall into disrepair, owner may appeal to courts challenging any "direction for
minimum compensation" under s.117.

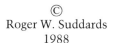

©
Roger W. Suddards
1988

TABLE 2

Options open to local authorities in respect of a building which is dangerous, defective, ruinous, dilapidated or unfit

Condition of building	Appropriate LA power	Possible problem if listed building (1)	Chapter section
Dangerous: urgent action needed (all building types)	Outside London: Public Health Act 1984, s.78(1)	PH Act 1961, s.83 and T.C.P.A. 1971, ss.54/55 may conflict. LA and owner affected	para. 7.14; (i) and para. 7.18
	London: London Building Acts (Amdt.) Act 1939	Apparently none	para. 7.15 and para. 7.20
Dangerous, but urgent action not needed (all building types)	Outside London: Building Act 1984, s.77 but see s.56C T.C.P.A. 1971	Poss. conflict as above. LBC may be needed for works. Owner affected	para. 7.14; (ii) and para. 7.19
	London: London Building Acts (Amdt.) Act 1939	Apparently none	para. 7.15 and para. 7.20
Defective (so as to be prejudicial to health, or a nuisance); and "urgent" (all building types)	All areas incl. London: Building Act 1984, s.76. (Defective Premises Notices)	LBC may be needed for works— interpretation of s.76(6) important	paras. 7.21–7.22
Defective (so as to be prejudicial to health, or a nuisance) but not urgent (all building types)	All areas inc. London. Public Health Act 1936, ss.93–95 (Abatement Notices)	LBC may be needed for works	paras. 7.21–7.22
Ruinous or dilapidated; and detrimental to amenity (all building types)	All areas other than at note (2): Building Act 1984, s.79 but see s.56C T.C.P.A. 1971	LBC may be needed for works—owner affected	paras. 7.23–7.24
	Areas as note (2): Powers as note (3)	As above	As above
Unfit or defective (dwellings only)	All areas: Housing Acts 1957 and 1974	LBC may be needed for certain works	para. 7.25

(1) or unlisted building in conservation areas.
(2) Inner London Boroughs, the City, and the Temples.
(3) London Government Act 1963, Sched. 11, Pt. II, para. 9.

©
Roger W. Suddards
1988

TABLE 3

Options open to owners of "redundant" listed buildings

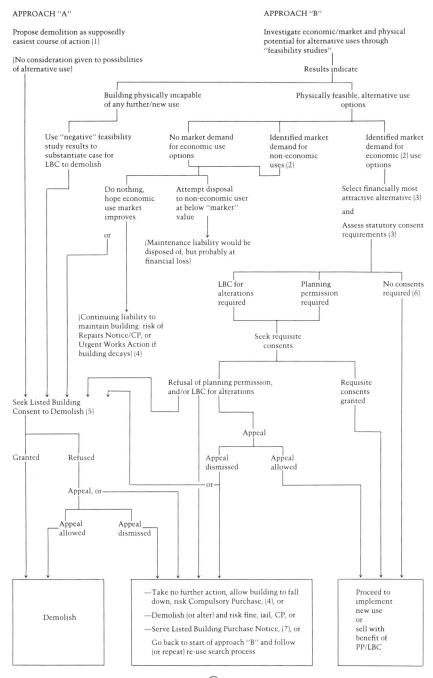

Roger W. Suddards
1988

(1) Approach "A" may appear to be the easiest, quickest and cheapest. However, evidence of DOE and local authority policy on demolition of listed buildings indicates that the only route to LBC for demolition is by way of proving that all alternative use possibilities have been fully explored, and that the results are negative. Thus Approach "B" is effectively the only practical approach. See also Chapter 4.

(2) "Economic" uses in this context are those in which the user pays either market value for the freehold, or a rent which properly reflects the owner's investment in the property. "Non-economic" uses are those in which the user, whilst requiring the type of floorspace available, cannot afford to pay a market price or rent, *e.g.* charities.

(3) Relevant inputs will be produced in the feasibility studies.

(4) Repairs Notice: Town and Country Planning Act 1971, s.115. Urgent Works Action: Town and Country Planning Act 1971, s.101. See para. 7.01, and Table 1.

(5) LBC procedure: see paras. 5.04–5.06 above.

(6) Situations may arise in which the introduction of a new use involves neither physical alterations requiring LBC, nor any change of use class, or any other works giving rise to the need for planning permission. It should however be noted that Building Regulations approval may be required.

(7) Listed building purchase notice: Town and Country Planning Act 1971, s.190. See paras. 5.18–5.19 above.

TABLE 4

Options open to the owner of a non listed building not in a conservation area, suspecting that it is of a type likely to be listed and wishing to avoid the consequences; building not in beneficial use

OPTION ONE : Undertake "alternative use feasibility study". If result positive, obtain necessary planning permission and then dispose of the building (Table 3 above)

OPTION TWO : Resolve to demolish the building

No listed building consent needed, *but*

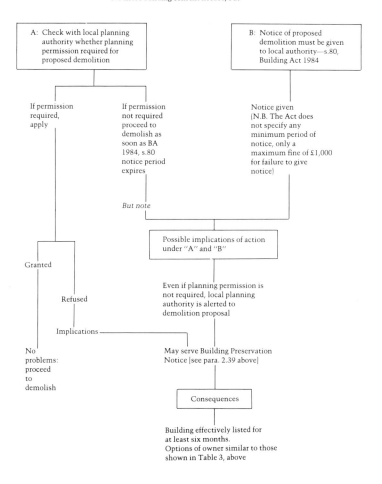

©
Roger W. Suddards
1988

TABLE 5

Options open to the owner of a non listed building not in a conservation area, suspecting that it is of a type likely to be listed and wishing to avoid the consequences; building in beneficial use but use change/demolition/major alteration possible in future

OPTION ONE : Do nothing and hope that if building is listed, listing will not adversely affect future use potential/proposals

OPTION TWO : Apply for planning permission for a wholly innocuous alteration, which the planning authority will have no reason to refuse. (No need for any *intent* to implement proposal. Planning application is solely to enable action for the next step)

Apply to the Secretary of State for a certificate under s.54(A) of the 1971 Act confirming that the building will *not* be listed for at least five years

Certificate not granted

Certificate granted

Take steps as suggested in Table 4 *before* implied probability of listing becomes a reality

or

Do nothng and hope as in option One above

Building is "safe" from listing or Building Preservation Notice for at least five years

But note:

It is entirely possible that before the Secretary of State responds to the s.54(A) certificate application (and the Act does not specify any response period) the local planning authority may still, on the basis of the planning application, conclude that *in their opinion* the building is of "architectural or historic interest . . . and . . . in danger of demolition or (adverse) alteration," and serve a s.58 Building Preservation Notice *before* the SoS issues a s.54(A) certificate

The Building Preservation Notice will be valid until the SoS notifies the local planning authority (under s.58(3)) of no intention to list. Until such action the building would effectively be listed (see paras. 2.49–2.50 above).

©
Roger W. Suddards
1988

TABLE 6

Options open to an owner of a non listed building which is unlikely to be listed but which is located in an area likely to be designated as a conservation area

POSSIBILITIES RELATIVE TO FUTURE OF BUILDING	IMPLICATIONS OF CONSERVATION AREA DESIGNATION
Change of use probable	(i) No implications if change of use does not affect character of area adversely
	(ii) Possible difficulties in obtaining planning permission if new use is "bad neighbour" (T.C.P.A. 1971, s.26) *or* affects character of area adversely (*e.g.* by creating increased traffic)
Major alterations likely to be required	(i) No implications if alterations are sympathetic to character or appearance of the area of special architectural or historic merit, but wise to obtain planning permission before designation
	(ii) Planning permission problems likely for "non sympathetic" alterations. Therefore seek planning permission prior to designation, or adapt proposals to gain approval
Major extensions	Implications as for major alterations
Major alterations involving demolition of significant parts of the building	Conservation area consent will be required for demolition aspects of proposals
	[See Chapters 4 (Criteria for consent to demolish) and 5 (Mechanics of consent)]

Roger W. Suddards
1988

179

8. Ancient Monuments

1. GENERAL SUMMARY

8.01   The law relating to ancient monuments has had a welcome clarification in the Ancient Monuments and Archaeological Areas Act 1979 (in *this* chapter referred to as "the Act"), all the provisions of which, relating to ancient monuments, are now in force. The Act relates to England and Wales and (with appropriate modifications) to Scotland. Although the Act provides an almost complete code in relation to ancient monuments, it still carries forward some of the provisions of the earlier legislation. It may therefore be useful to recapitulate on the progress of legislation relating to ancient monuments, which in fact pre-dates the legislation as to listed buildings by some 60 years or so.

The parliamentary campaign for the protection and preservation of the nation's ancient monuments began in the 1870s and was led by Sir John Lubbock, who was a Member of Parliament for Maidstone, a Trustee of the British Museum and a keen antiquarian. He steered on to the statute book the Ancient Monuments Acts of 1882 and 1900, though not without some difficulties—in the House of Lords, despite the pleas for "modest protection," Lord Francis Hervey asked why we should retain anything from our barbarous past. He refused to recognise our ancestors, who "stained themselves blue, ran about naked and practised absurd, perhaps obscene, rites under the mistletoe." The latter Act contained a schedule of ancient monuments. A Royal Commission reported in 1908, there was a further Act in 1910, and finally, the Ancient Monuments Consolidation and Amendment Act 1913 was passed. Amongst other things the 1913 Act provided for an Ancient Monuments Board with Inspectors and Commissioners of Works who were required to prepare a list of monuments, the preservation of which was of national importance. The Board was also empowered to prepare a list of other monuments which were of less than national importance but which should be preserved in the public interest, a distinction which might perhaps be helpful in considering the criteria for preservation under the 1979 Act.

By 1931 some 3,000 ancient monuments had been listed and the number **8.02** controlled by the Commissioners was then 200. The 1913 Act was found to be inadequate, and strengthening powers were given in the 1931 Act, in particular in relation to schemes for the purpose of preserving the amenities of an ancient monument. The next Act was the Historic Buildings and Ancient Monuments Act 1953 which brought under control not merely the ancient monument, but its owner. The range of ancient monuments was widened to include monuments which had a reference to industrial archaeology by virtue of that Act. Running throughout the legislation from 1900 onwards was the provision for a list of ancient monuments to be maintained. It is this element which is preserved in the 1979 Act (substantially amended by the National Heritage Act 1983). At December 1985 there were 12,875 scheduled ancient monuments—an increase of 58 during the year. Now that the re-survey of listed buildings is coming to an end, the Historic Buildings and Monuments Commission is starting an equivalent exercise for scheduled monuments, known as the Monuments Protection Programme. The intention is not only for legal action against the indiscriminate destruction of archaeological remains to be stepped up, but also for financial incentives to be offered to those agreeing not to harm relics on their land. It will take up to ten years during which, it is thought, the number of scheduled monuments is likely to rise to at least 60,000.[1]

The 1979 Act introduced a number of new phrases and definitions, and it is essential to see the differences between these definitions.

First, a *"monument"* is defined in section 61(7) as meaning:

"(a) any building, structure or work, whether above or below the surface of the land, and any cave or excavation;

(b) any site comprising the remains of any such building, structure or work or of any cave or excavation; and

(c) any site comprising, or comprising the remains of, any vehicle, vessel, aircraft, or other moveable structure or part thereof which neither constitutes nor forms part of any work which is a monument within paragraph (a) above.

and any machinery attached to a monument shall be regarded as part of the monument if it could not be detached without being dismantled."

This section specifically provides that references in the Act to a monument include references to the site of the monument in question and to a

---

[1] Reported in *SPAB News,* Autumn 1987, and in *The Sunday Times,* November 15, 1987.

group of monuments or any part of a monument or group of monuments.[1a] Further, it provides that references in the Act to the site of a monument are references to the monument itself where it consists of the site, and in any other case include references to the monument itself.[2]

8.03　There are, however, exclusions from the definition of a monument, and the exclusions relate to the definition above. There is excluded from subsection (7)(a) any ecclesiastical building for the time being used for ecclesiastical purposes[3]; subsection (7)(c) does not apply to a site comprising any object or its remains unless the situation of that object or its remains in that particular site is a matter of public interest,[4] nor to a site comprising, or comprising the remains of, any vessel which is protected by an order under the Protection of Wrecks Act 1973.[5]

Thus the above is the basic definition of a monument, and a monument cannot become either a scheduled monument or an ancient monument, or a protected monument, unless the hurdles of the definition above are overcome.

A *"scheduled monument"* is defined by section 1 of the 1979 Act as "any monument which is for the time being included in the Schedule." The Schedule is the schedule of monuments compiled and maintained for the purposes of the Act by the Secretary of State. The Secretary of State is obliged on first compiling the Schedule to include therein any monument included in the last list published under the 1913 Act[6] and any monument in respect of which the Secretary of State has served notice in accordance with the 1931 Act of his intention to include it in a list to be published under that Act, the service of such notice being prior to October 9, 1981 (the commencement date for Part I of the Act).[7]

In addition to those monuments which must of necessity be included in the schedule, the Secretary of State may on first compiling the Schedule or at any time thereafter include therein any monument which appears to him to be of national importance,[8] with the proviso that he shall consult the Commission before including a monument situated in England.

The only exception is that he may not include a structure which is occupied as a dwelling house by any person other than a person employed as a caretaker thereof or his family.[9]

8.04　An *"ancient monument"* is wider than the category of scheduled monuments and is defined in section 61(12) as meaning any scheduled monument and any other monument which in the opinion of the Secretary of State is of public interest by reason of the historic, architectural, traditional, artistic or archaeological interest attaching to it.[10]

[1a] s.61(10).

[2] s.61(11).

[3] s.61(8).

[4] s.61(8)(a).

[5] s.61(8)(b). An example of the problems under this Act is found in a letter to *The Times*, March 7, 1988.

[6] s.1(2)(a) and (b).

[7] *Ibid.*

[8] s.1(3), (as amended by the N.H.A. 1983, Sched. 4).

[9] s.1(4).

[10] In s.34(3) of the N.H.A. 1983 the phrase is defined more specifically as any structure, work, site, garden or area being of such public interest.

A *"protected monument"* (the definition for which appears to be included solely to define those monuments in respect of which an offence can occur by damaging them) means any scheduled monument and any monument under the ownership or guardianship of the Secretary of State, the Commission or a local authority by virtue of the 1979 Act.[11]

To complete the range of definitions, it is as well to remember that *"a protected place"* is defined in section 42(2) (the section dealing with the restrictions on the use of metal detectors) as any place which is either the site of a scheduled monument or of any monument under the ownership or guardianship of the Secretary of State, the Commission or a local authority, or is a place situated in an area of archaeological importance. An *"area of archaeological importance"* is defined in section 33 as an area which the Secretary of State may, having consulted the Commission, from time to time by order designate as such if "any area . . . appears to him to merit treatment as such for the purposes of this Act."

It will be seen that there are a number of different criteria for admission to protection. A monument appears to be any building at all which the Secretary of State thinks fit so to define. Unless, however, it is on a list under the 1913 Act or has been subject to a notice under the 1931 Act, the Secretary of State must not include in the schedule any monument until he has consulted the Commission and unless it "appears to him to be of national importance." Further, if the monument is in category (c) of section 61(7), namely a "moveable" monument, it may only by definition be a monument if the site comprising any object or its remains "is a matter of public interest."[12] **8.05**

The ancient monument definition embraces the scheduled monument and "any other monument which in the opinion of the Secretary of State is of public interest by reason of the historic, architectural, traditional, artistic or archaeological interest attaching to it." This therefore appears to define more closely the definition of "public interest," and it is perhaps worthy of note that the word here used is "historic" and not "historical," a distinction which for practical purposes may be of no significance but which a grammarian might justify. It will be seen that, for instance, in the powers of entry provisions in section 6 the powers of entry relate to inspecting the land with a view to recording any matters of archaeological or historical interest. Presumably therefore the powers of entry would not be available for use if it were sought to record architectural, traditional or artistic interest; whether or not the fine distinction between "historic" and "historical" could be drawn here must await a decision.

The draftsman of the Act must be assumed to have used these differing criteria deliberately. There are no definitions of the phrases such as "public interest", "national importance," "historic, architectural, traditional, artistic or archaeological interest." It would seem that there have been no decided cases on previous legislation which would throw any light on these criteria, although it is perhaps of interest to note the distinction which was drawn in section 12 of the 1913 Act between monuments of national importance and "other monuments which were of less than national importance but should be preserved in the public interest."

---

[11] s.28(3), (as amended by the N.H.A. 1983).
[12] s.61(8)(a).

8.06   In practical terms, the distinctions operate in the following way. The Act will not bite on any building which is not a monument. If it is a monument it may, in the manner above indicated, become a scheduled monument. A scheduled monument is protected in Part I of the 1979 Act under which it is a criminal offence to do certain works to a scheduled monument without scheduled monument consent[13]; there are provisions for compensation for refusal of scheduled monument consent.[14] There is also a provision for the execution of works for preservation of a scheduled monument by the Secretary of State in cases of urgency. An ancient monument (the definition of which is wider than that of a scheduled monument[15]) is subject to a code under Part I which permits of compulsory acquisition, or acquisition by agreement or gift.[16] Ancient monuments may be placed under guardianship which has the effect of the Secretary of State, the Commission or a relevant authority being required to maintain the ancient monument until determination.[17] The criminal offence section[18] in relation to damage to an ancient monument brings in the even wider definition of the protected monument. Finally, the designation of areas of archaeological importance[19] (a code not dissimilar to the conservation area code) gives a wider definition, which is also used in relation to the restrictions on the use of metal detectors under section 42, in what is described as a "protected place": see Table 7, para. 8.49 below.

8.07   It will be seen that the definition of a monument is a wide one. As indicated above there would appear to be no logical reason why any building or site should not rank as a monument provided it passes the relevant criterion. Prior to the coming into force of the 1979 Act, the broad definition of ancient monument was the only one which was applicable. The English Tourist Board carried out an interesting survey as at December 1985 of categories of objects which constituted ancient monuments. The list was not expressed to be exhaustive, but the variety and relative range, even within this list, is perhaps of interest. The 11 categories gave rise to 12,875 ancient monuments. Burial mounds and megalithic monuments accounted for 29 per cent.; camps and settlements for 15 per cent.; Roman remains for 7 per cent.; ecclesiastic ruins for 6 per cent.; crosses and inscribed stones for 5 per cent.; castles and fortifications for 9 per cent.; deserted villages and moated sites 8 per cent.; linear earthworks 3 per cent.; ancient bridges 4 per cent.; industrial monuments 2 per cent.; and other secular sites and buildings 12 per cent.

A few well known examples of ancient monuments are the castles of Edinburgh, Caernarvon and Conway, the Tower of London, Fountains Abbey and Glastonbury Abbey, Stonehenge and Hadrian's Wall. An example of a less famous ancient monument, and perhaps more unexpectedly scheduled as such, is the Anderton Boat Lift connecting the Trent and Mersey Canal to the Weaver Navigation in Cheshire (now in the course of restoration to full working order).

---

[13] s.2(1) and (2).
[14] s.7.
[15] s.61(12).
[16] ss.10 and 11.
[17] s.12.
[18] s.28.
[19] s.33.

2. THE MECHANICS OF SCHEDULING

These are set out in section 1 of the 1979 Act. The Secretary of State has, **8.08** in effect, three powers, namely that of including any monument in the schedule, amending the schedule in relation to any monument, and excluding any monument from the schedule. As we have seen, there are certain mandatory monuments to be included in the first listing[20]; thereafter so long as a monument appears to the Secretary of State to be of national importance, it may be included so long as it is not a structure which is occupied as a dwelling-house by any person other than the person employed as a caretaker thereof or his family,[21] nor is an ecclesiastical building used for the time being for ecclesiastical purposes,[22] nor a vessel protected under the Protection of Wrecks Act 1973. However, if there is no order made under section 1 of the Protection of Wrecks Act 1973, a monument in territorial waters can be an ancient monument by virtue of section 53 of the 1979 Act which provides that "a monument situated in, on, or under the sea bed within the seaward limits of the United Kingdom territorial waters" may be included in the schedule.

On including, amending or excluding any monument, the Commission is required to inform the owner and (if the owner is not the occupier) the occupier of the monument and any local authority in whose area the monument is situated, and in the event of an inclusion or an amendment, the Commission must send to him or them a copy of the entry or of the amended entry in the schedule.[23]

An entry in the schedule recording the inclusion therein of a monument **8.09** situated in England and Wales must be entered as a local land charge. Although section 1(9) refers only to the "inclusion" of a monument, it is thought that the effect of this subsection would be that the provisions of the Local Land Charges Act 1975 will apply to all entries in the schedule relating to monuments in England and Wales.

Scheduling proposals can originate from almost anyone, but typically they come from local archaeologists and their associations, local authorities, universities, etc. In England the Commission's inspectors of ancient monuments who are its professional archaeologists then review the evidence and probably visit the site (the submitted evidence may include details and photographs which render a visit superfluous) to assess whether the site or monument appears to be of national importance—which is the sole criterion laid down by statute for inclusion in the list or schedule of ancient monuments—and put forward a recommendation if they think it qualifies. At this point the owner is notified of the intention to schedule and the details of the proposal are checked. The recommendation is passed to the Ancient Monuments Advisory Committee for review, followed by endorsement by the full Commission. The Department of the Environment then formally confirms or rejects the proposed scheduling and the owner is finally notified by the Commission. This procedure is currently under review by the Commission.

---

[20] s.1(2).
[21] s.1(4).
[22] s.61(8).
[23] s.1(6).

8.10   In each of the three countries the appropriate Secretary of State is required from time to time to publish a list of all the monuments which are for the time being included in the schedule, whether as a single list or in sections containing the monuments situated in particular areas. There is no obligation to publish area lists simultaneously, and the Secretary of State may maintain for the purposes of the Act the schedule in such form as he thinks fit. It may be helpful to note that while the publication is officially the List of Ancient Monuments, it is always referred to as the Schedule, and the process of adding to it is called scheduling, because the original list was published as the schedule to the first Ancient Monuments Act of 1882, and nowadays because it provides a convenient and very useful distinction from the list of buildings of special architectural or historic interest under the Planning Acts.

The Secretaries of State have power to (but are not obliged to) publish amendments of any list,[24] and there is provision in section 1 that any such lists (as amended) shall be evidence of th inclusion in the schedule for the time being.[25] The question of what precisely constitutes the Schedule is currently under review by the Commission. There is some legal doubt whether monuments not included in the last published list are currently scheduled, and the Commission is now drawing up a comprehensive entry to avoid this doubt.

3. THE ORGANISATION OF THE ANCIENT MONUMENTS ADMINISTRATION[26]

8.11   In England the work of the Department of the Environment on ancient monuments and the general administration of the service is carried out by the Commission. Internally, the Commission has its work organised into two broad groups, one of which deals with properties in its own care, the other dealing with properties in the care of other owners. Both groups have multi-disciplinary teams incorporating inspectors.

The Commission's inspectors work closely with its architects in preserving and displaying the monuments in the Commission's care, and confer with them on the technical measures to be taken. They also give advice to private owners and local authorities when requested. The preparation of lists of monuments worthy of being scheduled, for submission to the Ancient Monuments Advisory Committee, is another important duty of the inspectors, and in this they rely substantially on co-operation and information from local archaeologists.

The inspectors also scrutinise plans for new development such as building, quarrying, roads and pipelines which might interfere with ancient sites and structures. They also arrange, and in some cases personally supervise, the excavation of such sites in order to ensure that the archaeological evidence of monuments which cannot be permanently preserved is properly examined and recorded before destruction.

---

[24] s.1(8).

[25] *Ibid.*

[26] We are much indebted to the DOE Ancient Monument Section for the information on the administration of the Act.

The ancient monuments laboratory provides the necessary scientific back-up to the work of the inspectors and other bodies undertaking archaeological excavations on behalf of the Commission. It also maintains the collections on display at the museums established at certain monuments. Its staff are trained in a variety of scientific disciplines and, under the direction of the head of the ancient monuments laboratory, work in four main subject areas—geophysics, environmental studies, early technology and conservation.

The work of the inspectors' staff includes preparing the standard guidebooks and also editing for publication the reports of archaeological excavations.

Advice and architectural services related to ancient monuments and historic buildings are given to the Commission by its own architects, and the greater part of the work on the monuments is carried out by a directly employed labour staff. Craftsmen in most of the building trades are employed, some of whom have spent a lifetime in the service of the DOE.

8.12 The Commission's architects are responsible for the preparation of reports on monuments prior to being taken into care, in which they assess the condition of the monument, recommend the treatment necessary for its preservation, maintenance and display to the public, and estimate the cost of so doing. However, their primary function is the structural preservation of monuments taken into the Commission's care. The techniques used in this work are the result of the experience gained over many years combined with constant research into new methods. It is the Commission's policy so to treat the ancient monuments for which it is responsible that they are not only structurally safe for the future but retain unimpaired the historical significance which justifies their preservation.

The architects and craftsmen are additionally responsible for the maintenance, management and custody of the sites, and the ancillary buildings associated with them. The aim is to maintain the condition of the sites to the high standard and provide the service that the visiting public have come to expect. These responsibilities are partly shared with the presentation branch of the Commission.

Public services in the form of car parks, ticket offices, site museums, toilets and refreshment rooms where these are provided, are planned and designed by the Commission's architects. With the growth of the tourist industry and greater public appreciation of the heritage, there is an ever increasing commitment to provide more sophisticated public facilities raising new problems of visual integration with historic sites.

Architects and technical staff are also called upon to give advice on monuments not in the Commission's care, and, in certain cases, work for private owners of monuments is carried out by the Commission's direct labour staff, the costs being recovered from the owner.

The architectural group includes civil, mechanical and electrical engineers, and quantity surveyors, and is able to call upon other servicing divisions for their assistance when required.

Another department of the Commission is responsible for publicising monuments in the Commission's care, and for making recommendations on the need for the provision of shops and any other services which may be needed at these sites. This publicity work is carried out in liaison with tourist authorities, travel agencies and coach operators and with the National Trust and owners of historic houses.

Similar arrangements apply in Scotland and Wales where the administration is a function of the Scottish and Welsh Offices respectively.

4. THE CONSEQUENCES OF SCHEDULING

(a) No appeal against scheduling

8.13   The monument remains in the schedule until it is excluded or amended by order of the Secretary of State. There is no provision for appealing against inclusion in the schedule, but, as with listed buildings, there is nothing to stop an owner applying to the Secretary of State for exclusion or amendment which the Secretary of State has power to do by section 1. However, there is no appeal against the refusal of the Secretary of State to exclude or amend, and the owner would then only have the power to apply for scheduled monument consent (see paras. 8.16–8.17 below).

(b) Unauthorised works may be an offence

8.14   Inclusion in the schedule gives rise to the control of works affecting the scheduled monument. Section 2 provides that if any person executes or causes or permits to be executed any works to which that section applies he shall be guilty of an offence unless the works are authorised, *i.e.* unless he has scheduled monument consent either specifically given in relation to the scheduled monument, or given under section 3 (by which section the Secretary of State has power to make a general order not dissimilar to the General Development Order under the Town and Country Planning Act 1971).[27]

The Ancient Monuments (Class Consents) Order 1981[28] came into operation on October 9, 1981 and gave scheduled monument consent for the execution of works comprising the following classes:

    I certain agricultural, horticultural or forestry works being works of the same kind as works previously executed in the same field or location during the period between October 10, 1976 and October 9, 1981;

    II works executed more than 10 metres below ground level by the National Coal Board or its licensees;

    III certain works executed by the British Waterways Board;

    IV works for the repair or maintenance of machinery which do not involve material alteration to a monument;

    V works which are essential for the purposes of health or safety; and

    VI works executed by the Commission.

There are several separate matters which could give rise to an offence,

---

[27] See para. 8.17 below.

[28] S.I. 1981 No. 1302. For Scotland, a similar order came into operation on November 30, 1981 (S.I. 1981 No. 1468) (as amended by S.I. 1984 No. 222).

namely works resulting in the demolition or destruction of, or damage to, a scheduled monument; works for the purpose of removing or repairing a scheduled monument or any part of it, or of making any alterations or additions thereto; and flooding or tipping operations on land in, on or under which there is a scheduled monument.[29] There is no definition of what is destruction or damage, but presumably the distinction between demolition and damage on the one hand and destruction on the other is that in demolition the parts are removed and parts retained, in destruction the fabric of the monument is physically destroyed. "Flooding or tipping operations" are defined respectively as covering land with water or any other liquid or partially liquid substance, and tipping soil or spoil or depositing building or other materials or matter (including waste materials or refuse) on any land.

There are four defences to the claim that an offence has been commit- **8.15**
ted.[30] They are:

(i) That the defendant took all reasonable precautions and exercised all due diligence to avoid contravening the conditions of a scheduled monument consent where failure to comply with any condition attached to such consent is alleged;

(ii) Where demolition destruction or damage is alleged the defendant can prove that he took all reasonable precautions and exercised all due diligence to avoid or prevent damage to the monument;

(iii) Where demolition, destruction, damage, flooding or tipping is alleged it is a defence for the accused to prove that he did not know, and had no reason to believe, that the monument was within the area affected by the works, or (as the case may be) that it was a scheduled monument;

(iv) The last defence is for the defendant to prove that the works were urgently necessary in the interests of safety or health, and that notice in writing of the need for the works was given to the Secretary of State as soon as was reasonably practicable. It is arguable that such notice can be given after the works are done so long as it is given as soon as reasonably practicable. The words "need for the works" suggests a prior notice, but nowhere is it specifically stated.

Defence number (iv) above is comparable with the defence available under section 55(6) (as amended) of the Town and Country Planning Act 1971, relating to listed buildings, though drafted less restrictively. Moreover, the three other defences set out above are not available in relation to listed buildings. Particularly it should be noted that, unlike the provisions under the 1971 Act, offences with regard to scheduled monuments are not absolute offences.

(c) Need to obtain scheduled monument consent for works

The person executing, causing or permitting to be executed any works to **8.16**
which section 2 applies shall not be guilty of an offence if he has a scheduled monument consent (in writing) for the execution of the works and the

[29] s.2(2).
[30] s.2(6)–(9).

works are executed in accordance with the terms of the consent and of any conditions attached to the consent.[31]

Despite the transfer of some of the functions formerly exercised by the Secretary of State to the Commission, it is the Secretary of State who grants the scheduled monument consent. In the year to December 1985 there were 710 applications for scheduled monument consent—29 were refused, 105 were granted subject to terms and 328 were granted unconditionally. At present, the Secretary of State must consult with the Commission before determining applications involving works to scheduled monuments. It is believed that the Commission feels that this duplication of work, where the advice-giving and decision-taking functions are separated, is cumbersome and adds to delay and misunderstanding; and that a better system would be for the Secretary of State to transfer his responsibilities to the Commission. The Commission itself receives advice from the Ancient Monuments Advisory Committee. The procedure might well be reviewed and changed.

The phrase "the terms" seems to be wider than merely the general provisions of the scheduled monument consent—in section 8(3) there is a provision whereby the Secretary of State may grant a scheduled monument consent "on terms" that no works in respect of which compensation has been paid are to be executed in pursuance of the consent until the recoverable amount has been repaid to the Secretary of State or secured to his satisfaction.

The provision for scheduled monument consent closely follows the principles of LBC on which code it appears to have been modelled. There are two types of scheduled monument consent—the consent relating specifically to a particular monument granted by the Secretary of State on application by a person who has a relevant interest in that monument, and the scheduled monument consent granted by the Secretary of State by order under section 3—a section which seems to have been modelled on the principles of the General Development Order.

8.17   A "specific" scheduled monument consent is applied for under section 2(11) which refers to Part I of Schedule I of the Act which provides for the detailed machinery dealing with applications for scheduled monument consent. The Ancient Monuments (Applications for Scheduled Monument Consent) Regulations 1981[32] prescribes a form of application for scheduled monument consent, requires that the application be accompanied by plans and drawings, and obliges the applicant to supply such further information as the Secretary of State may request. The regulations provide for the form of certificate which should accompany the application and the form of notice which has to be given to all persons who were owners of the monument 21 days before the submission of the application. The owner is the fee simple owner or is a person entitled to a certain tenancy of which not less than seven years remain unexpired. The procedure is not unlike the procedure for LBC and requires notices to be given to the owners of the monument where the applicant is not the owner, or a certificate as to the inability to issue such a certificate; there is provision for the Secretary of State to cause a public local inquiry to be held or to afford the applicant or any other person to whom it appears expedient the opportunity of appearing before

[31] s.2(3).
[32] S.I. 1981 No. 1301. For Scotland, a similar order came into operation on November 30, 1981 (S.I. 1981 No. 1467).

and being heard by a person appointed by the Secretary of State for the purpose. There is an obligation on the Secretary of State to consider any representations and the report of any inquiry of hearing[33]; and the Secretary of State's decision may be challenged in the High Court on a point of law.

Objections have in fact been raised to what appears to be the "secretive" nature of the process, compared to the procedures relating to listed buildings. There is no obligation to advertise the application; the decision is not made public; nor, apparently, may any party other than the owner, the Commission or the Secretary of State express a view on an application as a matter of right.[34] Indeed the local planning authority may be unaware of the proposal.

(d) Time limits applicable to scheduled monument consent

Section 4(1) provides that if no works to which a scheduled monument **8.18** consent relates are executed or started within a period of five years, beginning with the date on which the consent was granted or such longer or shorter period as may be specified in the order for the purposes of section 4(1), the consent shall cease to have effect at the end of that period unless it has been previously revoked. There is also a provision by which the scheduled monument consent may specifically be stated to cease to have effect at the end of a period specified in the consent.[35]

(e) Scheduled monument consent may be modified or revoked

There is a provision for the Secretary of State to modify or revoke a sched- **8.19** uled monument consent to any extent which he considers expedient[36] (which includes specifying or altering any period). Part II of Schedule I to the Act has effect with respect to directions under the section for modifying or revoking a scheduled monument consent and a procedure exists which is not unlike the modification or revocation procedures in respect of a planning permission. Where the direction would affect a monument in England, the Secretary of State is required to consult with the Commission before he gives such a direction.

(f) Compensation may be payable on refusal of scheduled monument consent

There is also a provision for compensation for refusal of scheduled monu- **8.20** ment consent. The provisions are fairly restrictive, largely as a result of the decision in *Hoveringham Gravels Ltd.* v. *Secretary of State for the Environ-*

---

[33] Sched. I, Pt. I, para. 3.
[34] Michael Farley, *The Times*, January 25, 1986.
[35] s.4(2).
[36] s.4(3) (as amended).

ment[37] where it was held that likely harm to an ancient monument may be a consideration in refusing planning permission, and that without planning permission there could be no claim for compensation. The upshot is that, unless express or implied planning permission is granted before a monument is scheduled, compensation is limited to works which are reasonably necessary for the continuation of any existing use of the monument.

The provision is found in section 7 and there are four requirements which must be satisfied before compensation will be awarded. They are:

   (i) The claimant must have an interest in the whole or any part of the monument;

   (ii) The claimant must have incurred expenditure or otherwise sustained loss or damage;

   (iii) The expenditure or loss or damage must have been incurred or sustained in consequence of the refusal or the granting subject to conditions of the scheduled monument consent; and

   (iv) The scheduled monument consent must relate to works of a description mentioned in section 7(2).

An interest to qualify for compensation must be in accordance with regulations prescribing interest qualifications as provided for in section 47 of the Act. As yet, no such regulations have been made.[38]

8.21   The works which will qualify for compensation are:

   (i) Works which are reasonably necessary for carrying out any development for which planning permission had been granted (otherwise than by a General Development Order) *before* the time when the monument in question became a scheduled monument and was still effective at the date of the application for scheduled monument consent;

   (ii) Works which do not constitute development or constitute development such that planning permission is granted therefor by a General Development Order; and

   (iii) Works which are reasonably necessary for the continuation of any use of the monument for any purposes for which it was in use immediately before the date of the application for scheduled monument consent save that any use in contravention of any legal restrictions for the time being applying to the use of the monument shall be disregarded.[39]

The distinction between (i) and (ii) appears to be that compensation is payable where, at the time of scheduling of a monument, there is a planning permission specifically outstanding and unimplemented in respect of the monument so scheduled. Compensation will not be paid in respect of a planning permission granted after scheduling of the monument, but compensation will always be paid for prevention of the carrying out of General Development Order permission or for works which do not constitute development. As the General Development Order permission or the definition of what does not constitute development would be applicable both before or

---

[37] [1975] Q.B. 754.

[38] Regulations as to claims for compensation for land in Scotland: See S.I. 1981 No. 1469, operative November 30, 1981.

[39] s.7(2).

after the scheduling of the monument, the question of time in this respect is irrelevant.

Section 7(3) provides that compensation payable under (i) above shall be limited to loss sustained by virtue of the fact that any development for which the planning permission was granted could not be carried out without contravening section 2(1), in consequence of the Secretary of State's decision.

The applicant is not entitled to compensation under (ii) above if the works in question or any of them would or might result in the total or partial demolition or destruction of the monument unless those works consist solely of operations involved in or incidental to the use of the site of the monument for purposes of agriculture or forestry (including afforestation).[40] Presumably the reasoning for this is that at all events total demolition or destruction of the monument would result in a more valuable site than one which is encumbered with a scheduled monument.

Similarly, where scheduled monument consent is granted subject to conditions, a person will not be entitled to compensation by virtue of (iii) above unless compliance with those conditions would in effect make it impossible to use the monument for the purpose there mentioned.[41]

There are provisions which build in an assumption to the valuation that any subsequent application for a scheduled monument consent in relation to works of a like description will be determined in the same way (no doubt to defeat the argument that it would be likely that a wider scheduled monument consent would be made available) and a requirement that the valuation reflects any undertaking by the Secretary of State on refusing consent to grant consent for some other works affecting the monument in the event of an application being made in that behalf.[42]

(g) Compensation may be payable for depreciation

There are some provisions which apply to compensation for depreciation **8.22** generally under Part I to be found in section 27, and in particular valuation assumptions in relation to land subject to a mortgage in respect of depreciation of the value of the interest subject to the mortgage.

(h) Compensation may be recovered on subsequent grant of scheduled monument consent

There is a provision in section 8 for the recovery of any compensation **8.23** paid out under section 7 on a subsequent grant of consent. Thus, if compensation was paid on a section 7 claim and there is a subsequent grant of a scheduled monument consent, or a scheduled monument consent is modified so that if the consent was subject to conditions these conditions or any of them cease to apply to the execution of all or any of the works in respect

[40] s.7(4).
[41] s.7(5).
[42] s.7(6).

of which compensation was paid, then there is a repayment provision on condition, first, that the compensation paid exceeded £20 and, secondly, that the Commission (in Scotland and Wales, the Secretary of State) have caused notice of the payment of compensation to be deposited with the appropriate local authority.[43] There is a provision for appeal to the Lands Tribunal by a person who has an interest in the whole or any part of the monument where he is aggrieved by the amount recoverable by the Secretary of State.[44] A notice deposited in the case of a monument situated in England and Wales must have been entered as a local land charge.[45]

(i) Compensation may be payable for "abortive expenditure"

8.24   Where works affecting a scheduled monument have been authorised (*i.e.* by a scheduled monument consent, or consent given under a scheduled monument consent order under section 3) and subsequently cease to be authorised (*e.g.* by a modification or revocation) then any person who has an interest in any part of the monument who has incurred expenditure in carrying out works which are rendered abortive by the fact that further works have ceased to be so authorised or has otherwise sustained a loss or damage which is directly attributable to that fact, may apply to the Commission or outside England to the Secretary of State who shall be required to pay that person compensation in respect of that expenditure, loss or damage.[46]

Where under section 9 the work ceases to be authorised by virtue of the fact that a scheduled monument consent granted by order under section 3 ceases to apply to any scheduled monument, the applicant is not entitled to compensation unless he specifically applies for a scheduled monument consent for the works in question and consent is refused, or is granted subject to conditions other than those which previously applied under the order.

(j) "Urgent works" may be undertaken by the Secretary of State

8.25   There is a provision whereby the Secretary of State (or, on his authorisation, the Commission) may, if it appears to him that any works are urgently necessary for the preservation of any scheduled monument, enter the site of the monument and execute the works after giving the owner and (if the owner is not the occupier) the occupier of the monument not less than seven days notice in writing of his intention so to do.[47] There is no recharging provision here. If the Secretary of State (or the Commission on his behalf) undertakes this work, he undertakes it at his own expense. If

---

[43] s.8(2).
[44] s.8(4).
[45] s.8(6).
[46] s.9.
[47] s.5(1).

194

however there is any compensation order made in respect of payment of compensation by a convicted person under the Powers of Criminal Courts Act 1973, the order is made in favour of the Secretary of State,[48] which is as far as the Secretary of State appears to want to go in relation to recoupment.

(k) Extensive powers of entry are applicable

There are substantial powers of entry contained in section 6 for the vari- **8.26** ous stages of ascertaining the condition of a scheduled monument for viewing works to which a scheduled monument consent relates and for recording matters of archaeological or historical interest. These powers of entry and recording are dealt with in Chapter 11.

5. ACQUISITION OF AN ANCIENT MONUMENT

There are three ways in which an ancient monument can be acquired: by **8.27** compulsory acquisition, by agreement, or by gift.[49] The Secretary of State has power to acquire compulsorily and by agreement, and may accept a gift.[50] The Commission (with the consent of the Secretary of State) or a local authority, however, may only acquire by agreement or accept a gift.[51] The gift in either case may be either by deed or by a will.

If the Secretary of State wishes to acquire compulsorily, he must first consult with the Commission. He may acquire any ancient monument but only for the purposes of securing its preservation, and in practice the Secretary of State will only acquire compulsorily if it is the only way of securing the preservation of the monument. The Acquisition of Land Act 1981 applies, and there is a built-in assumption in respect of the compensation, namely that it is to be assumed that scheduled monument consent would not be granted for any works which would or might result in the demolition, destruction or removal of the monument or any part of it.[52]

In so far as section 11 is concerned (acquisition by agreement or gift) the provisions of Part I of the Compulsory Purchase Act 1965 (with some exceptions) are applicable.

There is a further provision in section 15 which permits land adjoining or in the vicinity of an ancient monument to be acquired compulsorily if it appears to the Secretary of State or the Commission to be reasonably required for the purpose of maintenance of the monument or its amenities, providing or facilitating access, the exercise of proper control or management, the storage of equipment or materials, and the provision of facilities and services for the public for or in connection with affording public access to the monument. Wide powers under this section are given to the Secretary of State and the Commission in respect of this land so acquired.

---

[48] s.5(2).
[49] ss.10 and 11.
[50] Ibid., and see also para. 9.19 above as to the taxation consequences.
[51] s.11(2) and (3).
[52] s.10(2) and (4).

6. GUARDIANSHIP OF ANCIENT MONUMENTS

8.28   As an alternative to acquisition of an ancient monument there is provision for guardianship (the early practice of compulsory guardianship having proved unsuccessful). The broad intention of guardianship is that the legal estate in the land is left with those who own it, but that the Secretary of State, the Commission or the local authority become the guardians of the land (and in particular the monument). An ancient monument need not be a scheduled monument before it is taken into guardianship. There is a duty on the guardian (be it the Secretary of State, the Commission or the local authority) to maintain the monument, for which it has full control and management powers.[53] There is an obligation (with some safeguards) to permit the public access to the monument under guardianship.[54] Guardianship orders are not new—indeed the original guardianship provisions were contained in the 1913 Act and have been effectively used for the last 75 years. There are now over 400 monuments in the care of the Commission alone.

The power is given to a person who has an interest either in the fee simple, in the leasehold estate or an interest in possession, being an estate or interest for a term of which not less than 45 years are unexpired or renewable for a term of not less than 45 years, or an interest in possession for his own life or on the life of another, to constitute the Secretary of State (with his consent) or the Commission (with its and the Secretary of State's consent) by deed the guardian of the monument. With regard to a monument situated in England, the Secretary of State must consult with the Commission before consenting to guardianship.[55] As an alternative, a person with such an interest in an ancient monument may with the consent of any local authority in or in the vicinity of whose area the monument is situated, constitute that authority by deed guardians of the monument.[56] There is a prohibition against consenting to guardianship of a structure which is occupied as a dwelling house except by a caretaker or his family occupying as such.[57]

8.29   There is an overriding restriction on both guardianship provisions whereby a person who is not the occupier of the ancient monument may not establish guardianship unless the occupier is also a party to the deed executed with the guardian.[58] Any person who has an interest in an ancient monument may be a party to the deed in addition to the person establishing the guardianship of the monument and the occupier. It may be prudent for such a person so to enter into the arrangements which would give him some (although rather limited) rights if the guardianship is sought to be terminated under the provisions of section 14. The person who has such an interest must at the time of the proposal to terminate be "immediately affected by the operation of the guardianship deed"—it is difficult to see how he could not be—and in practical terms his presence as a party under the deed would no doubt result in his being properly consulted.

The effect of the guardianship is dealt with in section 13. The main effect

[53] s.13.
[54] s.19.
[55] s.12(3).
[56] s.12(2).
[57] s.12(10).
[58] s.12(4).

is that the guardian is under a duty to maintain the monument (at its own expense). (There is a specific provision defining maintenance as including fencing, repairing and covering in of a monument and the doing of any other act or thing which may be required for the purpose of repairing the monument or protecting from decay or injury.)[59] In return, the guardian has full control and management of the monument and powers to do all things as may be necessary for the maintenance of the monument and for the exercise by it of proper control and management with respect to the monument. In particular the guardian may examine, open up, excavate or remove the whole or any part of the monument. The access by the public to the monument must be over and along a defined route indicated on a plan annexed to the guardianship agreement "with or without horses, carts and mechanically propelled vehicles." Little else is included in the standard agreement. All the provisions of section 13 are subject to any provision to the contrary contained in the guardianship deed.

Having accepted guardianship of an ancient monument it is less easy for the guardian to get rid of the responsibility. Under section 14, the guardian (if it is a local authority it must consult the Secretary of State before entering into any agreement under this section, but if it is the Secretary of State he must consult with the Commission) may by agreement with the persons "who are for the time being immediately affected by the operation of the guardianship deed" exclude any part of the monument from guardianship or renounce guardianship of the monument.[60] But it shall remain under guardianship (unless the monument is acquired by its guardian) until the occupier of the monument who is entitled to terminate the guardianship gives notice in writing to that effect to the guardian of the monument. **8.30**

The occupier is in a stronger position because he is entitled to terminate the guardianship if he has any interest in the monument which would qualify him to establish guardianship under section 12 of the Act (i.e. fee simple, leasehold estate for 45 years, interest in possession for life or life of another),[61] and if he is not bound by the guardianship deed. This is the effect of the provision of section 14(1). It is thought that the word "bound" must mean that he is not bound adversely by any provision in the guardianship deed to the contrary. He will be presumably bound by the deed if under section 12(5) he enters into it, and the provisions of the guardianship deed, being a local land charge, will be binding on a subsequent occupier.

However, the guardian may not enter into any such agreement unless it is satisfied with respect to the part of the monument, or, as the case may be, with respect to the whole of the monument in question, that satisfactory arrangements have been made for securing its preservation after termination of the guardianship or that it is no longer practicable to preserve it (whether because of the cost of preserving it or otherwise).[62]

There is a provision to take into guardianship, by virtue of section 15, land in the vicinity of an ancient monument if it appears to the guardian to be reasonably required for the purpose of maintenance, access, control or management, storage of equipment or materials, or facilities and services to the public for or in connection with affording public access.

---

[59] s.13(7).
[60] s.14(1).
[61] s.12(3).
[62] s.14(3).

In addition there is a provision for the acquisition of easements or other similar rights over land in the vicinity of an ancient monument whereby the Secretary of State may acquire by agreement or compulsorily any easement "which appears to him to be necessary" for any of the purposes relating to the monument mentioned in section 15(1) (*e.g.* maintenance, access, control or management, etc.) or for the use of any land associated with that monument for any of those purposes.[63] The Commission or a local authority may by agreement acquire easements, but they have no compulsory powers in this respect.[64]

7. AGREEMENTS CONCERNING ANCIENT MONUMENTS AND LAND IN THEIR VICINITY

8.31   The Secretary of State and the Commission have a general power in section 17 to enter into an agreement with the occupier of an ancient monument or of any land adjoining or in the vicinity of an ancient monument. The local authority has a similar power. In 1985–86 the Commission concluded 44 of these management agreements, which they regard as particularly valuable in preserving field monuments. "Limited owners," being persons defined by section 18 as a body corporate or corporation sole and any other persons who have a limited interest such as a tenant for life or statutory owner or trustees for sale, have power under section 18 to enter into such agreements and guardianship agreements.

8. PUBLIC RIGHTS

8.32   The public is given rights of access under section 19 to any monument under the ownership or guardianship of the Secretary of State, the Commission or local authority by virtue of the 1979 Act. Restrictions are imposed so that the Secretary of State,the Commission or local authority may nevertheless control the times of the normal public access by regulations made under the section, and the power of a local authority entirely to exclude the public from access to any monument shall only be exercisable with the consent of the Secretary of State. The regulations may provide the times at which the public is to have access and provision may be made for the preservation of the monument and regulations prohibiting or regulating any act or thing which would tend to injure or disfigure any monument.[65] There is provision also for the Secretary of State, the Commission and a local authority to make charges and to refuse admission to any person believed to be likely to do anything which would tend to disfigure or injure the monument or its amenities. There is a penalty provision in section 19(7) in respect of any person contravening or failing to comply with the provisions of section 19. The Act also makes provision for facilities for the public—power is given to the Secretary of State and any local authority to

---

[63] s.16(1).
[64] s.16(2).
[65] s.19(4).

provide facilities to the public and information for or in connection with affording public access to any monument.[66] (See also Chapter 12).

These statutory public access rights have given rise to the well-known difficulties at Stonehenge where it fell to the Commission to attempt to balance such rights against the danger of damage or disfigurement to this popular landmark. In the words of the Commission's chairman, Lord Montagu: "Stonehenge is one of the great European ancient monuments—indeed it has a worldwide significance. We must care for it and equally improve the visitor facilities to enable the public to understand it better, to recognise its unique quality and to marvel at its age and beauty. Many plans have been brought forward in the past. The Commission has decided to take a fresh look at the problem and strive for a long-term solution and we intend to direct sustained efforts to finding that solution as quickly as possible and implementing it."[67]

9. ANCIENT MONUMENTS BOARDS[68]

There were three Ancient Monuments Boards originally constituted under the 1913 Act: one for England, one for Scotland and one for Wales. Section 39(2) of the National Heritage Act 1983 abolished the Ancient Monuments Board for England, whose functions were taken over by the Historic Buildings and Monuments Commission for England, established by the 1983 Act. The Commission for England and the Ancient Monuments Board for Wales consist of members representing the bodies specified in section 22 of the 1979 Act. For England, these are, the Royal Commission on Historical Monuments (England), The Society of Antiquaries of London, The Royal Academy of Arts, the Royal Institute of British Architects, the Trustees of the British Museum, and the British Academy; for Wales, the Royal Commission on Historical Monuments (Wales), The National Museum of Wales, and The Cambrian Archaeological Assocation. In each case they are joined by such other members as the Secretary of State may appoint. The function of the Commission and the Ancient Monuments Boards for Scotland and Wales is to advise the Secretaries of State in respect of the exercise of his functions under the Act, whether generally or in relation to any particular case or classes of case.[69] The Ancient Monuments Boards for Scotland and Wales (but not the Commission) are each required by section 23 of the 1979 Act to produce annual reports, and these are laid before Parliament and published as House of Commons Papers.

8.33

It should be remembered that by section 33 of the National Heritage Act 1983, the general functions of the Commission are to preserve, and to promote the public enjoyment and awareness of, ancient monuments and historic buildings; to provide educational facilities and give advice; and for the purpose of exercising these functions, it is empowered to enter into contracts and to acquire and dispose of land and other property. The Com-

---

[66] s.20.

[67] Speech made at the Banqueting House, April 2, 1984 (Stonehenge Study Group Report).

[68] See also para. 13.02 below.

[69] s.22(6).

mission, then, is very much more than an advisory body, having major executive functions in its own right.

10. GENERAL POWERS

8.34   There are a number of general powers in the 1979 Act. Section 24 provides that the Commission may defray or contribute towards the cost of the acquisition by any person of any ancient monument. Section 25 provides that the Commission may give advice with reference to the treatment of any ancient monument and superintend any work in connection with a scheduled monument, if in its opinion it is advisable, and may make a charge for giving that advice and superintendence, or may give it free of charge as it thinks fit. There are a number of powers of entry,[70–71] all of which are dealt with in Chapter 11. There is a general power for the transfer of ancient monuments between local authorities and the Commission,[72] and there is a power given to the Secretary of State or a local authority to dispose of land acquired by them under the Act.[73] The Secretary of State or local authority may receive voluntary contributions under section 31 towards the cost of any expenditure incurred by him under Part I of the Act. The Commission may also undertake (section 45) or assist in, or defray, or contribute towards the cost of any archaeological investigation of any land, as may the local authority. There is power for the Secretary of State, the Commission or the local authority to publish the results of archaeological investigation undertaken, and (in Scotland) there is provision for the Secretary of State or the Commission[73a] to make grants to the Architectural Heritage Fund, whose terms of reference are described below in para. 13.13.

11. DUTIES IMPOSED IN THE ACT

8.35   There are certain duties imposed in the Act. Under section 46 there is a requirement for the Secretary of State or the Commission or other authority on whose behalf an archaeological investigation has been carried out to pay compensation for any damage to land or to chattels on application being made within the time and in the manner prescribed, disputed amounts of compensation being referred to the Lands Tribunal. Anyone who enters land under any of the powers of the Act may take "temporary custody" of any objects of archaeological or historical interest they may find there and take them away for examination, preservation or recording. Unless the owner gives his consent, the article can only be retained for such period as the Secretary of State may think desirable for the purpose of archaeological investigation or analysis.[74]

[70–71] s.26.
[72] s.21.
[73] s.30.
[73a] s.49.
[74] s.54.

12. ARCHAEOLOGICAL AREAS

Section 33 of the Act contains a new provision for the designation and **8.36**
control of operations affecting "areas of archaeological importance." This
gives specific powers over areas as opposed to specific monuments. Part II of
the Act covers these areas, which are to be designated selectively. So far
some five areas have been designated.

The introduction of the concept of "areas" of archaeological potential
appears to have proved a successful alternative to the problems thrown up
by the old "condition-based" approach. According to the latter approach,
where planning permission is granted for development which might affect a
non-scheduled monument or an area of known or supposed archaeological
interest not designated as such, the local planning authority may impose
conditions on that permission, designed to protect the monument or to
allow access for archaeologists during the course of the development.[75]
However, it has been argued that this procedure fails to recognise that
sometimes important archaeological discoveries are made that could not
have been reasonably predicted before excavations began. Nor does the
"condition-based" procedure give adequate notification to non-statutory
archaeological organisations as to when development is going to commence, allowing them to make their own work arrangements in proper time
and ensuring that the excavation work does not unduly delay the commencement of building works. The "archaeological area" approach, on the
other hand, allows for an initial evaluation at the application stage and if
this demonstrates that the site is of national importance, the application
can be refused. This, certainly, has been the experience of the Reading
Borough Council, whose policy has been to divide their area into sites of
high and low archaeological potential.[76] The British Archaeologists and
Developers Liaison Group, the sponsoring bodies of which are the British
Property Federation and the Standing Conference of Archaeological Trust
Managers, have produced a helpful, but voluntary, code of conduct relating
to a realistic understanding between archaeologists and developers.[76a]

(a) Making of designation orders

The basis of the control is a designation order made by the Secretary of **8.37**
State who may from time to time by order designate as an area of archaeological importance any area "which appears to him to merit treatment as such
for the purposes of this Act."[77] The Commisssion has power to designate
such an area within Greater London, and a local authority has a similar
power in relation to its own area. Five areas have so far been designated,
comprising areas containing the historic centres of Canterbury, Chester,
Exeter, Hereford and York. The Secretary of State has power to vary or
revoke a designation order, but the power to vary is confined to reducing the

[75] Circular 1/85, "The Use of Conditions in Planning Permissions," para. 61 and see
the discussion on s.52 agreements at para. 3.16 above.
[76] See Philip Joyce, *Planning* (August 15, 1986), p. 101.
[76a] Copies available from BPF, 35 Catherine Place, London SW1E 6DY.
[77] s.33(1).

area.[78] There is no similar variation or revocation order in respect of the Commission or a local authority. There is no appeal against inclusion in a designation order although, as might be expected, informal discussions with the local authorities were held prior to designation. Schedule 2 of the Act has effect with regard to the making and the variation and revocation of designation orders. There are notification procedures and a requirement of the local authority to submit a designation order to the Secretary of State for confirmation.[79] Finally, a designation order is registrable as a local land charge.[79a]

(b) Investigating authorities: appointment and powers

8.38   The Secretary of State may at any time appoint any person whom he considers to be competent to undertake archaeological investigations to exercise in relation to any area of archaeological importance the functions conferred by Part II of the Act.[80] The persons so appointed are known as the "investigating authority," possibly (but not necessarily) an independent archaeological unit attached to a university, or perhaps one forming part of the local authority. Appointments of investigating authorities may be cancelled at any time; the Secretary of State must consult with the Commission and notify each local authority for whose area an investigating authority is appointed of the appointment and of any cancellation thereof; and an investigating authority may authorise any other person to act on his behalf in exercising the functions conferred by the Act.[81] Investigating authorities have extensive powers of entry to and investigation of sites.[82]

(c) Controls and offences in designated areas

8.39   The method by which control is exercised over operations affecting land which is included in a designation order is contained in section 35 of the Act which is the kernel of Part II. Section 35 makes it an offence for any person (referred to somewhat tendentiously as "the developer") to carry out or cause or permit to be carried out on designated land (i.e. within an area of archaeological importance) any operations involving disturbance of the ground, flooding or tipping without first having served an "operations notice" on the district (or London borough) council in whose area the "site" is situated, and second, having allowed six weeks to expire after service of the operations notice. Nowhere in the Regulations is there provision for the amount of information which should be provided with the operations notice. If "the developer" is a local authority, the notice must be served on the Secretary of State. "Site" includes buildings and other structures on the site. The developer must in the notice specify the nature of the proposed

---

[78] s.33(4).
[79] Sched. 2, para. 13.
[79a] s.33(5).
[80] s.34(1).
[81] s.34(2)(3) and (5).
[82] s.38.

operations, the estimated date of the commencement of work and a certificate satisfying the provisions of section 36. This in effect is the consent of the person having an interest in the site of the operations or having compulsory purchase rights or issued by a statutory undertaker. An operations notice can be served in respect of operations which have to be carried out after clearance of any site. In these circumstances the developer must notify the investigating authority immediately on completion of the clearance operations.[83] The investigating authority then has a right to enter and inspect the site, observe any operations, and/or carry out any excavations,[84] but the investigating authority only has a right to excavate the site of the operations if before the end of the period of *four weeks*, beginning with the date of the service of the operations notice, the authority serves notice in the prescribed form of its intention to excavate and serves a copy of that notice on any council served with an operations notice.[85] The period allowed for excavation is a period of four months and two weeks beginning with the date immediately following the end of the *six week* period beginning with the date of the service of the operations notice.

Thus, the developer must serve his notice and must do nothing for *six weeks*. If he does, he commits a criminal offence. If, in the *first four weeks* of that six weeks, the investigating authority notify, under section 38, that they intend to inspect or excavate, then the developer is stopped from doing anything until the investigating authority carry out that work, which cannot be extended beyond the period of four months and two weeks from the end of the six-week period. Thus effectively no development can be delayed by statute beyond six months. Where there is a possibility of a site of archaeological interest being discovered, it is no doubt prudent to write into the standard form of building contract a provision whereby work may be held up for the six months.[86] It will also be noted that there are no emergency powers in the Act equivalent to the building preservation notice procedure which imposes a six months "listed" status on unlisted buildings pending a decision by the Secretary of State. There is no equivalent in ancient monuments legislation to the "stop" notice provisions in general planning law.

The investigating authority can, after the six weeks, carry out excavations provided it does not obstruct the execution on the site by the developer of clearance operations.[87] This provision only applies where the period allowed for the excavation begins at a later date than the six weeks beginning with the date of the service of the operations notice. This would only apply where the operations specified in the operations notice are to be carried out after the clearance of the site when, it has been seen, the developer is under an obligation to notify the investigating authority of the completion of the clearance of the site.[87a] In practice there has evolved an agreed

---

[83] s.35(7).

[84] s.38(1).

[85] s.38(3).

[86] But, as to antiquities, fossils and other objects of interest or value, see *e.g.* cl. 34 of the J.C.T. local authorities contract with quantities 1980, and Emden on *Building Contracts* (December 1986).

[87] s.38(5).

[87a] The forms of notice are contained in the Operations in Areas of Archaeological Importance (Forms of Notice, etc.) Regulations 1984 (S.I. 1984 No. 1285).

programme: often the archeology societies undertake part of the site clearance as part of the programme.

(d) Investigation of sites compulsorily acquired

8.40   There is power under section 39 for the investigating authority to investigate in advance of the service of an operations notice any site which may be acquired compulsorily. There are supplementary powers of entry contained in section 44, and the provision in section 46 in relation to compensation for damage caused by exercise of this power will no doubt be taken into account by the investigating authority before exercising these powers.

(e) Power of entry where operations notice served

8.41   Where an operations notice is served, section 40 confers powers on a person duly authorised in writing by the Secretary of State to inspect the site and record matters of archaeological or historical interest and a person duly authorised in writing by the Royal Commission on Historical Monuments for similar inspection and recording.

(f) Exemptions from operations notice controls

8.42   The Secretary of State may by an order[88] direct that section 35 shall not apply to the carrying out, or the carrying out by any class or description of persons specified in the order, of operations of any class or description specified in the order. Thus operations undertaken in compliance with such an order (an order which is not unlike a permission under the Schedule to the General Development Order under the 1971 Act) will not constitute an offence under section 35. The Areas of Archaeological Importance (Notification of Operations) (Exemption) Order 1984 has been made which gives exemption (*inter alia*) to certain operations in connection with agriculture, forestry, landscaping, tunnelling, mining, repair and maintenance of highways, waterways and mains services, and their installation.

(g) Defences to prosecution

8.43   In any proceedings for an offence under section 35 for carrying out or causing or permitting to be carried out any operations which disturb the ground, it is a defence for the accused to prove that he took all reasonable precautions and exercised all due diligence to avoid or prevent the disturbance of the ground.[89]

[88] s.37.
[89] s.37(5).

In any proceedings under section 35 it is a defence for the accused to prove either that he did not know and had no reason to believe that the site of the operations was within an area of archaeological importance, or that the operations were urgently necessary in the interests of safety of health and that notice in writing of the need for the operations was given to the Secretary of State as soon as reasonably practicable.[90] It is to be observed that this defence is in contrast to the absolute nature of offences in relation to listed buildings.

(h) Emergency actions prohibiting operations: powers of local authorities

There is a provision contained in section 35(10) whereby a district council **8.44** may institute High Court proceedings for an injunction for an offence under this section in respect of operations on any site wholly or partly within their area if it appears to any such council that any such operations are being, or are about to be, carried out in contravention of section 35, and the site contains or is likely to contain anything of archaeological or historical interest which will be disturbed, damaged, destroyed or removed without proper archaeological investigation.

(i) Anticipated problems

A major problem in the present economic climate continues to be the **8.45** financing of archaeological investigations. There is no mandatory obligation to provide grants, nor can the planning authority impose conditions requiring a financial contribution towards the cost of excavation. The provisions for designating areas of archaeological importance are discretionary unlike, *e.g.* the duty on local authorities to keep under review the designation of conservation areas. Moreover, statutory protection and financial assistance are not always enough to prevent monuments from being damaged, sometimes through ignorance. Specific threats include commercially sponsored "treasure hunts" which involve digging for a prize. Besides earmarking a substantial portion of available funds (£7.4 million in 1986–7) for rescue archaeology, as the work is known, the Commission is conscious of the vital importance of increasing public awareness and understanding of the constant threat to the archaeological heritage.

13. CROWN LAND

Where proposed Crown development affects a scheduled ancient monu- **8.46** ment or one held in guardianship under the provisions of the Ancient Monuments and Archaeological Areas Act 1979, or any known archaeological remains, the developing department is required to notify the Depart-

---

[90] s.37(6).

ment of the Environment (Heritage Sponsorship Division) or the Welsh Office (Conservation and Land Division). In England they must also consult the Commission.

14. METAL DETECTORS

8.47   There is also a provision in the Act whereby if a person uses a metal detector in a *protected place* without the written consent of the Commission he shall be guilty of an offence and liable for a fine not exceeding £200.[91] A *protected place* means any place which is either the site of a scheduled monument or any monument in the ownership or guardianship of the Secretary of State or situated in an area of archaeological importance.[92] It is a defence to the charge to prove that the metal detector was used for a purpose other than detecting or locating objects of archaeological or historical significance. There is a further offence for removing any object of archaeological or historical interest.[93] Consent for removal of such an object may be given by the Secretary of State for the purposes of the section.[94] These provisions form part of the "rights" of the public, and, as such, are considered in detail in Chapter 11.

The law of treasure trove remains unchanged by the 1979 Act: broadly, that only objects of pure gold or silver, orginally hidden by their owner with the intention of recovering them, are to be classed as such. The finder of treasure trove is entitled to the full market value, and the artifact goes to the Crown; otherwise it belongs to the owner of the land on which it was found, who may dispose of it as he likes. Whereas many archaeologists would like the definition of treasure trove to be broadened, others fear this would open up a black market in discovered antiquities.[95]

15. CRIMINAL OFFENCES

8.48   There are a number of criminal offences created in the Act, *e.g.*: carrying out works without consent: s.2(10); contravention of public access regulations: s.19(7); destroying or damaging a protected monument: s.28(1); carrying out without permission operations in areas of archeological importance: s.35(9); issuing a false certificate to accompany operations notice: s.36(4); using without authority a metal detector: s.42(5); intentionally obstructing powers of entry: s.44(8); and failing to give information as to interests in land: s.57(2).

[91] s.42(1).
[92] s.42(2).
[93] s.42(3).
[94] s.42(4).
[95] In 1985 the Department of the Environment issued a Consultation Paper on "Portable Antiquities" which at the time of going to press was still under consideration.

TABLE 7

Types of Monuments

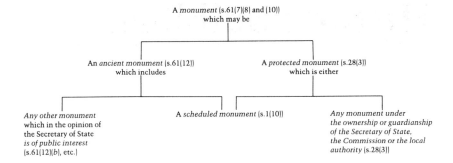

A *monument* (s.61(7)(8) and (10))
which may be

An *ancient monument* (s.61(12))
which includes

A *protected monument* (s.28(3))
which is either

Any other monument
which in the opinion of
the Secretary of State
is of public interest
(s.61(12)(*b*), etc.)

A *scheduled monument* (s.1(10))

*Any monument under
the ownership or guardianship
of the Secretary of State,
the Commission or the local
authority* (s.28(3))

©
Roger W. Suddards
1988

9. Taxation and Historic Buildings

1. GENERAL SUMMARY

9.01   In view of the importance of our country's national heritage, the taxation laws give sympathetic treatment to historic buildings in the shape of special reliefs and exemptions. These are designed to ensure that such buildings are conserved for the nation's benefit by remaining in private hands, the owners being encouraged to maintain the properties and allow public access. Where this is not possible, owners are encouraged to transfer the properties to national bodies set up to hold and maintain them.

This chapter describes these special reliefs and also summarises the taxation implications should an owner repair, improve, sell or give away a listed building, or receive income from letting it or opening it up to the public, or die owning it.

Unfortunately the tax laws of this country are very complicated, and if recent Finance Acts are anything to go by this complexity will not abate but increase. Accordingly, this chapter can only give a broad summary of those parts of our tax laws which affect listed buildings. If further information is required on any particular aspect, the reader should not hesitate to seek professional advice. Also, the Inland Revenue has published a useful booklet—"Capital Taxation and the National Heritage" (I.R. 67)—which outlines the law relating to capital taxation and its affect on the national heritage.

The taxes which affect listed buildings and which are described below comprise value added tax, capital gains tax, income tax and inheritance tax; the special position of maintenance funds is also covered.

This chapter is written on the basis of the law and practice in force on August 1, 1987.

2. VALUE ADDED TAX ("VAT")

(a) Introduction

Until June 1, 1984 work carried out by builders in making alterations (but **9.02** not repairs) to property was zero-rated. The result was that builders could recover the VAT which they suffered on their costs (such as materials purchased), but did not have to add VAT to their charges, so that the work was carried out for the owner of the building entirely free of VAT.

This relief from VAT was generally withdrawn from June 1, 1984, but a new relief was introduced for certain work carried out in connection with "protected buildings."

In outline, zero-rating is available for the following supplies:

(i) services of builders in carrying out "approved alterations" to a "protected building", and goods (such as materials) supplied with those services; and

(ii) the sale of a "protected building" (or the grant of a long lease) where this is carried out in the course of a business and the vendor (or grantor of the lease) has substantially reconstructed the building.[1]

Thus the person carrying out non-approved alterations, or repairs, to a listed building has to add VAT at 15 per cent. to his charges.

The new reliefs are hedged with conditions and complications, some of which are covered below. It should particularly be borne in mind that relief is not available for the services of architects, etc., nor for materials supplied by a person not also providing zero-rated services (*e.g.* a builder's merchant).

In practical terms, it will often be necessary to provide detailed evidence to H.M. Customs and Excise, and obtain appropriate rulings, in order to persuade builders and developers to zero-rate their supplies, or to ensure zero-rating on a future disposal of a protected building owned by a business.

The views of H.M. Customs and Excise in connection with listed buildings are contained in VAT Leaflet 708/1/85.

Where a building is opened to the public (see paras. 9.14–9.15 below), advice as to the necessity to register for VAT should be taken, as, if registration is necessary, this will involve not only VAT on the takings, but also a reclaim of VAT on the expenses of running the house to the extent they relate to business as opposed to private use. Such apportionment will need to be agreed by H.M. Customs and Excise. If registration is required, VAT is likely to be due on subsequent sales of many of the items associated with the running of the house (for example, antiques). Removal of items from display can also attract VAT.

(b) Definitions

It will be seen from the above summary that the terms "protected build- **9.03** ing" and "approved alteration" are vital in determining whether relief from VAT is available.

A "protected building" is:

---

[1] V.A.T.A. 1983, Sched. 5, Group 8A.

(i) a listed building within the meaning of the Town and Country Planning Act 1971, or the Scottish and Northern Irish equivalents; or

(ii) a scheduled monument within the meaning of the Ancient Monuments and Archaeological Areas Act 1979 or the Historic Monuments Act (Northern Ireland) 1971.[2]

In general, an "approved alteration" is an alteration for which listed building consent both:

(i) is required; and
(ii) has been obtained.[3]

In the case of buildings on Crown or Duchy land, an approved alteration is one for which listed building consent would have been required had it been situated elsewhere.[3]

If the protected building is a church and is still used as such, any alteration is an approved alteration.[4]

Works of repair or maintenance are never regarded as alterations or as approved alterations.[5] The distinction between a work of alteration and a work of repair or maintenance has been an area of dispute in the VAT tribunals for many years, and has never been fully resolved. In case of doubt, professional advice should be sought.

Where the work consists partly of approved alterations and partly of other works, the charge must be apportioned.[5] Only the part relating to approved alterations may be zero-rated.

Example: Builder's invoice

To: works at XYZ House:

	£	VAT £
Approved alterations	2,000	Zero
Other alterations	1,000	150
Repairs	500	75
	3,500	£225
VAT	225	
Total	£3,725	

(c) Zero-rating for approved alterations

9.04   Zero-rating is available for:

(i) services supplied in the course of approved alterations to protected buildings, other than services of architects, surveyors, and others acting as consultants or in a supervisory capacity[6]; and

[2] V.A.T.A. 1983, Sched. 5, Group 8A, Note 1.
[3] V.A.T.A. 1983, Sched. 5, Group 8A, Note 3(c).
[4] V.A.T.A. 1983, Sched. 5, Group 8A, Note 3(a).
[5] V.A.T.A. 1983, Sched. 5, Group 8A, Note 6.
[6] V.A.T.A. 1983, Sched. 5, Group 8A, Item 2.

(ii) supplies of materials, etc. provided by a person also supplying services which are zero-rated as in para. 9.02 above, and supplied in connection with those services.[7]

It will be seen from the above that a supply of goods in isolation is incapable of being zero-rated, and that there are restrictions on the supplies of goods which can be zero-rated. These are generally confined to materials, builders' hardware, sanitary ware, and other articles of a kind ordinarily installed by builders as fixtures.[8]

Specifically excluded from zero-rating are supplies of fitted furniture (or materials for the construction thereof) other than kitchen furniture.[9] A VAT liability will therefore arise if, say, fitted wardrobes are provided.

Domestic electrical and gas appliances are also excluded from zero-rating, other than space heaters and water heaters.[10]

The restriction of zero-rating for services of architects, etc. might sometimes be avoided by employing a builder to carry out the overall work on a "design and build" basis, and letting the builder hire the architect.[11] This will usually be disadvantageous on commercial grounds, as it breaks the contractual link between property owner and professional adviser, and may make it more difficult to obtain recompense if things go wrong.

(d) Building used as a private residence

Special care is needed if the listed building is a private house. Approved **9.05** alterations made to the house itself will qualify for zero-rating. However, no zero-rating will be available for work on other buildings within the grounds unless they are themselves self-contained dwelling houses. Zero-rating is not even available for the construction, from scratch, of such secondary buildings.[12]

If it is desired that the facilities of a listed dwelling house be improved, it will often be preferable (from a VAT point of view) to achieve this by extending the existing house, rather than by refurbishing outbuildings or by erecting new buildings in the grounds.

(e) Sale of a protected building

As indicated above, there is zero-rating for the sale of a protected building, **9.06** or the grant of a long lease over it, by a person who has substantially reconstructed the building.[13]

This zero-rating is only relevant where it is done in the course of a business, in which case it will enable the builder or developer to obtain a refund of VAT on expenses incurred to the extent that these are not zero-rated.

---

[7] V.A.T.A. 1983, Sched. 5, Group 8, Item 3.
[8] V.A.T.A. 1983, Sched. 5, Group 8, Item 3(a).
[9] V.A.T.A. 1983, Sched. 5, Group 8, Note 2A(a) and (b).
[10] V.A.T.A. 1983, Sched. 5, Group 8, Note 2A(c).
[11] Leaflet 708/2/85, para. 11.
[12] V.A.T.A. 1983, Sched. 5, Group 8A, Note 7, and Group 8, Note 2(a).
[13] V.A.T.A. 1983, Sched. 5, Group 8A, Item 1.

No general definition is given as to what is involved in "substantially reconstructing" a building, so this must be interpreted in terms of the general meaning of these words. In the past, H.M. Customs and Excise have been prepared to accept a building as substantially reconstructed if the cost of the works carried out (excluding any repair element) has exceeded half the estimated cost of constructing a similar building from the ground upwards.

The VAT legislation applies one of two additional, or secondary, tests before zero-rating is available.

If at least 60 per cent. of the cost of the works involved in carrying out the reconstruction qualifies for zero-rating as described above (or would qualify, if the suppliers were VAT registered), then zero-rating is available.[14]

Alternatively, zero-rating will be granted if all that remains of the original listed building are the *external* walls and other *external* features of architectural or historic interest.[15]

It should be borne in mind that the general test (of a substantial reconstruction having taken place) must always be met for zero-rating to apply. This is scarcely likely to be a problem where the latter of the secondary tests above is relied upon.

(f) Practical points

9.07   There is often uncertainty as to whether the conditions for zero-rating are met and, more particularly, as to the extent to which work carried out constitutes approved alterations as opposed to other alterations or works of repair or maintenance.

The best way of dealing with this uncertainty is by approaching H.M. Customs and Excise for a ruling. Provided that *all* of the relevant facts are disclosed to H.M. Customs and Excise, a ruling that the work is zero-rated will be honoured even if it subsequently turns out to have been incorrect.[16] Care should be taken to present the information in writing and to insist on a written ruling, so that there is evidence of the ruling and of the basis on which it was made. The application for a ruling should normally be made to the local VAT office which deals with the building contractor.

As indicated above, an approved alteration means an alteration for which listed building consent was both needed and obtained. In practice, if consent is obtained H.M. Customs and Excise generally accept that it was needed. When seeking listed building consent, therefore, it is wise to ensure that it embraces as much as possible of the work being undertaken.

Whilst the proposal must be clearly stated, nevertheless the form of words used in the application for listed building consent, and in the consent itself, can often affect the likelihood of obtaining zero-rating. It is often difficult to distinguish between works of alteration and works of repair or maintenance. If the consent uses words like "alteration," "improvement" and "extension," this will generally enhance the chances of obtaining zero-rating. The use of words like "repair" and "replacement" tend to colour

---

[14] V.A.T.A. 1983, Sched. 5, Group 8A, Note 2(a).
[15] V.A.T.A. 1983, Sched. 5, Group 8A, Note 2(b).
[16] *Hansard* (July 21, 1978), Col. 426 and 1978 V.A.T.T.R. 278.

thinking in the opposite direction, and will almost invariably result in zero-rating being denied.

It is possible for part only of a building to be listed. Accordingly, work carried out on the non-listed part (or on non-listed outbuildings) would not qualify for the VAT relief for listed buildings. In appropriate cases, therefore, it is advisable to check the extent of the listing and, if possible, seek to have it widened.[16a]

Where work to be carried out to a listed building involves its extension, it is arguable that the new extension is by definition not covered by the existing listing and thus not eligible for zero-rating. However, H.M. Customs and Excise may not take this point, although if an extension is contemplated consideration should be given to seeking an extension of the terms of the listing prior to the construction of the extension.[16a]

If alterations are made to a listed building owned by a business, it is important to establish at the time whether zero-rating will be available in the event of a subsequent sale. If a sale takes place some years after the alterations were carried out, it might then be difficult to assemble sufficient evidence to obtain zero-rating.

If work done to a listed building is incorrectly zero-rated without the protection of a ruling from H.M. Customs and Excise, the question arises of who is to bear the unexpected VAT liability which subsequently arises. If the contract for the works was expressed as being for a fixed sum of money, with no mention of VAT, the agreed price is taken to include VAT.[17] The legal liability to pay the tax therefore falls on the builder. Where the contract specifies a price "plus VAT if applicable," the builder has the primary liability to pay H.M. Customs and Excise, but can recover the tax from the customer.[17a]

(g) European Commission infraction proceedings

At the time of writing, the European Commission is involved in proceedings against the U.K. government, claiming that certain UK zero-ratings contravene Community law. Depending on the results of those proceedings, it is possible that the U.K. law will be amended to withdraw zero-rating in respect of listed buildings, or in respect of listed buildings other than dwelling houses. Any such changes would be likely to take effect in 1988 or 1989.   **9.08**

3. CAPITAL GAINS TAX ("CGT")

(a) Introduction

CGT is charged at the rate of 30 per cent. on gains accruing to individuals from the disposal of assets, including listed buildings.[18] Broadly, the gain is calculated by deducting from the net sale proceeds the aggregate of the orig-   **9.09**

[16a] Such a check must include an analysis of what is included in the curtilage—see paras. 2.17–2.20.

[17] V.A.T.A. 1983, s.10(2).

[17a] The VAT rules tend to encourage owners to alter or replace rather than to repair (which the conservationist would prefer).

[18] C.G.T.A. 1979, ss.1–3.

inal sum paid for the building and any expenditure subsequently incurred in improving it.[19] Also, to recognise the effects of inflation since March 1982 (or the date the building was acquired if later) an indexation allowance is deducted.[20]

CGT liability can also arise when capital sums are derived from assets, such as sums received for surrendering rights or claims for damages.[21] However, the CGT may be deferred if, broadly, the compensation received for damage to property is wholly applied in restoring it.[22]

There is currently, unlike the position in previous years, no special tax on development value attaching to land or buildings, such value merely attracting CGT liability as described above.

Capital losses are computed in more or less the same way as capital gains, and can be deducted from capital gains realised in the same or succeeding tax years.[23] A capital loss can arise when a building is destroyed or its value becomes negligible, although in these circumstances the owner is regarded as having sold (and re-acquired) at market value the site of the building together with any land occupied for purposes ancillary to the use of the building.[24]

Subject to the reliefs described below, a building is regarded as having been disposed of for CGT purposes at market value if it is given away or transferred into a trust[25]; similar remarks apply if trustees transfer a building to beneficiaries of the trust.[26] No CGT liability arises on any unrealised gain if the owner of a building dies—his or her beneficiaries are treated for CGT purposes as acquiring the building at market value on the date of death.[27]

For 1987–88 net gains of individuals of up to £6,600 (£3,300 for most trusts) are exempt.[28]

The following reliefs and exemptions contained in the CGT code may be relevant as regards listed buildings and historic houses.

(b) Private residence

9.10   Full exemption from CGT is available if a building has been the owner's only or main residence throughout his period of ownership.[29] Relief is given, not only for the house itself, but also for garden or grounds of up to one acre, including the site of the house; in certain cases relief may be given for a larger area if it is required for the reasonable enjoyment of the house having regard to its size and character.[30]

---

[19] C.G.T.A. 1979, s.32.
[20] F.A. 1982, ss.86, 87.
[21] C.G.T.A. 1979, s.20.
[22] C.G.T.A. 1979, s.21.
[23] C.G.T.A. 1979, s.29.
[24] C.G.T.A. 1979, s.22.
[25] C.G.T.A. 1979, s.29A and 53.
[26] C.G.T.A. 1979, s.54.
[27] C.G.T.A. 1979, s.49.
[28] C.G.T.A. 1979, s.5.
[29] C.G.T.A. 1979, s.102.
[30] C.G.T.A. 1979, s.101(1)–(4).

Similarly, the exemption can apply to a trustee where the house is the only or main residence of a person entitled to occupy it under the terms of the settlement.[31] Somewhat similar relief is available to an executor who sells a private residence.[32]

The exemption can be restricted where part only of the building is used as a private residence,[33] where the property has not been used as the owner's only or main residence throughout his period of ownership,[34] or where part of the property is used exclusively for business purposes.[35] On the other hand, relief is available in certain circumstances where the property is let residentially,[36] and a special relief exists if the property is let commercially as furnished holiday accommodation.[37]

(c) Gifts and transfers to and from settlements

In general, gifts of property by one individual to another, or to and from settlements, are treated as taking place at market value for CGT purposes, with the result that CGT can be payable on a "deemed" gain.[38] **9.11**

However, so as not to discourage the spreading of wealth within a family, an election can be made in the above circumstances to "hold-over" any capital gain.[39] This means that the transferee inherits the history of the property from the transferor, and also his base CGT cost of the property and indexation allowance, so that any unrealised gain at the time the property is transferred is deferred until it is subsequently disposed of.

Similarly, if property is given to a charity or to certain national and local bodies concerned with the preservation of the national heritage,[40] no capital gain arises at the date of gift and any charge to tax is deferred by carrying forward the gain until there is a later disposal of the property.[41]

On the other hand, *complete* exemption from CGT is available in certain circumstances for buildings of outstanding historic or architectural interest (including essential surrounding amenity land) provided they are formally designated following the receipt of an undertaking that they will be preserved and the public allowed reasonable access.[42] The circumstances in which such CGT exemption is available are:

(i) gifts and private sales to certain national and local bodies concerned with the preservation of the national heritage;

---

[31] C.G.T.A. 1979, s.104.
[32] Extra statutory Concession D5.
[33] C.G.T.A. 1979, ss.101(1)(a) and 103(2).
[34] C.G.T.A. 1979, s.102.
[35] C.G.T.A. 1979, s.103(1).
[36] F.A. 1980, s.80.
[37] F.A. 1984, s.50 and Sched. 11.
[38] C.G.T.A. 1979, ss.29A, 53, 54.
[39] F.A. 1980, s.79; F.A. 1982, s.82.
[40] These bodies are listed in Sched. 3 to the Inheritance Tax Act 1984 (see also "Capital Taxation and the National Heritage" (December 1986), p. 61, published by the Board of Inland Revenue).
[41] C.G.T.A. 1979, s.146.
[42] C.G.T.A. 1979, s.147.

(ii) gifts made for public benefit to a non-profit making body; and

(iii) property accepted in lieu of inheritance tax.

(d) Charities

9.12   If a listed building is owned by a charity, no capital gain arises on its sale provided the gain is applied for charitable purposes.[43]

Charities also enjoy a measure of relief from income tax.[44] This is also referred to in para. 9.17 below.

4. INCOME TAX

(a) Introduction

9.13   The income tax rules offer few concessions of assistance to the individual who is the owner or occupier of a listed building or historic house. On the other hand, if the building is owned by a charity there are extensive income tax reliefs, and these are described below.

(b) Operation as a business

9.14   If an historic building is opened to the public and run on a commercial basis and with a view to profits, the owner is treated for tax purposes as carrying on a trade.[45] This means that the various reliefs applicable to traders in the tax legislation are available (e.g. losses,[46] retirement annuities,[47] capital gains tax roll-over[48] and retirement relief.[49]).

In addition, the running costs of the enterprise can be set off against the income received in assessing taxable income, such expenses including upkeep of the house, contents and gardens (excluding any part set aside exclusively for private use),[50] together with capital allowances in respect of plant or machinery provided for maintaining the house, contents and gardens.[51]

There are certain Inland Revenue guidelines governing the question of whether a house open to the public is "managed on a commercial basis and with a view to the realisation of profits," and therefore whether it should be treated as a business and its running costs allowed in computing taxable income. The factors taken into account are:

---

[43] C.G.T.A. 1979, s.145.
[44] I.C.T.A. 1970, s.360.
[45] I.C.T.A. 1970, s.110(3).
[46] I.C.T.A. 1970, ss.168–175.
[47] I.C.T.A. 1970, ss.226–228.
[48] C.G.T.A. 1979, ss.115–121.
[49] F.A. 1985, ss.69–70 and Sched. 20.
[50] I.C.T.A. 1970, s.130.
[51] F.A. 1971, ss.40–50.

(i) the extent to which the property is likely to attract visitors having regard, *inter alia*, to its historic, architectural and, in the case of gardens, horticultural interest;

(ii) how much of the property is set aside as a show place; a substantial part of the property should be open to visitors but appropriate allowance will be made for utility and other rooms of little interest to the public, and for those houses where the delicate condition of the fabric prevents part from being shown;

(iii) the number of days on which the property is open to the public. This would usually have to be a substantial number of days in the year but must be compatible with the aim of making a profit from opening. For example, where opening on 75 days or less might be expected to show a higher return than, say, 125 days, then the former figure would satisfy this requirement. Days on which the house is open by appointment to groups and parties can also be taken into account; and

(iv) the amount of organisation for the attraction and reception of visitors (*e.g.* adequate advertising and publicity, the provision of ticket offices, car parks, refreshments and guides, the sale of post cards and guide books); it must be shown in general that a definite organisation has been set up for attracting and dealing with visitors.[52]

It is of underlying importance that the house is opened with the intention **9.15** of making a profit. If the opening is for purely altruistic reasons, or merely with a view to obtaining tax relief for what are in reality private expenses, the Revenue will not treat the enterprise as a business. The fact that the house has made a loss will not necessarily prevent it from being treated as a business provided the Revenue are satisfied that the intention is to make a profit, although the continuation of the enterprise in the face of prolonged losses might cause the Revenue to reconsider whether the property is indeed being managed on a commercial basis and with a view to the realisation of profits.

The stringency of this approach is modified where a house is first opened to the public; it is accepted that a house which may eventually be a commercial success might not attract a sufficient number of visitors to make a profit at the outset. It will be sufficient to show that there is a reasonable prospect of profits being made in the future. As a guideline, the Revenue accept that a property which subsequently achieves 15,000 visitors per year from regular opening should be treated as having been opened on a commercial basis from the outset. It is stressed that the figure of 15,000 is not a rigid minimum to be achieved in every case, and factors such as the size and accessibility of the property and the delicate condition of its fabric could lead to this figure being lowered.

Receipts from incidental activities such as tea rooms and the sale of souvenirs are added to receipts from entrance charges for the purpose of establishing profitability.

If the Revenue are not satisfied that the house is being run commercially to make profits, then whilst they will undoubtedly tax any net surpluses,

[52] "Tax Treatment of Historic Houses and Gardens Open to the Public" (November 1980), T1617/5/1970.

they are likely to insist on any deficiencies merely being carried forward to be set off only against future profits from running the house.

The VAT position is referred to in para. 9.02 above.

(c) Letting of historic house

9.16   Where a house is merely let out to a lessee or tenant, the rents received less maintenance, repair, insurance and management costs are assessable.[53]

(d) Ownership by a charity

9.17   Listed buildings and historic houses are often owned by charities. In these circumstances rents and most other forms of income are exempt from tax provided they are applied for charitable purposes only.[54]

Trading profits are similarly exempt from tax provided they are applied solely for charitable purposes and, *inter alia*, the trade is exercised in the course of the actual carrying out of a primary purpose of the charity.[55] Thus income from amusement machines, sale of items not connected with the educational or cultural activities of the historic house, funfairs, etc. (but not normally cafeteria refreshments or vending machines) is not exempt, although exemption can effectively be achieved if a company owned by the charity carries on these activities and covenants its profits to the charity.

5. INHERITANCE TAX ("IHT")

(a) Introduction

9.18   IHT, formerly known as capital transfer tax, was introduced in the 1974 budget as a replacement for estate duty. Since its inception 80 years previously in 1894, estate duty had become increasingly easier to avoid so as to earn the description of the "voluntary tax." As will be seen from the remarks below, as a result of the fundamental changes to IHT made by the Finance Act 1986 estate duty has almost, but not quite, returned.

Prior to the Finance Act 1986, IHT could be described as a tax at progressive rates on the total of an individual's lifetime gifts (cumulated with those made within the previous 10 years), with a final charge to the tax on the value of the assets he possessed when he died. Furthermore, not only could a charge to IHT arise when property was transferred into a trust, it could also arise when property left a trust and, in the case of a "discretionary trust," at regular intervals during its life.

The changes made by the Finance Act 1986 were fundamental. In general,

[53] I.C.T.A. 1970, ss.67–78.
[54] I.C.T.A. 1970, s.360.
[55] I.C.T.A. 1970, s.360(1)(e)(i).

gifts to other individuals made on or after March 18, 1986 are totally exempt unless the donor dies within seven years of the gift. In these circumstances the value of the gift when it was made will be added to the value of the estate on death and tax charged accordingly, but with tapering rates of tax payable on gifts made more than three years before death. Thus a gift made, say, six years before death will suffer a lower rate of tax than the same gift made within, say, two years of death.

Similar remarks apply to a transfer to a special form of trust known as an "accumulation and maintenance" trust, to trusts for the disabled and to transfers into and out of life interest trusts.

On the other hand, transfers to other types of trust, such as discretionary trusts, and transfers out of such trusts, will still attract liability when they are made, and the regular periodic charge will remain. However, in calculating the liability on such transfers, which is at progressive rates, they will only be aggregated with non-exempt transfers made in the previous seven years.

The main reason behind the relaxation in IHT made by the Finance Act 1986 was to give individuals the freedom to pass their wealth to other individuals, in particular to enable a family business or other assets to be handed down to the next generation free of tax. Previous Finance Acts have also assisted in this by enabling such transfers to take place free of capital gains tax and stamp duty.

(b) Exemptions and reliefs for historic buildings

Provided undertakings are given—usually by the new owner—that agreed **9.19** steps will be taken to secure reasonable access to the public and also that the property will be preserved and maintained, IHT relief is available both to individuals and trustees against the IHT that would otherwise arise on death, and also against that which would have arisen on a lifetime transfer provided the donor or his spouse owned the building for at least six years before the transfer.[56]

However, the relief is withdrawn and an IHT liability arises if, broadly, these undertakings are broken or the property is sold, given away or the owner dies, although the sale or gift can be to one of the bodies concerned with the preservation of the national heritage or the new owner can renew the above undertakings without the relief being lost.[57] Where such a sale is made, the vendor and purchasing body share the tax exemption. Also, relief is retained if the property is accepted by the Revenue in satisfaction of IHT, in which event no capital gains tax, stamp duty or VAT arises.[58]

Similarly, if an historic building is transferred outright to a UK charity, or to a body concerned with the preservation of the national heritage, or to an approved non-profit making body, no IHT arises.[59] However, this exemption is only available if any occupation of the building by the donor or his family is at a full arm's length rent.

The above reliefs are available not only in respect of the buildings them-

---

[56] I.H.T.A. 1984, s.31.
[57] I.H.T.A. 1984, ss.23, 25, 26, 32.
[58] I.H.T.A. 1984, s.231.
[59] See n. 57 above.

selves, but also for their essential amenity land and objects historically associated with them.[60]

Further information on the IHT aspects can be found in the booklet "Capital Taxation and the National Heritage" (I.R. 67), and "Inheritance Tax" (I.H.T. 1), both of which are published by the Inland Revenue.

(c) Buildings eligible for relief

9.20   As regards those buildings which qualify for IHT relief, if a grant has been given under section 3A of the Historic Buildings and Ancient Monuments Act 1953 (as introduced by the National Heritage Act 1983) for a particular building, that will be a *prima facie* indication that it will be accepted as outstanding for IHT purposes. If a building has been listed under the Town and Country Planning Acts, the grading will give an indication of its merits; but any building or ancient monument is eligible for consideration.[61]

Before a decision is taken on whether or not a building is eligible, the Capital Taxes Office of the Inland Revenue consults the Commission, or the appropriate department in Scotland, Wales or Northern Ireland, which will in turn consult the relevant Historic Buildings Council.[61]

6. MAINTENANCE FUNDS

(a) Introduction

9.21   A maintenance fund is a trust fund set up during lifetime or on death by the owner of an historic building in order to maintain and preserve it, also to allow the public reasonable access to it. As the owner indirectly benefits from the fund, it cannot be set up as a charity.

Income producing assets, which often include land, are transferred to the trust, and provided various conditions are met there are favourable IHT and income tax consequences. These are described below.

The maintenance fund must be set up to preserve a building of special architectural or historic interest, including its essential amenity land and objects historically associated with it. The building must be supported by the undertakings as to maintenance and access referred to in para. 9.19 above, and it must be eligible for relief as an outstanding building as described in para. 9.20 above.[62]

---

[60] See n. 56 above.

[61] "Capital Taxation and the National Heritage", p. 17, published by the Inland Revenue.

[62] I.H.T.A. 1984, Sched. 4, para. 3(3).

(b) Inheritance tax reliefs

If the maintenance fund itself satisfies the conditions described in para. **9.22**
9.25 below, no IHT arises when cash or other investments are transferred
into the fund,[63] the ten-yearly IHT charge on discretionary trusts is inappli-
cable,[64] and the use or extraction of capital from the fund for a purpose connected with the relevant building does not result in IHT liability.[65]
However, other transfers out of the fund to beneficiaries can result in IHT
liability unless, broadly, they are made to the person who originally created
the maintenance fund,[66] or the beneficiary immediately transfers the funds
to a new approved maintenance fund,[67] or the beneficiary is a charity or
other approved body.[68]

(c) Income tax relief

In the absence of special income tax relief, the income of a maintenance   **9.23**
fund would normally be assessable on the person who created it, as he has
an effective interest in the fund since its assets can be used to repair and
improve a building he owns or occupies. In these circumstances where the
person creating the trust has an interest, direct or indirect, in it, the tax laws
treat the trust's income as assessable on him.[69]

However, the trustees can elect that the above treatment is not to apply,
whereupon the income of the fund will be assessable to income tax on them
at the rate (for 1987–88) of 45 per cent.—*i.e.* 27 per cent. basic rate and 18
per cent. additional rate—and the trustees can also use the trust funds to
maintain, etc. the building without this involving the owner in tax liability.[70] Whether such an election is beneficial will depend on the owner's
marginal tax rate.

If no election is made, the fund's income will be assessed on the owner of
the building, assuming he set up the trust, although he will incur no further
tax liability if the trustees use the trust funds to maintain, etc. the building.[71]

If the trustees use funds for a purpose unconnected with the historic
building (*e.g.* for the personal use of a beneficiary) in circumstances where
the above election has been made so that the fund's income is being taxed at
45 per cent. as opposed to the higher rate that is likely to be payable by the
person who created the fund, that income is then subjected to a further
income tax charge of 30 per cent. to compensate, to the extent it has not
been used to maintain, etc. the historic building.[72] Similar remarks apply
where Inland Revenue approval of the fund is withdrawn.[72]

---

[63] I.H.T.A. 1984, s.27(1).
[64] I.H.T.A. 1984, s.58(1)(*c*).
[65] I.H.T.A. 1984, s.76(1) and Sched. 4, para. 8(2).
[66] I.H.T.A. 1984, Sched. 4, para. 10.
[67] I.H.T.A. 1984, Sched. 4, para. 9.
[68] I.H.T.A. 1984, s.76.
[69] I.C.T.A. 1970, ss.447, 448.
[70] F.A. 1977, s.38(2).
[71] F.A. 1977, s.38(3).
[72] F.A. 1980, s.52.

(d) Capital gains tax relief

9.24   No CGT need arise when assets are transferred into or out of a maintenance fund in view of the availability of the "hold-over" election referred to
in para. 9.11 above. On the other hand, sales of assets by the maintenance
fund trustees can result in CGT liability.

(e) Conditions to be satisfied for above favourable tax treatment

9.25   To prevent abuse of the above tax reliefs, the Revenue must be satisfied as
to the following matters.[73]

(i) The assets transferred to the fund must be of an appropriate character and amount having regard to the requirements of the historic
building and also other sources of upkeep available to the owner.
Stock exchange securities or agricultural property are normally
ideal.

(ii) The trustees must be approved by the Revenue, they must include
at least one professional trustee, and the majority must be resident
in the U.K.

(iii) For the first six years from the time the assets are put into the
maintenance fund (or the settlor's death, if earlier), any of the
fund's assets can only be used to maintain the building (including
maintenance and improvement of non-historic properties transferred to the maintenance fund), provide public access to it, pay the
trustees' expenses, or be paid to a national heritage body or heritage
charity. After the expiry of that six year period, capital in the fund
can be used for any purpose, although income must continue to be
used for the above purposes.

The Revenue can enforce the trusts of a maintenance fund,[74] can withdraw their approval[75] (in which event IHT and income tax liability could
arise), and will expect to receive annual reports and accounts.[76]

---

[73] I.H.T.A. 1984, Sched. 4, paras. 1–4.
[74] I.H.T.A. 1984, Sched. 4, para. 7.
[75] I.H.T.A. 1984, Sched. 4, para. 5.
[76] I.H.T.A. 1984, Sched. 4, para. 6.

10. Grant and Loan Facilities

1. INTRODUCTION

It is perhaps fortunate that the vast majority of listed buildings are gain- **10.01**
fully and usefully occupied, and that though a large number of ancient
monuments cannot be said to be usefully occupied, some are at least gain-
fully utilised. It is fortunate because in a country which has over 400,000
listed buildings and ancient monuments there is little financial resource
available from public sources to help support their maintenance and repair.
Ever since the early ancient monuments legislation, successive govern-
ments have appeared to try to avoid shouldering the burden of maintenance
and repair, and have left it with the owners of such buildings. Perhaps it is
for this reason that some local authorities do not pursue powers which they
have against the owners of listed buildings quite so vigorously as some
would wish them to do.

Many of those who own or have responsibility for listed buildings wish
that a greater share of the national economy was devoted to the maintenance and upkeep of historic buildings. Many contend that there should be
(as in the United States) a greater tax incentive to owners of such buildings;
the Finance Act 1980 went some way towards meeting that objection.

Nonetheless, successive Parliaments over the last 70 years have recognised that there must be made available some money in particularly important or deserving cases. In doing so, however, they have succeeded in
creating a web of powers for the making of grants and loans for historic
buildings and areas, which is not readily intelligible to the layman, and
which even for the professional engaged in the building conservation field,
presents a formidable array of possibilities for securing assistance where it
is needed.

This chapter seeks to review the current position in respect of grant aid relating to, *inter alia*, listed buildings, adjacent land and gardens, ancient monuments and conservation areas. New legislation has continued to add to the range of grants and loans available to both private individuals and local authorities. The position is constantly changing with several important alterations having been made in recent years in respect of the powers of various bodies to make grants. Of particular significance was the transfer, on April 1, 1984, of all the Secretary of State's powers to make grants towards the costs of repairs to buildings of architectural or historic interest and for works in conservation areas in England, to the Commission.

The overall position on grants and loans is summarised in Table 8 at para. 10.29 below. This not only summarises the range of grant and loan aid available, but identifies its statutory derivation. The scope of each grant/loan is briefly described, together with any specific methods or conditions of payment if applicable.

The summary table is intended to give owners assistance in making a provisional assessment of the possible eligibility of their buildings for financial assistance from various sources and where to make the initial approach. Further details are set out in the following pages of the legislation from which each grant or loan derives its status.

Finally, we consider briefly the statutory provisions relating to the acquisition by agreement of historic buildings by government, the National Trusts, and local authorities.

The following statutory provisions are given at length, but for further reference the reader should consult the commentary to the sections in the *Encyclopedia of Planning Law and Practice.*

2. HISTORIC BUILDINGS AND ANCIENT MONUMENTS ACT 1953[1]

Under the provisions of this Act there are made available grants and loans limited to the repair of buildings (and of land or objects associated with them) which, individually or as part of a group, are of outstanding historic or architectural interest. The Act also provides for the recovery of such grants where attached conditions are not complied with, and for grants to local authorities and the National Trust for the acquisition of such properties.

"Grants and loans for preservation of historic buildings

10.02   **3A.**—(1) The Commission may make grants for the purpose of defraying in whole or in part any expenditure incurred or to be incurred in the repair or maintenance of a building which is situated in England and which appears to the Commission to be of outstanding historic or architectural

---

[1] As amended by T.C.A.A. 1974, s.12 and A.M.A.A.A. 1979, s.48(2) which section with s.49 was brought into operation by S.I. 1979 No. 786—The Ancient Monuments and Archeological Areas Act 1979 (Commencement No. 1) Order 1979. Also by the N.H.A. 1983 to incorporate reference to the Commission and to land situated in England.

interest, or in the upkeep of any land which is situated in England and which comprises, or is contiguous or adjacent to, any such building, or in the repair or maintenance of any objects ordinarily kept in any such building or in the upkeep of a garden or other land which is situated in England and which appears to the Commission to be of outstanding historic interest but which is not contiguous or adjacent to a building which appears to the Commission to be of outstanding historic or architectural interest.

(2) The power conferred by subsection (1) of this section to make grants for the purposes there mentioned shall include power to make loans for those purposes.

(3) Where a grant under this section is made to the National Trust for Places of Historic Interest or Natural Beauty, the grant may, if the Commission think fit, be made by way of endowment, subject to such provisions, by way of trust, contract or otherwise, as may appear to the Commission to be requisite for securing that, so long as it is reasonably practicable to give effect to the purposes of the endowment, the sum granted will be retained and invested by the Trust and used as a source of income for defraying the expenditure in respect of which the grant is made.

(4) A grant or loan under this section may be made subject to conditions imposed by the Commission for the purpose of securing public access to the whole or part of the property to which the grant or loan relates, or for other purposes, as the Commission may think fit.

(5) A loan made under this section shall be made on such terms as to repayment, payment of interest and otherwise as the Commission may determine.

Grants for preservation of historic buildings, their contents and adjoining land[2]

4.—(1) The Secretary of State may, out of moneys provided by Parliament, **10.03** make grants for the purpose of defraying in whole or in part any expenditure incurred or to be incurred in the repair or maintenance of a building which is not situated in England and which appears to the Secretary of State to be of outstanding historic or architectural interest, or in the upkeep of any land comprising, or contiguous or adjacent to, any such building, or in the repair or maintenance of any objects ordinarily kept in any such building or in the upkeep of a garden or other land which is not situated in England and which appears to the Secretary of State to be of outstanding historic interest but which is not contiguous or adjacent to a building which appears to him to be of outstanding historic or architectural interest.

(2) Where a grant under this section is made to the National Trust for Places of Historic Interest or Natural Beauty or the National Trust for Scotland for Places of Historic Interest or Natural Beauty, the grant may, if the

---

[2] Also eligible for these grants are "places of worship in use." Although not excluded from the provisions of section 4, grants under the section for such buildings were not made until 1977. Although there was always the power to use this provision in respect of Church of England places of worship in use, it never was so exercised because of the arrangements made in 1913 with the Church of England whereby no state aid was made available in return for "the ecclesiastical exemption." It is understood that cathedrals are not included in the scope of the Department's provisions in this respect.

Secretary of State thinks fit, be made by way of endowment, subject to such provisions, by way of trust, contract or otherwise, as may appear to the Secretary of State to be requisite for securing that, so long as it is reasonably practicable to give effect to the purposes of the endowment, the sum granted will be retained and invested by the Trust and used as a source of income for defraying the expenditure in respect of which the grant is made.

(3) A grant under this section may be made subject to conditions imposed by the Secretary of State for the purpose of securing public access to the whole or part of the property to which the grant relates, or for other purposes, as the Secretary of State may think fit.

(4) Before making any grant under this section the Secretary of State shall consult with the appropriate Council under this Act, both as to the making of the grant and as to the conditions subject to which it should be made:

Provided that this subsection shall not apply in a case where the making of a grant appears to the Secretary of State to be a matter of immediate urgency.

Recovery of grants under sections 3A and 4

10.04   **4A.**—(1) This section applies to any grant under section 3A or 4 of this Act made on terms that it shall be recoverable under this section; but any such grant shall only be regarded for the purposes of this section as so made if before or on making the grant the Commission or (as the case may be) the Secretary of State gives to the grantee notice in writing—

  (a) summarising the effect of this section; and
  (b) specifying the period during which the grant is to be recoverable in accordance with subsection (4) below in the case of a grant made for the purpose there mentioned.

(2) The period specified under subsection (1)(b) above in the case of any grant shall be a period beginning with the day on which the grant is made and ending not more than ten years after that day.

(3) If any condition subject to which a grant to which this section applies was made is contravened or not complied with the Commission or (as the case may be) the Secretary of State may recover the amount of the grant or such part of it as they think or (as the case may be) he thinks fit from the grantee.

(4) If, during the period specified under subsection (1)(b) above in the case of a grant to which this section applies made to any person for the purpose of defraying in whole or in part any expenditure on the repair, maintenance or upkeep of any property, the grantee disposes in any manner mentioned in subsection (5) below of the interest, or any part thereof, held by him in the property on the day on which the grant is made (referred to below in this section as "the relevant interest") the Commission or (as the case may be) the Secretary of State may recover the amount of the grant or such part of it as they think or (as the case may be) he thinks fit from the grantee.

(5) Subsection (4) above only applies where the grantee disposes of the relevant interest or any part of it by way of sale or exchange or lease for a term of not less than twenty-one years.

(6) If a person becomes entitled by way of gift from the grantee, whether directly or indirectly (but otherwise than by will) to a part of the relevant

interest, a disposal by the donee in any manner mentioned in subsection (5) above of the interest so acquired by him in the property, or any part of that interest, shall be treated for the purposes of subsection (4) above as a disposal by the grantee of a part of the relevant interest.

(7) If a person becomes entitled by way of any such gift to the whole of the relevant interest subsection (4) above shall have effect (except for the purpose of determining the relevant interest) as if the donee were the grantee.

(8) Nothing in subsection (3) or (4) above shall be taken as conferring on the Secretary of State a right to recover (by virtue of a breach of more than one condition or disposals of several parts of an interest in property) amounts in the aggregate exceeding the amount of the grant.

Grants to local authorities and National Trust for acquisition of historic buildings

5B.—(1) The Commission may make grants for the purpose of defraying   **10.05** in whole or in part any expenses incurred by a local authority in England in the acquisition of property situated in England under section 114 or 119(1)(b) or (c) of the Town and Country Planning Act 1971 (under which buildings of special architectural or historic interest may in certain cases be acquired by a local authority).

(2) The Commission may also make grants to the National Trust for Places of Historic Interest or Natural Beauty for the purpose of defraying in whole or in part any expenses incurred by them in the acquisition of—

  (a) any building which is situated in England and which appears to the Commission to be of outstanding historic or architectural interest;
  (b) any land which is situated in England and which comprises, or is contiguous or adjacent to, any such building; or
  (c) any garden or other land which is situated in England and which appears to the Commission to be of outstanding historic interest but which is not contiguous or adjacent to a building which appears to the Commission to be of outstanding historic or architectural interest.

Grants to local authorities and National Trusts for acquisition of historic buildings

6.—(1) The Secretary of State may, out of moneys provided by Parliament,   **10.06** make grants for the purpose of defraying in whole or in part any expenses incurred by a local authority in the acquisition of property under section 114 of the Town and Country Planning Act 1971, or section thirty-eight of the Town and Country Planning (Scotland) Act 1947 (under which sections buildings of special architectural or historic interest may in certain cases be acquired by a local authority).

(2) The Secretary of State may also, out of moneys so provided, make grants to the said National Trusts for the purpose of defraying in whole or in part any expenses incurred by them in the acquisition of buildings which appear to the Secretary of State to be of outstanding historic or architectural interest.

(3) Before making any grant under this section the Secretary of State shall consult with the appropriate council under this Act:

Provided that this subsection shall not apply in a case where the making of a grant appears to the Secretary of State to be a matter of immediate urgency.

(4) This section applies only where the property or buildings are not situated in England."

3. LOCAL AUTHORITIES (HISTORIC BUILDINGS) ACT 1962[3]

10.07 *This Act makes provision for contributions by Local Authorities towards the repair and maintenance of buildings of historic or architectural interest and the upkeep of gardens occupied therewith and for other purposes connected therewith.*

"Power of local authority[4] to contribute to preservation of historic buildings

1.—(1) A local authority in England or Wales may by grant or loan—

   (a) contribute towards the expenses incurred or to be incurred in the repair or maintenance of a building[5] which is situate in or in the vicinity of their area and is for the time being included in a list of buildings of special architectural or historic interest compiled or approved under section 54 of the Town and Country Planning Act 1971; and

   (b) . . . contribute towards the expenses incurred or to be incurred in the repair or maintenance of a building in their area appearing to them to be of architectural or historic interest, other than such a building as is referred to in the foregoing paragraph,

and, at the time of making a contribution under this section towards the expenses of the repair or maintenance of a building may also, by grant or loan, contribute towards the expenses incurred, or to be incurred in the upkeep of any garden occupied with the building and contiguous or adjacent thereto.

(2) A contribution by way of loan under the foregoing subsection may be made upon such terms and conditions as the local authority may determine including, without prejudice to the generality of the foregoing words, a term that the loan shall be free of interest; and the local authority may at any time renounce their right to repayment of the loan or any interest for the time being outstanding, and, by agreement with the borrower, may otherwise vary any of the terms and conditions on which the loan is made.

---

[3] Amended and updated consequent upon the provisions of L.G.A. 1963 and T.C.P.A. 1971.

[4] Local authority within the context of the Act, as read relative to the Acts referred to in note 3, above and L.G.A. 1972, means a county council, a district council, or a joint planning board (L.G.A. 1972, s.182), or a London Borough Council (L.G.A. 1963, s.4). The view is taken that in this context "local authority" includes a Park Planning Board.

[5] As to the meaning of "building" see subsection (4) below.

(3) A local authority may require as a condition of the making by them of a contribution under this section by way of grant towards the expenses of the repair or maintenance or upkeep of any property that the person to whom the grant is made shall enter into an agreement with them for the purpose of enabling the public to have access to the property or part thereof during such period and at such times as the agreement may provide.

(4) In this section—

"building" includes any structure or erection and any part of a building as so defined;

"local authority" means the council of a county, . . . borough or . . . district, and a joint planning board constituted under section 1 of the said Act of 1971. . . .

Recovery of grants on disposal of property within three years

2.—(1) If, during the period of three years beginning with the day on which a grant is made under this Act to a person towards the repair or maintenance or upkeep of any property, that person disposes of the interest, or any part thereof, held by him in the property on that day by way of sale or exchange or lease for a term of not less than twenty-one years, the local authority may recover from that person, in any court of competent jurisdiction, the amount of the grant, or such part thereof as to them seems fit. **10.08**

(2) If, in the case of property towards the repair or maintenance or upkeep of which a grant is made under this Act, a person becomes entitled by way of gift from the grantee, whether directly or indirectly (but otherwise than by will), to a part of the interest held by the grantee in the property on the day on which the grant is made, a disposal by the donee in any manner mentioned in the foregoing subsection of the interest so acquired by him in the property, or any part of that interest, shall be treated, for the purposes of that subsection, as a disposal by the grantee of a part of the interest so held by him, and, if, in the case of any such property, a person becomes entitled by way of such a gift to the whole of the interest held by the grantee therein on the day aforesaid the foregoing subsection shall have effect as if the grant had been made to the donee instead of to the grantee and that interest had then been held by the donee.

(3) Subsection (1) of this section shall not be taken as conferring on a local authority a right to recover, in the event of proceedings thereunder being brought in relation to disposals of several parts of an interest in property, amounts in the aggregate exceeding the amount of the grant."

4. INNER URBAN AREAS ACT 1978[6]

Improvement area grants

Although these grants are not specifically designed to provide for build- **10.09** *ings of architectural or historic interest or for buildings in conservation areas, they do provide another source of finance which may be available for such purposes.*

---

[6] As amended by L.G.P.L.A. 1980, s.191.

"Loans and grants for improving amenities

5.—(1) Where a designated district[7] authority are satisfied that the carrying out by any person of any works mentioned in subsection (2) below on land situated within an improvement area would benefit that area, they may make a loan or a grant or both to that person for the purpose of enabling him to carry out those works.

(2) The works referred to in subsection (1) above are as follows—

- (a) the construction of fencing or walls;
- (b) landscaping and the planting of trees, shrubs and plants;
- (c) the clearance or levelling of land;
- (d) the cleansing of watercourses, whether natural or artificial, or the reclamation of land covered with water;
- (e) the cleaning, painting, repair or demolition of structures or buildings; and
- (f) the construction of parking spaces, access roads, turning heads or loading bays.

(3) Subsections (2) and (3) of section 3 above[7a] shall apply in relation to the making of loans or grants under this section as they apply in relation to the making of loans or grants under that section.

Grants for converting or improving buildings

10.10   **6.**—(1) Where a designated district authority are satisfied that the carrying out by any person of any works mentioned in subsection (2) below on land situated within an improvement area would benefit that area, they may make a grant to that person for the purpose of enabling him to carry out those works.

(2) The works referred to in subsection (1) above are as follows—

- (a) the conversion, extension, improvement or modification of industrial or commercial buildings; and
- (b) the conversion of other buildings into industrial or commercial buildings.

(3) The amount of a grant under this section shall not exceed 50 per cent. of the cost of carrying out the works.

(4) Subsections (2) and (3) of section 3 above[7b] shall apply in relation to the making of grants under this section as they apply in relation to the making of grants under that section.

(5) In this section "industrial or commercial building" means a building in use or intended for use for industrial or commercial purposes."

---

[7] "Designated districts" under the Act are specified in the Inner Urban Areas (Designated Districts) (England and Wales) Order 1978 (S.I. 1978 No. 1314). In England the districts included in the Order are those referred to as Partnership and Programme Authorities in Table 8 at para. 10.29 below. (In Wales the designated districts are Blaenau, Gwent, Cardiff, Newport, Rhondda and Swansea).

[7a] *i.e.* empowering the Secretary of State and a local authority as to the imposition of conditions, *e.g.* as to repayment in certain circumstances.

[7b] See n. 7a above.

5. ANCIENT MONUMENTS AND ARCHAEOLOGICAL AREAS ACT 1979[8]

"Expenditure by Secretary of State or local authority on acquistion and preservation of ancient monuments etc.

24.—(1) Subject to subsection (3A) below the Secretary of State may **10.11** defray or contribute towards the cost of the acquisition by any person of any ancient monument.

(2) Subject to subsection (3A) below the Secretary of State may undertake, or assist in, or defray or contribute towards the cost of the removal of any ancient monument or of any part of any such monument to another place for the purpose of preserving it, and may at the request of the owner undertake, or assist in, or defray or contribute towards the cost of the preservation, maintenance and management of any ancient monument.

(3) Subject to subsection (3A) below the Secretary of State may contribute towards the cost of the provision of facilities or services for the public by a local authority under section 20 of this Act.

(3A) As respects a monument situated in England, subsections (1) to (3) above shall apply as if "Commission" were substituted for "Secretary of State."

(3B) References to an ancient monument in subsections (1) and (2) above, as amended by subsection (3A) above, shall be construed as if the reference in section 61(12)(b) of this Act to the Secretary of State were to the Commission.

(4) Any local authority may at the request of the owner undertake or assist in, or defray or contribute towards the cost of the preservation, maintenance and management of any ancient monuments situated in or in the vicinity of their area.

(5) No expenses shall be incurred by the Secretary of State or the Commission or any local authority under this section in connection with any monument which is occupied as a dwelling house by any person other than a person employed as the caretaker thereof or his family."

6. NATIONAL HERITAGE ACT 1980

The National Heritage Act 1980 enables the Trustees of the National **10.12** *Memorial Fund to make grants or loans towards the acquisition, maintenance or preservation of any land, building, structure object or group of objects, which in the opinion of the Trustees is of outstanding scenic, historic, aesthetic, architectural or scientific interest.*

Full details are given in section 3 of the National Heritage Act 1980 as follows.

"Grants and loans from the Fund

3.—(1) Subject to the provisions of this section, the Trustees may make grants and loans out of the Fund to eligible recipients for the purpose of assisting them to acquire, maintain or preserve—

---

[8] As amended by N.H.A. 1983, Sched. 4.

(a) any land, building or structure which in the opinion of the Trustees is of outstanding scenic, historic, aesthetic, architectural or scientific interest;

(b) any object which in their opinion is of outstanding historic, artistic or scientific interest;

(c) any collection or group of objects, being a collection or group which taken as a whole is in their opinion of outstanding historic, artistic or scientific interest;

(d) any land or object not falling within paragraph (a), (b) or (c) above the acquisition, maintenance or preservation of which is in their opinion desirable by reason of its connection with land or a building or structure falling within paragraph (a) above; or

(e) any rights in or over land the acquisition of which is in their opinion desirable for the benefit of land or a building or structure falling within paragraph (a) or (d) above.

10.13   (2) The Trustees shall not make a grant or loan under this section in respect of any property unless they are of opinion, after obtaining such expert advice as appears to them to be appropriate, that the property (or, in the case of land or an object falling within paragraph (d) of subsection (1) above, the land, building or structure with which it is connected or, in the case of rights falling within paragraph (e) of that subsection, the land, building or structure for whose benefit they are acquired) is of importance to the national heritage.

(3) In determining whether and on what terms to make a grant or loan under this section in respect of any property the Trustees shall have regard to the desirability of securing, improving or controlling public access to, or the public display of, the property.

(4) In making a grant or loan under this section in respect of any property the Trustees may impose such conditions as they think fit, including—

(a) conditions with respect to—
  (i) public access to, or the public display of, the property;
  (ii) the maintenance, repair, insurance and safe keeping of the property;
  (iii) the disposal or lending of the property; and

(b) conditions requiring the amount of a grant and the outstanding amount of a loan to be repaid forthwith on breach of any condition.

(5) A grant under this section for the purpose of assisting in the maintenance or preservation of any property may take the form of a contribution to a trust established or to be established for that purpose.

(6) Subject to subsection (7) below, the eligible recipients for the purposes of this section are—

(a) any museum, art gallery, library or other similar institution having as its purpose or one of its purposes the preservation for the public benefit of a collection of historic, artistic or scientific interest;

(b) any body having as its purpose or one of its purposes the provision, improvement or preservation of amenities enjoyed or to be enjoyed by the public, or the acquisition of land to be used by the public;

(c) any body having nature conservation as its purpose or one of its purposes;

(d) the Secretary of State acting in the discharge of his functions under section 5 of the Historic Buildings and Ancient Monuments Act 1953 or section 11(1) or 13 of the Ancient Monuments and Archaeological Areas Act 1979; and

(e) the Department of the Environment for Northern Ireland acting in the discharge of its functions under so much of section 1(1) of the Historic Monuments Act (Northern Ireland) 1971 as relates to the acquisition of historic monuments by agreement, section 4 of that Act or Article 84 of the Planning (Northern Ireland) Order 1972.

(7) The institutions referred to in paragraph (a) of subsection (6) above include any institution maintained by a Minister or Northern Ireland department; but neither that paragraph nor paragraph (b) or (c) of that sub-section applies to any institution or body established outside the United Kingdom or established or conducted for profit."

Authors note. Applications for assistance should be made to the Trustees at 10 St. James Street, London, SW1A 1FF (01–930 0963).

7. LOCAL GOVERNMENT ACT 1985

This Act makes financial provisions for the Greater London Area, follow- **10.14**
ing the abolition of the Greater London Council, in respect of listed build-
ings, conservation areas and ancient monuments; the details are set out at
Schedule 2 to the Act as follows.

"Other functions

3.—(1) The Historic Buildings and Monuments Commission for England (in this paragraph and paragraph 4 below referred to as "the Commission") may—

(a) acquire by agreement any building or place of historical or architectural interest in Greater London;

(b) undertake, or contribute towards, the cost of preserving, maintaining and managing any such building or place;

(c) acquire by agreement any work of art;

(d) agree with any person for the production by that person of a work of art for acquisition by the Commission;

(e) erect and maintain, or contribute towards the provision, erection and maintenance of, any work of art in any place in Greater London.

(2) For the purposes of providing for the accommodation, exhibition and preservation of works of art or objects of historical, antiquarian or other public interest which may for the time being be in the possession of the Commission by virtue of any gift, loan or discovery, or by virtue of this Act, the Commission may adapt, furnish and maintain any premises given to and for the time being vested in it for the purposes of this sub-paragraph.

(3) The Commission may let any building vested in it for the purposes of sub-paragraph (2) above on such terms and conditions as to payment or otherwise as it thinks fit and may make charges for admission to any such

building which may for the time being be under its management and control.

(4) The Commission may in the case of any building in Greater London cause investigations to be made, and information to be published, with respect to the history of the building.

4. The Commission may in Greater London, and a London borough council may in its borough—

> (a) provide; and
> (b) on any conspicuous part of a house, building or place, with the consent of its owner, erect,

a commemorative plaque, tablet or sign indicating an event or matter of public interest in connection with the house, building or place or its site, and may in that area, with the like consent, maintain any such plaque, tablet or sign erected by it or by any other person or body, whether before or after the passing of this Act."

8. HOUSING ACT 1985

10.15   *Housing Act grants derive their status from sections 460 and 462 of the Housing Act 1985 as follows:*

"PART XV

GRANTS FOR WORKS OF IMPROVEMENT, REPAIR AND CONVERSION

Main forms of grant assistance

460. General description of the main grants

(1) The following grants are payable by local housing authorities[9] in accordance with the following provisions of this Part—

> improvement grants (sections 467 to 473),
> intermediate grants (sections 474 to 482),
> special grants (sections 483 to 490), and
> repairs grants (section 491 to 498)[10];

and references in this Part to grants, without more, are to those grants.

---

[9] s.1: "Local housing authority" is defined as a district or London borough council or the Common Council of the City of London, or the Council of the Isles of Scilly.

[10] s.492(1) provides that an application for a repairs grant shall only be approved "if it is made in respect of an old dwelling, as defined by order of the Secretary of State." The Grants by Local Authorities (Repairs) Order 1982 (S.I. 1982 No. 1205) applies here, article 4 of which defines "old dwelling" for the purposes of this section as a dwelling which is, or forms part of, a building which was erected before October 3, 1961 if the relevant works satisfy the requirements elsewhere in the Order (*q.v.*).

(2) The grants are payable towards the cost of works required for—

(a) the provision of dwellings by the conversion of houses or other buildings,
(b) the improvement of dwellings,
(c) the repair of dwellings, and
(d) the improvement of houses in multiple occupation.

(3) The grants are not payable where the provision, improvement or repair is by—

a local authority,
a new town corporation, or,
the Development Board for Rural Wales. . . .

462. Preliminary condition: the age of the property

(1) A local housing authority shall not entertain an application for—

(a) an improvement grant in respect of works required for the provision of a dwelling by the conversion of a house or other building which was erected after October 2, 1961, or
(b) any grant for the improvement or repair of a dwelling which was provided after October 2, 1961,

unless they consider it appropriate to do so.

(2) The authority's discretion to entertain such applications is subject to such general or special directions as may be given by the Secretary of State."

Sections 467 to 498 of the Act (see section 460(1) above) deal in detail with the provisions quoted, and should also be referred to.

These provisions do not specifically apply to listed buildings, but nevertheless form an alternative source of finance which may be available for repairs and maintenance works to owners of listed buildings.

9. TOWN AND COUNTRY PLANNING (AMENDMENT) ACT 1972[11]

The following sections of this Act provide the specific statutory authority for conservation area and town scheme grants, and for the recovery of such grants where under certain circumstances the grantee disposes of his interest in the property.

[11] As amended by A.M.A.A.A. 1979, s.48(1), and L.G.P.L.A. 1980, Sched. 15, para. 27, and N.H.A. 1983, Sched. 4.

(a) Conservation areas

"Grants and loans for preservation or enhancement of character or appearance of conservation areas

10.16   **10.**—(1) Subject to subsection (1AA) of this section the Secretary of State may out of money provided by Parliament make grants or loans for the purpose of defraying in the whole or in part expenditure incurred or to be incurred in or in connection with, or with a view to the promotion of, the preservation or enhancement of the character or appearance of any conservation area or of any part of a conservation area, in any case where in his opinion the expenditure in question has made or will make a significant contribution towards preserving or enhancing the character or appearance of that area or part.

(1A)[12] In subsections (1) and (1AA) of this section "conservation area" means any area designated as a conservation area under section 277 of the Act of 1971 (areas of special architectural or historic interest).

(1AA) Subsection (1) of this section does not apply in relation to a conservation area (or part) situated in England, but the Commission may make grants or loans for the purposes of defraying in the whole or in part expenditure incurred or to be incurred in or in connection with, or with a view to the promotion of, the preservation or enhancement of the character or appearance of any conservation area (of part) situated in England, in any case where in their opinion the expenditure in question has made or will make a significant contribution towards preserving or enhancing the character or appearance of that area or part.

(2) A grant or loan under this section may be made subject to such conditions as the Secretary of State or (as the case may be) the Commission may think fit to impose.

10.17   (3) Any loan under subsection (1) of this section shall be made on such terms as to repayment, payment of interest and otherwise as the Secretary of State may with the approval of the Treasury determine; and all sums received by the Secretary of State by way of interest on, or repayment of, such a loan shall be paid by him into the Consolidated Fund.

(3A) Any loan under subsection (1AA) of this section shall be made on such terms as to repayment, payment of interest and otherwise as the Commission may determine.

(3B) In this section "the Commission" means the Historic Buildings and Monuments Commission for England.

(4) Before making any grant or loan under this section, the Secretary of State shall consult, both as to its making and as to the conditions subject to which it should be made, with the appropriate Council, that is to say, according as the conservation area in question is in Scotland or Wales (including Monmouthshire), the Historic Buildings Council for Scotland, or the Historic Buildings Council for Wales:

Provided that this subsection shall not apply in a case where the making

---

[12] Prior to the L.G.P.L.A. 1980, s.10(1) provided that such grant was available only in respect of "outstanding" conservation areas, designated and accepted as such on the advice of the (then) Historic Buildings Council, although a small proportion of the fund available annually was committed to similar purposes in "non-outstanding" conservation areas.

of a grant or loan appears to the Secretary of State to be a matter of immediate urgency.

(5) The Secretary of State may out of moneys provided by Parliament pay to any member of any of the Councils referred to in subsection (4) above by whom services are rendered in connection with any question as to the exercise of his powers under this section such remuneration and allowances as the Secretary of State may with the approval of the Minister for the Civil Service determine:

Provided that, in the case of any such member who is also a member of the House of Commons, the payments which the Secretary of State may make under this subsection shall extend only to allowances in respect of travelling and subsistence expenses, and any other expenses necessarily incurred by that member in connection with the rendering of the services in question.

Recovery of grants under section 10

10A.[13]—(1) This section applies to any grant under section 10 above made on terms that it shall be recoverable under this section; but any such grant shall only be regarded for the purposes of this section as so made if before or on making the grant the Secretary of State or (as the case may be) the Commission gives to the grantee notice in writing—

    (a) summarising the effect of this section; and

    (b) specifying the period during which the grant is to be recoverable in accordance with subsection (5) below in the case of a grant made for the purpose mentioned in subsection (4) below.

10.18

(2) The period specified under subsection (1)(b) above in the case of any grant shall be a period beginning with the day on which the grant is made and ending not more than ten years after that day.

(3) If any condition subject to which a grant to which this section applies was made is contravened or not complied with, the Secretary of State or (as the case may be) the Commission may recover the amount of the grant or such part of it as he thinks or (as the case may be) they think fit from the grantee.

(4) The following provisions of this section have effect where a grant to which this section applies is to any person for the purpose of defraying in whole or in part any expenditure in relation to any particular property; and references in those provisions to the relevant interest are references to the interest held by the grantee in that property on the day on which the grant is made.

(5) If, during the period specified for the purposes of the subsection under subsection (1)(b) above, the grantee disposes of the relevant interest or any part of it by way of sale or exchange or lease for a term of not less than twenty-one years, the Secretary of State or (as the case may be) the Commission may recover the amount of the grant or such part of it as he thinks or (as the case may be) they think fit from the grantee.

(6) If a person becomes entitled by way of gift from the grantee, whether directly or indirectly (but otherwise than by will) to a part of the relevant interest, a disposal by the donee in any manner mentioned in subsection (5)

---

[13] Amendment inserted by A.M.A.A.A. 1979 (n. 11).

above the interest so acquired by him in the property, or any part of that interest, shall be treated for the purposes of that subsection as a disposal by the grantee of a part of the relevant interest.

(7) If a person becomes entitled by way of any such gift to the whole of the relevant interest subsection (5) above shall have effect as if the donee were the grantee.

(8) Nothing in subsection (3) or (5) above shall be taken as conferring on the Secretary of State or (as the case may be) the Commission a right to recover (by virtue of a breach of more than one condition or disposals of several parts of an interest in property) amounts in the aggregate exceeding the amount of the grant.

(9) In this section "the Commission" means the Historic Buildings and Monuments Commission for England."

(b) Town schemes

"Grants for repair of buildings in town schemes

10.19 **10B.**—(1) Subject to subsection (1A) below the Secretary of State may, out of money provided by Parliament, make grants for the purpose of defraying in whole or in part any expenditure incurred or to be incurred in the repair of a building which—

> (a) is comprised in a town scheme; and
> (b) appears to him to be of architectural or historic interest.

(1A) Subsection (1) above does not apply in relation to a building situated in England, but the Commission may make grants for the purpose of defraying in whole or in part any expenditure incurred or to be incurred in the repair of a building which is so situated and which—

> (a) is comprised in a town scheme; and
> (b) appears to the Commission to be of architectural or historic interest.

(2) For the purposes of this section a building is comprised in a town scheme if—

> (a) it is in an area designated as a conservation area under section 277 of the Act of 1971; and
> (b) it is included in a town scheme list or shown on a town scheme map.

(3) In subsection (2) above—
> "town scheme list," means a list, containing buildings which are to be the subject of a repair grant agreement and compiled (in the case of buildings situated in England) by the Commission and one or more English local authorities or (in the case of buildings situated in Wales) by the Secretary of State and one or more Welsh local authorities after consultation with the Historic Buildings Council for Wales;

"town scheme map" means a map, showing buildings which are to be the subject of such an agreement and prepared (in the case of buildings situated in England) by the Commission and one or more English local authorities or (in the case of buildings situated in Wales) by the Secretary of State and one or more Welsh local authorities after such consultation.

(4) In subsection (3) above—

"repair grant agreement" means an agreement between the Secretary of State (or, as the case may be, the Commission) and any authority who have participated in the compilation of a town scheme list or the preparation of a town scheme map under which the Secretary of State (or, as the case may be, the Commission) and the authority or authorities who have so participated have agreed that a specified sum of money shall be set aside for a specified period of years for the purpose of making grants for the repair of the buildings included in the town scheme list or shown on the town scheme map.

(5) A grant under this section may be made subject to conditions imposed **10.20** by the Secretary of State or (as the case may be) the Commission for such purposes as he or they may think fit.

(6) Subject to subsection (7) below, before making any grant under this section the Secretary of State may consult with the Historic Buildings Council for Wales, both as to the making of the grant and as to the conditions subject to which it should be made.

(7) Subsection (6) above shall not apply where the making of a grant appears to the Secretary of State to be a matter of immediate urgency.

(8) The Secretary of State or the Commission may pay any grant under this section to an authority participating in a town scheme and may make arrangements with any such authority for the way in which the scheme is to be administered.

(9) Arrangements under subsection (8) above may include such arrangements for the offer and payment of grant under this section as may be agreed between the Secretary of State (or the Commission) and any authority or authorities participating in a town scheme.

(10) Section 2 of the Local Authorities (Historic Buildings) Act 1962 (recovery of grants made by local authorities on disposal of property within three years) shall apply to a grant made by the Secretary of State or the Commission under this section as it applies to a grant for the repair of property made by a local authority under that Act; and any reference to a local authority in this section shall accordingly be construed, in relation to a grant under this section, as reference to the Secretary of State or (as the case may be) the Commission.

(11) In this section—

"local authority" means—

(a) a county council;

(b) a district council;

(c) a London borough Council or the Common Council of the City of London;

(d) the Greater London Council; and

(e) the Council of the Isles of Scilly.

(12) In this section "the Commission" means the Historic Buildings and Monuments Commission for England."

10. ACQUISITION BY AGREEMENT OF HISTORIC BUILDINGS AND AREAS

10.21   *The Historic Buildings and Ancient Monuments Act 1953, as amended,[14] makes the following provisions in the following respect:*

"Acquisition by the Secretary of State of historic buildings, their contents and adjoining land

5.—(1) Subject to subsection (4) of this section, the Secretary of State shall have power to acquire by agreement, whether by purchase, lease or otherwise, or to accept a gift of—

(a) any building appearing to him to be one of outstanding historic or architectural interest;

(b) any land comprising, or contiguous or adjacent to, any such building.

(2) Subject as aforesaid, the Secretary of State shall have power to purchase by agreement, or to accept a gift of, any objects which are or have been ordinarily kept in—

(a) a building which, or any interest in which, is vested in the Secretary of State, or a building which is under his control or management being in either case a building appearing to the Secretary of State to be of outstanding historic or architectural interest; or

(b) a building of which the Secretary of State is guardian under the Ancient Monuments and Archaeological Areas Act 1979; or

(c) a building which, or any interest in which, is vested in either of the said National Trusts.

(3) Subject as aforesaid, the Secretary of State may make such arrangements as he may think fit as to the management or custody of any property acquired or accepted by him under this section, and as to the use of any such property, and may dispose of or otherwise deal with any such property as he may from time to time determine.

(3A) The Commission may be a party to such arrangements as are mentioned in subsection (3) of this section if the arrangements relate to property situated in England.

(4) The Secretary of State shall consult with the appropriate Commission or Council under this Act before acquiring or accepting any property under this section, and before taking any step by way of disposing of or otherwise dealing with any property so acquired or accepted, other than any step taken by him in the course of managing or keeping the property and making arrangements as to its use:

Provided that this subsection shall not prevent the Secretary of State from acquiring or accepting any property without consultation with the said Commission or Council in a case where the acquisition or acceptance thereof appears to him to be a matter of immediate urgency.

(5) Any expenses incurred by the Secretary of State under this section

---

[14] T.C.P.A. 1971, Sched. 24; A.M.A.A.A. 1979, Sched. 4; N.H.A. 1983, Sched. 4.

shall be defrayed out of moneys provided by Parliament, and any receipts of the Secretary of State under this section shall be paid into the Exchequer.

Acquisition by the Commission of historic buildings, etc.

5A.—(1) Subject to subsection (4) of this section, the Commission shall **10.22** have power to acquire by agreement, whether by purchase, lease or otherwise or to accept a gift of—

    (a) any building which is situated in England and which appears to them to be one of outstanding historic or architectural interest;

    (b) any building which is situated in England and in an area designated as a conservation area under section 277 of the Town and Country Planning Act 1971 and which appears to the Commission to be of special historic or architectural interest;

    (c) any land which is situated in England and which comprises, or is contiguous or adjacent to, any building mentioned in paragraph (a) or (b) of this subsection;

    (d) any garden or other land which is situated in England and which appears to the Commission to be of outstanding historic interest but which is not contiguous or adjacent to a building which appears to the Commission to be of outstanding historic or architectural interest.

(2) The Commission shall have power to purchase by agreement, or to accept a gift of, any objects which it would (within the meaning of subsection (5) of this section) be historically appropriate to keep in—

    (a) a building which, or any interest in which, is vested in the Commission, or a building which is under their management or in their custody, being in either case a building appearing to the Commission to be of outstanding historic or architectural interest; or

    (b) a building of which the Commission are guardian under the Ancient Monuments and Archaeological Areas Act 1979; or

    (c) a building situated in England which, or any interest in which, is vested in the National Trust for Places of Historic Interest or Natural Beauty.

(3) The Commission may make such arrangements as they think fit as to the management or custody of any property acquired or accepted by them under this section, and as to the use of any such property, and may dispose of or otherwise deal with any such property as they may from time to time determine.

(4) The Commission shall not acquire or accept any property under subsection (1) of this section without the consent of the Secretary of State, which may be given subject to such conditions as he thinks fit.

(5) For the purposes of subsection (2) of this section, any object is one which it would be historically appropriate to keep in a building if—

    (a) it is or has been ordinarily kept in the building; or

    (b) it is historically associated with the building or connected with a person or event historically associated with the building; or

    (c) objects of its kind were produced or used in a period falling within the lifetime of the building; or

241

(*d*) the Commission are of opinion that it would for some other reason be historically appropriate to keep in the building.

Grants to local authorities and National Trusts for acquisition of historic buildings

10.23   **5B.**—(1) The Commission may make grants for the purpose of defraying in whole or in part any expenses incurred by a local authority in England in the acquisition of property situated in England under section 114 or 119(1)(*b*) or (*c*) of the Town and Country Planning Act 1971 (under which buildings of special architectural or historic interest may in certain cases be acquired by a local authority).

(2) The Commission may also make grants to the National Trusts for Places of Historic Interest or Natural Beauty for the purpose of defraying in whole or in part any expenses incurred by them in the acquisition of—

(*a*) any building which is situated in England and which appears to the Commission to be of outstanding historic or architectural interest;

(*b*) any land which is situated in England and which comprises, or is contiguous or adjacent to, any such building; or

(*c*) any garden or other land which is situated in England and which appears to the Commission to be of outstanding historic interest but which is not contiguous or adjacent to a building which appears to the Commission to be of outstanding historic or architectural interest.

Grants to local authorities and National Trusts for acquisition of historic buildings

10.24   **6.**—(1) The Secretary of State may, out of moneys provided by Parliament, make grants for the purpose of defraying in whole or in part any expenses incurred by a local authority in the acquisition of property under section 114 of the Town and Country Planning Act 1971, or section thirty-eight of the Town and Country Planning (Scotland) Act 1947 (under which sections buildings of special architectural or historic interest may in certain cases be acquired by a local authority).

(2) The Secretary of State may also, out of moneys so provided, make grants to the said National Trusts for the purpose of defraying in whole or in part any expenses incurred by them in the acquisition of buildings which appear to the Secretary of State to be of outstanding historic or architectural interest.

(3) Before making any grant under this section the Secretary of State shall consult with the appropriate council under this Act:

Provided that this subsection shall not apply in a case where the making of a grant appears to the Secretary of State to be a matter of immediate urgency.

(4) This section applies only where the property or buildings are not situated in England.

Power of Secretary of State to accept endowments of historic buildings

8.—(1) Where any instrument coming into operation after the passing of **10.25**
this Act contains a provision purporting to be a gift of property to the Secretary of State upon trust to use the income thereof (either for a limited time
or in perpetuity) for or towards the upkeep of—

- (a) a building acquired or accepted by the Secretary of State under
  section five of this Act, or a building which the Secretary of State
  proposes so to acquire or accept, or
- (b) a building which at the coming into operation of the trust instrument is or will shortly be vested in or under the control or management of the Secretary of State, being a building which appears to
  him to be one of outstanding historic or architectural interest, or
- (c) a building of which at that time the Secretary of State is or will
  shortly be guardian under the Ancient Monuments and Archaeological Areas Act 1979,

or for or towards the upkeep of any such building together with other property, the Secretary of State may accept the gift, and, if he does so, and the
provision does not constitute a charitable trust, the following provisions of
this section shall have effect.

(2) The validity of the gift and of the trust to use the income as aforesaid
(hereinafter referred to as "the endowment trust") shall be deemed not to
be, or ever to have been, affected by any rule of law or equity which would
not have affected their validity if the trust had been charitable.

(3) In relation to the property (of whatsoever nature) comprised in the gift
and any property for the time being representing that property (hereinafter
collectively referred to as "the trust fund") the Secretary of State shall during the continuance of the endowment trust have the like powers of management, disposition and investment as, in the case of land held on trust for
sale, are conferred by law on the trustees for sale in relation to the land and
to the proceeds of sale thereof:

Provided that this subsection shall have effect without prejudice to any
additional or larger powers conferred on the Secretary of State by the trust
instrument.

(4) If while the endowment trust continues an event happens such that
immediately thereafter the Secretary of State is neither entitled to any
interest in the building to which the trust relates, nor has the building
under his control or management, nor is guardian of the building under the
said Act of 1979 and apart from this subsection the endowment trust would
not then be determined or be deemed to have failed, then on the happening
of that event the endowment trust shall cease by virtue of this subsection
and the trust fund shall devolve accordingly as on a failure of the trust.

(5) If the trust instrument contains a provision whereby on the failure or
determination of the endowment trust the trust fund purports to be given,
or to be directed to be held, on charitable trusts, the validity of that gift or
direction shall be deemed not to be, or ever to have been, affected by any
rule of law or equity relating to perpetuities.

(6) *Scotland.*

(7) Where the Commission are requested in pursuance of subsection (3) of
this section to manage any property the income from which is applicable for

or towards the upkeep of property situated in England, they may undertake the management.

Power of Commission to accept endowments

10.26 8A.—(1) Where any instrument coming into operation after the establishment of the Commission contains a provision purporting to be a gift of property to the Commission upon trust to use the income thereof (either for a limited time or in perpetuity) for or towards the upkeep of—

(a) a building acquired or accepted by the Commission under section 5A of this Act, or a building which the Commission propose so to acquire or accept, or

(b) a building which at the coming into operation of the trust instrument is or will shortly be vested in or under the management or in the custody of the Commission, being a building which is situated in England and which appears to them to be one of outstanding historic or architectural interest, or

(c) a building of which at that time the Commission are or will shortly be guardian under the Ancient Monuments and Archaeological Areas Act 1979,

or for or towards the upkeep of any such building together with other property situated in England, the Commission may accept the gift, and if they do so, and the provision does not constitute a charitable trust, the following provisions of this section shall have effect.

(2) The validity of the gift and of the trust to use the income as aforesaid (hereinafter referred to as "the endowment trust") shall be deemed not to be, or ever to have been, affected by any rule of law or equity which would not have affected their validity if the trust had been charitable.

(3) In relation to the property (of whatsoever nature) comprised in the gift and any property for the time being representing that property (hereinafter collectively referred to as "the trust fund") the Commission shall during the continuance of the endowment trust have the like powers of management, disposition and investment as, in the case of land held on trust for sale, are conferred by law on the trustees for sale in relation to the land and to the proceeds of sale thereof; but this subsection shall have effect without prejudice to any additional or larger powers conferred on the Commission by the trust instrument.

(4) If while the endowment trust continues an event happens such that immediately thereafter the Commission are neither entitled to any interest in the building to which the trust relates, nor have the building under their management or in their custody nor are guardian of the building under the said Act of 1979, and apart from this subsection the endowment trust would not then be determined or be deemed to have failed, then on the happening of that event the endowment trust shall cease by virtue of this subsection and the trust fund shall devolve accordingly as on a failure of the trust.

(5) If the trust instrument contains a provision whereby on the failure or determination of the endowment trust the trust fund purports to be given, or to be directed to be held, on charitable trusts, the validity of that gift or direction shall be deemed not to be, or ever to have been, affected by any rule of law or equity relating to perpetuities.

Endowment of gardens

8B.—(1) Where any instrument coming into operation after the establish- **10.27** ment of the Commission contains a provision purporting to be a gift of property to the Commission upon trust to use the income thereof (either for a limited time or in perpetuity) for or towards the upkeep of a garden or other land acquired or accepted by the Commission under section 5A(1)(d) of this Act, or a garden or other land which the Commission propose so to acquire or accept, or for or towards the upkeep of any such garden or other land together with other property situated in England, the Commission may accept the gift, and if they do so, and the provision does not constitute a charitable trust, the following provisions of this section shall have effect.

(2) The validity of the gift and of the trust to use the income as aforesaid (hereinafter referred to as "the endowment trust") shall be deemed not to be, or ever to have been, affected by any rule of law or equity which would not have affected their validity if the trust had been charitable.

(3) In relation to the property (of whatsoever nature) comprised in the gift and any property for the time being representing that property (hereinafter collectively referred to as "the trust fund") the Commission shall during the continuance of the endowment trust have the like powers of management, disposition and investment as, in the case of land held on trust for sale, are conferred by law on the trustees for sale in relation to the land and to the proceeds of sale thereof; but this subsection shall have effect without prejudice to any additional or larger powers conferred on the Commission by the trust instrument.

(4) If while the endowment trust continues an event happens such that immediately thereafter the Commission are not entitled to any interest in the garden or other land to which the trust relates, and apart from this subsection the endowment trust would not then be determined or be deemed to have failed, then on the happening of that event the endowment trust shall cease by virtue of this subsection and the trust fund shall devolve accordingly as on a failure of the trust.

(5) If the trust instrument contains a provision whereby on the failure or determination of the endowment trust the trust fund purports to be given, or to be directed to be held, on charitable trusts, the validity of that gift or direction shall be deemed not to be, or ever to have been, affected by any rule of law or equity relating to perpetuities."

11. THE ROLE OF PRIVATE CHARITABLE BODIES[15]

In certain circumstances assistance towards the cost of maintenance, **10.28** repair, or preservation of historic buildings, or even the acquisition of such buildings, may be available from a number of private charitable trusts.

For details of the various charities involved in this field, the "Directory of Grant-Making Trusts" published by the Charities Aid Foundation, and available in most reference libraries, should be consulted.

---

[15] See also Chap. 13, "Interested Bodies."

TABLE 8

TABLE OF TYPES OF GRANT

TYPE OF GRANT	STATUTORY DERIVATION	SCOPE	METHOD OF PAYMENT
Section 3A	s.3A Historic Buildings & Ancient Monuments Act 1953 (as amended) (Inserted by National Heritage Act 1983, s.33 & Sched. 4, para. 4) brought into force 1/4/84 S.I. 1984 No. 208.	Provision of grants and loans for— i) repair or maintenance of buildings in England of outstanding historic interest. ii) upkeep of land in England which comprises, is contiguous or adjacent to any such building. iii) repair or maintenance of objects kept in such buildings. iv) upkeep of garden or land in England which is not contiguous or adjacent to any such building but appears to be of outstanding architectural or historic interest.	May be by endowment if grant given by National Trust.
Section 4	s.4, Historic Buildings & Ancient Monuments Act 1953 (as amended).	As s.3A, but excludes land/buildings in England.	As s.3A
Section 5B	s.5B Historic Buildings & Ancient Monuments Act 1953 (as amended) (Inserted by National Heritage Act 1983, s.33 & Sched. 4, para. 4) brought into force 1/4/84 S.I. 1984 No. 208.	i) Provision of grants for Local Authorities in England towards costs of acquiring property in England, under s.114 or s.119(1),(b) or (c) of the Town & Country Planning Act 1971. ii) Provision of grants to National Trust for acquisition of buildings, land or gardens of outstanding historic or architectural interest (applies to England only).	
Section 6	s.6 Historic Buildings & Ancient Monuments Act 1953 (as amended).	As s.5B but excludes properties/buildings in England.	

TABLE 8—*cont.*

TABLE OF TYPES OF GRANT—*cont.*

CONDITIONS OF PAYMENT	METHOD OF OBTAINING GRANT OR LOAN & RECOVERY PROCEDURE	ADMINISTRATOR	PARAGRAPH REFERENCE IN TEXT
Conditions may be imposed to secure public access to all or part of the property.	Consult the Commission.	The Commission.	10.02
As s.3A.	Consult "appropriate council" (s.9(1) refers, prior to grant or loan, except in cases of emergency). Grant may be recovered for non-compliance with conditions or upon the disposal of the grantee's interest in the property during a period of up to 10 years.	Secretary of State.	10.03–10.04
		The Commission.	10.05
		Secretary of State.	10.06

247

TABLE 8—*cont.*

TABLE OF TYPES OF GRANT—*cont.*

TYPE OF GRANT	STATUTORY DERIVATION	SCOPE	METHOD OF PAYMENT
Local Authority Grant	Local Authorities (Historic Buildings) Act 1962.	Provision of grant or loan towards expenses in the repair or maintenance of buildings (and gardens) of architectural or historic interest (whether or not they are listed) located in or in the vicinity of the authority area.	s.1(2) makes provision for any loan to be free of interest, if the authority agree.
Improvement Area grants	ss.5–6 Inner Urban Areas Act 1978 (as amended by Local Government, Planning & Land Act 1980).	Loans and grants for improving amenities within a designated "improvement area" and grants for converting or improving buildings therein, not restricted to listed buildings.	
Ancient Monument	s.24 Ancient Monuments & Archaeological Areas Act 1979.	Contributions to costs of acquisition of Ancient Monument, or its resiting, preservation, maintenance and management. s.45 also provides for contributions towards the cost of any archaeological investigation of any land.	
National Heritage Memorial Fund	s.3 National Heritage Act 1980.	Grants or loans towards the acquisition, maintenance, or preservation of any land, building or structure which is of outstanding scenic, historic, aesthetic, architectural or scientific interest (in opinion of the trustees).	
Local Government Act	Sched. 2, para. 3(i) Local Government Act 1985.	Grants for the repair of any building within the Greater London Area which appears to be of architectural or historic interest (whether or not they are listed).	

TABLE 8—*cont.*

TABLE OF TYPES OF GRANT—*cont.*

CONDITIONS OF PAYMENT	METHOD OF OBTAINING GRANT OR LOAN & RECOVERY PROCEDURE	ADMINISTRATOR	PARAGRAPH REFERENCE IN TEXT
Authorities will require that the building will not only be repaired but also adequately maintained. A requirement may be made regarding limited public access to property but this depends upon the significance of the property.	Approach local authority. Contribution may be paid in advance of expenditure but will normally be paid after the work has been satisfactorily completed (where necessary by instalments). s.2 provides for recovery of grant if agreed conditions are not met.	Local authority.	10.07–10.08
In respect of buildings, the amount of grant shall not exceed 50% of the cost of carrying out the works.		Secretary of State Partnership & Programme Authority.	10.09–10.10
Does not apply to any ancient monument occupied as a dwelling (except as caretaker thereof).	Request from owner to relevant local authority.	In England: The Commission Elsewhere: Secretary of State.	10.11
	By application to the trustees.	Trustees of the National Heritage Memorial Fund.	10.12–10.13
			10.14

249

TABLE 8—*cont.*

TABLE OF TYPES OF GRANT—*cont.*

TYPE OF GRANT	STATUTORY DERIVATION	SCOPE	METHOD OF PAYMENT
Housing Act Grants	ss.460 & 462, Housing Act 1985.	*Improvement Grants* can be provided for the conversion and improvement of older substandard properties and can include an element for repair works. *Intermediate Grants* provide for the installation of specific standard amenities. *Repairs Grants* are available for structural repairs to dwellings erected before 1919. The above relates to all types of building but higher eligible expense limits have been specified for improvement and repairs grants where listed buildings are involved.	
Section 10	s.10, Town and Country Planning (Amendment) Act 1972 (as amended by Local Government, Planning & Land Act 1980).	Provision of grants where the expenditure to be incurred will make a significant contribution towards preserving or enhancing the character or appearance of a conservation area. (Applications should fall within categories identified in para. 140 of Circular 8/87). *Subs. 1* does not apply to conservation areas in England. *Subs. 1AA* applies to all conservation areas. *NOTE* Grant aid is no longer limited to outstanding conservation areas.	
Section 10B (town scheme)	s.10B Town & Country Planning (Amendment) Act 1972 (as amended by Local Government, Planning & Land Act 1980).	Provision of grants for expenditure in the repair of a building which is in a town scheme and appears to be of architectural or historic interest. Subs. 1 does not apply to buildings in England.	s.10B (1) and (1)(A) suggest that payment can either be made in advance or retrospectively.

TABLE 8—*cont.*

TABLE OF TYPES OF GRANT—*cont.*

CONDITIONS OF PAYMENT	METHOD OF OBTAINING GRANT OR LOAN & RECOVERY PROCEDURE	ADMINISTRATOR	PARAGRAPH REFERENCE IN TEXT
At discretion of local authority. Qualifying conditions must be met.	Application to local authority prior to undertaking works.	Local authority	10.15
	Procedures for the recovery of grant embodied in s.10A.	*Subs. 1:* Secretary of State. *Subs. 1AA:* The Commission.	10.16–10.18
May be subject to conditions imposed by the Secretary of State or Commission as they see fit.		*s.1:* Secretary of State. *Subs. 1A:* The Commission. The local authority allocates money on annual basis for purpose of making grants towards the repair of buildings covered by the scheme. Contributions are shared equally with Secretary of State (or Commission).	10.19–10.20

11. Rights of Entry of Officers and Officials

1. IN RELATION TO LISTING AND LISTED BUILDING CONTROLS

11.01   A number of powers are conferred by section 280 of the 1971 Act upon the Secretary of State, local authorities and (in relation to a building situated in Greater London) the Commission, to authorise persons to enter land for purposes connected with the listing of buildings, the control of works affecting listed buildings, and the surveying of listed buildings appearing to be in need of repair. The powers in section 280 are qualified by section 281 referred to at para. 11.05 below.

(a) Entry for compilation of lists of buildings

Persons duly authorised in writing by the Secretary of State may at any reasonable time enter on land for the purpose of surveying any building in connection with a proposal to include it in a list of buildings of architectural or historic interest under section 54 of the 1971 Act.[1]

As "land" includes a building[2] this power includes the power to enter the building as well.

(b) Entry for purpose of surveying in connection with listed buildings

11.02   Persons duly authorised in writing by the Secretary of State or by a local planning authority may at any reasonable time enter land in order to survey it in the course of preparing to serve certain orders or notices under specified parts of the Act, and to ascertain whether or not the requirements of such orders or notices have been complied with.[3]

---

[1] T.C.P.A. 1971, s.280(2).
[2] T.C.P.A. 1971, 290(1).
[3] T.C.P.A. 1971, s.280(1)(c) and 280(8).

Insofar as listed buildings are concerned, this includes:

(i) survey in connection with any proposal to serve a building preservation notice under section 58.[4] (As to the actual service of a building preservation notice, section 58(6)[5] empowers a local planning authority "if it appears . . . to be urgent that a building preservation notice should come into force" to "affix the notice conspicuously to some object on the building." This action may well involve entering on land upon which the building stands, and whilst neither section 280 nor section 58 specifically confer any right to enter for the purpose of affixing such a notice, this right appears implicit in section 58(6).)

(ii) survey in connection with any proposal to serve a repairs notice under section 115 as the necessary preliminary to the taking of compulsory purchase powers in respect of listed buildings appearing to be in need of repair.[6]

(c) Entry for investigation of alleged offences under the Act

Persons duly authorised in writing by the Secretary of State or a local **11.03** planning authority may at any reasonable time enter any land[7] in order to ascertain whether, with respect to any buildings on the land, an offence has been, or is being, committed under the following sections of the Act[8]:

(i) Section 55—unauthorised works of demolition, alteration or extension of a listed building.[9]

(ii) Section 57—acts[10] causing, or likely to result in damage to a listed building.[11]

(iii) Section 98—non-compliance with the terms of a listed building enforcement notice.[12]

(d) Entry in connection with urgent works powers

Persons duly authorised in writing by the Secretary of State or a local **11.04** authority may at any reasonable time enter any land (including a building—see para. 11.01 above) in order to ascertain whether it should exercise any of the functions conferred by section 101 of the Act (the making of urgent

---

[4] See paras. 2.37–2.39 above (Deemed listing).

[5] Inserted by T.C.P.(A).A. 1972, s.7(1).

[6] Powers under T.C.P.A. 1971, ss.114 and 115. See paras. 7.02–7.09 above.

[7] "Land" includes a building, see n. 2, above.

[8] T.C.P.A. 1971, s.280(3).

[9] See paras. 2.43–2.44 above and Chapter 5.

[10] Other than "excepted works," *e.g.* where LBC has been granted: see T.C.P.A. 1971, s.57(2).

[11] T.C.P.A. 1971, s.280(4)(a). Entry for this purpose may be authorised by a local authority (as opposed to a local planning authority).

[12] Listed building enforcement notice—s.96. See paras. 5.40–5.43 above.

works for the repair of unoccupied listed buildings), and may enter the land in order to effect those repairs[13] (entry for *undertaking* the works must be preceded by seven days' notice to the owner—section 101(4)[14]).

(e) Provisions supplementary to section 280

11.05   Rights of entry conferred by section 280 of the 1971 Act, referred to in the previous paragraph (but excluding rights of entry pursuant to section 58(6) of the Act referred to at para. 11.02 above) are subject to provisions contained in section 281(1) which requires that

> "A person authorised under section 280 of this Act to enter any land shall, if so required, produce evidence of his authority, and shall not demand admission as of right to land which is occupied, unless twenty-four hours' notice of the intended entry has been given to the occupier."

It will be noted that as this provision applies to occupied land, no such notice is required for *investigations* in pursuance of powers under section 101 (above) which by definition relates only to unoccupied buildings.

Further provisions in section 281 relate to offences by authorised persons communicating trade secrets learned in the process of entry in pursuance of the powers quoted[15]; and compensation for damage resulting from entry under section 280.[16]

It is an offence for any person wilfully to obstruct a person acting with due authority in pursuance of powers under section 280 of the Act.[17]

(f) Entry in connection with applications for LBC

11.06   It is interesting to note that the 1971 Act does not provide any specific rights of entry to land for persons—*e.g.* planning officers—engaged in the processing and consideration of applications for LBC. Whilst section 280(1)(b) provides for authorisation of entry of authorised persons in connection with applications under Part III of the 1971 Act (*i.e.* planning applications), applications under Part IV of the Act, which include those for LBC, are not similarly provided for, either within section 280, or in any other section of the Act, or so far as can be ascertained, within any other or subsequent Act or regulations.

Notwithstanding what can only be surmised to be an omission from the Act, it will be apparent that if an officer of a planning authority to whom an application for LBC has been submitted, requires to gain access to the building the subject of the application in the process of considering the application, but is denied such access, then he may not be able to make any recommendation as to how the application should be determined (on the basis of having insufficient information on which to make a recommen-

---

[13] T.C.P.A. 1971, s.280(4)(b).
[14] See paras. 7.10–7.13 above.
[15] T.C.P.A. 1971, s.281(3).
[16] T.C.P.A. 1971, s.281(4) and (5).
[17] T.C.P.A. 1971, s.281(2).

dation). It is therefore in the interest of applicants for LBC to permit access to officers considering their applications, if access is requested. However, the problem of an applicant being an owner but having an unwilling tenant will remain.

2. IN RELATION TO ANCIENT MONUMENTS AND ARCHAEOLOGICAL AREAS

The Ancient Monuments and Archaeological Areas Act 1979 confers **11.07** upon the Secretary of State for the Environment, and upon the Commission and other persons authorised by the Secretary of State, a number of powers of entry to land for the pursuance of powers and duties under the Act, with respect to scheduling of monuments, works concerning scheduled monuments, ancient monuments, and areas of archaeological importance. With the exception of the power described in para. 11.08 below, all other powers quoted are qualified by the provisions of section 44 of the Act (see para. 11.14 below).

(a) Entry in process of scheduling a monument

Section 1 of the 1979 Act, which places a duty on the Secretary of State to compile a schedule of monuments, does not itself confer any power on the Secretary of State to enter any land for the purpose of ascertaining whether any monument on the land[18] should be included in the Schedule. The relevant power for such entry is contained in section 26 of the Act, and extends to any person duly authorised in writing by the Secretary of State. Such a person "may at any reasonable time enter any land in, on or under which the Secretary of State knows or has reason to believe there is an ancient monument for the purpose of inspecting the land (including any building or other structure on the land) with a view to recording any matters of archaeological or historical interest."

As such investigation could reasonably be expected to be a necessary stage in the determination of whether or not to include an ancient monument in the schedule, it would seem reasonable to deduce that this power provides for entry necessary to effect the scheduling prescribed by section 1.

(b) Entry for works urgently needed to protect a scheduled monument

Section 5(1) of the 1979 Act empowers the Secretary of State to enter the **11.08** site of a scheduled monument[19] for the purpose of executing works which he considers urgently necessary for the preservation of the monument. He must give the owner and, if the owner is not the occupier, the occupier

---

[18] Or in or under the land.
[19] Definition of scheduled monument: A.M.A.A.A. 1979, s.1(11).

seven days' notice in writing of his intention to enter and carry out the works. (It is interesting to note that section 5(1) refers to the Secretary of State, and not to a person authorised by the Secretary of State, except in England where the Secretary of State may authorise the Commission to enter and evaluate the works.)

(c) Entry to permit inspection of condition of a scheduled monument

11.09   Section 6(1) of the 1979 Act empowers any person duly authorised in writing by the Secretary of State to enter land at any reasonable time for the purpose of inspecting any scheduled monument in on or under the land with a view to ascertaining its condition and

>   (i) whether any works affecting the monument are being carried out in contravention of section 2(1) of the Act[20]; or
>   (ii) whether it has been or is likely to be damaged (by any such works or otherwise).

(d) Entry in relation to applications for scheduled monument consent and to inspect works connected therewith

11.10   Any person duly authorised in writing by the Secretary of State may at any reasonable time enter any land in on or under which a scheduled monument exists for the following purposes:

>   (i) inspecting the monument in connection with any application for scheduled monument consent for works affecting that monument[21];
>   (ii) inspecting the monument in connection with any proposal by the Secretary of State to modify or revoke a scheduled monument consent[22];
>   (iii) observing the execution of works to which a scheduled monument consent relates[23];
>   (iv) inspecting the condition of the land and the scheduled monument after the completion of any such works[24];

and in respect of any land on which any works authorised by a scheduled monument consent are being carried out:

>   (v) inspecting the land (or buildings or structures on it) with a view to recording any matters of archaeological or historical interest; and
>   (vi) observing the execution of the works with a view to examining and

---

[20] See paras. 8.14–8.15 above.
[21] A.M.A.A.A. 1979, s.6(2)(a).
[22] A.M.A.A.A. 1979, s.6(2)(b).
[23] A.M.A.A.A. 1979, s.6(3)(a).
[24] A.M.A.A.A. 1979, s.6(3)(b).

recording any objects or other material of archaeological or historical interest, and recording any such matters discovered in the
course of the works.[25]

(e) Entry for posting of notices and markers

Any person authorised in writing by the Secretary of State may enter any **11.11**
land in on or under which a scheduled monument is situated, with the consent of the owner and, if the owner is not the occupier, the occupier, in order
to erect or maintain on or near the site of the monument such notice boards
and marker posts as appear to the Secretary of State to be needed to preserve
the monument from accidental or deliberate damage.[26]

(f) Concurrent powers of the Commission

The Commission have powers with regard to land in England which are
broadly concurrent with those of the Secretary of State in paras. 11.09–11.11
above, and in addition have powers to determine whether or not to
prosecute.[27]

(g) Entry in pursuance of operations notice powers—areas of archaeological importance

There are a number of powers of entry in connection with actions arising **11.12**
from operations notices under section 35 of the Act in respect of areas of
archaeological importance.[28] These powers are contained in sections 38, 39
and 40 of the Act, and are considered at paras. 8.36–8.45 above.

(h) Powers of entry for survey and valuation

Section 43 of the Act provides for any person authorised under the section **11.13**
at any reasonable time to enter any land to survey it or estimate its value in
connection with any proposal to acquire it or any other land under the Act,
or in connection with a claim for compensation under the Act in respect of
any such acquisition or any damage to that or other land (resulting from the
operation of the Act).[29]
Persons authorised under section 43 are:

  (i) officers of the Valuation Office of the Inland Revenue Department,
  or

---

[25] A.M.A.A.A. 1979, s.6(4)(a) and (b).
[26] A.M.A.A.A. 1979, s.6(5).
[27] A.M.A.A.A. 1979, s.6A.
[28] A.M.A.A.A. 1979, Pt. II, ss.33–41.
[29] A.M.A.A.A. 1979, s.43(1).

(ii) a person duly authorised in writing by the Secretary of State or other authority proposing to make the acquisition which is the occasion of the survey or valuation or from whom compensation is recoverable.[30]

(i) Supplementary provisions with respect to powers of entry

11.14
(i) A person may not in the exercise of any power of entry under the Act, other than that conferred by section 43, enter any building or part of a building occupied as a dwelling house, without the consent of the occupier.[31]

(ii) Other than in connection with powers of entry under section 5 of the Act (para. 11.08 above)) a person exercising any of the powers of entry under the Act may not demand admission as of right to any land which is occupied unless prior notice has been given to the occupier, as follows:

(a) where the purpose of entry is to carry out works (other than excavations under sections 26 [where there is believed to be an ancient monument] or 38 [where an operations notice has been served]), not less than 14 days notice;

(b) in any other case, 24 hours before admission is demanded.[32]

(iii) An authorised person seeking to enter land must produce evidence of authorisation if required to do so[33];

(iv) Section 44 prescribes a number of other supplementary provisions relating to the taking onto land of equipment necessary for the purpose to which the entry relates[34]; removing samples required for archaeological analysis[35]; and co-operation with persons undertaking works on the land.[36]

It is an offence for any person to obstruct the entry onto land of any person duly authorised to do so under the Act.[37]

(j) Recording the building

11.15
The Royal Commissions on the Historical Monuments of England (and separately, Wales and Scotland) which were founded by Royal Warrants in 1908 (which bodies should not be confused with the HBMC) have apparently no powers of entry: but much is achieved by the wording suggested by paragraph 117 of Circular 8/87 for inclusion in LBCs about the notice to be given to the Royal Commission by the applicant at least one month following the grant of consent to enable the Commission to make a record (see para. 5.14).

[30] A.M.A.A.A. 1979, s.43(2).
[31] A.M.A.A.A. 1979, s.44(1).
[32] A.M.A.A.A. 1979, s.44(2)(a), (b).
[33] A.M.A.A.A. 1979, s.44(3).
[34] A.M.A.A.A. 1979, s.44(4).
[35] A.M.A.A.A. 1979, s.44(5).
[36] A.M.A.A.A. 1979, s.44(6), (7).
[37] A.M.A.A.A. 1979, s.44(8).

12. Buildings, Conservation Areas and Ancient Monuments— Public Rights

1. PUBLIC RIGHTS IN RELATION TO THE PROTECTIVE MEASURES

(a) Listing of buildings

The procedures for the listing of buildings are dealt with in Chapter 2. **12.01**
Members of the public have no rights to demand the inclusion of a building in a list, nor its exclusion from it. However individuals, civic societies, and other groups interested in the built environment, are at liberty to suggest to the Secretary of State buildings they consider suitable for inclusion in the list. Paragraph 34 of Circular 8/87 indicates that such suggestions will be welcomed, and, in paragraph 39, indicates the nature of information to be submitted with such suggestions.

Under the provisions of section 54A of the 1971 Act at any time after an application for planning permission has been made, or granted, in respect of a building which is not listed, any person may at the same time as the planning application apply to the Secretary of State for a certificate, known as an "Immunity Certificate."[1] The issue of such a certificate will mean that the building cannot be listed or a building preservation notice issued in respect of it, for at least five years. Non-issue of such a certificate will, according to paragraph 41 of Circular 8/87, mean that the building will be listed forthwith.

---

[1] See paras. 2.49–2.50 above.

Whilst this provision has been introduced in order to avoid situations such as that which gave rise to the *John Walker* case refered to in Chapter 2, above, the fact that any person may apply for an immunity certificate (provided he also applies for planning permission) must inevitably increase the capacity of members of the general public to influence the listing of buildings by bringing cases to the notice of the Department in a way which requires a decision to be made.

(b) Designation of conservation areas

12.02   The procedures for designation of conservation areas are dealt with in Chapter 3.

The public has no *statutory* right to be consulted or to make comments on proposals to designate conservation areas. In practice, however, it is rare for a planning authority not to mount some informal pre-designation publicity exercise, or to ignore representations made as a result (see paras. 3.05–3.08 above).

(c) Scheduling of monuments

12.03   The procedures for scheduling of monuments are dealt with in Chapter 8.

As with listed buildings, the public has no right to demand the scheduling of a monument, or the exclusion of a monument from the schedule; equally, the public is at liberty to suggest monuments for scheduling.

(d) Designation of areas of archaeological importance

12.04   The procedures for areas of archaeological importance designation are dealt with in Chapter 8. Five areas have been designated, being areas containing the historic centres of Canterbury, Chester, Exeter, Hereford and York. There seems no reason why the public should not suggest other areas.

2. PUBLIC RIGHTS IN RELATION TO THE STATUTORY CONTROLS

(a) Applications for LBC

12.05   When an application has been made for LBC for works (other than works affecting only the interior of a Grade II (unstarred) listed building), the local planning authority has a duty to publicise the application. It must advertise the application both in a local newspaper and by means of a site notice, afford members of the public reasonable opportunity to inspect the plans, and to make representations, and take such representations as are received within prescribed time limits into account when determining the application. The authority may not determine the application before the expiry of 21 days after the publication of the press notice or the first day of display of the site notice.[2]

Thus, with the exception of applications for interior works to unstarred Grade II buildings, the public has a right to be notified of the existence of LBC applications, to have a reasonable period in which to inspect and to comment on them, and to have such comments taken into account in their determination.

Interior works to unstarred Grade II buildings are excluded from these publicity requirements.

This position does not, however, preclude members of the public from making representations in such cases, nor preclude the local planning authority from considering them. Although the public does not have to be officially notified of such applications, most local planning authorities ensure that their weekly or monthly lists of applications received are supplied to the local press, and that neighbours are notified; thus ample opportunity appears to be afforded for making the public aware of such applications, and to respond accordingly if they so desire.

(b) LBC applications "called-in" by the Secretary of State

It is interesting to note that whereas the Secretary of State, in determining applications for planning permissions which he has "called in," is obliged[3] to take into account any representations received in response to any advertisement of such applications required by section 26 of the Act, the same statutory obligation does not apply to LBC applications which he calls in, the advertisement procedures and requirements for which closely correspond with those for planning applications affected by section 26 requirements. **12.06**

That the Secretary of State does take into account representations made as a result of regulation 5 advertisement,[3a] when determining LBC applications which he has called in, is not disputed; there is ample case evidence to confirm that he does so. The rights of the public to have their views heard irrespective of whether the decision on the application is by the local authority or the Secretary of State are therefore assured in practice, if not by statute or regulations arising from statute.

It is nonetheless strange that the Act, in dealing with procedures for "called-in" planning applications, clearly specifies the matters (relating to consideration of representations arising from statutory notices) which the Secretary of State must consider, whilst the same Act in dealing (in Schedule 11, paras. 4–7) with comparable procedures for "called-in" LBC appli-

---

[2] Town and Country Planning (Listed Buildings and Buildings in Conservation Areas) Regulations 1987, reg. 5 (S.I. 1987 No. 349).

[3] By T.C.P.A. 1971, s.35(4).

[3a] See n. 2 above.

cation, makes no comparable references, and none are to be found in the relevant regulations.

(c) Planning applications affecting the setting of a listed building

12.07   When an application for planning permission for any development of land is made to a local planning authority and the development, if implemented, would in the opinion of the authority, affect the setting of a listed building, section 28(2) and (3) of the 1971 Act make exactly the same provisions for publicity as are prescribed by regulation 5 of the Listed Buildings Regulations 1987, in respect of applications for LBC considered above.

This provision is an amendment of section 28 of the 1971 Act, inserted by section 4(1) of the Town and Country Amenities Act 1974. Additionally, section 56(3) of the Town and Country Planning Act 1971 (inserted by paragraph 9 of Schedule 15 to the Local Government Planning and Land Act 1980) requires that

> "in considering whether to grant planning permission for development which affects a listed building or its setting and in considering whether to grant listed building consent for any works, the local planning authority or the Secretary of State as the case may be, shall have special regard to the desirability of preserving the building or its setting or any features of special architectural or historic interest which it possesses."

(d) Appeals concerning applications for LBC

12.08   It is difficult for members of the public to ascertain what their rights are in such matters. Few appellants and, proportionately, even fewer members of the public know that the statutory sources of such rights which do exist lie in:

  (i) Section 56(6), Schedule 9, and paragraph 8 of Schedule 11 to the 1971 Act;
  (ii) Regulations 5 and 8 of, and Schedule 2 to the Town and Country Planning (Listed Buildings and Buildings in Conservation Areas) Regulations 1987 (S.I. 1987 No. 349);
  (iii) The Town and Country Planning (Determination of Appeals by Appointed Persons) (Prescribed Classes) Regulations 1981 (S.I. 1981 No. 804), as amended by (S.I. 1986 No. 623);
  (iv) The Town and Country Planning Appeals (Determination by Appointed Persons) (Inquiries Procedures) Rules 1974 (S.I. 1974 No. 420), as amended by (S.I. 1986 No. 420)

or that the principal source of advice on LBC appeal procedures is contained in the 16 lines of paragraph 118 of Circular 8/87, the only relevant part of which, so far as this consideration is concerned, reads:

"The procedure for these appeals corresponds with that for ordinary planning appeals under section 36 of the 1971 Act."

This statement is correct. Yet reference to section 36, and cross-reference to rules and regulations relating to that section (principally the last two referred to above) produces an equally daunting maze, and hardly helps either the appellant or the public to ascertain their rights. Unless, that is, they know of the existence of Circular 71/73 which contains by reference (in paragraphs 20 and 21) to publicity for appeals in general, the only available simple guidance on public "rights" in such matters. The Circular says:

"20. Appeals may be dealt with either by way of a local inquiry or by written representations. Where there is any substantial local objection an inquiry will usually be necessary and there will be local publicity. The Secretaries of State rely on local planning authorities to warn them if local concern in an appeal is known to be sufficient to justify an inquiry. Where the appeal is to be the subject of a local inquiry, the authority is asked to give as much public notice of the inquiry date as possible—not less than four weeks unless there are very special circumstances.

21. Many appeals are now decided on written representations by the parties, even where there is some third party interest, *e.g.* near neighbours. Where it has been agreed that an appeal should be conducted by written representations the planning authority will be asked to notify local residents or others who may be affected as soon as possible that the Secretary of State or the person deciding the appeal will take into account any views which are put to him in writing, provided those views are disclosed to the planning authority and the appellant. The statement of case sent by the authority to the Secretary of State should be made available for inspection locally, as should the appellant's "grounds of appeal," unless there are special reasons for withholding all or part of it, *e.g.* where he has given details of his personal circumstances."

Referring back to statute, rules and regulations on appeals, it is found that **12.09** the only persons who have a right to be notified of the lodging of an appeal and the fact that it is to be considered are "section 29 parties." Such parties are those who have to be notified of the making of an application, by virtue of section 27 of the 1971 Act, namely, owners of the land and agricultural tenants.

Circular 71/73 encourages the Secretary of State (and the local authority) to acknowledge and have regard to public opinion in such matters, but neither the Secretary of State nor the local authority is under any statutory duty to give publicity to the lodging of an appeal. There is not even any statutory requirement for persons who made representations as a result of a regulation 5 advertisement, to be notified officially of the existence of an appeal.

The same absence of statutory rights applies if the appeal goes to inquiry. Nobody other than the appellant or the local planning authority can ask for an inquiry (referred to in the Act as a "hearing"). There is, however, a safeguard, obviously inserted to provide for the airing of public opinion when neither appellant nor local authority elects to have a hearing. Under paragraph 5(1) of Schedule 9 to the 1971 Act, the person appointed to determine the appeal has the discretion to cause a local inquiry to be held if neither appellant nor local authority asks for one. Additionally under this paragraph the Secretary of State can direct that a local inquiry be held.

Thus, when public opinion manifests itself sufficiently strongly with or without the prompting of such discretionary publicity as Circular 71/73 recommends, the right for such opinion to be taken into account is to some extent provided for.

However, even if public opinion does result in a decision to hold a local inquiry, the way in which it may be brought out in the inquiry is itself subject to limitations. Only certain parties have a *right* to appear at an inquiry (and thus give evidence or otherwise make their views known). Rule 9(1) of the 1974 Rules[4] specifies who these persons may be:

12.10 "(1) The persons who are entitled to appear at the inquiry shall be:
   (a) the appellant;
   (b) the local planning authority;
   (c) where the land is not in Greater London or a metropolitan county the council of the administrative county in which the land is situated, if not the local planning authority;
   (d) where the land is not in Greater London, the council of the district in which the land is situated (or the Council of the Isles of Scilly, as the case may be) if not the local planning authority;
   (e) where the land is in a National Park, the National Park Committee (if any), if not the local planning authority;
   (f) any joint planning board constituted under section 1 of the Act (or any joint planning board or special planning board reconstituted under Part I of Schedule 17 to the Act of 1972), where that board is not the local planning authority;
   (g) where the land is in an area designated as the site of a new town, the development corporation of the new town;
   (h) section 29 parties [e.g. owners (being the freeholder, or the holder of a lease with seven years to run), and tenants of an agricultural holding];
   (i) the council of the parish or community in which the land is situated, if that council has made representations to the local planning authority in respect of the application in pursuance of a provision of a development order made under section 24 of the Act;
   (j) any persons on whom the Secretary of State or the appointed person has required notice to be served under rule 5(2)(b).
   (k) where the application was required to be notified to the Commission [in respect of a listed building in Greater London], the Commission."

12.11 It is within group (j) above that we find hidden the route to effective public representation in an inquiry, even if it is an indirect route. Rule 5(2)(b) empowers the Secretary of State to require the local planning authority to serve notice of the inquiry on such persons or classes or persons as he may specify. Moreover, according to the direction contained in paragraph 81 of Circular 8/87, at the application stage the local planning authority should already have notified the various bodies and amenity societies referred to in

---

[4] Town and Country Planning Appeals (Determination by Appointed Persons) (Inquiries Procedure) Rules 1974 (S.I. 1974 No. 420), amended by S.I. 1986 No. 420.

that direction.[5] Assuming that representations arising from such notifications have (as required in the direction) been taken into account, and assuming that representations arising from discretionary publicity or common public knowledge of the appeal have reached the ears of the Secretary of State, either directly or indirectly, herein lies the opportunity for the Secretary of State to allow that opinion a formal place in the inquiry. If the civic society, residents association, etc., make strong enough representations, there is a reasonable chance that they may secure an appearance at the inquiry.

There is one further safeguard. Rule 9(2) of the 1974 rules states quite simply:

"Any other person may appear at the inquiry at the discretion of the [Inspector]."

(e) Applications for scheduled monument consent

Applications for scheduled monument consent (Chapter 8) are made   **12.12**
direct to the Secretary of State, and his decision is final. However, the 1979 Act[6] requires that before granting scheduled monument consent the Secretary of State shall either:

"(a) cause a public local inquiry to be held, or
(b) afford to the applicant, and to any other person to whom it appears to the Secretary of State expedient to afford it, an opportunity of appearing before and being heard by a person appointed by the Secretary of State for the purpose."[7]

Additionally,

"Before determining whether or not to grant scheduled monument consent on any application therefor the Secretary of State—
(a) shall in every case consider any representations made by any person with respect to that application before the time when he considers his decision thereon (whether in consequence of any notice given to that person in accordance with any requirements of regulations made by virtue of paragraph 2 (of the Schedule) or of any publicity given to the application by the Secretary of State, or otherwise)."[8]

(f) Modification or revocation of scheduled monument consent

There is a similar procedure for an inquiry as in para. 12.12 above.   **12.13**

---

[5] See para. 5.05 above.
[6] A.M.A.A.A. 1979.
[7] A.M.A.A.A. 1979, Sched. I, para. 3(2), and see para. 8.17 above.
[8] A.M.A.A.A. 1979, Sched. I, para. 3(3).

(g) Operations notices in respect of areas of archaeological importance

12.14   As an operations notice required under section 35 of the Ancient Monuments and Archaeological Areas Act 1979 is a notice of intent to undertake works, and not an application for consent to do so, it would appear that the public has no formal rights in respect of making known its views on such proposed works.

3. ACCESS TO BUILDINGS AND SITES: PUBLIC ACCESS RIGHTS

12.15   This is an area of no little importance bearing in mind the scale of recent statistics. It is reported that, in particular, there were some 51 million visits made to historic buildings in England in 1986, with an estimated 10 million visits a year made to English parish churches; and that in that year there were about 206 millions visits made to sightseeing attractions in general.[9]

(a) In respect of buildings of architectural or historic interest

12.16   The inclusion of buildings in lists compiled by the Secretary of State under section 54(1) of the 1971 Town and Country Planning Act does not confer upon the public any right of access to such buildings or to the land on which they stand.

The only circumstances in which it is possible that the owner of a listed building, or one which, whilst not listed, is regarded as being of local interest, might be required to grant rights of access to a building not normally open to the public, are cases where the repair or maintenance of such a building has been assisted by way of a grant (but not a loan) made under the statutory provisions for financial assistance considered in Chapter 10.

Grants made by the Secretary of State under sections 3A and 4 of the Historic Buildings and Ancient Monuments Act 1953, and by local authorities under section 1(1) of the Local Authorities (Historic Buildings) Act 1962 may be made subject to public access conditions. The Secretary of State is advised on the nature of appropriate access conditions by the Commission when the grant application is being considered. The actual criteria by which such access conditions are applied in the case of section 4 grants are not publicly specified, but some guidance as to their nature might be derived from Circular 8/87. Appendix VI of the Circular, in dealing with local authority grants under the 1962 Act,[10] considers the application of access conditions under section 1(3) of that Act whereby:

"A local authority may require as a condition of the making by them of

[9] *English Heritage Monitor* 1987, p. 7.
[10] Local Authorities (Historic Buildings) Act 1962, s.1.

> a . . . grant towards the expenses of the repair or maintenance or upkeep of any property, that the person to whom the grant is made shall enter into an agreement with them for the purpose of enabling the public to have access to the property or part thereof during such period and at such times as the agreement may provide."

Circular 8/87 advises that:

> "A requirement as to access will not be appropriate in all cases. Some buildings may not be sufficiently large or significant to justify this. Sometimes the value of the building attracting a grant may lie in its external appearance seen from a street or other public place. On the other hand, where the building is not reasonably visible from a public place or where its value lies partly or wholly in its interior, opportunities for public access at specified times or by appointment . . . should be considered. . . .[11]
>
> The extent and duration of public access must clearly be decided with regard to the circumstances of each case. A requirement that would be so onerous upon the owner or occupier of the building as to discharge the acceptance of a grant would, of course, tend to defeat the object of the Act. . . .[12]
>
> Arrangements should be made to give notice when the public may have access. The authority might arrange for the display of notices in libraries and other public buildings. In the case of large grants, the recipient might also reasonably be expected to arrange for a number of announcements in the local press."[13]

In respect of sections 3A and 4 grants (and it may be deduced, in respect of section 1(1) grants also) standards of access which arise as the result of the appropriate application of conditions, fall into four categories. These are described in the English Heritage Monitor (1987). 59 per cent. of the buildings assisted during 1985–86 are open to the public for a minimum of 28 days a year, 23 per cent. are open by appointment; 15 per cent. are open by reason of the use of their interiors (e.g. hotels and theatres), and 3 per cent. qualify through being visible from public thoroughfares.

(b) In respect of access to buildings in conservation areas

Access conditions do not normally appear to be applied in the case of grants made by the Secretary of State under section 10 of the Town and Country Planning (Amendment) Act 1972 ("Grants and loans for preservation or enhancement of character or appearance of conservation areas") although section 10(2) (as amended) thereof would appear to provide the opportunity for so doing: **12.17**

> "A grant or loan under this section may be made subject to such conditions as the Secretary of State may think fit to impose."

This situation is undoubtedly a reflection of the basic aim of this grant-

[11] Circular 8/87, para. 7, Appendix VI.
[12] Circular 8/87, para. 8, Appendix VI.
[13] Circular 8/87, para. 9, Appendix VI.

aiding provision, namely the visual enhancement of areas of buildings to which the public normally has access. Even when such grant is applied to buildings, its purpose is their external, rather than internal, improvement, and such improvements can be expected to be visible to the passing public in the normal course of events.

(c) In respect of ancient monuments and archaeological areas

12.18   There is no automatic public right of access to ancient monuments, other than in the case of monuments under the ownership or guardianship of the Secretary of State or a local authority. In such circumstances the provisions of section 19 of the Ancient Monuments and Archaeological Areas Act 1979 apply; these are considered at para. 8.32 above.

In addition to the section 19 duty of the Secretary of State or local authorities, section 17 of the 1979 Act provides for the Secretary of State or a local authority to enter into agreements with occupiers of ancient monuments (not just scheduled monuments—see paras. 8.01–8.07 above) and land adjoining them or in their vicinity, for, amongst other purposes, the purpose of providing:

> "public access to the monument or land and the provision of facilities and information or other services for the use of the public in that connection."

The designation of an "Area of Archaeological Importance" under section 33 of the 1979 Act (paras. 8.36–8.45 above) does not confer any public rights of access in respect of those parts of such an area to which the public does not normally have rights of access. Such areas of archaeological importance may be broadly compared in concept with conservation areas (Chapter 3) and can be expected to include areas (*e.g.* streets, footpaths, commons) to which the public normally has access.

(d) In respect of the use of metal detectors

12.19   Advances in electronics and growing public interest in "treasure hunting" have produced considerable concern amongst archaeologists and there is strong evidence of the indiscriminate use of metal detectors ruining valuable, unexcavated archaeological sites.

Primarily because of this concern, section 42 of the 1979 Act[13a] as amended by the National Heritage Act 1983 prohibits the use of such equipment within areas of archaeological importance designated under section 33 without the consent of the Secretary of State. There is a defence provision built into section 42 whereby an accused might prove that he used the metal detector for a purpose other than detecting or locating objects of archaeological or historic interest. The statutory protection is, of course, additional to all other legal limitations covering such treasure hunting activities on all land, of which limitations the majority of members of the public are probably unaware. Some helpful general leaflets have been pro-

[13a] A.M.A.A.A. 1979.

duced by the Commission and the Council for British Archaeology. "Buried Treasure"[14] contains sound advice and is produced in an attractive lay fashion. It makes the following points:

1. The operator of a metal detector needs permission from the owner and tenant of the land for access, except in the case of public open space. Without this permission he is committing an act of trespass.
2. He needs permission from the owner (not only the tenant) to remove objects on or in the ground. Without such permission the removal of such objects may be an act of theft. Even common lands are governed by owners, often the local authority.
3. Unauthorised damage to property or land during the recovery of objects located by a metal detector could be the subject of litigation under the Criminal Damage Act 1971.
4. Disturbance of the ground may lead to accidents involving third parties, for which the landowner would be liable, e.g. holes dug near footpaths in public parts, etc.

However, the continuing damage caused by persons using metal detectors underlines the need for tighter legal control in this area. Various suggestions have been put forward.[14a] Fines should be commensurate with the offence, making it impossible for an offender who is fined, say, in the magistrates' court then to profit from an award for his "find" at a coroner's inquest. The definition of treasure trove (i.e. Crown property) should be widened to include more than simply gold or silver and in such a way as not to depend on the original owner's intention. There should be a statutory obligation to report finds to a museum or empowered archaeologist. It has also been suggested that the government should re-introduce the system of Home Office licences for metal detectors, which practice was discontinued in 1980.[15]

---

[14] The Commission at 23 Savile Row, London W1X 2HE, The Council for British Archaeology, 112 Kennington Road, London SE11 6RE, and at Manor House Museum, Castle Yard, Ilkley LS29 9DT.

[14a] The Department of the Environment issued in 1988 a Conservation Paper on Portable Antiquities which at the time of going to press is still under consideration.

[15] See Sunday Telegraph November 22, 1987.

13. Interested Bodies

1. INTRODUCTION

13.01 The growth of interest in conservation has been matched by the growth of bodies who will help and support various specialised interests. Some of these bodies have received a statutory recognition. There is reproduced a selective list of those bodies who can offer technical support and in certain instances funds towards certain classes of buildings. It must be emphasised that this list is not comprehensive—perhaps no list could be—but is assembled with the particular aim of helping those concerned with listed buildings to obtain information and support. The statutory requirements and recommendations are set out in Table 9.

2. THE STATUTORY BODIES

(a) The Historic Buildings and Monuments Commission for England[1]

13.02 The Commission has inherited many of the functions formerly exercised by the Secretary of State for the Environment and the advisory functions of the Ancient Monuments Board for England and the Historic Buildings Council for England. Both the Board and the Council ceased to exist on April 1, 1984 when the Commission began to exercise its public functions.

The general duties of the Commission are so far as practicable:

(a) to secure the preservation of ancient monuments and historic buildings situated in England;

(b) to promote the preservation and enhancement of the character and appearance of conservation areas situated in England; and

---

[1] See also para. 1.05 above.

270

(c) to promote the public's enjoyment of, and advance their knowledge of, ancient monuments and historic buildings situated in England and their preservation.

The Commission's specific functions involve giving advice in relation to ancient monuments, historic buildings and conservation areas situated in England, including advice to the Secretary of State on the inclusion of buildings in the statutory list of buildings of special architectural or historic interest and the scheduling of ancient monuments; grants and loans may be made in relation to historic buildings, land and gardens, conservation areas, ancient monuments, and in respect of archaeological investigation. With the consent of the Secretary of State, the Commission may acquire historic buildings, land or gardens, and acquire or become the guardian of ancient monuments. In Greater London, the Commission carries out, with some modifications, the functions formerly exercised by the Greater London Council. It also manages about 400 monuments on behalf of the Secretary of State.

Address: Fortress House, 23 Savile Row, London, W1X 2HE (01–734 6010)

(b) The Historic Buildings Councils for Scotland and Wales

The Historic Buildings Councils for Scotland and Wales were established by sections 2 and 3 respectively of the Historic Buildings and Ancient Monuments Act 1953. Their membership is at the discretion of the appropriate Secretary of State, who is responsible for appointing the Councils and their Chairmen.
The Councils have broadly the same functions in their respective areas as has the Historic Buildings and Monuments Commission in England.
The addresses of their respective headquarters are:

Scotland: 20 Brandon Street, Edinburgh, EH3 5DX (031–226 2570)
Wales: Brunel House, 2 Fitzalan House, Cardiff, CF2 1UY (0222 465511)

(c) The Ancient Monuments Boards for Scotland and Wales

These were originally constituted under the Ancient Monuments Consolidation and Amendment Act 1913, and consist of members representing the bodies specified in section 22 of the Ancient Monuments and Archaeological Areas Act 1979. For Scotland, these are: the Royal Commission on the Ancient and Historical Monuments of Scotland, the Royal Incorporation of Architects in Scotland, and the Society of Antiquaries of Scotland; for Wales: the R.C.H.M. (Wales), the National Museum of Wales, the Cambrian Archaeological Association and the R.I.B.A. In each case they are joined by such other members as the Secretary of State may appoint. The function of the Ancient Monuments Boards is to advise the Secretary of

271

State in respect of the exercise of his functions under the 1979 Act, whether generally or in relation to any particular case or classes of case.

Their respective addresses are:

> Scotland: 17 Atholl Crescent, Edinburgh, EH3 8HA (031–229 9321)
> Wales: Crown Buildings, Cathays Park, Cardiff, CF1 3NQ (0222 825111)

3. ROYAL COMMISSIONS

(a) The Royal Commissions on historical monuments

13.03   There have been established for England, for Wales, and for Scotland, Royal Commissions on Historical Monuments. Their full titles are, respectively:

> The Royal Commission on the Ancient and Historical Monuments and Constructions of England;
> The Royal Commission on Ancient and Historical Monuments in Wales;
> The Royal Commission on the Ancient and Historical Monuments of Scotland.

The Royal Commission for England was established by King Edward VII on October 28, 1908, with the following terms of reference:

> " . . . to make an inventory of the Ancient and Historical Monuments and constructions connected with or illustrative of the contemporary culture, civilisation and conditions of life of the people of England, excluding Monmouthshire, from the earliest times to the year 1700, and to specify those which seem most worthy of preservation."[2–3]

The work of compiling the inventories referred to in the Commission continues even after 70 years, although this is not now the sole role of the Commissioners.

Each Royal Commission has to be consulted on applications to demolish listed buildings in the national area for which it is established[4] and, upon the grant of LBC to demolish, the Commissioners must be given notice of at least one month prior to the demolition being carried out, and be afforded reasonable access to the building for the purpose of recording it, unless they have stated in writing that they have completed their recording and do not wish to record the building.[5]

Additionally, each Royal Commission is a constituent member (through a nominated representative) of the HBMC and of the Ancient Monuments Board for its national area.[6]

[2–3] Abstract of copy of paragraph 1 of the Commission document—Yorkshire Archaeological Society, Leeds.

[4] Circular 8/87, para 81, consequent on T.C.PA. 1971, Sched. 11, para. 7(2) applies to England.

[5] T.C.P.A. 1971, section 55(3).

[6] See para. 8.33 above.

Within each Royal Commission, an executive arm referred to as the National Monuments Record has the role of compiling, and maintains for public reference, complete records of the architecture of the country concerned and of its archaeological sites. They each also maintain an index of architectural records in public and private possession.

The addresses of the Royal Commissioners and their respective National Monuments Record headquarters are:

England: Fortress House, 23 Savile Row, London, W1X 1AB (01–734 6010)

Wales: Edleston House, Queens Road, Aberystwyth, Dyfed, SY23 2HP (0970 4381)

Scotland: 52/54 Melville Street, Edinburgh, EH3 7HF (031–225 5994)

(b) The Royal Fine Art Commissions

The Royal Fine Art Commission and the Royal Fine Art Commission for **13.04** Scotland are consultative bodies responsible for advising government departments on matters of public amenity or artistic importance. The Royal Commissioners are consulted on matters appertaining to proposals involving major new buildings, or which may affect buildings of national importance, but they are not "statutory consultees" in respect of demolition proposals affecting listed buildings. Whilst they make recommendations, they have no direct powers of control.

The addresses of the Royal Fine Art Commissioners are:

England and
Wales: 7 St. James Square, London, SW17 4JU (01–839 6537)

Scotland: The Royal Fine Art Commission for Scotland, 22 Melville Street, Edinburgh, EH3 7NS (031–227 1109)

4. STATUTORY CONSULTEES

In accordance with powers under paragraph 7(2) of Schedule 11 to the **13.05** 1971 Act the Secretary of State has directed, in paragraph 81 of Circular 8/87, that local planning authorities should notify the following bodies of all applications for consent to demolish listed buildings and of the decisions taken thereon:

The Ancient Monuments Society. Founded in 1924 for the "Study and Conservation of Ancient Monuments, Historic Buildings and Fine Old Craftsmanship," the Society concerns itself with protecting historic buildings of all ages and types against unjustified demolition. It publishes an annual volume of transactions containing papers on many aspects of architectural history.

Address: St. Andrew-by-the-Wardrobe, Queen Victoria Street, London, EC4V 5DE (01–236 3934)

The Council for British Archaeology. National representative body for archaeology, concerned with the safeguarding of ancient monuments, his-

273

toric buildings, and industrial monuments at both amateur and professional levels.

Address: 112 Kennington Road, London, SE11 6RE (01–582 0494)

The Georgian Group. Promotes public interest in Georgian architecture and town planning.

Address: 37 Spital Square, London, E1 6DY (01–377 1722)

Scottish Georgian Society. Similar aims to those of The Georgian Group. Statutory consultee on applications to demolish listed buildings in Scotland.

Address: 5b Forres Street, Edinburgh, EH3 6BJ (031–225 9724)

The Society for the Protection of Ancient Buildings. Founded by William Morris in 1877, the S.P.A.B. was the first national organisation to acknowledge, and campaign for, the protection or our built heritage. Mr. Morris' dictum:

"We are only the trustees for those who come after us"

is still the motto of the Society for the Protection of Ancient Buildings. The Society performs a wide range of functions, including the provision of technical advice, the making of reports on neglected old buildings, and the organisation of courses on historic building conservation and repair for architects, builders, craftsmen, etc. The Society is concerned with the maintenance of originality and the avoidance of pastiche in the maintenance and repair of buildings. The Society recently instituted a private prosecution in respect of the demolition of the Welby Almshouses in Grantham, Lincs.

Address: 37 Spital Square, London, E1 6DY (01–377 1644)

Victorian Society. Founded in 1958 "to preserve the best of Victorian and Edwardian architecture and also to study the art and history of the period." It is particularly concerned to protect important nineteenth century and early twentieth century buildings, both public and private, industrial monuments, and historical areas. Co-operates with, and assists, the Department of the Environment over listing of buildings of the period. Active at appeals and inquiries, and advises local planning authorities on conservation area designation. The Society has a number of active regional groups who fight local casework issues and organise regional activities.

Address: 1 Priory Gardens, London, W4 1TT (01–994 1019)

Royal Commission on Historical Monuments (England). See para. 13.03 above.

5. PRIVATE, VOLUNTARY, AND EDUCATIONAL INTERESTS: NATIONAL AND REGIONAL BODIES

13.06   Since at least the latter quarter of the nineteenth century, the growth of public awareness of the built environment has generated a substantial number of voluntary bodies concerned with the protection, preservation or improvement of what has come to be called the "built heritage." The vast majority of such bodies have essentially local interests, if a common aim, but a number operate at national or regional level, dealing with particular aspects of building and archaeological conservation, or providing an "umbrella" function for the local groups.

A small number of these national bodies (referred to in para. 13.05 above) have a statutory right to be consulted on proposals involving the demolition of listed buildings. The others form a comprehensive and frequently formidable lobby on all aspects of built heritage conservation, and the following references include some of the leading bodies in this national field.

(a) Historic Buildings and Architectural Interests

Association for Studies in the Conservation of Historic Buildings. **13.07** Comprises an invited membership of those professionally engaged in historic building conservation work. Involved in setting up training courses in this field. Founded 1968.

> Address: Institute of Archaeology, 31/34 Gordon Square, London, WC1H 0PY (01–387 6052).

Building Conservation Trust. Formed to provide the proper conservation, maintenance, alteration and use of buildings of all types and ages. Encourages sympathetic conservation of the architectural heritage, the employment of professional expertise and craft skills, and the correct use of materials and products as exemplified by its permanent "Care of Buildings" Exhibition at Hampton Court.

> Address: Apartment 39, Hampton Court Palace, East Molesey, Surrey, KT8 9BS (01–943 2277).

Central Committee for Architectural Advisory Panels. Local branches of the Royal Institute of British Architects (para. 13.12 below) jointly organise architectural advisory panels, consisting essentially of local architects and environmentalists concerned with architecture, to assist local planning authorities by providing expert technical advice on architectural standards. The Central Committee provides a co-ordinating source for these panels.

> Address: 66 Portland Place, London, W1N 4AD (01–580 5533).

The Civic Trust. Founded in 1957, the Trust is a recognised charity supported by voluntary contributions. It encourages the protection and improvement of the environment. By means of conferences, practical projects, films and reports it focuses attention on major issues in planning and architecture. It publishes a bi-monthly journal, *Heritage Outlook*, and maintains a library and photographic collection. It makes awards for good development of all kinds. Among some particular concerns have been the initiation of co-operative street improvement schemes; the promotion of new techniques for transplanting semi-mature trees; industrial dereliction and urban wasteland; and the problems of damage and disruption caused by heavy lorries. The Trust encourages the formation of local amenity

275

societies and gives advice and support to nearly 1,200 such societies now on its register. Its proposals led to the creation of the Lee Valley Regional Park Authority. It was closely associated with the drafting of the Civic Amenities Act 1967, which created the concept of the conservation area and of the Town and Country Amenities Act 1974. At the request of the government, it provided the United Kingdom Secretariat for European Architectural Heritage Year 1975. It administers the Architectural Heritage Fund, an independent charity which provides loan capital to local buildings preservation trusts; and on behalf of the Department of the Environment, the work of the Heritage Education Group. Since 1976 the Civic Trust has administered government grant-aid to conservation projects in "non-outstanding" conservation areas on behalf of the Department of the Environment.

Address: 17 Carlton House Terrace, London, SW1Y 5AW (01–930 0914).

Scottish Civic Trust. Involved throughout Scotland with heritage conservation and general environmental matters. It has been given the right by the Scottish Development Department to provide authoritative comment where planning permissions to demolish or radically alter listed buildings are concerned. It encourages the formation of, and supports with advice, local civic and amenity societies. The Trust provides the Secretariat to the Scottish Environmental Education Committee and publishes the quarterly magazine The Scottish Review: Arts and the Environment in conjunction with the Saltire Society and the National Trust for Scotland, and with the support of the Scottish Arts Council.

Address: 24 George Square, Glasgow, G2 1EF (041–221 1466).

13.08 *Civic Trust for the North East (CTNE).* A trust associated with, but independent from, the Civic Trust, and with similar aims. Operates principally in Northumberland, Durham, Tyne & Wear, Cleveland and parts of North Yorkshire.

Address: 3 Old Elvet, Durham, DH1 3HL (0385 61182).

Civic Trust for the North West (CTNW). Similar aims to Civic Trust and CTNE. Operates primarily in Greater Manchester, Lancashire, Merseyside, Cheshire, Cumbria and High Peak, Derbyshire. Useful reference service provided through its Granada Environment Library.

Address: Environmental Institute, Greaves School, Bolton Road, Swinton, Manchester, M27 2UX (061–794 9314).

Civic Trust for Wales/Treftadaeth Cymru. An independent body, supported by voluntary contributions, which operates in the principality of Wales. Its aims are similar to those of the Civic Trust.

Address: 46 Cardiff Road, Llandaff, Cardiff, CF5 2DT (0222 552388).

Historic Houses Association. Represents the interests of the owners and guardians of over 1,000 historic houses, parks, gardens and places of interest, in private ownership, throughout Great Britain; provides practical advice and professional services to owners. The "Friends of the HHA" offers free admission to over 250 HHA member's houses, on payment of annual subscription.

Address: 38 Ebury Street, London, SW1W 0LU (01–730 9419).

Institute of Advanced Architectural Studies, University of York. Graduate Institute undertaking research, education practice in architectural studies and the building industry. Nationally recognised post-graduate Diploma in Conservation Studies one year course, plus regular short courses.

Address: The Secretary, The King's Manor, York, YO1 2EP (0904 24919).

National Trust for Places of Historic Interest or Natural Beauty. An **13.09** independent charitable organisation relying on voluntary support with membership open to the public on annual subscription. Established in 1895 to promote the permanent preservation, for the benefit of the nation, of lands and tenements (including buildings) of beauty or historic interest and—as regards land—for the preservation so far as is practicable of natural aspects, features and animal and plant life. Owns over 240 historic buildings and 450,000 acres in England, Wales and Northern Ireland. Receives grants from the Secretary of State for the acquisition of buildings or land of outstanding architectural or historic interest.[7]

Address: 36 Queen Anne's Gate, London, SW1H 9AS (01–222 9251).

National Trust for Scotland for Places of Historic Interest or Natural Beauty. Founded 1931 for purposes similar to the National Trust (above). An independent charity, with public membership by subscription.

Address: 5 Charlotte Square, Edinburgh, EH2 4DU (031–226 5922).

SAVE Britain's Heritage. Established 1975 by a group of journalists, architects, planners and historians. Campaigns vigorously for the retention and re-use of old buildings and areas. Authoritative reports on conservation problems. Takes a hard hitting approach to issues in which it involves itself.

Address: 68 Battersea High Street, London, SW11 3HX (01–228 3336).

Thirties Society. The Thirties Society was founded in 1979 to campaign for the protection of buildings built after 1914. It seeks to arouse public interest in the fate of inter-war buildings and has taken an active part in extending the Department of the Environment's policy of giving protection to the best of what was built after the First World War. The casework officer regularly advises local authorities on planning applications that affect buildings of the period. The Society organises a wide range of events, lectures and study tours. It has organised a number of conferences and publishes an annual journal and quarterly newsletter.

Address: 3 Park Square West, London, NW1 4LJ.

Town and Country Planning Association. National pressure group primarily concerned with influencing central and local government, and public opinion in national and regional planning matters. Widely respected and

---

[7] H.B.A.M.A. 1953, s.6(2).

consulted. Operates a national Planning Aid Service primarily for community groups and voluntary organisations with planning problems, operates the National Council for Urban Studies Centres, and promotes environmental education. Membership open to anyone interested in its aims.

Address: 17 Carlton House Terrace, London, SW1Y 5AS (01–930 8903).

(b) Special ecclesiastical interests

13.10   The following bodies represent the various church interests on a national basis. It should also be remembered that there are many diocesan or county church preservation bodies, details of which may be obtained from their national counterparts.

The Church Commissioners. Responsibilities include, amongst others, pastoral reorganisation and deciding the future of redundant churches of the Church of England.

Address: 1 Millbank, London, SW1P 3JZ (01 222 7010).

Council for the Care of Churches. A permanent advisory Commission of the Church of England General Synod, which in addition to statutory responsibilities under the Pastoral Measure 1968 and to the Faculty Jurisdiction Measure 1964, is the central co-ordinating body for the Diocesan Advisory Committees for the Care of Churches. The Council also provides information and advice on all matters concerning churches and their furnishings, and allocates grant aid for the conservation of furnishings and works of art in churches. A further role is the promotion of high standards of craftmanship and conservation; to this intent the Council maintains a register of artists and craftsmen.

Address: 83 London Wall, London, EC2M 5NA (01–638 0971)

Friends of Friendless Churches. A trust whose main object is to save churches of architectural or historic interest, especially those threatened with collapse or demolition or conversion to unsympathetic use. The Trust does not normally help churches in ordinary use.

Address: 12 Edwardes Square, London, W8 6HG (01–602 6267).

Historic Churches Preservation Trust. The Trust is an independent non-denominational charity and relies entirely on voluntary financial support. Subject to availability of funds enquiries about grants can be considered on behalf of any church or chapel in use which in the opinion of the Trust is worthy, on grounds of architectural merit or historic interest, of preservation.

Address: Fulham Palace, London, SW6 6EA (01–736 3054)

Redundant Churches Fund. Established 1969 by Pastoral Measure, the Church of England's equivalent of an Act of Parliament, with the object of preserving "in the interests of the nation and the Church of England" churches or parts of churches of historic or architectural interest transferred to the fund. Transfer to the fund is effected by a legal process which may follow the initial legal procedure for formally declaring a church (of the Church of England only) redundant.

The Fund is financed largely by the State and the Church of England in equal shares.

Address: St Andrews-by-the-Wardrobe, Queen Victoria Street, London, EC4V 5DE (01–2481 7461).

(c) Archaeological interests

Association for Industrial Archaeology. Concerned with the promotion of the study of industrial archaeology and industrial monuments, and their recording and conservation.   **13.11**

Address: Ironbridge, Telford, Shropshire, TF8 7AW (095–245 3522).

Institute of Archaeology. Institute of the University of London. Closely associated with the Association for Studies in the Conservation of Historic Buildings. Major institute for professional archaeological training and interests.

Address: 31/34 Gordon Square, London, WC1H 0PY (01–387 6052).

Rescue (British Trust for Archaeology). Promotes the recording and preservation of Britain's archaeological remains. Concerned with and involved in rescue archaeology, education, publicity, and public awareness.

Address: 15A Bull Plain, Hertford, Herts. SG14 1DX (0992 58170).

(d) Professional interests

The Chartered Institute of Building. Professional institution of the building industry. Seeks to establish and maintain standards of competence and professional conduct. Entry by examination.   **13.12**

Address: Englemere, Kings Ride, Ascot, Berks, SL5 8BJ (0990 23355).

The Incorporated Society of Valuers and Auctioneers. Professional institute for valuers and auctioneers.

Address: 3 Cadogan Gate, London SW1X 0AS (01–235 2282)

The Landscape Institute. Professional institute for landscape architects and those engaged in land science and landscape management. Entry by examination. The Institute proves a "clients advisory service," nominating practices experienced in specific types of landscape work.

Address: 12 Carlton House Terrace, London, SW1Y 5AH (01–839 4044).

The Law Society. Professional institution of the solicitors' branch of the legal profession. There is a Standing Committee on Planning and Development Law.

> Address: The Law Society's Hall, 113 Chancery Lane, London, WC2A 1PL (01–242 1222).

Royal Institute of British Architects. The professional institute for architects in the United Kingdom. In addition to having regard to its members interests and professional standards and qualifications, it is concerned to increase public interest in and understanding of architecture. Numerous "local" branches. Architectural library and bookshop at headquarters, regular RIBA exhibitions at the Heinz Gallery, Portman Square, W.1. Clients advisory service will suggest suitable architects for specific work.

> HQ Address: 66 Portland Place, London, W1N 4AD (01–580 5533).

Royal Institution of Chartered Surveyors. Principal representative body of the surveying profession in Great Britain. The Institution has seven practice divisions: Building Surveyors; General Practice; Land Agency and Agriculture; Land Surveyors; Minerals Surveyors; Planning and Development; and Quantity Surveyors. Co-organiser in association with *The Times* of annual Conservation Awards. Strong interest in the promotion of positive conservation of old buildings. Library facilities and technical information services.

> HQ Address: 12 Great George Street, Parliament Square, London, SW1P 3AD (01–222 7000).

Royal Town Planning Institute. Aims to promote high standards of town planning and education in the subject, in addition to providing codes of practice and conduct for its members. Provides limited planning aid service at branch level.

> HQ Address: 26 Portland Place, London, W1N 4BE (01–639 9107).

(e) Other related interests

13.13   *Architectural Heritage Fund.* An independent charity administered by the Civic Trust on behalf of a council of management. Its purpose is to provide short-term loan capital to help building preservation trusts and other appropriate charitable bodies to acquire and restore any building which merits conservation.

> Address: Civic Trust, 17 Carlton House Terrace, London, SW1Y 5AW (01–930 0914).

Council for Small Industries in Rural Areas (CoSIRA). Main agent of the government's Development Commission, whose prime objective is to re-generate the rural areas of England through the stimulation and promotion of small rural businesses and village industries. Provides consultancy, training and financial services, the latter including provision of loans for converting existing rural buildings into workshops—a possible contribution to the effective re-use of old buildings.

Address: 141 Castle Street, Salisbury, Wilts. SP1 1EX (0722 6255).

(CoSIRA only operates in England. Similar services to rural businesses are offered in Wales by the Small Businesses Section of the Welsh Development Agency (Treforest Industrial Estate, Pontypridd, CF37 5UT (044 385) 2666) and in Scotland by the Small Business Division of the Scottish Development Agency (102 Telford Road, Edinburgh, EN4 2NP (031 343) 1911/6)).

Council for the Protection of Rural England (CPRE). Seeks to protect rural scenery and the amenities of county towns and villages. Active and effective county branch organisation, with over 30,000 members. These branches, and their affiliated village and town branches, are actively concerned with conservation matters and especially with monitoring planning applications. (See also para. 13.14 below).

National Office
      Address: 4 Hobart Place, London, SW1W 0HY (01–235 9481).

Council for the Protection of Rural Wales/(CPRW) Cymdeithas Diogelu Harddwch Cymru (CDHC). Similar aims and operation to CPRE.

      HQ Address: 14 Broad Street, Welshpool, Powys, SY21 7SD (0938 2525).

Friends of the Earth Ltd. Non-charitable company with primary objectives of promoting understanding and appreciation of the need for conservation, protection and restoration of natural resources and beauty, of pressing for environmentally sound legislation, and of working for the enhancement and rational use of the environment, well informed and powerful lobby in major environmental issues, *e.g.* Windscale, Belvoir.

      Address: 9 Poland Street, London, W1V 3DG (01–437 6121).

Garden History Society. The Society is dedicated to the preservation of historic gardens and landscape parks and to the study of the various aspects of garden history which include botany, landscape design, horticulture, architecture and forestry.

      Address: 66 Granville Park, London, SE13 7DX.

National Heritage Memorial Fund. An independent body set up by the National Heritage Act 1980 in succession to the National Land Fund. It is empowered to assist, through grants or loans, the preservation, maintenance and acquisition of buildings, land, works of art and other objects or structures of outstanding interest which are also of importance to the national heritage. The eligible recipients for assistance from the Fund are non-profit making institutions in the arts, libraries, land and building worlds, or any other non-profit making body whose main objective lies in the conservation of the national heritage. The Fund is vested in and run by eleven independent trustees, appointed by the Prime Minister and representing the four home countries of the UK.

      Address: Church House, Great Smith Street, London, SW1P 3BL (01–212 5414).

6. PRIVATE VOLUNTARY SECTOR INTERESTS: LOCAL AMENITY SOCIETIES

13.14   Local amenity societies form the "backbone" of the amenity movement and the post-war period has seen a considerable acceleration in the rate of their formation. Many have arisen as a result of general interest in the protection and improvement of the local environment; many have been formed in order to contest proposals considered prejudicial to its well-being.

According to The Civic Trust (which amongst its other functions (see para. 13.07 above) acts as the central registration agency for civic and amenity societies, registration being voluntary, not mandatory) by September 1987 there were some 1,097 (registered) local amenity societies and trusts, with a total membership of over 300,000.

Vociferous but nevertheless increasingly well informed and organised, these societies are a powerful lobbying voice in local politics and with key members often including solicitors, architects, surveyors and planners they can have an authoritative voice in development proposals, and in the outcome of conservation schemes and projects.

Indeed, notwithstanding the statutory requirements for local authorities to consult the bodies listed above at para. 13.05, positive encouragement is also given in Circular 8/87 for local authorities to bring local amenity societies into the consultation process on matters relating to listed buildings and conservation areas (paragraphs 68 and 70; also paragraph 8).

There are few areas of the United Kingdom without some form of local amenity society; most local libraries will be able to provide names and addresses of secretaries etc. Alternatively, details can be obtained from the Civic Trust, or one of the Regional Civic Trusts (paras. 13.07–13.08 above) or the Council for the Protection of Rural England.

TABLE 9

Involvement of "interested bodies" in the listed building consent application process (excluding the Greater London area) (1)

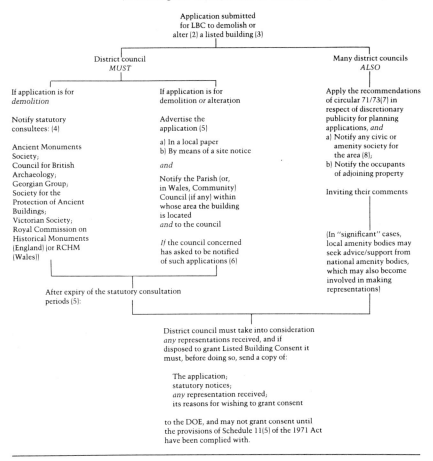

Application submitted for LBC to demolish or alter (2) a listed building (3)

District council
MUST

Many district councils
ALSO

If application is for *demolition*

Notify statutory consultees: (4)

Ancient Monuments Society;
Council for British Archaeology;
Georgian Group;
Society for the Protection of Ancient Buildings;
Victorian Society;
Royal Commission on Historical Monuments (England) (or RCHM (Wales))

If application is for demolition *or* alteration

Advertise the application (5)

a) In a local paper
b) By means of a site notice

and

Notify the Parish (or, in Wales, Community) Council (if any) within whose area the building is located *and* to the council

If the council concerned has asked to be notified of such applications (6)

Apply the recommendations of circular 71/73(7) in respect of discretionary publicity for planning applications, *and*
a) Notify any civic or amenity society for the area (8);
b) Notify the occupants of adjoining property

Inviting their comments

(In "significant" cases, local amenity bodies may seek advice/support from national amenity bodies, which may also become involved in making representations)

After expiry of the statutory consultation periods (5):

District council must take into consideration *any* representations received, and if disposed to grant Listed Building Consent it must, before doing so, send a copy of:

The application;
statutory notices;
any representation received;
its reasons for wishing to grant consent

to the DOE, and may not grant consent until the provisions of Schedule 11(5) of the 1971 Act have been complied with.

Notes

(1) For Greater London area provisions see Circular 8/87, paras. 83(ii), 86II, 88.

(2) Other than works affecting only the interior of a Grade II (unstarred) building which has not been subject of a grant under Section 4 of the Historic Buildings & Ancient Monuments Act 1953. In such cases the requirements for notification of consultees, public advertisement, and reference to the DOE do not apply: T.C.P.A. 1971, Sched. 11, and Circular 8/87, paras. 80, 81, 82(i).

(3) Excluding churches in use and ancient monuments: T.C.P.A. 1971, s.56.

(4) T.C.P.A. Act 1971, Sched. 11, and Circular 8/87, para. 81.

(5) T.C.P.A. (Listed Buildings and Buildings in Conservation Areas) Regulations 1987, reg. 5.

(6) Local Government Act 1972, Sched. 16(20).

(7) "Publicity for Planning Applications."

(8) Many such bodies also receive the Council's weekly list of applications submitted.

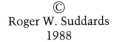

Appendix

1. A SHORT GUIDE TO THE TOWN PLANNING SYSTEM

14.01 Town planning is a "creature of statute," *i.e.* all the powers of Secretaries of State, and local planning authorities derive from the powers given by Parliament in successive Acts of Parliament ("the Planning Acts")—in particular the Town and Country Planning Act 1971 as subsequently amended.

The listed building legislation is part of that Act as is the conservation area legislation. Listed buildings are seen as part of the whole town planning process. So in fact is the ancient monuments legislation, although its origins—again in statute—are from a separate piece of legislation: the Ancient Monuments and Archaeological Areas Act 1979.

Under the Planning Acts a *Secretary of State* for the Department of the Environment is appointed "with the duty of securing consistency and continuity in the framing and execution of a national policy with respect to the use and development of land throughout England and Wales."[1] In carrying out this function the Secretary of State acts through and is advised by the civil servants in the Department of the Environment. Therein lies a range of skills including professional town planners, experts in land and land values and those knowledgeable and experienced in historic buildings. The Secretary of State frames new planning legislation and brings it before Parliament. He confirms structure plans (which often include important policy statements of the local authorities on historic buildings)—which will not be operative until so confirmed.

Appeals against decisions of local planning authorities on listed building or conservation area issues are heard and determined by the Secretary of State, although in practice the vast majority of these appeals are now delegated by him for determination to his inspectors (who are sometimes called the "appointed persons"). Sometimes the Secretary of State removes the

---

[1] Minister of Town and Country Planning Act 1943, s.1. There is an argument that this section has been repealed: but this is the basis on which the Secretary of State acts.

decision making or the appeal decision making from the local planning authority or the appointed person. This is generally known as the "call-in" procedure.

The main headquarters of the Department is in Marsham Street, West- **14.02** minster, London, but the Department has *regional offices* each of which has delegated to it important functions and which is under the control of a regional officer. The main purpose of each regional officer is to be the spokesman of the Secretary of State locally, but in a more particular sense it is the office which decides appeals on listed buildings and conservation area cases where these are not decided by the appointed persons.

The establishment of the *Historic Buildings and Monuments Commission* has separated some of the functions formerly carried out by the Secretary of State. Now the Commission carries out many planning functions (including some listed building functions) in Greater London but also acts throughout England as an advisory body to the Secretary of State who Parliament has determined, in many cases, must not act in the absence of such advice.

There is power in the Planning Acts for the Secretary of State to make or submit for approval to Parliament certain subsidiary legislation. These are usually *Regulations* or *Orders*. Thus the Town and Country Planning (Listed Buildings and Buildings in Conservation Areas) Regulations 1987 were "made" by the Secretary of State on March 4, laid before Parliament on March 11, and came into force on April 1, 1987. These Regulations cover a wide range of administrative procedures, from applications for listed building consent to applications by local planning authorities. When an Act of Parliament is passed it is common practice today for Parliament to enact that it will come into force (sometimes on different dates for different sections) "on such day as may be appointed by the Secretary of State by order made by statutory instrument." Thus the Housing and Planning Act 1986 (Commencement No. 4) Order 1987 (which dealt with listed buildings and conservation areas) was "made" by the Secretary of State on March 4, 1987. As Parliament had given him the power to make the Order he did not (as opposed to the Regulations mentioned above) need to "lay" his Order before Parliament. It merely came into effect.

Similarly the two important town planning provisions—the General Development Order and the Use Classes Order—were made by the Secretary of State without parliamentary approval. The former grants planning permission in certain limited cases without the necessity of a formal application and decision; the latter enables, in certain limited cases, one use to be substituted for another.

The Secretary of State may in certain cases issue a *Direction*. For **14.03** instance, not all non-listed buildings in a conservation area need conservation area consent—the Secretary of State issued a direction[2] that this provision should not apply, *e.g.* to any building with "a total cubic content not exceeding 115 cubic metres or any part of such building . . ."

The Secretary of State may, and frequently does, issue *Circulars*. The Circular 8/87 entitled "Historic Buildings and Conservation Areas—Policy and Procedures" is a careful and embracing analysis of the government's view on these subjects. Copies of a Circular are available for sale to the public from the HMSO Bookshops, but it is actually addressed by the relevant

---

[2] Direction contained in paragraph 97 of Circular 8/87.

department (in this case by the Department of the Environment) to all relevant local authorities and government departments. The status of a Circular is interesting. It has obviously strong persuasive value: those who fly in the face of the advice must be ready to explain their action on a planning appeal. Farquarson J. in 1985 summed up the matter thus:

> "It should be emphasised that these circulars are intended to give advice to local planning authorities and, while they may represent government policy at the time, the Minister is in no sense bound by them, save to the extent that he should consider their relevance in appropriate cases."

The provision of a new Circular will replace previous Circulars on that same topic, provided it says so; reference should be made to the end of the Circular where amendments, cancellations, withdrawals, etc. will be found set out. Otherwise the reader must also refer back to previous circulars. Circulars are also useful and important vehicles to set out the terms of a *Direction*. Several Directions including the one mentioned above were incorporated, *e.g.*, in Circular 8/87. Such Directions are printed in bold type and obviously a reader who is affected by the provisions of a circular must pay special attention when he encounters a paragraph set out in this way.

14.04 Indeed, it is perhaps worthwhile to mention the correct terminology relating to the instruments already described:

> *Statutes* contain sections;
> *Orders* contain articles;
> *Schedules* contain paragraphs;
> *Circulars* contain paragraphs;
> *Regulations* contain regulations.

Although this note seeks to set out the basis of the statutory system, it is of necessity a sketch only.[3] Much of importance in the system of planning and listed buildings is left on a non-statutory basis. The grading of listed buildings, for example, is referred to extensively in Directions and Circulars and constitutes a much-used administrative guideline. But it is not part of the statutory order.

Much of the statutory and advisory material regarding listed building consent applications seems to place an emphasis on the problems of demolition. But the consent to alter or extend can frequently be of far greater importance. This is so not least in the case of interiors which, while not being environmentally visible so to speak, are important as part of the heritage of our country. Thus it is possible, for example, to imagine circumstances in which the preservation of a staircase in a Grade II building could be of greater significance than the disappearance of a Grade II* building. Like so many decisions which authorities—be they central or local—are required to take, the ultimate issue depends on a delicate balance, requiring the exercise of knowledge and judgment in such matters as architectural taste and historical significance, every bit as much as the precise interpretation of the legislation.

In this note we have barely mentioned the *local planning authorities*. As the book throughout will have made clear, however, their role is fundamental. They receive all this "guidance"—Orders, Directions and Guidelines. In

---

[3] For a comprehensive treatment of planning law generally, see Sir Desmond Heap, "*Outline of Planning Law*" (9th ed., S. & M., 1987).

fact, it is the local authorities themselves—to be precise their chief executives—who are the actual addressees of Circulars. The reason why this is so is because listed building consent applications, and also of course planning applications, invariably start and for the most part also end with the planning departments and the planning committees of district councils and their equivalents.

Planning officers are professional people, and are usually deeply concerned with the consequences which their work may have for their environment. It is hoped that this book and especially this note will be useful in helping them sort out the sometimes subtle legal differences between the statutory obligation, the directions and the advice.

2. THE TOWN AND COUNTRY PLANNING ACT 1971

Below is a list of the important provisions of the 1971 Act relating to **14.05** listed buildings and conservation areas. It is not comprehensive. The provisions themselves, as amended, are to be found fully set out and annotated in the *Encylopedia of Planning Law and Practice*.

Section
Numbers

28	Publicity for applications affecting conservation areas
54	Lists of buildings of special architectural or historic interest
54A	Issue of certificate that building is not intended to be listed
55	Control of works for demolition, alteration or extension of listed buildings
56	Provisions supplementary to s.55
56A	Limit of duration of listed building consent
56B	Application for variation or discharge of conditions
56C	Dangerous structure orders in respect of listed buildings
57	Acts causing or likely to result in damage to listed buildings
58	Building preservation notice in respect of building not listed
58A	Special provision for listed buildings in Greater London
58AA	Power to restrict exemption of certain ecclesiastical buildings
96	Power to serve listed building enforcement notice
97	Appeal against listed building enforcement notice
97A	Appeals against listed building enforcement notices—supplementary
98	Penalties for non-compliance with listed building enforcement notice
99	Execution and cost of works required by listed building enforcement notice
99A	Effect of listed building consent on listed building enforcement notice
99B	Concurrent functions in London
100	Enforcement by, or by direction of, the Secretary of State

3. THE ANCIENT MONUMENTS AND ARCHAEOLOGICAL AREAS ACT 1979

As for the 1971 Act, the important provisions of the above Act are listed **14.07** below. Again, further reference should be made to the *Encyclopedia*.

Section
Numbers

PART I

4. DOE CIRCULAR 8/87—HISTORIC BUILDINGS AND CONSERVATION AREAS—POLICY AND PROCEDURES

A summary of the provisions of this important Circular is given below.   **14.10**
The *Encylopedia* (*q.v.*) contains the provisions set out in full.

Introduction [paras. 3–32]	General policy advice and information; the legislative framework; the Historic Buildings and Monuments Commission for England—its duties and functions; new uses for old buildings and conservation aspects of planning control.
Part I [paras. 33–52]	Listed buildings; how buildings of special architectural or historic interest are selected for inclusion in the list; building preservation notices; certificates of immunity from listing and the differences between ancient monuments and listed buildings.
Part II [paras. 53–71]	Conservation areas; the designation procedure and general advice on policy matters.
Part III [paras. 72–123]	Listed building control; the procedures and policy involved in dealing with applications for listed building consent and conservation area consent; prosecutions; the ecclesiastical exemption; enforcement; and associated subjects.
Part IV [paras. 124–138]	Buildings in need of repair; urgent repairs notices (s.101 of the 1971 Act), repairs notices (section 115) and compulsory purchase orders (ss.114–117).
Part V [paras. 139–152]	Financial matters, grants, etc.
Conclusion [paras. 153–154]	

Index

All references are to paragraph numbers.